The Sexual State

The Sexual State

Sexuality and Scottish Governance, 1950–80

Roger Davidson and Gayle Davis

EDINBURGH
University Press

For Colin Davidson and Jean Davis,
who have always been there for us

© Roger Davidson and Gayle Davis, 2012, 2014

First published in hardback in 2012
This paperback edition 2014

Edinburgh University Press Ltd
The Tun – Holyrood Road
12 (2f) Jackson's Entry
Edinburgh EH8 8PJ
www.euppublishing.com

Typeset in Sabon by
3btype, and
printed and bound in Great Britain by
CPI Group (UK) Ltd, Croydon CR0 4YY

A CIP record for this book is available
from the British Library

ISBN 978 0 7486 4560 2 (hardback)
ISBN 978 0 7486 9406 8 (paperback)
ISBN 978 0 7486 4943 3 (webready PDF)
ISBN 978 0 7486 4945 7 (epub)

The right of Roger Davidson and Gayle Davis to be
identified as authors of this work has been asserted
in accordance with the Copyright, Designs and
Patents Act 1988 and the Copyright and Related
Rights Regulations 2003 (SI No. 2498).

CONTENTS

TABLES

ACKNOWLEDGEMENTS

Many people have helped us in the preparation of this book. We are greatly indebted to the Wellcome Trust whose financial support underpinned the project from 2001 to 2006. In addition, the award by the Leverhulme Trust of an Emeritus Fellowship to Professor Roger Davidson in 2007 greatly facilitated additional research for section IV of the study, and the completion of the manuscript.

In our quest to explore the sexual concerns and ideologies of the Scottish policy community we have also received invaluable support from many archivists and librarians. In particular, we would wish to thank the staff of the British Medical Association Archives, Church of Scotland Archives, Edinburgh Central Library, Edinburgh City Archives, Edinburgh University Centre for Research Collections, Glasgow City Archives, Lothian Health Services Archive, National Archives of Scotland (now National Records of Scotland), NHS Greater Glasgow and Clyde Archives, National Library of Scotland, New College Library, Northern Health Services Archives, The National Archives (Public Record Office, Kew) and the Wellcome Library for the History and Understanding of Medicine. Thanks are also due to the Keeper of Public Records and the Keeper of the Records of Scotland for permission to quote from central government archives. In addition, we are indebted to Dr Sandy McMillan and the late Dr Alastair Batchelor for access to the papers of the Medical Society for the Study of Venereal Diseases, Scottish Branch, and of Dr R. C. L. Batchelor, respectively. Finally, the chapters relating to abortion, family planning and sexual health drew upon valuable oral testimony and we wish to thank those members of the medical community who very kindly agreed to be interviewed for the purposes of our study.

We have benefited enormously from the shared expertise of many historians and social scientists, in particular Lynn Abrams, Michael Anderson, Mike Barfoot, Angela Bartie, Allan Beveridge, Esther Breitenbach, Anne Crowther, Brian Dempsey, Kirsten Elliott, Trevor

Griffiths, Lesley Hall, Louise Jackson, Bob Morris, Graeme Morton, Malcolm Nicolson, Lutz Sauerteig, Steve Sturdy and Simon Taylor. We have also enjoyed a very supportive departmental environment. In particular, we are beholden to Stana Nenadic and Martin Chick who, as heads of the then Department of Economic and Social History, gave us every encouragement and selflessly protected our research agenda against the encroachment of other duties. In addition, we wish to thank Dr Helen Coyle for her work on the content of Scottish newspapers in 1950 and 1980 that furnished the basis of an introductory overview of shifting moral perspectives within Scottish society. Above all, we have to thank our respective families, who have endured many years during which our preoccupation with the history of sex and sexuality has lowered the tone of many a social occasion.

As the book has evolved over a number of years, parts of the material have been published in earlier versions. Parts of Chapter 2 appeared as '"A festering sore on the body of society": the Wolfenden Committee and female prostitution in mid-twentieth-century Scotland', *Journal of Scottish Historical Studies*, 24: 1 (2004), 80–98 (Edinburgh University Press). Chapters 3 and 4 draw on '"A field for private members": the Wolfenden Committee and Scottish homosexual law reform, 1950–67', *Twentieth Century British History*, 15: 2 (2004), 174–201 (Oxford University Press) and 'Sexuality and the state: the campaign for Scottish homosexual law reform, 1967–80', *Contemporary British History*, 20: 4 (2006), 533–58 (Taylor and Francis). Some of the material in Chapters 5 and 8 originally appeared as '"A fifth freedom" or "hideous atheistic expediency"? The medical community and abortion law reform in Scotland, c. 1960–1975', *Medical History*, 50: 1 (2006), 29–48 (Wellcome Trust) and as '"This thorniest of problems": school sex education policy in Scotland 1939–80', *Scottish Historical Review*, 84: 2 (2005), 221–46 (Edinburgh University Press). Finally, some of our conclusions were first sketched out in 'The sexual state: sexuality and Scottish governance, 1950–80', *Journal of the History of Sexuality*, 13: 4 (2004), 500–21 (University of Texas Press).

ABBREVIATIONS

ACC	Assistant Chief Constable
ALRA	Abortion Law Reform Association
A-SC	Alliance-Scottish Council
BBFC	British Board of Film Censors
BCS	Broadcasting Council for Scotland
BMA	British Medical Association
CCC	Consultative Committee on the Curriculum
CHE	Campaign for Homosexual Equality
CLRC	Criminal Law Revision Committee
DHS	Department of Health for Scotland
ECA	Edinburgh City Archives
ECL	Edinburgh Central Library
EHSSD	Edinburgh Health and Social Services Department
EIS	Educational Institute of Scotland
EMC	Edinburgh Magistrates' Committee
EPHD	Edinburgh Public Health Department
EUL	Edinburgh University Library
FCS	Free Church of Scotland
FPA	Family Planning Association
FPCS	Free Presbyterian Church of Scotland
GACS	General Assembly of the Church of Scotland
GAFCS	General Assembly of the Free Church of Scotland
GAUFCS	General Assembly of the United Free Church of Scotland
GCA	Glasgow City Archives
HC	House of Commons
HL	House of Lords
ITA	Independent Television Authority
MOH	Medical Officer of Health
MSSVDSB	Medical Society for the Study of Venereal Diseases, Scottish Branch
NBCA	National Birth Control Association

NHSA	Northern Health Services Archives
NRS	National Records of Scotland
PLC	Proceedings of the Lane Committee
PP	Parliamentary Papers
PRO	The National Archives, Public Record Office, Kew
PWC	Proceedings of the Wolfenden Committee on Homosexual Offences and Prostitution
RCOG	Royal College of Obstetricians and Gynaecologists
RHWSS	Report on Health and Welfare Services in Scotland
RWC	Report of the Wolfenden Committee on Homosexual Offences and Prostitution
SBCEA	Scottish Branch of the Cinema Exhibitors' Association
SCCL	Scottish Council for Civil Liberties
SCHE	Scottish Council for Health Education
SED	Scottish Education Department
SFPA	Scottish Family Planning Association
SHD	Scottish Home Department
SHEU	Scottish Health Education Unit
SHHD	Scottish Home and Health Department
SHRG	Scottish Homosexual Rights Group
SMG	Scottish Minorities Group
SPUC	Society for the Protection of the Unborn Child
SRCWPO	Social Responsibility Committee Working Party on Obscenity
SSS	Secretary of State for Scotland
STD	Sexually Transmitted Disease
UFCS	United Free Church of Scotland
USFI	Union for Sexual Freedom in Ireland
VD	Venereal Disease

1

INTRODUCTION

HISTORIOGRAPHY

As Jeffrey Weeks has observed, the state has played a central role in the social construction of sexuality in modern society:

> Through its role in determining legislation and the legal process it constitutes the categories of the permissible and the impermissible, the pure and the obscene. Through its symbiosis with the forces of moral regulation (from the churches to the medical profession) it can shape the climate of sexual opinion . . . The state can shape through its prohibitions and punishments. It can also organize and regulate through its positive will and injunctions, and influence through its omissions and contradictions.[1]

The social politics of sexual health and reproduction and the regulation of 'dangerous sexualities' in post-1945 Britain, and the medical, legal and moral discourses that shaped the role of the state, have been the subject of extensive research by historians and social scientists. Some authorities have mainly viewed sexual governance in this period as a subsidiary theme in the broader history of changing sexual attitudes and behaviour, and accompanying 'moral panics',[2] or in relation to cultural shifts in the nature of personal relationships and intimacy.[3] Others have focused more closely on the response of post-war governments to moral anxieties arising from a more affluent society and the decline of religion.[4] Finally, a range of studies has explored specific areas of policy making relating to sexual offences, sexual health and sexual reproduction.[5] Such studies have frequently related the governance of sexual issues to more general changes in gender and class relationships within British society, and to changing public and professional (especially medical) perceptions of sexuality and sexual identity.

Within this growing historiography, certain key areas of attention may be discerned. The proceedings of the Wolfenden Committee on Homosexual Offences and Prostitution (1954–7) have generated considerable debate. For commentators such as Jeffrey Weeks, the Wolfenden Report 'was a crucial moment in the evolution of liberal moral attitudes', offering the 'outline of a new moral economy' that was to underpin 'the limited, but symbolically significant, social reforms of the 1960s' and to provide 'the framework for all the major "official" proposals on morality throughout the 1970s'.[6] Other authorities emphasise more the coercive and regulatory implications of the report, often within a Foucauldian framework of analysis. Thus, for Frank Mort, one of its most significant features was the extent to which, in privileging the language of legal and medical regulation rather than that of moral hygiene and vigilance, it recast the contours of sexual pathology.[7] Meanwhile, a growing literature has sought to explore the implications of the Wolfenden Report for the history of female sexuality and its relationship to the law.[8]

A second major area of research has centred upon the degree to which the so-called 'permissive' legislation of the 1960s and early 1970s redefined the relationship of the state to the moral domain of the private citizen. Several studies of the policy-making process in the period have sought to demystify the notion of 'permissiveness' and to review the historiography surrounding it.[9] In particular, they have investigated how the ideology shaping legislation related to shifts in sexual attitudes and behaviour within British society that were subsequently to be interpreted by many observers as a 'sexual revolution'.[10] Other studies have viewed this legislation either in the context of the development of sexual citizenship within modern consumer society,[11] or as a preamble to the contentious politics of public and private morality pursued by the Thatcher Government after 1979.[12]

What emerges from such studies is the ambivalence of sexual politics in Britain after 1950. While there was a major reassessment of the role of the state in matters affecting sexual attitudes and behaviour, evidence suggests that radical pressures for sexual permissiveness were met, both in the central and local state, by the countervailing ideologies of both the traditional purity movement and, after the late 1960s, a new 'moral authoritarianism'. What also emerges is the degree to which, as in previous periods, the state did not have a 'strategic and concerted agenda' in confronting sexual issues.[13] Rather, the state itself continued to be 'a locale of struggle over the meaning of sexuality'.[14] Policy was often hesitant, piecemeal and/or contradictory, and continued to be shaped by the 'constant interplay of "reactionary", "progressive" and apathetic forces'.[15]

However, a further distinctive feature of the historiography surrounding sexual governance in the period from 1950 to 1980 is the degree to which the literature has centred on the policy-making process in England, and specifically Westminster and Whitehall. Largely missing from it are regional and local studies of the interface between sexuality and the state. In part, this is because of the impor- tance attached by cultural historians to the sexual politics of London in configuring national debate over sexual issues.[16] As Lesley Hall suggests, it is also because 'the history of sexual attitudes and behav- iour is itself a relatively new and somewhat controversial area'.[17]

This lack of a devolved focus is particularly serious in the case of Scotland, given its separate traditions of law, local government and medical practice, as well as, arguably, its distinctive civic and sexual culture. As a number of studies on nineteenth- and early twentieth- century Scottish society suggest, the ideology of Scottish law officers and administrators, the content of local Burgh Police Acts and bye- laws, the prejudices of local presbyteries and purity activists, and the whims of local magistrates and police commissioners were often as effective as national legislation in regulating sexual behaviour and the spaces deemed harmful to sexual hygiene and racial health, whether they be ice-cream parlours, cinemas, parks or public conveniences.[18] Such studies indicate that, in Scotland at least, the local state had for long played a critical role in shaping the nature of moral governance.

In recent years, scholars have paid increasing attention to the interplay between sexuality and national consciousness. Narratives of sexual 'purity', 'hygiene' and 'degeneracy', often in the context of resistance to colonial or metropolitan values, have been shown to be instrumental in the social construction of nationhood and gendered relations of power.[19] According to Finlayson, 'representations of sexuality infuse ideas on national identity that help constitute the state and its citizens'.[20] Similarly, Mayer contends that sexual control and repression (specifically, but not exclusively, of women and homosexuals) are frequently linked with 'national ego'.[21] A study of the history of policy making in Scotland may therefore also serve to illuminate the extent to which the governance of sexual issues and associated norms surrounding sexuality and sexual behaviour both reflected and reinforced national identity north of the Border.

AIMS AND CONTENT

This study draws upon a very wide range of central and local government archives, along with the records of the leading medical, religious and educational institutions that helped shape Scottish civil society after 1950. Court records are explored, as are the leading Scottish newspapers, and the papers of women's organisations and moral vigilante groups. Where possible, a limited amount of oral testimony with respect to the dynamics of policy making has also been garnered.

The central aim of this volume is to furnish a new perspective on the sexual politics of the period 1950–80 by exploring seven strands of sexual governance in Scotland: prostitution, homosexuality, abortion, family planning, sexually transmitted diseases, sex education and censorship. In so doing, it will seek to discover just how innovative Scottish policy makers actually were and the degree of continuity and/or change between sexual governance in 1950 and 1980. How far, for example, did the proceedings of the Wolfenden Committee mark a watershed in the relationship of the Scottish state and legal system to issues affecting private morality? To what extent did the mindset of policy makers subsequently shift from a moral to a social scientific approach toward sexual issues and from a legal to a more permissive socio-medical approach when they defined sexual offences? How far did the weight of moral conservatism traditionally associated with Scottish Presbyterian society continue to impact upon policy? How much did policy makers actually acknowledge and empower a broader range of sexual behaviours and identities, and to what degree, if any, did they moderate the traditional employment of surveillance and censure to target female sexuality? Finally, in what respects did Scotland's distinctive legal, medical and cultural identity affect policy-making decisions and its constitutional position inhibit its engagement with sexual issues?

This volume addresses four main, often overlapping, areas of Scottish policy making relating to sexual issues in the period 1950–80. Part I deals with the response of the central and local state to prostitution and homosexual offences. Chapter 2 focuses on the incidence of female prostitution in Scotland and developments in the prosecution and treatment of soliciting and related offences. Particular attention is paid to the Scottish evidence to the Wolfenden Committee, to the omission of Scotland from the 1959 Street Offences Act and to the subsequent efforts of policy makers and law officers to confront the issue of prostitution. Chapter 3 explores the history of homosexual law reform in Scotland in the period 1950–67. Prominence is again accorded to the proceedings of the Wolfenden Committee and to the subsequent response of Scottish public and professional opinion to its recommendations, culminating in the exclusion of Scotland from the 1967 Sexual Offences Act. Thereafter, Chapter 4 reviews the campaign to introduce homosexual law reform to Scotland in the period 1967–80. It focuses on the interface between the Scottish Minorities Group and Scottish governance and how it shaped the fortunes of a succession of measures designed to advance the legal status of homosexuals north of the Border.

Part II concentrates on issues relating to sexual reproduction. Chapter 5 explores the history of abortion law reform in Scotland. It focuses on Scottish legal and medical practice relating to abortion prior to the 1967 Abortion Act, the input of Scottish medicine to the politics surrounding the Act and the subsequent debate over its scope and implementation as evidenced in the proceedings of the Lane Committee (1971–4) and parliamentary attempts to restrict/ amend its provisions. Chapter 6 also addresses the relationship of the state to reproductive strategies by examining the impulses and constraints that shaped family planning provisions and policy in Scotland. The social, cultural and medical factors influencing the growth and content of contraceptive advice are investigated, in addition to the social politics surrounding the 1967 Family Planning Act. The response of the policy community and medical profession in Scotland to the growing demand for the free and universal provision of contraceptive advice and treatment, including the contraceptive pill, receives particular attention, as do the ideological and administrative tensions arising out of health education initiatives that sought to promote greater awareness of reproductive issues and options.

The dynamics of sexual health and sex education policy making form the subject of Part III. Chapter 7 outlines contemporary concerns and perceptions surrounding sexually transmitted diseases and the response of policy makers to the rising incidence of a new generation of infections. A range of policy options – both potential and realised – are reviewed, including the introduction of compulsory notification and treatment, health education initiatives, the development of contact tracing and the enhanced resourcing of sexual health services in Scotland. Thereafter, Chapter 8 turns to the contentious issue of sex education in Scottish schools during the period, examining the role of the central and local state in shaping the sexual knowledge of the young, and the interplay between a range of competing moral, medical and educational agencies within this contested area of social politics.

Part IV of the book (Chapters 9–11) is devoted to the history of moral censorship and the state in Scotland after 1950 in relation to theatre, film, broadcasting and literature (ranging from novels to pornography). It focuses on the legal and cultural factors that produced a distinctive reaction to legislation within the policy community north of the Border. Particular attention is paid to the Scottish response to projected reforms of theatre censorship and of the law relating to indecency and obscenity. The role of local statute and civic authorities in determining the nature and degree of censorship of plays, films and written material is also fully explored. As with other sections of this volume, this section seeks to identify the main fears and assumptions surrounding sexuality and sexual behaviour that underlay the policy-making process within both the Scottish Office and local government.

A concluding chapter, Chapter 12, explores the more general implications of this study for an understanding of the response of Scottish governance to sexual issues in the period 1950–80.

Two disclaimers are necessary. First, this volume does not address issues such as marital breakdown and divorce where the sexual aspects of personal behaviour, such as sexual violence or impotence, might well have had a bearing on legal cases but were essentially tangential to the central concern of policy makers. More importantly, there are sexual issues such as child sexual abuse, rape and infertility that are not included in our study.[22] These are omissions that were dictated in part by purely pragmatic considerations of time and space but primarily by the sensitivity of the policy files involved and associated problems of access and publication. We feel, however, that the wide range of themes encompassed within the book provides an ample basis for assessing the role of the Scottish state in sexual politics after 1950.

PERSPECTIVES – 1950 AND 1980

Insofar as the press both reflects and reinforces the dominant concerns of civil society, a content analysis of Scottish newspapers indicates that specifically sexual issues were low on the agenda of public debate in 1950.[23] Yet such an analysis would also suggest that underpinning contemporary debate was a basic concern to restore a set of Christian moral values fractured by the Second World War, values that related in part, at least implicitly, to sexual issues and behaviour.

Several strands of this concern can be identified. First, the press in 1950 strongly articulated the fears of church and civic leaders that society was descending into secularism and in danger of losing its 'moral compass' in the face of scientific and technological progress, and the increasing intrusion of a more disinhibited media.[24] Second, the press reflected a post-war consensus to rebuild a sense of 'citizenship' as a means of restoring the moral integrity of the nation, drawing upon a mix of religious and eugenic ideals of social purity and hygiene. Implicit in this process was a reassertion of Christian, heterosexual and marital norms for sexual activity. The need to address the rising incidence of marital breakdown was central to this agenda, as was the issue of how far the law should facilitate divorce.[25]

However, by far the strongest strand of this concern, reflected in the press in 1950, was the impact of war and post-war disruption on the morality of the younger generation. Often, as with newspaper coverage of the effects of cinema attendance, this was couched in general terms of 'delinquency' or 'demoralisation' rather than specific forms of sexual behaviour. The contentious issue of sex education was also mainly related to contemporary anxieties over the apparent alienation of youth culture from religious and family values.[26]

As Foucault has observed, 'silence' constitutes a powerful discursive practice,[27] and there were many silences surrounding sex and sexuality in the Scottish press of 1950. There was, for example, virtually no reference to sexual pleasure or diversity. Apart from isolated legal reports, from which explicit details of offences were excised, there was no reference to abortion, prostitution or homosexuality. Similarly, the more salacious aspects of films and literature banned or prosecuted by local magistrates were rarely reported. Issues relating to contraception and family planning were seldom directly addressed except as a discreet aside in articles relating to demographic trends and marital relationships.[28] Where, in 1950, public health venereal disease (VD) propaganda was published, the message merely employed the rhetoric of social hygiene, depicting VD as 'a grave menace to the future of the race' that could only be contained by 'clean living'.[29] Explicit reference to sex or sexual promiscuity was rare. Sex education was the one area of press coverage where the word 'sex' was routinely employed, perhaps because the discussion remained focused around narrow biological issues and avoided explicit discussion of sexual initiation and practice.

The treatment of sexual issues by the Scottish press in 1980 was in marked contrast to that of 1950, in terms of coverage, content and delivery. The column inches devoted to sexual themes had increased dramatically, as had the range of sexual concerns that were addressed. Previous areas of 'silence' had been slowly eroded. Vague concepts of 'permissiveness' and 'immorality' were unpacked into a broader taxonomy of sexual proclivities and behaviours. Instead of a narrow focus on a cluster of issues relating to public morality, sexual hygiene and citizenship, such as prostitution, VD and sex education, the agenda had broadened to engage also with the increasingly problematic role of the central and local state in shaping individual patterns of sexual choice and consumption. Thus, concerns relating to abortion, contraception and family planning were afforded extensive coverage, as were issues relating to pornography and censorship.

Discussion of sexual themes in 1980 was far more explicit. Euphemisms such as 'the social evil' and 'moral laxity' were dispensed with and sexual practices and preferences more openly identified and intimately explored, if not always condoned. The details of cases involving sexual offences were more fully reported, often with sensational headlines.[30]

Moreover, a process of secularisation had taken place. Although the views of the Scottish churches continued to be faithfully reported, they were now just one strand of a more inclusive public debate, embracing not only professional interest groups but also a wide spectrum of lay opinion within the general community. In 1950, comment on issues of sexual morality was largely restricted to the proceedings of presbyteries or synods, whereas, by 1980, on issues such as abortion and homosexual law reform, teenage pregnancy and contraception, or the regulation of 'sex shops', the press reproduced the views of civic leaders, women's organisations, medical and legal experts, educationists, sociologists, social workers and civil liberty groups, along with the – often intemperate – reflections of individual correspondents.

At the same time, the discourse surrounding sexual politics, as reflected in the Scottish press, was also less imbued with religious imagery and aspirations, in line with cultural shifts elsewhere in society. The Christian rhetoric of 'sin' and redemption that had informed press coverage in 1950 was not entirely absent, but it had been largely replaced in the framing of sexual issues with the medical and sociological language of pathology and dysfunction.[31] Nonetheless, in its treatment of sex, the press continued to reaffirm traditional heterosexual norms within the framework of marriage and procreation, and to reflect enduring concerns over the potential threat to the moral integrity of the nation's youth posed by exposure to sexual ambiguity or diversity.

In dealing with sexual issues over the period 1950–80, Scottish governance was therefore called upon to address a sexual culture and agenda that, while retaining aspects of continuity, were undergoing significant change. This volume explores how the Scottish state responded to this challenge and sought to balance the continuing demands of public health, public order and public decency with a growing regard for personal sexual space and empowerment.

Notes

1 Weeks, *Making Sexual History*, 133.
2 See, for example, Ferris, *Sex and the British*, chs 8–12; Hall, *Sex, Gender and Social Change*, chs 9–10; Haste, *Rules of Desire*, chs 6–10; McLaren, *Twentieth-Century Sexuality*, ch. 9.
3 See, for example, Collins, *Modern Love*, chs 3–6; Cook, *The Long Sexual Revolution*.
4 See, for example, Jarvis, *Conservative Governments, Morality and Social Change*; Holden, *Makers and Manners*; Weeks, *Sex, Politics and Society*, chs 12–14.
5 See, for example, Evans, 'Sexually transmitted disease policy', 237–52; Hampshire and Lewis, 'The ravages of permissiveness', 290–312; Jeffery-Poulter, *Peers, Queers & Commons*; Leathard, *The Fight for Family Planning*, chs 11–21; Self, *Prostitution, Women and the Misuse of the Law*; Sheldon, *Beyond Control*; Travis, *Bound and Gagged*; Weeks, *Coming Out*, chs 10–18.
6 Weeks, *Sex, Politics and Society*, 239–42; Weeks, *Coming Out*, 164.
7 Mort, 'Mapping sexual London', 92–110. See also Moran, *The Homosexual(ity) of Law*, part 2.
8 See, for example, Smart, 'Law and the control of women's sexuality', 40–60; Self, *Prostitution, Women and the Misuse of the Law*.
9 See especially Newburn, *Permission and Regulation*; Weeks, *Sexuality and its Discontents*, ch. 2; Collins, 'The Permissive Society and its enemies', in Collins (ed.), *The Permissive Society*, 1–40.
10 For a discussion of the broader debate over whether the 1960s and 1970s constituted a 'sexual revolution', see especially Garton, *Histories of Sexuality*, ch. 11.
11 See, for example, Evans, *Sexual Citizenship*, ch. 3.
12 See, for example, Durham, *Sex and Politics*.

13 M. Cook, 'Law', in Cocks and Houlbrook (eds), *The Modern History of Sexuality*, 71–2.

14 Weeks, *Making Sexual History*, 136.

15 Hall, *Sex, Gender and Social Change*, 8.

16 Most recently, Mort, *Capital Affairs*; Swanson, *Drunk with the Glitter*.

17 Hall, *Sex, Gender and Social Change*, 8.

18 See, for example, Barrie, *Police in the Age of Improvement*; Cree, *From Public Street to Private Life*, ch. 2; Davidson, *Dangerous Liaisons*, ch. 2; Mahood, *The Magdalenes*, part 3.

19 See, for example, Carver and Mottier (eds), *Politics of Sexuality*; McClintock, *Imperial Leather*; Mayer (ed.), *Gender Ironies of Nationalism*.

20 Finlayson, 'Sexuality and nationality: gendered discourses of Ireland', in Carver and Mottier (eds), *Politics of Sexuality*, 91–101.

21 Mayer, 'Gender ironies of nationalism', in Mayer (ed.), *Gender Ironies*, 1–2.

22 Research into the social, medical and political response to infertility in later twentieth-century Scotland is currently being conducted by Dr Gayle Davis at the University of Edinburgh.

23 The following is based on a content analysis undertaken by Dr Helen Coyle of the leading Scottish newspapers for the years 1950 and 1980.

24 Typical headlines included 'Nation's Moral Condition', 'Moral State of Country Denounced' and 'People Drifting into Paganism' [*The Scotsman*, 2 June 1950; *Inverness Courier*, 24 May 1950; *Dundee Courier and Advertiser*, 24 May 1950].

25 See, for example, the series entitled 'Marriage and Morals', (*Edinburgh*) *Evening Dispatch*, 12–25 May 1950.

26 See, for example, *Glasgow Herald*, 15 February 1950, 6 May 1950; *The Scotsman*, 27 May 1950.

27 Foucault, *History of Sexuality*, vol. 1, 27.

28 See, for example, (*Edinburgh*) *Evening Dispatch*, 14 January 1950.

29 See, for example, (*Edinburgh*) *Evening Dispatch*, 21 January 1950.

30 For example, 'Sex Mag too Hot to Handle'; 'Aberdeen's Sex Shop is there to Stay'; 'Nine Years for "Bestial" Rape'; 'Abortion: Face the Ugly Facts' [*Dumfries and Galloway Standard and Advertiser*, 8 February 1980; *Aberdeen Press and Journal*, 27 September 1980; *Dundee Courier and Advertiser*, 9 December 1980; (*Edinburgh*) *Evening News*, 21 November 1980].

31 See, for example, *The Scotsman*, 15 January 1980; (*Edinburgh*) *Evening News*, 10 July 1980.

PART I
Sexual Offences

2

FEMALE PROSTITUTION

INTRODUCTION

The history of the state's response to female prostitution in later twentieth-century Britain has been viewed from a variety of historical perspectives. A largely narrative approach has located legislative changes within a wider story of shifting social mores and moral anxieties.[1] In addition, many social historians and sociologists have focused upon the regulatory aspects of the Wolfenden Report on Homosexual Offences and Prostitution (1954–7) and the Street Offences Act of 1959. Thus, for Jeffrey Weeks, by redefining the relationship of the law to the private moral terrain of the citizen, they enabled a reaffirmation of the policing of public space in the interests of order and decency.[2] Meanwhile, other commentators have advanced a more specifically feminist interpretation of events, viewing government initiatives as enshrining the desire to contain female sexuality within a patriarchal society.[3]

However, historical research into the law relating to sexual offences since the Second World War has focused on social politics in Westminster and Whitehall. In order to chart the Scottish experience, this chapter explores six main themes. First, it surveys the evidence for female prostitution in Scotland during the first half of the 1950s. Second, it explores the provisions existing in Scotland for the prosecution and treatment of female prostitutes. The written and oral evidence presented to the Wolfenden Committee by a range of Scottish civil servants, law officers, medical experts and social workers is then used to capture the forces and arguments both for and against new legislation north of the Border. A further section examines the reaction of Scottish opinion to the recommendations of the Wolfenden Report and to the subsequent exclusion of Scotland from the 1959 Street Offences Act. Finally, this chapter documents the incidence of female prostitution in Scotland in the 1960s and 1970s and the views and policies adopted by both central and local government in response to its perceived threat to public order and public morality.

Evidence suggests that female prostitutes were operating in all the major urban centres of Scotland in the early 1950s. In Glasgow, prostitution was considered to be well established within the city centre. For example, one former procurator fiscal recollected that in the immediate past:

> You had your square – Oak Street, Renfrew Street and Gordon Street – where you could say you had at least 20 prostitutes – who just went round and round that square – stood at the street corners for a few minutes, and were regularly there, and were regularly accosting individuals who passed . . .[4]

There was also evidence of a so-called 'dirty rank' of taxis used by prostitutes to conduct their business.[5]

However, by the 1950s, the main focus of prostitution in Glasgow was reported to be at the coffee stalls in the central business area of town, which operated from 11pm to 3am and where prostitutes seeking clients 'could capture crowds coming from late dances and picture houses' and then, charging on average about £1 a transaction, use the nearby closes for their business.[6] Although 'the lodging house type – the aged hag' – might still patrol the dock area, in the view of Glasgow's Assistant Chief Constable, in the central area the '"old shawlie" type of prostitute' had been largely superceded by a better-dressed, more sophisticated type.[7] At the same time, it was observed that there was an absence in Glasgow of the type of 'high-class prostitute' prevalent in parts of London.[8]

Yet, despite some history of vice rings and evidence of so-called 'call-girl rackets' in Glasgow, it was claimed that prostitution was not generally organised or closely involved with the criminal fraternity.[9] James Adair, a former procurator fiscal for Glasgow and prominent member of the Wolfenden Committee, attributed this to the fact that 'the social and economic conditions were different [from London] and there was not the cosmopolitan factor', one of many references to the alleged role of immigrants – especially Greek Cypriots – in organised vice.[10]

In Edinburgh, the Crown Agent's view was that 'there [were]

certain streets where one would know where to look' for prostitutes – for example, in the Leith Dock area and Saxe-Coburg Street in Stockbridge – but that it was not comparable to the problem in London and, 'except in some of the quieter streets', there was not 'much accosting going on'.[11] The coffee stalls that proved such a focus for prostitution in Glasgow had been abolished in Edinburgh after the war. As in Glasgow, there was, he claimed, evidence of an influx of prostitutes when major exhibitions and other events were held in the city – notoriously the General Assembly of the Church of Scotland – and they 'occasionally follow[ed] the fleet up from Plymouth'. However, there were, he stressed, no 'serious problems' in Edinburgh cafés or public houses and little evidence of organised brothels.[12] In his experience, the main issues of public concern were the prevalence of kerb crawling in Queen Street and the West End, and the association of very young girls with American servicemen.

Other evidence suggests that the Edinburgh police authorities were almost certainly in some considerable degree of denial when testifying to the Wolfenden Committee. Their view was not shared by the Edinburgh Magistrates' Committee who believed there had been a significant shift of 'certain activities . . . from the streets to public houses and other places of public resort'.[13] One commentator later recorded that at the Imperial Hotel in Leith Walk 'there would be fifteen hookers and the place would be absolutely stinking of hairspray and beehives'. At Deep Sea Fish and Chip:

> It was all communal tables and the loo opened directly into the dining room and you could sit there and see everybody going out and in and the whores would drag in whatever trick they had managed to grab. There was a subterranean lavvy outside . . . and the gay guys and the hookers all just used it, slipped downstairs and used the boxes. I think money more than likely passed hands from the hookers to the police.[14]

The brothel operated by Dora Noyce at 17 and 17a Danube Street was also notorious. It was reputed to have supported '15 resident girls with a further 25 coming in on a regular shift basis'. When the American navy was in port, 'extra hands were brought on deck at Danube Street' and with 'bluejackets queuing in the street, girls arrived in taxis from as far away as Grangemouth and Falkirk'.[15]

Very little was recorded of the incidence of prostitution elsewhere in Scotland. While there was reportedly no 'resident problem' in the

West of Scotland outside Glasgow, it was alleged that trainloads of prostitutes did migrate to the area from Glasgow when 'a troopship was due in Greenock or an American vessel arrive[d]'.[16] Similar migrations were associated with the American base near Prestwick and with the dockyard at Rosyth.[17] Certainly, Mary Cohen, one of three Scottish members of the Wolfenden Committee, regarded 'the crowds of women and girls rushing to naval ports and various camps' in Scotland as 'equally degrading spectacles in their respective areas' as the 'Common Prostitutes in Curzon Street', while her fellow committee member, James Adair, was concerned to extend existing burgh legislation relating to soliciting to cover military establishments in rural areas.[18] Some evidence suggested that, outwith Glasgow and Edinburgh, the problem lay more with 'amateur good-time girls' rather than professional prostitutes.[19]

However, while acknowledging the existence of prostitution north of the Border, the weight of Scottish evidence presented to the Wolfenden Committee was that its prevalence did not present 'the same magnitude of problem' as in London with regard to either street offences or the conduct of brothels. Echoing the views of his Chief Constable, Bailie Duncan of Glasgow considered that its problem was 'the least for an industrial city', while the Assistant Chief Constable of Edinburgh considered that prostitution in Edinburgh 'was no problem whatever'.[20] For their part, the Faculty of Advocates testified that:

> They do not consider that there is any reason to suppose that, in Scotland [Street Offences] are carried on to such an extent or in such a manner as to affect general standards of conduct, or so as to give grounds for apprehension that these types of immorality are on the increase.[21]

Such arguments were strongly reinforced by statistics supplied by the Scottish Home Department (SHD) on the incidence of prosecutions for female importuning in Scotland.[22] These indicated a long-term decline in prosecutions, with the annual average number of cases for the years 1950–5 representing only about one-third of that for the inter-war period. This was in marked contrast to the apparent threefold rise in recorded offences of female solicitation in England and Wales.[23]

Scottish Committee members and witnesses presented a range of explanations for this divergence. Adair considered that it was due less to differences in legal procedures than to the relative size of 'urban concentrations',[24] while Cohen attributed it to the fact that 'the Scottish way of life . . . even in the big cities [was] much simpler and altogether there [was] not so much night life of any kind in Scotland'.[25] J. Anderson, Deputy Secretary of the SHD, suggested that, *prima facie*, the heavier penalties in Scotland and the absence of a need to prove 'annoyance' might be crucial factors but there was a lack of any conclusive evidence.[26] Meanwhile, Glasgow Magistrates' Committee submitted that, while the media might focus 'more on sex', standards of morality had in fact risen in Scotland and the incidence of prostitution had been reduced by 'the higher physical standard of the community and the greater degree of economic security women [had] generally'.[27]

THE PROSECUTION AND TREATMENT OF FEMALE PROSTITUTES IN THE 1950S

In the 1950s, female solicitation was prosecuted in Scotland primarily in the police courts and Burgh Courts, under either the Burgh Police (Scotland) Act of 1892 or a variety of local corporation orders in the major cities. The usual charge was that, 'being a common prostitute or streetwalker', the accused 'loiter[ed] about or importune[d] for the purposes of prostitution'.[28] A wide range of byelaws regulating public parks, pleasure grounds, links, seashores and other places of public resort included provisions against soliciting.[29] The Licensing Acts were also employed to reduce the number of prostitutes operating out of hotels and public houses, while the byelaws governing docks and harbours often contained clauses designed to prevent prostitutes infiltrating ships in port. In addition, some police authorities, such as Edinburgh, were prepared to charge kerb crawlers with disorderly behaviour and to employ 'girls in plain clothes as *agents provocateurs*'.[30]

There is some evidence that prostitution was primarily targeted by the police in city-centre areas where it was most visible to the general public and visiting tourists. Certainly, in Edinburgh some 90 per cent of prosecutions related to offences in Princes Street and the surrounding area of the New Town, including George Street, Frederick Street, Queen Street and Rose Street. In contrast, the few prosecutions recorded for female solicitation in Leith would suggest that the area was being treated virtually as a 'tolerance zone'.[31]

Penalties varied across the country. Outside the cities, the maximum penalty for a first offence would typically be 40/- with imprisonment for up to twenty days for non-payment. In Edinburgh, however, the penalty might be as much as £10 for a first offence, or alternatively imprisonment for up to sixty days. Imprisonment was used more extensively in Scotland than in England and Wales, with some 20 per cent of proven charges for female importuning in Scotland in the early 1950s incurring imprisonment, either for repeat offences or non-payment of fines.[32]

Several other significant features distinguished the law and practice relating to female prostitution in Scotland. First, whereas in England and Wales an offence of soliciting had to be 'to the annoyance of the inhabitants or passengers', this requirement was absent from Scots law, greatly facilitating the prosecution process and avoiding the manufacture of false charges by the police, which was a perennial complaint south of the Border. Second, accusations of police corruption and discrimination surrounding issues of vice were less frequent in Scotland because a procurator fiscal and not the police had the responsibility of initiating prosecutions in the public interest, and the uncorroborated evidence of one witness was not sufficient to prove a charge, as was the case in England and Wales.[33]

Third, in Scotland, only after surveillance and several cautions was a woman charged in court as a 'common prostitute', a process previously recommended for the whole of the United Kingdom by the 1927 Macmillan Committee on Street Offences.[34] Thus, in Glasgow, if a woman was suspected of being a prostitute, her behaviour was monitored by the police, and if she was seen to importune or accost three or more individuals, she was warned that, if she persisted, she might be apprehended. Particulars of this caution were recorded by the officer in his official notebook. If the woman repeated the offence, she was apprehended and taken to the police station where she was formally cautioned. Only if, after both cautions, she repeated the offence was she brought before the court, where the record of her conduct served as presumptive evidence that she was a 'common prostitute'.[35] A similar system operated in Edinburgh, but here the woman was given two cautions on the street before being taken to the police station.[36] In some parts of Scotland the cautionary process started afresh if a woman was free from conviction for two years.

Furthermore, a major feature of the Scottish cautioning system was its close association with the 'rescue work' of moral welfare agencies. In Glasgow, there was a long-standing liaison between the police authorities and the Women's Help Society. Representatives of the Society regularly patrolled at night with the plain-clothes police and obtained particulars of girls being warned or cautioned. The information was used to facilitate follow-up visits, especially to the younger women observed loitering on the streets.[37] The police also liaised with the National Vigilance Association of Scotland in an effort to 'rescue' vulnerable girls arriving at bus, train and shipping terminals from the clutches of pimps and brothel keepers.[38] In addition, at various stages of the cautioning and prosecution processes, the police would routinely refer suspected prostitutes to the voluntary societies in the hope of some form of moral reclamation. Similarly close links between moral welfare agencies and the Burgh Courts existed in Edinburgh and Dundee, with a social welfare officer employed by the Church of Scotland to counsel women cautioned or charged with street offences.[39]

However, elements of care and compassion in the treatment of female soliciting were often counterbalanced, not only by concerns for the policing of public space and the avoidance of public nuisance, but also by anxieties over public health. The body of the prostitute long continued to preoccupy policy makers as the key vector of venereal disease (VD), with a consequent erosion of her civil liberties.[40] Under the Criminal Justice (Scotland) Act of 1949, courts were empowered to remand sexual offenders for a medical examination, or to make it a condition of bail.[41] As a result, in the 1950s, women convicted of soliciting were frequently remanded in custody for medical examination and treatment for VD, irrespective of whether they had any symptoms.[42] Similarly, under the Children and Young Persons (Scotland) Act of 1937, girls and young women whose sexual promiscuity was thought to presage a life of prostitution were often subjected to medical investigation at VD clinics as part of the custodial process.[43] It is noteworthy that, while the Criminal Justice Act was commonly used to refer homosexual offenders in Scotland for psychiatric appraisal, which frequently mitigated the sentences imposed, this option was rarely adopted in cases of female solicitation despite significant advances in the psychopathology of prostitution.[44]

THE WOLFENDEN COMMITTEE – EVIDENCE FAVOURING FRESH LEGISLATION

One of the two main tasks entrusted to the Wolfenden Committee, appointed in August 1954, was to 'consider the law and practice relating to offences against the criminal law in connection with prostitution and solicitation for immoral purposes'.[45] The lack of deterrence in existing sentencing was a criticism frequently levelled during its proceedings. Scottish members of the Wolfenden Committee, and a range of Scottish witnesses giving evidence, regarded the prevailing tariff of penalties for soliciting as derisory. The penalty of a £2 fine for a first offence imposed in most Scottish burghs was regarded as 'totally inadequate as a deterrent' and 'nothing short of a laughing stock'.[46] Many witnesses endorsed the view of James Adair that the regular prostitute 'invariably had her 40/- fine tucked away, to be produced at the police station if she was arrested; she could then get her release on bail. The fine was part of the oncost.'[47] It was claimed that, as a result, coupled with the fact that, as in London, the police only operated a system of rotating arrests, there was a high degree of recidivism, and prostitution in the major Scottish cities was effectively being condoned.

However, for many witnesses before the Committee the solution was not just an increase in the level of fines, which might merely serve as an incentive for prostitutes to increase the number of their clients, but imprisonment. Although imprisonment was used more extensively in Scotland for street offences relating to prostitution, Scottish law officers and the police strongly urged that prison sentences should be more regularly imposed on offenders as a deterrent. According to the Glasgow Magistrates, 'the only thing that [would] disturb their quiet serenity [was] imprisonment',[48] while women police and prison officers in Scotland wanted prison sentences extended as they claimed that short sentences tended to be treated 'as a rest cure'.[49] An additional benefit, it was argued, was that the prostitute was effectively compelled, if imprisoned, to submit to examination and treatment at a VD clinic, to the benefit of public health.

Many of the Scottish churches, along with women's organisations and moral welfare agencies, also advocated a greater use of imprisonment for soliciting offences, although their rationale was more a concern to secure for first offenders a period of self-reflection and moral rehabilitation before they progressed to being 'hardened prostitutes'. Thus, Christine Mackenzie, Warden of the Glasgow Women's Help Committee, advocated a sixty-day prison sentence for a first offence: 'I feel very strongly about it. I do feel there are some who could see another way of living if they were just removed for sixty days.'[50]

This strongly resonated with the views of Mary Cohen, another Scottish member of the Wolfenden Committee, former Chairman of the Scottish Association for Girls' Clubs and long-standing member of the National Vigilance Association for Scotland, who proposed that prostitutes under the age of 21 on first conviction should:

> not be fined but put under probation and detained in a centre for some days for social and medical examination (partly to detect venereal disease and mental defectiveness); during this time probation officers and others would have an opportunity to talk with the girl and rescue her.[51]

Perhaps the greatest consensus amongst Scottish Committee members and witnesses was the need for increased penalties for pimps, procurers and property owners living on immoral earnings. There was a widespread concern that the law should anticipate the greater organisation and off-street commercialisation of prostitution consequent on street offences legislation. A range of proposals for countering the growth of so-called 'call-girl rackets' included the increase of penalties for procuring, previously established under the 1885 Criminal Law Amendment Act and the 1902 Immoral Traffic Act, the hearing of such cases before more senior courts and more stringent targeting by the law of landlords who let accommodation for the purposes of prostitution.[52]

However, underlying some of the Scottish evidence to the Wolfenden Committee there was an additional strand of disquiet at the moral assumptions and double moral standards underpinning the existing law and legal procedures. Women's organisations, such as the Scottish Standing Committee of the National Council of Women, the Women Citizens' Association, the Association for Moral and Social Hygiene and the Equal Citizenship Group, protested on a number of counts at the gender discrimination inherent in the existing system of prosecution in Scotland.

First, women's organisations considered that the courts were heavily prejudiced against women offenders 'by reason of the statutory nature of the offence'. The words 'being a common prostitute or street-walker', which appeared in the charge, were said 'to create an impression of guilt'. Accordingly, in line with the recommendations of the 1927 Street Offences Committee, such organisations called for the law of solicitation to be framed so as to apply only to the generic offence and not the offender, without any specific reference to his/her 'character or sex'.[53]

Second, female witnesses were outraged that although in Scotland the Immoral Traffic Act, and local statutes such as the Glasgow Police Act, applied to importuning by both men and women, they were, in practice, invariably deployed against women. Thus, Christine Mackenzie protested that she had been over thirty-three years in the Glasgow police courts and never once seen a man prosecuted under the Police Act. She added with some passion: 'I am not a feminist – I would like to say that I am definitely not – but I do feel terrifically strongly when they [men] are a menace, as they are at the moment, and nothing happens.'[54] Similarly, Elizabeth Abbott, a Scot and veteran of the Association for Moral and Social Hygiene, urged the Committee to focus more on the problem of 'male immorality' in their deliberations and to end the systemic discrimination in the application of the law.[55]

While not directly testifying to the Committee, many of the Scottish churches endorsed such sentiments. In particular, the United Free Church associated itself with the concerns of the Association for Moral and Social Hygiene over gender inequalities in the law on solicitation, and it called upon the Government to ensure that legislation 'apply on an equal basis to men and women alike' and that procedures should maintain 'the right of all accused to be assumed innocent before conviction'.[56] Likewise, the Congregational Union of Scotland wanted clearer recognition in law that solicitation was also a function of male demand.[57]

THE WOLFENDEN COMMITTEE – EVIDENCE FAVOURING THE STATUS QUO

Despite such reservations, the majority of Scottish witnesses before the Wolfenden Committee did not perceive the problem of female prostitution in Scotland as sufficiently acute to merit fresh legislation.[58] Moreover, many witnesses considered that the existing Scottish penalties and procedures for dealing with female solicitation were both more efficient and humane, and generally more consistent with civil liberties, than those operating in England and Wales. Scots law and practices on the issue were perceived more as a template for action south of the Border than as a suitable case for revision.

Thus, testimony focused on the degree to which the different laws of evidence and prosecution procedures in Scotland not only facilitated legal action against prostitution in Scotland but also reduced the number of allegations of corruption levelled at the police in their regulation of vice.[59] The higher level of fines and prison sentences imposed by Scottish courts for female solicitation was also cited in defence of the status quo.[60] The SHD and the police authorities were satisfied that they had procedures in place to deal with more recent developments in the 'vice trade'. In particular, they were convinced that the powers devolved under the Licensing and Public Order Acts were sufficient to curb the use of hotels and public houses for prostitution and the prevalence of kerb crawling.[61]

Scottish law officers were also hostile to the proposals of women's organisations and moral welfare agencies to extend the provisions of probation and remand for 'rescue' purposes. They concurred with Adair's view that 'non-punitive detention could not be defended'.[62] In fact, the Scottish police did 'not think that the intervention of moral welfare workers [had] much effect'.[63] In many respects the evidence of moral welfare workers themselves served to undermine the strength of their recommendations. They conveyed the strong impression that the new generation of prostitutes was better off and 'more sophisticated', and that it was motivated more by idleness than economic necessity and resistant to traditional rescue work. Young prostitutes in particular were perceived as deliberately choosing prostitution as a way of life and as 'unlikely to respond to moral persuasion'.[64] The limited evidence presented by Scottish psychologists merely served to reinforce such impressions. Thus, in the view of Winifred Rushforth, founder of the pioneering Davidson Clinic in Edinburgh, established in 1940 to provide psychotherapeutic treatment to the general public, prostitutes were 'usually unsuitable patients' for treatment. In her view, they were often 'unintelligent, dull or psychopathic' and she had 'never found them at all helpful' in her counselling work.[65]

In addition, the evidence of senior Scottish law officers, including the Crown Agent, and strongly supported by Adair, favoured the retention of the designation 'common prostitute' in the charge for soliciting, as an essential protection against 'an innocent woman' being charged. They refused to acknowledge that the habitual male client should be in an analogous legal position.[66] Despite clear evidence of the lack of prosecutions against men for soliciting, the law officers stressed that in Scotland, in contrast to England and Wales, male importuning of women and children was expressly an offence. However, the main thrust of their resistance on this issue was that Scottish legal procedures ensured that the status of 'common prostitute' could only be designated after an extensive process of surveillance and cautioning which involved close liaison with the moral welfare agencies.[67] Again, the existing treatment of female prostitutes in Scotland was upheld as an example for the rest of Britain in balancing care and coercion in the regulation of what were deemed to be 'dangerous sexualities'.

THE WOLFENDEN REPORT AND ITS AFTERMATH IN SCOTLAND, 1954–60

In its eventual report to Parliament in September 1957, the Wolfenden Committee recommended a mix of punitive and reformatory measures designed to facilitate the prosecution of street offences, increase the penalties for repeated solicitation and bring the law to bear more effectively against brothel keepers and landlords living on immoral earnings. More specifically, the Committee proposed that there should no longer be a need to establish 'annoyance' in the prosecution of soliciting; that the maximum penalties for street offences be increased and a system of progressively higher penalties for repeated offences be introduced; that stricter powers should be introduced, enabling the courts to rescind the tenancy rights of those using premises for the purposes of habitual prostitution and to indict landlords who charged exorbitant rents for such premises with living on immoral earnings; that a more formal system of cautioning prostitutes, as in Edinburgh and Glasgow, should be introduced prior to prosecution and that particulars of a prostitute cautioned for the first time should be referred to a moral welfare worker; that courts be given explicit power to remand, in custody if need be, for not more than three weeks, a prostitute convicted for the first or second time of a street offence, in order that a social or medical report might be obtained; and that more research be conducted into the aetiology of prostitution.[68]

At Westminster, some Scottish peers and MPs objected to the tenor of the Wolfenden Report, many proposals of which were contained in a Street Offences Bill, introduced into the House of Commons in December 1958.[69] For example, Lord Kilmuir acknowledged that the presence of prostitutes on the street was 'offensive to the ordinary citizen's sense of decency' and 'injurious' both as an example to girls and as a needless temptation to their male clients. However, he considered that, in addition to specific measures, there was an urgent need 'to raise the social and moral outlook of society as a whole'.[70] Somewhat more eccentrically, Lord Saltoun, while opposed to the propensity of the British public in its 'virtuous brutality' to 'harry the whore' off the streets, counselled a curious mix of Christian charity and a regularised system of maisons tolérées that might accord British prostitutes 'some sort of respect'.[71]

More orthodox liberal objections came from the Liberal leader, Jo Grimond, and Lord Balfour of Burleigh. Jo Grimond criticised the Wolfenden Report and draft legislation for callously ignoring the systemic economic and social causes of prostitution, for under-valuing the civil liberties of female prostitutes and for failing to address the moral and legal liability of male clients and the likely emergence of more sophisticated and exploitative call-girl rackets.[72] In similar vein, Lord Balfour of Burleigh dismissed the Street Offences Bill as 'a Pimp's Benefit Bill' that, he argued, resonated with the bigotry of 'former centuries [that] approved the whipping of the harlot at the cart's tail'. Like Grimond, he considered that the bill infringed civil liberties in its retention of the designation 'common prostitute' and its asymmetry in the treatment of male and female importuning. For the first time, he protested, it wrote 'the double standard of morality into the Statute Book'.[73]

However, insofar as Scottish opposition *was* articulated in the parliamentary debates surrounding the Street Offences Bill, the argument was primarily directed at the comparative equity and effi-ciency of existing legal and social work practices relating to female solicitation north of the Border and at the consequent lack of need for Scotland to be included in fresh legislation.[74] This strongly echoed the views of the Home Office and the SHD. Both departments drew a clear conclusion from the Wolfenden Report that the problem was essentially a metropolitan one and that the incidence of prostitution in Scotland could be contained by means of existing measures. Considering the issue in late October 1957, the Secretary of the SHD advised the Secretary of State for Scotland that:

> As regards prostitution, the Committee made few criticisms of the existing Scottish law, and their main recommendations were desig-ned to bring the English law closer to the Scottish, which does not require annoyance to be established before an offence is committed, provides higher penalties (including imprisonment) for repeated offences, and automatically terminates any lease of premises used as a brothel or for the purposes of habitual prostitution.[75]

Although the Wolfenden Report had recommended higher and more uniform penalties for solicitation and an amendment of regulations covering places of refreshment, the permanent officials believed that this could readily be effected in Scotland by local legislation and bye-laws.[76] The one area where they anticipated Scots law being out of line was in respect of persons living on immoral earnings, where the maximum sentence recommended by the Committee was five years, as compared with the two years operating in Scotland. In public, the SHD rationalised this likely discrepancy on the somewhat disingenuous grounds that there was no evidence that the existing law was 'insufficiently severe'.

However, the main reason why both the Scottish law officers and the Government wanted to preserve the status quo was that the relevant legislation relating to immoral earnings for Scotland, the Immoral Traffic Act 1902, Section 1, also applied to importuning by males, including for homosexual purposes. As a result, there was acute concern that to alter the penalties for living on immoral earnings north of the Border would simply reactivate public debate over the issue of homosexual law reform and the Government's contentious decision not to decriminalise homosexual practices in accordance with the recommendations of the Wolfenden Committee.[77]

In contrast, some sections of the Scottish media were heavily critical of the omission of Scotland from the Street Offences Bill. A series of articles in *The Scotsman* in June 1959 questioned the validity of official statistics on the incidence of Scottish prostitution, arguing that it 'remained a festering sore on the body of society', casting 'its infection in many directions' and requiring additional powers for police and public health authorities.[78] Its reporter found compelling evidence of a rise in female prostitution across Scotland. In Edinburgh, despite the removal of the obvious congregating points such as the old coffee stalls in Princes Street, he encountered a taxi driver who could 'reel off without the slightest hesitation 30 addresses where he knew prostitution could readily be found, in flats near the centre'. He also found widespread evidence of a rising use of bars and cafés for prostitution, often frequented at the weekend by women from the housing schemes and the Lothians, driven into the sex industry by poverty due to unemployment and credit arrears. In Glasgow, similar trends were identified, with 'as many as 40 prostitutes in a limited area of the centre of the City . . . quite brazen about their purpose, standing in groups on the corners of streets'. Apart from the dockside bars, prostitutes were reported to be colonising the poorer tenements in areas such as the Gorbals and Charing Cross where the 'old social order' was disintegrating. There were also indications of a call-girl system operating in the city.[79]

Evidence was also produced that cast doubts on official claims that prostitution was largely absent elsewhere in Scotland. In Dundee, it was claimed that the dramatic rise in the rate of new cases of VD closely reflected the increase in open soliciting both in the streets and in bars in the area adjacent to the docks, with some sixty women known to the police authorities, many controlled by pimps and/or operating from brothels. In addition, prostitution was said to have gravitated to some of the housing schemes on the outskirts of Dundee as a result of the slum clearances in the city centre. Aberdeen, Perth and Inverness were reported as witnessing similar 'sexual license', fuelled by the demands of the workforces on the local hydroelectric schemes, while the presence of American bases was predicted to have a similar impact on other towns such as Ayr.[80]

In the event, the Street Offences Act of 1959 applied only to England and Wales, and excluded Scotland and Northern Ireland. Heavier and more graduated penalties were introduced for soliciting and significantly longer terms of imprisonment for living on immoral earnings. While a woman cautioned for soliciting might, under the Act, apply for the caution to be expunged from the public record, powers of caution and arrest were simplified to enable any constable to act without proof of annoyance, as in Scotland. In addition, the Licensing Acts were further deployed to penalise the use of public houses and other places of refreshment for the purposes of prostitution.

Ironically, despite figuring so prominently in the debates surrounding the Wolfenden Report, the Scottish system of cautioning prostitutes and of routinely referring particulars to a moral welfare officer was not incorporated into the Street Offences Act. The Metropolitan Commissioner was not persuaded of the value or appropriateness of such referrals (in part, as a result of the clear ambivalence of the Scottish police authorities in their evidence to the Committee) and preferred to leave it to the Court Probation Officer 'to deal with incipient prostitutes'.[81] More seriously, English law officers doubted the legality of the cautioning system operated by the Scottish police. As a Home Office memorandum warned:

> The Scottish police can point to no authority except practice for taking prostitutes to the station for the second caution, and it is believed that in England, at any rate, it would be unlawful to arrest a prostitute and take her to the station unless it was intended to charge her and bring her before a magistrate.[82]

Given the degree to which Scottish legal and police procedures had been lauded throughout the debate surrounding street offences legislation, there was more than a hint of relish in the postscript that this should not be publicised 'because it might throw doubt on the legality of the Scottish practice'.

THE INCIDENCE OF FEMALE PROSTITUTION IN SCOTLAND, 1960–80

Civic leaders and the media in Scotland continued to perceive female prostitution as a social problem during the 1960s and 1970s. Although official crime statistics for the period are difficult to interpret and are further complicated by the reorganisation of local government and police authorities, evidence would suggest that the incidence of offences 'made known to the police' involving prostitution rose dramatically after 1955, with a further substantial rise in the early 1960s (see Table 2.1). Thereafter, the number of offences levelled out before beginning to decline in the early 1970s.

Table 2.1 Reported offences of female prostitution in Scotland: five-yearly averages, 1955–74

Period	Number of crimes reported
1950–4	158
1955–9	287
1960–4	429
1965–9	440
1970–4	417

Source: SHD/SHHD, *Criminal Statistics Scotland, Annual Reports for 1950–74*, Table 5.

The figures for brothel keeping were separately recorded. Again, they show a rise (some 50 per cent) between the late 1950s and early 1960s, peaking at twenty-four offences reported in 1964, with a fairly constant level of cases maintained in the late 1960s before a dip after 1970.[83]

The official crime statistics indicate that, in terms of age distribution, those accused of prostitution tended to get younger over time. In 1950, the proportion of persons convicted of prostitution in summary courts in the age groups 17–21 and 21–30 was 11 per cent and 47 per cent respectively, whereas the comparable shares for 1970 had increased to 16 per cent and 59 per cent. Conversely, the proportion aged over 30 had declined from 42 per cent to 25 per cent.[84]

As Table 2.2 indicates, virtually all the recorded offences that involved prostitution were located within the four Scottish cities. Glasgow had by far the largest, and increasing, share of reported crimes, with levels of prosecutions for soliciting in the 1960s more than double that for the 1950s.[85] In an attempt to reduce a major area of soliciting, after prolonged pressure from local councillors and social workers many of the city-centre stalls, including those in St Vincent Place and St Vincent Street, had been closed in 1959.[86] Faced with clear evidence of a sharp rise in prostitution in the early 1960s, Glasgow City Police also introduced a more rigorous policy of prosecuting offenders.[87] However, court reports indicate that, despite such initiatives, prostitution was thriving in Glasgow in the 1960s. Typically, a prostitute could make up to £150–£200 a week, arranging appointments by phone, soliciting kerb crawlers or picking up business around Wellington Street, St Vincent Street, West Campbell Street and Blythswood Square, otherwise known as 'the big beat' or 'the drag'.[88] According to witness statements, many of the prostitutes had Maltese partners who were also their pimps and had migrated north from London or Manchester because they had been informed that, compared with life under the 1959 Street Offences Act in England, Glasgow 'was OK for business'.[89] As one sheriff concluded in 1966, 'it is perfectly apparent the age-old and classical vices flourish with an odd luxuriance in this city'.[90]

Table 2.2 Persons proceeded against for female prostitution, percentage distribution by city: five-yearly averages, 1950–74

Period	Aberdeen	Dundee	Edinburgh	Glasgow	Other
1950–4	5	2	16	70	7
1955–9	7	8	21	62	2
1960–4	2	7	21	65	5
1965–9	1	4	11	81	3
1970–4	6	7	5	80	2

Source: SHD/SHHD, *Criminal Statistics Scotland, Annual Reports for 1950–74*, Table 5.

Estimates varied of how many female prostitutes were operating in Glasgow. In the mid-1970s, the Glasgow Police Authorities calculated that there were '30–40 regular girls' but the Secretary of the Glasgow United Evangelical Association considered this to be an underestimate. He stressed that, apart from a small core of professionals, there were now many more casual prostitutes, young girls who were 'simply tempted by the big money involved'.[91] What particularly concerned him was that they were, in his view, 'ordinary girls', many of whom were 'smart, tidy and of normal intelligence'.

Glasgow would also appear to have been a recruiting ground for brothels elsewhere in Scotland. Thus, in 1963, twenty-two girls from the Glasgow area gave evidence in a case involving the provision of sexual services to US sailors in Dunoon.[92] The use by Dora Noyce of taxi loads of Glasgow prostitutes to meet unusual demand at her Danube Street brothel in Edinburgh was legendary.[93] A few Glasgow 'girls' also migrated to Aberdeen in the 1970s to capitalise on opportunities generated by the North Sea oil boom. However, according to a resident prostitute, they appeared to underestimate the local police force: 'The lassies frae Glasgow were jist walkin' on the streets, and on to the ships . . . They were arestit [sic] and sent back.'[94]

The recorded incidence of offences involving prostitution in Edinburgh was far more modest. While the number of persons proceeded against in Edinburgh in 1960 was almost double that for 1955, after peaking in 1962, there was a steady decline to 1970, with a further reduction thereafter.[95] Commenting on this trend, the Chief Constable remarked that 'prostitution on the streets' appeared to be 'on the wane', although he surmised that other methods of soliciting, by phone and by contacts in bars and dance halls, might well be continuing undetected.[96] Another explanation may be that, as prostitution migrated in the 1970s away from the central business and tourist areas of the city, the police were less concerned to prosecute.[97]

Outwith Glasgow and Edinburgh, reported cases of prostitution were relatively few, but they nonetheless often became a focus in the media and council chambers for broader anxieties surrounding sexual morality. In 1960, a call-girl racket was exposed in the West of Scotland involving a number of prostitutes having sex with US servicemen in Ayr, Prestwick, Troon and Dumfries, leading to an official inquiry as to the level of vice in the area.[98] In Aberdeen, a sharp rise in the early 1970s of prosecutions for soliciting triggered a similar moral panic. The Social Work Committee for Aberdeenshire and

Kincardineshire received reports that as many as sixty prostitutes had been attracted from the 'South' to Aberdeen and Peterhead by the prospect of a wealthy clientele of offshore oil workers, and that some were actually being smuggled onto the rigs.[99] The Lord Provost of Aberdeen discounted such stories as scaremongering, observing that the presence of a foreign fishing fleet in port had always attracted some degree of prostitution. However, in 1975, according to one local prostitute – alluded to as 'Maggie: Frontier Working Girl' in the press – the oil industry had certainly inflated the number of prostitutes in the area, with ten in Aberdeen 'and more in Peterhead . . . from Edinburgh, Orkney, Stirlin [sic] and Leith – some from [the] South and some big black lassies'.[100] In her view, the problem for the police was that younger girls could be picked up in the dance halls for the purposes of prostitution and were not visible on the streets.

FEMALE PROSTITUTION AND THE LAW IN SCOTLAND, 1960–80

During the period 1960–80, as in other areas of sexual governance in Scotland, shifts in policy with respect to prostitution were predominantly initiated at the level of the local state. In Edinburgh, the vice duties performed by the police were reorganised at the end of the 1950s so as to enable the force to adopt a more efficient and coordinated approach to offences such as prostitution and brothel keeping.[101] Subsequently, the Edinburgh Corporation Order Confirmation Acts of 1961 and 1967 raised the level of penalties for prostitution, slightly broadened and modernised the definition of importuning and soliciting, and rendered the offence equally applicable to men and women.[102] Evidence also suggests that the Edinburgh police continued in the 1960s to charge kerb crawlers who frequented the city centre with a breach of the peace.[103]

Compared with Glasgow's police authorities, the Edinburgh police adopted a relatively tolerant attitude towards brothel keeping. It was not regarded as 'a serious threat' and for the most part the authorities contented themselves with prosecuting Dora Noyce, the madame of the Danube Street brothel.[104] Despite being fined the maximum of £250 at regular intervals, with occasional spells of imprisonment, Noyce continued to operate her establishment undeterred until her death in 1977, with as many as thirty 'girls' available from 6 or 7pm. Much to her delight and to the dismay of the Edinburgh Tourist Office, it had an international reputation. It was especially busy when ships on NATO exercises berthed in the Firth of Forth and when international rugby matches were being played. One local resident claimed that 'when the aircraft carrier USS John F. Kennedy was in port, there were sailors queuing almost the length of Danube Street'.

Despite the enduring opposition of other residents, who successfully claimed for a reduction in their rates given the impact of the brothel on surrounding property values, Dora Noyce became somewhat of a local hero in the press, and the story of her life was subsequently celebrated in a play written by Hector Macmillan for the Lyceum Theatre, entitled *Capital Offence*.

Meanwhile, Glasgow authorities were endeavouring to cope with the rising incidence of prostitution in the West of Scotland. Many councillors and magistrates were frustrated with the limited powers at their disposal and dismayed at the apparent migration of prostitutes and their pimps from south of the Border in search of a more lenient legal environment. One councillor lamented that the average fine for soliciting in Glasgow was only equivalent to taxing the offender's undeclared earnings and in no way constituted a deterrent.[105] In its Corporation Order Confirmation Act of 1960, Glasgow increased the penalties for those found guilty of loitering or soliciting for the purposes of prostitution, and in a local Act of 1971 further clarified the power of magistrates to imprison repeat offenders without option of a fine.[106] In addition, in the mid-1970s, Strathclyde Police Authority introduced dedicated anti-vice patrols in a number of divisions.[107] In 1980, Glasgow District Council did discuss a proposal for legalised brothels outside residential areas, following support for such a scheme from Falkirk District Council, but the police were adamant that existing laws were a preferable option.[108]

What was distinctive about the response of Glasgow police authorities was their increasing use of the Criminal Law Amendment Act (1885) and Immoral Traffic (Scotland) Act (1902) (and after 1976, the Sexual Offences (Scotland) Act) to prosecute brothel keepers and pimps, usually after extensive surveillance and the use of prostitutes as key witnesses.[109] The press made much of the colour and ethnicity of defendants, many of whom were West Indian or Maltese, and there were distinctly xenophobic, if not racist, overtones in the rhetoric of some of the court reporting.[110] Most of these cases were conducted in the Sheriff Court, thus attracting higher penalties and often periods of imprisonment. Indeed, it is significant that, across Scotland, whereas during the 1950s only 29 per cent of cases involving brothel keeping were prosecuted in the Sheriff Courts, in the 1960s they accounted for 79 per cent of such proceedings.[111]

However, as Table 2.3 indicates, even where a custodial sentence was within their powers to impose, there does not appear to have been any inclination on the part of Scottish magistrates to increase the incidence of prison sentencing for convicted prostitutes after 1960. On the contrary, while the proportion imprisoned fell from 19 per cent in 1950 to 7 per cent in 1970, the proportion either fined or admonished rose from 81 per cent to 93 per cent; albeit average fines had risen more than fourfold – from £2.18 to £9.40 over the same period.[112]

Table 2.3 Type of sentence imposed in Scottish summary courts for offences relating to prostitution

Year	% fined	% imprisoned	% admonished
1950	67	19	14
1955	77	17	6
1960	75	16	9
1965	79	6	15
1970	81	7	12

Source: SHD/SHHD, *Criminal Statistics Scotland, Annual Reports for 1950–74*, Table 9.

During the period 1960–80 there were no substantive changes to general statute law relating to prostitution in Scotland. Although modernising the language involved, the 1976 Sexual Offences (Scotland) Act merely consolidated existing provisions under the 1885 Criminal Law Amendment Act and 1902 Immoral Traffic (Scotland) Act designed to target procurers, brothel keepers and anyone living on immoral earnings.[113] It did not seek to address the miscellany of powers relating to sexual offences in Scotland under the Burgh Police and Local Acts.[114]

Instead, this became just one part of the protracted and complex task of the Working Party on Civic Government established in 1972 to plan for the demise of the Burgh Police Acts, scheduled for 1982. The Working Party surveyed a variety of issues relating to soliciting, importuning, kerb crawling and brothel keeping. It related its views specifically to proposals being advanced by a concurrent Working Party on Vagrancy and Street Offences set up by the Home Office to review the outcome and adequacy of the 1959 Street Offences Act in England and Wales.[115]

In general, the Working Party on Civic Government was resistant to any significant alteration in legal procedures and practices in Scotland. On the issue of loitering and importuning, it did not consider the desirability of extending the provisions of the 1959 Street Offences Act to Scotland but merely recommended that future legislation should be modelled on the Edinburgh Corporation Act of 1967.[116] With respect to the suppression of brothels, officials of the Scottish Home and Health Department (SHHD) argued that the issue was 'adequately covered by common law or general statutes'. Similarly, although the Home Office's Working Party pressed for the addition of a new offence of kerb crawling, both the Crown Office and the SHHD considered that such offences could be readily dealt with under the common law in Scotland as a breach of the peace.[117] It was also recommended that existing powers to prosecute those 'harbouring' prostitutes or 'persons of notoriously bad fame' in 'houses of refreshment' should be retained in line with the wording of the Edinburgh Order of 1967 as a means of deterring the use of public houses as a venue for prostitution. However, pressure to widen such powers to include all places of entertainment was resisted.[118]

The Working Party on Civic Government considered that the issue of reframing the existing law relating to sexual offences within the Burgh Police and Local Acts was one of 'great complexity'. Nonetheless, while they readily conceded that they were not qualified to explore the full legal and social implications of legal changes in this area, they 'reached one firm conclusion and made one observation':

> The conclusion was that it was necessary in the public interest that the offences of soliciting and importuning should be retained and we recommend that they should be included in the civic code. The observation was that there was no current controversy in Scotland about the present law and its workings, [and] it would appear that reenactment would be adequate.[119]

Section 447 of the Edinburgh Corporation Order of 1967 was recommended as a template for future legislation.

Subsequently, the relevant clauses of the long-awaited Civic Government (Scotland) Bill of 1982 closely adhered to the Working

Party's conclusions. The clauses were introduced as primarily a consolidation of existing provisions relating to prostitution. While senior law officers in Scotland were keen to penalise men who solicited women for the purposes of sexual gratification, it was concluded that such behaviour was adequately covered by the 1976 Sexual Offences (Scotland) Act and by the common law relating to breach of the peace.[120] As a result, no additional offence of kerb crawling was introduced. There were only two relatively minor changes. First, to avoid the criticism of sexual discrimination formerly levelled at legislation relating to street offences, it was made explicit that the offence of soliciting and importuning applied to both men and women. Second, the concept of 'public place' was more broadly defined to incorporate soliciting from the windows or doors of private property.[121] Thus, the law relating to prostitution in Scotland in the early 1980s had not fundamentally altered from that prevailing on the eve of the Wolfenden Committee.

Notes

1   See, for example, Hall, *Sex, Gender and Social Change*, ch. 9; Haste, *Rules of Desire*, ch. 7; Ferris, *Sex and the British*, ch. 8.
2   Weeks, *Sex, Politics and Society*, 243–4. See also Mort, 'Mapping sexual London', 94–5.
3   See, for example, Smart, 'Law and the control of women's sexuality', 40–60; Self, *Prostitution, Women and Misuse of the Law*.
4   The National Archives, Public Record Office, Kew (hereafter PRO), HO345/16, Proceedings of the Wolfenden Committee on Homosexual Offences and Prostitution (hereafter PWC), 9 April 1956.
5   *Edinburgh Evening News*, 15 July 1954.
6   Social workers and purity groups pressed for the closure of the coffee stalls but the police argued successfully for their retention on the grounds that they constituted a 'magnet' for criminal elements who they wanted to keep under surveillance.
7   PRO, HO345/16, PWC, Evidence of Assistant Chief Constable (hereafter ACC) for Glasgow, 10 April 1956.
8   Ibid., Evidence of Glasgow magistrates, 9 April 1956.
9   Ibid., Evidence of ACCs for Glasgow and Edinburgh, 10 April 1956.
10   PRO, HO345/6, PWC, Notes on general discussion, 21 February 1956.
11   PRO, HO345/16, PWC, Evidence of L. Gordon, Crown Agent, 9 April 1956.
12   Ibid.
13   Edinburgh City Archives (hereafter ECA), SL119/3/24, Minutes of

Magistrates' Committee, 18 November 1954. Edinburgh's City Prosecutor also observed a shift away from 'professional' street prostitution to the use of lower-class restaurants and public houses [National Records of Scotland (hereafter NRS), GD333/14, Minutes of the Executive Committee of the Edinburgh Women Citizens' Association, 27 March 1957].

14 Cant (ed.), *Footsteps and Witnesses*, 52.
15 *The Scotsman*, 23 December 1977.
16 PRO, HO345/16, PWC, Evidence of ACCs for Glasgow and Edinburgh, 10 April 1956.
17 Ibid.
18 PRO, HO345/5, PWC, M. Cohen to J. Wolfenden, 30 July 1956; HO345/10, Note of discussion, 29 January 1957.
19 PRO, HO345/16, PWC, Evidence of Crown Agent, 9 April 1956.
20 *Glasgow Herald*, 12 February 1955; PRO, HO345/16, PWC, Evidence of Glasgow Magistrates, 9 April 1956; Evidence of ACC for Edinburgh, 10 April 1956.
21 PRO, HO345/9, PWC, Evidence of Faculty of Advocates, 1956.
22 *Report of the [Wolfenden] Committee on Homosexual Offences and Prostitution* (hereafter *RWC*), 147.
23 Ibid., 143.
24 PRO, HO345/12, PWC, Committee proceedings, 15 October 1954.
25 Ibid.
26 Ibid., Evidence of Scottish Home Department (hereafter SHD), 15 October 1954.
27 PRO, HO345/16, PWC, Evidence of Glasgow Magistrates, 9 April 1956.
28 NRS, HH60/268, Memorandum by SHD on 'Prostitution and allied offences', October 1954.
29 Ibid.
30 PRO, HO345/16, PWC, Evidence of ACC for Edinburgh, 10 April 1956.
31 ECA, Edinburgh Burgh Court records for 1950–5.
32 NRS, HH60/268, Memorandum on 'Prostitution and allied offences', October 1954.
33 Ibid.
34 *Report of the Street Offences Committee*, 24.
35 PRO, HO345/16, PWC, Evidence of ACC for Glasgow, 10 April 1956.
36 Ibid., Evidence of ACC for Edinburgh, 10 April 1956.
37 *RWC*, 91; PRO, HO345/9, PWC, Memorandum by Christine Mackenzie, April 1956.
38 Glasgow City Archives (hereafter GCA), C/1/3/121, Minutes of the Glasgow Corporation Police Committee, 14 February 1950.
39 General Assembly of the Church of Scotland (hereafter GACS), *Report of Church and Nation Committee for 1958*, 421.

40 The role of prostitution in contemporary debates concerning VD and its containment is discussed more fully in Chapter 7 of this volume.

41 *Criminal Justice (Scotland) Act, 1949*, section 27.

42 NRS, HH57/568, Minutes by Dr I. D. Inch on 'The treatment of venereal diseases in prison', 10 January and 18 April 1961.

43 NRS, ED48/1364, Memorandum by the Home Office and SHD on 'The rehabilitation of young prostitutes', 1943; Davidson, *Dangerous Liaisons*, 276.

44 See, for example, Glover, *The Psycho-Pathology of Prostitution*.

45 *RWC*, 7.

46 PRO, HO345/4, PWC, Note by J. Adair, 1955.

47 PRO, HO345/6, PWC, Notes on general discussion, 21 February 1956; HO345/16, Evidence of Glasgow Magistrates and Christine Mackenzie, 9 April 1956.

48 Ibid., PWC, Evidence of Glasgow Magistrates, 9 April 1956.

49 PRO, HO345/15, PWC, Evidence of Director of Scottish Prison and Borstal Services, 1 November 1954.

50 PRO, HO345/16, PWC, Evidence of Christine Mackenzie, 9 April 1956.

51 PRO, HO345/10, PWC, Note of discussion, 29 January 1957. For similar views within the Church of Scotland, see GACS, *Report of Church and Nation Committee for 1958*, 421–2.

52 *RWC*, 123–4.

53 PRO, HO345/8, PWC, Evidence of Elizabeth Abbott, 1955; HO345/16, Evidence of Christine Mackenzie, 9 April 1956. For a more general discussion of the legal and cultural implications of the retention of the term 'common prostitute', see Smart, 'Law and the control of women's sexuality', 52.

54 PRO, HO345/16, PWC, Evidence of Christine Mackenzie, 9 April 1956.

55 PRO, HO345/8, PWC, Evidence of Elizabeth Abbott, 1955.

56 United Free Church of Scotland (hereafter UFCS), *Minutes of Proceedings of General Assembly for 1958*, 20.

57 Congregational Union of Scotland, *Annual Report of Temperance and Social Questions Committee for 1958–9*, 119.

58 Such evidence vindicated the view previously expressed in Cabinet by the Secretary of State for Scotland (hereafter SSS) that there was no justification for Scotland to be included in any public inquiry into street offences [PRO, CAB129/66, Memorandum on 'Sexual Offences', 17 February 1954].

59 NRS, HH60/268, PWC, Written submission of SHD, October 1954.

60 Ibid.

61 Ibid.; PRO, HO345/16, PWC, Evidence of ACCs for Edinburgh and Glasgow, 10 April 1956.

62 PRO, HO345/10, PWC, Notes of discussion, 29 January 1957.

63 PRO, HO291/123, Notes for debate on the Wolfenden Report, 1957–8.

64 Ibid., Notes for debates on Wolfenden: redemption of young prostitutes, 1957–8; HO345/16, PWC, Evidence of Christine Mackenzie, 9 April 1956.

65 PRO, HO345/7, HO345/16, PWC, Written and oral evidence of Dr Winifred Rushforth, 1955, 10 April 1956. Significantly, little evidence on the medical aetiology and treatment of prostitution was elicited by the Wolfenden Committee. Indeed, while the medical treatment of male homosexual offenders was explicitly part of its terms of reference, this was not the case with respect to female prostitutes.

66 PRO, HO345/7, PWC, Evidence of Glasgow Stipendiary Magistrate, 1955; HO345/16, Evidence of Crown Agent, and comment of J. Adair, 9 April 1956.

67 PRO, HO345/16, PWC, Evidence of Glasgow Magistrates and ACCs for Edinburgh and Glasgow, 9 and 10 April 1956.

68 *RWC*, 116–17.

69 *Hansard* [HC], vol. 597, 18 December 1958, col. 1,319.

70 *Hansard* [HL], vol. 206, 4 December 1957, cols 769–79.

71 *Hansard* [HL], vol. 217, 14 July 1959, cols 1,190–3.

72 *Hansard* [HC], vol. 598, 29 January 1959, cols 1,310–11.

73 *Hansard* [HL], vol. 216, 5 May 1959, cols 96–101; vol. 217, 14 July 1959, cols 1, 182–4. The Church and Nation Committee of the Church of Scotland also expressed concern that legislation that focused primarily on regulation 'might merely result in a hypocritical hiding away of prostitution and a convenient ignoring by the community of its existence as a social evil and a scandal' [GACS, *Report of Church and Nation Committee for 1958*, 420–1].

74 See, for example, *Hansard* [HL], vol. 206, 4 December 1957, cols 780–7; vol. 216, 5 May 1959, cols 78–9; [HC], vol. 596, 26 November 1958, col. 402.

75 NRS, HH60/265, Minute by Sir William Murrie, 30 October 1957.

76 Ibid., Notes for Commons debate on Wolfenden Report, 26 November 1958.

77 Ibid. For a full discussion of this decision and its implications for Scotland, see Chapter 3 of this volume.

78 *The Scotsman*, 2 and 4 June 1959.

79 Ibid.

80 Ibid., 3 June 1959.

81 NRS, HH60/265, Minute N. D. Walker to A. B. Hume, 11 October 1957.

82 PRO, HO291/123, Notes for debates on Wolfenden: redemption of young prostitutes, 1957–8.

83 SHD/SHHD, *Criminal Statistics Scotland, Annual Reports for 1950–74*, Table 5.

84 Ibid., Table 10.
85 Ibid. Evidence suggests that, in part, the concentration of reported cases in Glasgow reflected police practice. It was claimed that Glasgow Police Authorities were significantly more proactive in prosecuting prostitutes, even where there was no clear evidence of a public nuisance, sometimes as a means of inflating arrest figures [NRS, AD63/1514/19, Minutes of Scottish Standing Committee, 17 June 1982].
86 *Glasgow Herald*, 13 March, 28 July and 14 August 1959.
87 GCA, D-TC 7/19/2, *Report of the Chief Constable of the City of Glasgow for 1963*, 32.
88 *Glasgow Herald*, 3 March 1970.
89 Ibid., 28 May 1969, 4 June 1969, 3 March 1970.
90 Ibid., 5 May 1966.
91 Ibid., 17 November 1975.
92 Ibid., 15 October 1963.
93 Ibid., 29 November 1977.
94 Ibid., 20 October 1975.
95 *SHD/SHHD, Criminal Statistics Scotland, Annual Reports for 1950–74*, Table 5.
96 ECA, ED6/1/16, *Edinburgh City Police Annual Report for 1968*, 26.
97 Mapping the location of offences reveals an increasing shift away from Princes Street and the New Town towards Leith [ECA, Edinburgh Burgh Court records for 1970 and 1980].
98 *Glasgow Herald*, 25 May and 10 June 1960.
99 Ibid., 7 June 1973.
100 Ibid., 20 October 1975.
101 ECA, *Edinburgh City Police Annual Reports for 1959*, 15; *1960*, 15.
102 *Local Statutes, Edinburgh Corporation Order Confirmation Acts, 1961*, section 179; *1967*, section 447. The Orders dropped the phrase 'common prostitute or street walker' previously contained in the charge under the Burgh Police (Scotland) Act, 1892.
103 See, for example, ECA, Edinburgh Burgh Court records, papers relating to W.Q., 22 January 1963. On the application of Scots law to kerb crawling, see Gane, *Sexual Offences*, 158.
104 The following account is based upon *Glasgow Herald*, 22 September 1973, 19 and 20 July 1977, 11, 25 and 26 August 1977, 30 October 1977, 29 November 1977.
105 Ibid., 6 March 1970.
106 GCA, C1/3/160, Minutes of Glasgow Police Committee, 28 April 1970; *Local Statutes, Glasgow Corporation Consolidation (General Powers) Order Confirmation Acts, 1960*, sections 159, 188; *1971*, section 6.
107 GCA, SR22/1/1–2, *Reports of the Chief Constable of Strathclyde Police for 1975*, 31; *1976*, 16.
108 *Glasgow Herald*, 14 March 1980.

109 For details of the law in Scotland relating to brothel keeping, procuring and living on immoral earnings during the period 1960–80, see especially Gane, *Sexual Offences*, ch. 9; Gordon, *The Criminal Law of Scotland*, 909–19.

110 See, for example, *Glasgow Herald*, 5 May 1966, 30 September 1966, 3 February 1968, 10 May 1968, 3 March 1970, 23 September 1971, 12 January 1977. For the importance of race to contemporary fears relating to pimping and prostitution, see Mort, *Capital Affairs*, 311–12.

111 SHD/SHHD, *Criminal Statistics Scotland, Annual Reports for 1950–74*, Table 5.

112 Ibid., Table 9.

113 *Public General Acts, 1976*, ch. 67, sections 1–2, 11–14.

114 NRS, AD63/1293, Sexual Offences (Scotland) Bill 1976, Notes on clauses, 8 July 1976.

115 NRS, AD60/1214, Working Party draft report, 14 November 1975.

116 Ibid.

117 NRS, AD60/1214, A. M. Burnside to W. A. P. Weatherston, 4 December 1975.

118 Ibid., Draft report, 14 November 1975.

119 Ibid., Draft report, 5 December 1975.

120 NRS, AD63/1514/16, Civic Government (Scotland) Bill, House of Lords, notes on clauses, November 1981; AD63/1514/14, J. L. Jamieson to J. C. McCluskie, 5 July 1982; J. C. McCluskie to J. L. Jamieson, 9 July 1982.

121 *Public General Acts, Civic Government (Scotland) Act, 1982*, section 46. Gane, *Sexual Offences*, 156.

3

HOMOSEXUAL LAW REFORM, 1950–67

INTRODUCTION

The second major area of transgressive sexual behaviour that pre-occupied policy makers after 1950 was homosexuality. As with prostitution, contemporary debate surrounding homosexual offences was dominated by the proceedings and report of the Wolfenden Committee.[1] Subsequently, many historians have perceived the Committee, and the associated debate in Parliament and the media, as a watershed in the public awareness of homosexuality that was to be vital in the creation of a climate of opinion more receptive to law reform in the 1960s.[2] Others emphasise instead its role in the creation of a new taxonomy of sexual pathology 'conducted in the language of legal and professional regulation' and drawing upon not only the traditional expertise of medicine and the law but also the newer specialities of psychiatry and psychoanalysis 'in the interests of productive surveillance'.[3] A further group of social and legal commentators also stress the more illiberal aspects of the Wolfenden Report as reflected in its impact on public discourse and the 1967 Sexual Offences Act. They emphasise the regressive effects of the debate on the social labelling of homosexuals, and the very limited extent to which the utilitarian criteria adopted by the Committee, and its taxonomy of 'public' and 'private', advanced the social recognition of homosexuality.[4]

This chapter seeks to add a Scottish perspective to this historiography. First, it utilises the evidence presented by Scottish witnesses to the Wolfenden Committee to document the existing legal and medical provisions for the treatment of homosexual offences in mid-twentieth-century Scotland. Second, it investigates the forces and arguments both for and against the decriminalisation of homosexual practices as revealed in the Scottish testimony to the Committee. Third, it documents the views of the three Scottish members of the Wolfenden Committee in relation to its final report, and focuses in particular on the ideology and enduring influence of James Adair and his virulent opposition to its recommendation for the decriminalisation of consensual homosexual practices in private. Finally, the chapter surveys the wide-ranging opposition within Scottish civil society to such reform in Scotland in the decade following the Wolfenden Report, culminating in the exclusion of Scotland, along with Northern Ireland, from the 1967 Sexual Offences Act.

THE PROSECUTION AND TREATMENT OF HOMOSEXUAL OFFENCES IN THE 1950S

Table 3.1 sets out the law relating to homosexual offences in Scotland in the 1950s with the associated tariff of punishments.

Under Scots law, as in England and Wales, homosexual behaviour between males was an offence. The more serious cases were tried, often under common law, in a Sheriff Court or the High Court, while minor acts of indecency were dealt with as police offences in Burgh Courts under the Burgh Police (Scotland) Act of 1892.[5] In addition, many Scottish burghs had the power to make byelaws to prevent 'nuisances' and these were commonly employed to prevent soliciting.[6] Thus, in Edinburgh, 'cottaging' (homosexual activity between men in a public lavatory) was proceeded against under the cleansing byelaws which stipulated that: 'No person shall loiter in a public convenience or use the same for any purpose other than as a lavatory or toilet apartment.'[7] All cases of indecency where boys were involved were referred to the Lord Advocate's Department to determine the level of court proceedings. Where one of the parties was under 16, only the elder of the parties would be proceeded against, normally under common law. The sentences imposed for homosexual offences in Scotland were generally lighter than those imposed in England and Wales. Only 72 per cent of those convicted of sodomy and 20 per cent of those convicted of gross indecency incurred prison sentences, and such sentences were often of a year or less.[8]

Within the Scottish prison system, there was no general policy of segregating homosexual offenders. However, they were debarred from transfer to open prisons and efforts were made to allocate them separate accommodation where acute overcrowding prevailed. The Scottish Prison Department also admitted that 'passive homosexuals' were kept under unobtrusive attention by the staff and were, if possible, posted to work parties that could be closely supervised. Similarly, if an inmate of a borstal was suspected of homosexual tendencies, he might be allocated a single bedroom or transferred either to a particular training house or very occasionally to a closed institution.[9]

**Table 3.1 Law and practice relating to homosexual offences
in Scotland in the 1950s**

Offence	Statute	Where triable	Maximum punishment
Sodomy	Common law	High Court of Justiciary	Imprisonment for life
Attempted sodomy	Common law	ditto	Imprisonment for life
Indecent assault	Common law	Sheriff Court with jury	Two years' imprisonment
Lewd and libidinous practices	Common law	Sheriff Court with/without jury	Three months' imprisonment
Acts of gross indecency	Criminal Law Amendment Act 1885, Section 11, as applied by section 15	ditto	Two years' imprisonment/ Three months' imprisonment
Procuring acts of gross indecency	ditto	ditto	ditto
Attempting to procure acts of gross indecency	ditto	ditto	ditto
Persistent soliciting or importuning by male of males for homosexual purposes	Immoral Traffic (Scotland) Act 1902, Section 1; Criminal Law Amendment Act 1912, Section 7 (2) and (5)	Sheriff Court with jury or any court of summary jurisdiction	Two years' imprisonment/ Six months' imprisonment
Offences against byelaws involving indecency between persons of same sex	Various byelaws	Any court of summary jurisdiction	Fine of £5

Source: *RWC*, 30–1.

Evidence varies as to the extent to which medical considerations played a part in the sentencing of homosexual offenders. James Adair, formerly procurator fiscal in Glasgow, was of the opinion that: 'Some judges were very responsive to suggestions by medical men about treatment, while others agreed that these were not the concern of the judge.'[10] Certainly, under the Criminal Justice (Scotland) Act of 1949, courts had explicit powers both to call for medical reports on offenders and to prescribe medical treatment (although not its specific nature) as part of a probationary sentence. Thus, an offender could, with his consent, be required under a probation order to undertake remedial treatment as either a resident or a non-resident of an institution or as a patient of a named doctor.[11] Some law officers considered that there was an increasing trend in Scottish courts for medical reports to be used in cases involving homosexual offences and that the practice was 'much more the custom in Scotland than in England'.[12] Dr W. Boyd, Consultant Psychiatrist to the Scottish Prison and Borstal Services, testified that he was:

> in charge of a Mental Health Service where both the Procurators Fiscal and the Sheriffs were willing to recognise that we could have cooperation, and many of them [offenders] were placed on probation on the condition that they attended hospital.[13]

In line with the recommendation of the Scottish Advisory Committee on the Treatment and Rehabilitation of Offenders that psychotherapeutic and other medical treatment should be more widely available for convicted sexual offenders, the Scottish Home Department (SHD) had, by the mid-1950s, begun to expand psychiatric provisions within the Scottish prison system. The Department recommended that all male prisoners convicted of sexual offences, including homosexual offences, should be interviewed at some point by a psychiatrist and that, if the offender was suitable for treatment and was willing to undergo it during his sentence, he should be admitted to a psychiatric hospital as an in-patient or given treatment at a psychiatric clinic as an out-patient. Similar psychiatric examination and treatment was, in theory at least, available for all male borstal inmates.[14] However, Dr Inch, the Medical Adviser, maintained that the resources for treatment within Scottish prisons remained 'pitifully inadequate' and 'barely scratch[ed] the surface of the problem'.[15] Apart from Barlinnie, where a new medical psychiatric unit was being built, there were no special psychotherapeutic units in Scotland such as existed at Wormwood Scrubs and Wakefield, and many of the prisons were too small to justify in-house psychiatric provisions.[16]

Scotland differed from England and Wales in the type of prison treatment administered to convicted homosexual offenders. According to the evidence of Scottish Prison Medical Officers, no use was made of electroconvulsive therapy in Scottish prisons. Narcoanalysis (psychoanalysis conducted while the patient is in a drug-induced sleeplike state) had been used to a limited extent during the war but had been deemed unsuited to 'civil life'.[17] However, in contrast to England and Wales, where the practice had been discontinued as it was deemed too dangerous, oestrogen treatment had been used in Scottish prisons on sexual offenders for some time. It was only given to prisoners who signed an agreement to the procedure and then only under strict medical supervision. According to Inch, oestrogen treatment had never been pushed 'to its limits' – 'to the extent of producing atrophy of the testicles or gynaecomastia – but only to the point of eliminating or at least greatly reducing libido'.[18] The prime objective was to make the prisoners less anxious and more 'adaptable'. Significantly, such treatment regimes were not public knowledge. According to Inch, the Scottish Prison Service had 'never said anything'. 'We have,' he noted, 'just kept very quiet about it.'[19]

There is clear evidence of the Scottish police taking proactive measures against homosexuals in the early 1950s. Thus, the bulk of prosecutions under Section 11 of the Criminal Law Amendment Act for gross indecency were based on plain-clothes police observations on public lavatories. In Edinburgh, in cases where the police were unable to secure the necessary 'place of concealment' to prosecute under the Act, they made regular use of the local cleansing byelaws to penalise 'cottaging'. In Glasgow, there was a vigorous campaign to eliminate it. Lavatories were closed down or upgraded with attendants, and the procurator fiscal ordered that all such cases should be referred to Glasgow Sheriff Court rather than the lower Burgh Courts so that more serious charges might be brought. Some witnesses clearly considered that there had been a greater targeting of homosexual activities in recent years.[20] Indeed, during the media coverage of homosexual lifestyles in 1958, the *Daily Herald* later reported on a homosexual who had been forced to flee from Edinburgh to London due to 'a police clamp-down'.[21]

Nonetheless, there were distinctive features of the criminal procedures in Scotland that minimised the number of men prosecuted for homosexual offences in private with consenting adult partners.[22]

First, as all serious proceedings were instigated and the level of hearing determined, not by the police, but by the public prosecutor – the procurator fiscal – 'in the public interest', there was much greater uniformity of prosecution and sentencing. Second, as no proceedings could be initiated in respect of any statutory offence more than six months old in any court of summary jurisdiction, and older cases had to be reported to the Crown Office before proceedings could be brought, there was an automatic constraint on the prosecution of 'stale' offences, in contrast to the practice in many areas of England and Wales. Thus, in Scotland, even when criminal proceedings produced evidence of past homosexual behaviour, where it was evident that such behaviour was no longer 'active', charges were rarely brought.[23] Third, in Scotland, a higher standard of proof was required. No person could be convicted of any homosexual offence unless there was evidence of at least two witnesses implicating the person with the commission of the offence, or corroboration of one witness by irrefutable evidence. As a result, it was rarely possible to secure the necessary evidence with which to prosecute homosexual acts performed in private and between consenting adults. Moreover, while a written statement of guilt constituted corroboration, it was rarely elicited under Scottish legal proceedings. The police were not entitled to question a person with the object of causing him to incriminate himself and were not allowed to question a suspect after he had been cautioned. As a result, whereas in England and Wales some 94 per cent of men convicted for homosexual offences in the period 1953–6 were prosecuted on the basis of a written confession, this applied to only 11 per cent of such cases in Scotland.[24]

Moreover, in view of the high standard of proof required by Scottish criminal law, the Lord Advocate's Department had for many years adopted a policy of not prosecuting homosexual acts between consenting adults in private. There were occasional exceptions but, in the main, the Crown Office focused on offences committed in public places, especially in toilets, cinemas or parks, or on offences involving the seduction or 'debauching of the young';[25] an aspect of Scottish prosecution policy that was to prove central to the delay in homosexual law reform north of the Border.

THE WOLFENDEN COMMITTEE – EVIDENCE FAVOURING DECRIMINALISATION

As Patrick Higgins has rightly observed: 'It is not accurate to portray the arguments made before the Wolfenden Committee as a clash between reformers and reactionaries' because the overwhelming majority of witnesses favoured 'the reduction, and hopefully one day the elimination, of male homosexuality'.[26] However, there *were* Scottish witnesses who strongly advocated the decriminalisation of homosexual behaviour. Thus, a representative of the moral purity movement urged that while the law should always protect the young, it should not interfere with the personal morals of consenting adults, as this merely created a 'blackmailer's charter' and a *'police des mœurs'* with duties that were 'ugly, degrading and demoralising'. In her view, accusations of 'unnatural vice' were equally applicable to 'extravagances' within heterosexual relationships.[27] Similar views were expressed by Sheriff A. G. Walker. He favoured placing consenting homosexual acts in private between men over 25 'on the same legal base as adultery and fornication'. This would, in his view, 'enable the adult homosexual . . . to work out his difficult problems . . . in accordance with his own conscience and the religious or moral code to which he subscribe[d]' without the additional distraction of the fear of prosecution. At the same time, the full weight of the criminal law could be focused on the protection of boys and young men from predatory adults.[28]

The fullest and most compelling Scottish evidence in favour of homosexual law reform came from medical witnesses. Perhaps the most influential evidence was that submitted by Drs T. D. Inch and W. Boyd, respectively Medical Adviser and Consultant Psychiatrist to the Scottish Prison and Borstal Services.[29] Echoing the previous recommendations of the Scottish Advisory Council on the Treatment and Rehabilitation of Offenders, they aired serious doubts as to the value of imprisonment in reforming sexual offenders and favoured the decriminalisation of homosexual behaviour for consenting adults over 21. In their view, a range of alternative provisions was necessary. There needed to be more child guidance and child psychiatric clinics to 'treat deviation as early as possible before fixation occurred'. Courts should have routine psychiatric reports on all homosexual offenders prior to sentencing, supplied by a properly staffed University or Regional Hospital Board clinic, and more extensive use needed to be made of probationary orders for treatment of first offenders under the 1949 Criminal Justice (Scotland) Act. For the homosexual recidivist or 'homosexual psychopath', there should be a separate psychopathic institute, as in Denmark. Finally, treatment regimes had to be more effectively monitored and sustained by means of improved staff resources for aftercare and social work. Underlying their evidence was a belief that a less punitive policy would in fact produce a more liberal and sympathetic attitude to homosexuality in British society.

Evidence submitted by Drs Winifred Rushforth and W. P. Kraemer, respectively founder and Medical Director of the Davidson Clinic in Edinburgh, also favoured the decriminalisation of homosexual behaviour between consenting adults as integral to changing social attitudes and to a refocusing of public debate onto issues of aetiology rather than punishment.[30] Their case studies provided compelling evidence of the high incidence of blackmail experienced by homosexuals under existing law. Moreover, they considered that imprisonment merely reinforced the mental and social problems of homosexuals and should only be used for 'hardened offenders' who were 'a potential danger to young people'. They did not feel that prison predisposed homosexual offenders to effective treatment, and viewed the existing prison medical staff as unsuited to addressing sexual problems. At the very least, they advocated the general introduction of group psychotherapy for offenders. However, significantly, their evidence still identified homosexuals as fundamentally dysfunctional and anti-social and, in part, their opposition to legal coercion was that it served merely to magnify not only the homosexual's sense of social isolation but also his sexual ego. As Dr Kraemer testified:

> I feel that if we make them into heroes and put them into prisons ... it is not really doing very much good, and it gives them a wrong idea of self-importance ... If you do that I feel it is bad for society and for the character of these men, too.[31]

In his view, many such 'young heroes want[ed] to suck forbidden fruit' and prosecution often served to fuel a neurotic compulsion for punishment.

In his contribution to the British Medical Association's evidence to the Wolfenden Committee, John Glaister, Regius Professor of Forensic Medicine in the University of Glasgow, also conflated a somewhat pathological view of homosexuality with support for its limited decriminalisation. He was a vigorous supporter of coercive measures, including segregation in colonies, for 'the inveterate and degenerate sodomist, the debauchers of youth, and those who resort[ed] to violence to meet their desires'. Likewise, he endorsed a 'major attack by the law' on 'the confirmed invert and the male prostitute'.

However, he did not feel that the incidence of homosexuality threat-ened the nation with 'racial decadence' and considered that consenting acts of adults in private (not including sodomy) were a matter 'of private ethics' and should be outside the law. In his opinion, while society's disapproval was 'inevitable and desirable', and while homosexuality was certainly not something that should be encour-aged, incarceration was not the answer in the majority of cases that involved minor offences. Glaister viewed prison as 'the last place for homosexual treatment'. On the contrary, he emphasised its propensity 'to incubate and foster homosexual tendencies'. Moreover, he also considered that the risk of prosecution often acted as an aphrodisiac for offenders. 'Many homosexuals,' he averred, 'feel that to flout the law is fraught with adventure due to possible detection, and to their peculiar make-up this may tend to add a fillip to their sex life'.[32]

THE WOLFENDEN COMMITTEE – EVIDENCE FAVOURING THE STATUS QUO

However, the overwhelming consensus of Scottish evidence before the Wolfenden Committee was opposed to the decriminalisation of homosexual acts between consenting adults. In particular, two central and somewhat inconsistent arguments were advanced in favour of the status quo: first, that, in part because of its more demanding procedures relating to evidence and prosecution, the recorded incidence of homosexual offences in Scotland was compar-atively low and did not constitute a 'problem', and second, that the bulk of Scottish professional and public opinion was, in any case, fundamentally opposed to any liberalisation of the law.

As the Wolfenden Committee concluded: 'There was no precise information about the number of men in Great Britain who either [had] a homosexual disposition or engage[d] in homosexual behaviour'.[33] In Scotland, the problem of establishing the incidence of homosexual offences was compounded by the fact that the criminal statistics did not distinguish, as regards indecent assaults and lewd and libidinous practices, between offences committed with a male and those committed with a female. Prior to 1951, no statistics were available in respect of gross indecency between males under Section 11 of the 1885 Criminal Law Amendment Act, and there was therefore no basis for a historical comparison between the incidence of homo-sexual offences in Scotland and their incidence south of the Border.[34]

Witnesses were in no doubt that homosexuality and homosexual practices did exist in Scottish society. Scottish law officers made reference to 'habitual loci' for homosexual practices, 'some of long standing', including Glasgow Green and Calton Hill in Edinburgh, in addition to the regular use of certain public lavatories.[35] A number of blackmail and murder cases relating to homosexuality were also cited as evidence of its existence and vulnerability to exploitation by criminal elements.[36] In addition, several witnesses expressed a more nebulous fear that substantially more homosexual behaviour was lurking just below the surface of Scottish society. Thus, Glasgow's Procurator Fiscal of Police reflected that: '[A]s law officers we have a feeling that it goes on, we just do not know how far it goes on . . . There is a sort of iceberg of which only the top one-sixth is visible.'[37]

Moreover, such fears were reinforced by some of the medical evidence presented to the Committee. While Glaister doubted that the proportion of the population participating in a homosexual relationship at some time in their lives matched Kinsey's estimate for the USA of 10 per cent, he had little doubt that 'homosexual potentialities' existed in 'a very large number of male persons'.[38] For their part, Drs Rushforth and Kraemer considered that 'Kinsey's figures might easily work for Scotland'. On the basis of their casework, they were convinced that homosexual circles existed in all the Scottish cities and that homosexuality was 'an extremely common condition'.[39]

Nevertheless, the unequivocal view of the Scottish administration was that homosexuality did not constitute a significant problem north of the Border. Indeed, the Secretary of State for Scotland had advised the Cabinet as early as February 1954 that, although there had been a slight increase in the number of prosecutions for homosexual offences in the post-war period, 'The Scottish position did not justify an inquiry.'[40] Statistics presented by the SHD to the Wolfenden Committee endorsed this view. In 1955, only eighty convictions for homosexual offences were recorded in Scotland as compared with 2,293 in England and Wales. Moreover, for the period from March 1953 to March 1956, while 480 men in England and Wales aged 21 and over had been convicted of homosexual offences in private with other consenting adults, the comparable figure for Scotland was nine.[41]

Such statistics were reinforced by the general impressions of Scottish magistrates, law officers and senior policemen. Thus, in the view of Glasgow's Assistant Chief Constable and Procurator Fiscal of Police, homosexual practices in private were not 'a serious problem in the city' and there had been no 'noticeable increase in the amount of homosexual behaviour between grown men'.[42] Although such witnesses acknowledged that there were public conveniences where homosexuals tended to congregate, public importuning was not viewed as 'a major problem of public nuisance'. The Crown Agent testified that, in his experience: 'That offence does not appear to exist in this country to any extent, if at all.'[43] Remarking on the lack of prosecutions in Scotland, Dr Inch, Medical Adviser to the Scottish Prison and Borstal Services, observed that 'passive sodomists of the male prostitute type' had indicated that:

> it was not a popular and paying proposition north of the Border and the general tendency seems to be to make south, particularly for the bright lights of London. Apparently, the inducements, financial or otherwise, are less in Scotland.[44]

The low incidence of prosecutions for homosexual offences in Scotland was widely attributed to the more demanding and regularised system of legal process which operated under Scots law, which, it was argued, served to protect civil liberties and eliminate the arbitrary witch hunts conducted by local police authorities in England and Wales. Yet, as Lionel I. Gordon, the Crown Agent, was at pains to point out, this policy was a function of procedural constraints and did not in any way condone homosexuality or homosexual practices.[45] He insisted that, should sufficient evidence be to hand, homosexual behaviour would be prosecuted. He opposed the decriminalisation of homosexual acts as 'a retrograde step' that would undermine social standards and family values and be at odds with Scottish public opinion. In particular, he feared that the legalisation of private homosexual acts would prove a 'dangerous step' in giving a green light to the sexual predator given that, in his view, 'the practised homosexual look[ed] for new material in youth'.[46]

Such views were shared by the Faculty of Advocates,[47] and merely reflected broader homophobic prejudices within the Scottish legal establishment. The most extreme views were expressed by the sheriffs who presided over the bulk of the more serious cases relating to homosexual offences. Their evidence to the Wolfenden Committee was driven by a powerful set of fears and assumptions. First, concerns were expressed as to the dysgenic effects of homosexuality. Thus, Sheriff Prain (Perth and Kinross) warned that its decriminalisation would 'discourage the practice of heterosexuality' and would 'strike at the birth rate' and 'eventually lead to the deterioration of the race'.[48] Second, their evidence was informed by a perception of homosexuality as an essentially predatory and 'infectious' activity – a 'social evil' – even when conducted in private, with an initial sexual act engendering a cycle of debauchery. In their view, homosexual relationships were rarely confined to two individuals and invariably presented a danger to other members of society.[49] Third, some sheriffs were of the view that, in many instances, homosexuality was an issue of criminal wilfulness rather than medical dysfunction and should be addressed accordingly. Even where Scottish sheriffs advocated greater recourse to medical treatment, they were insistent that it be part of normal criminal proceedings so that the element of deterrence remained and offenders could be compelled to comply with appropriate therapies.

Nor was the evidence of medical witnesses entirely supportive of non-coercive measures. While they emphasised the importance of addressing homosexual offences as a medical rather than a moral issue, requiring remedial rather than punitive measures, they still portrayed homosexuality as quintessentially pathological and socially deviant and in some respects an insidious threat to civil society. Thus, for Dr Kraemer, homosexual networks presented 'a very great power like Freemasonry', and he warned that:

> We must not blind our eyes to it. There are influences everywhere. If people in certain ways of life want to get on, they had better give the impression that they are not opposed to homosexuality . . . That is the danger, I think, the undercurrent, the power it has.[50]

Indeed, much of the evidence presented on the effectiveness of existing medical treatments for homosexual conditions was far from compelling. The experience of the SHD was that, within the prison population, only a minority of homosexual offenders, some 30 per cent, were suitable for medical treatment and only 11 per cent prepared fully to cooperate with a course of psychotherapy. In particular, short-term prisoners proved reluctant to agree to a course of treatment that might be prolonged beyond the date of release.[51] Nor were the medical staff of the Scottish Prison and Borstal Services at all certain of the outcome of their therapies. It was never their aim to try to change the sexual identity of a homosexual, which they regarded as 'expensive, dangerous' and, almost certainly, impossible. However, even with the more limited aims of trying to reduce the levels of sexual urge and mental anxiety in homosexual offenders, the medical science was hazy. As Dr Inch freely admitted, 'we do not know what may be happening so far as the endocrine treatment is concerned and what the ultimate result may be', and he had never undertaken a controlled experiment 'to see whether aspirin would [have been] equally successful'.[52]

THE WOLFENDEN REPORT

In its report presented to Parliament in September 1957, the Wolfenden Committee advanced nine substantive recommendations relating to homosexual behaviour and the law: that homosexual behaviour between consenting adults in private be no longer a criminal offence, the age of adulthood being defined as 21; that, in line with Scottish procedures, no proceedings be taken in England and Wales in respect of any homosexual act (other than an indecent assault) committed in private by a person under 21 except with the sanction of the Attorney General; that the laws relating to living on the earnings of prostitution be applied to male as well as female prostitution; that the maximum penalties for buggery, gross indecency and indecent assaults be revised; that, except for some grave reason, proceedings should not be instituted in respect of homosexual offences revealed in the course of investigating allegations of blackmail; that, again in accordance with Scottish procedures, except for indecent assaults, the prosecution of any homosexual offence more than twelve months old be barred by statute; that psychiatric reports should be considered before any sentencing of a person under 21; that, subject to the approval of the prison medical officer, prisoners desirous of having oestrogen treatment should be permitted to do so in England and Wales, as in Scotland; and that research be instituted into the aetiology of homosexuality and the effects of various forms of treatment.[53]

Of the three surviving Scottish members of the Wolfenden Committee, two were broadly in agreement with its final recommendations. In private, the Marquess of Lothian had expressed a preference for 18 as the threshold for decriminalisation.[54] He also considered the retention of buggery as a separate offence as illogical but was convinced that this might help persuade public opinion to accept the more radical changes being proposed.[55] For her part, Mary Cohen was strongly opposed to buggery remaining a separate offence and joined the medical members of the Committee in a formal reservation to the Report on this issue.[56] It argued that many people were equally repelled by the heterosexual act of orogenital intercourse and that the medical evidence did not suggest that buggery did any more physical harm than other homosexual acts, nor did it simulate heterosexual intercourse so closely as to entice people from normal sexual behaviour.[57]

However, the most wide-ranging and influential reservation to the Report came from James Adair OBE, a former procurator fiscal, Chairman of the Scottish Council of the YMCA and a long-serving elder of the Church of Scotland. In his interrogation of witnesses, in his discussions within the Committee and in his final note of reservation, Adair marshalled a range of legal, moral and medical arguments against homosexual law reform.[58] In his view, homosexuality was 'a course of conduct which [was] contrary to the best interests of the community, and one which [could] have very serious effects on the whole moral fabric of social life'. In his opinion: 'No one interested in the moral, physical or spiritual welfare of public life wishe[d] to see homosexuality extending in its scope, but rather reduced in extent or at least kept effectively in check.' The removal of the law would merely be regarded 'as condoning or licensing licentiousness' and would open up 'for such people a new field of permitted conduct with unwholesome and distasteful implications', especially given the insidious tendency of homosexual practices to 'propagate themselves' and the existing breakdown in moral standards due to two world wars. The fact that sexual acts 'inherently hurtful to community life' were 'carried out clandestinely' did not justify their removal from the criminal code – the evocative parallel he drew being incest. Moreover, in a widely publicised warning, Adair predicted that a more liberal regime would lead to the corruption of youth: 'The presence in a district of . . . adult male lovers living openly and notoriously under the approval of the law is bound to have a regrettable effect on the young people of the community.'

Adair was especially scathing of the tendency of sociologists and psychiatrists to sentimentalise the problem of homosexuality and to downplay its predatory and paedophilic aspects, and its damage to physical health.[59] In his opinion, much of the evidence presented by 'mental specialists' was 'quite inexplicable and in not a few cases manifestly indefensible'.[60] Not only did he perceive homosexuality as being the latest disease 'fashion' or 'craze' of 'medical men', he also stressed the continuing uncertainties of medical and mental science 'and the limited knowledge and powers of the medical profession under existing circumstances to deal with homosexual patients'. In Adair's view, any medical strategies still needed to be underpinned by legal sanctions and the full 'moral force of the law'. It was not the threat of criminal proceedings that underlay the blackmail of homosexuals, but social stigma, the solution to which was self-control and either sexual conformity or abstinence.

THE AFTERMATH OF WOLFENDEN IN SCOTLAND, 1957–67

In the ten years following the Wolfenden Report, Adair's 'Reservation', effectively amounting to a minority report, was to have a significant impact on the sexual politics surrounding homosexual law reform in Britain and, in particular, its application to Scotland. It was widely cited in the press, in Parliament (across a wide spectrum of political opinion) and by moral pressure groups, including the Scottish churches.[61] Moreover, in policy briefings within the Scottish Office and the Cabinet, his concerns were regularly interpreted as reflecting wider opposition within Scottish society to any liberalisation of the law relating to homosexual offences.[62]

The major platform for airing his views was the Church of Scotland. Curiously, unlike the Church of England, the Church of Scotland sent neither memoranda nor delegation to the Wolfenden Committee. Nevertheless, at the instigation of Adair, the Church and Nation Committee had appointed a sub-committee to investigate the issue of homosexuality in June 1955 that took advice 'from the spheres of psychology, medicine, social service and the law'. In an interim report in 1956, the Church and Nation Committee conceded that the operation of the existing laws encouraged blackmail and intimidation, created 'a class of social outcasts' and discouraged homosexuals from seeking advice and treatment. It even argued that, although from the Christian standpoint homosexual practices were 'a sin from which the individual must be dissuaded and redeemed', it was probable that 'the sins of adultery and fornication present[ed] a greater danger to the social well-being of this country'. However, the Committee was also persuaded of the 'social harm' of any radical change in the criminal law and focused instead on the need for the provision of special detention centres for 'serious and persistent cases' with specialist treatment regimes.[63]

The sub-committee finally reported in December 1957 in favour of the decriminalisation of homosexual acts between consenting adults, in line with the Wolfenden Report. However, drawing heavily on both the concerns and jeremiads of Adair's report, the Church of Scotland's Church and Nation Committee overruled its sub-committee by seventeen votes to five. In its report to the General Assembly, the Committee challenged the philosophy of the Wolfenden Report that the law should not be concerned with the private moral behaviour of the individual provided that such behaviour did not involve the corruption of the young or was otherwise socially injurious. In its view, duly endorsed by the General Assembly:

The criminal law must of necessity reflect the standards of morality generally accepted by the nation . . . In a Christian country . . . the law should reflect as far as possible the generally accepted standards and principles of Christian ethics . . . In our opinion there are certain kinds of behaviour that are so contrary to Christian moral principles, and so repugnant to the general consensus of opinion throughout the nation that, even if private and personal, they should be regarded as both morally wrong and legally punishable . . . Homosexual offences seem to us to fall within this category. If so, it is surely right that they should be regarded not only as sinful but as criminal.[64]

A fundamental concern of the Church and Nation Committee was that, although a homosexual was deserving of the same pity and help as 'other cripples', unlike them 'he [was] apt to be proud of his disability and to spread what [was] properly called perversion'. It was for this reason that, while acknowledging the need for specialist counselling and medical treatment and the importance of redemption, a policy of 'repression' was advocated. In particular, it considered that homosexual law reform would merely reinforce the post-war decline in ethical standards and what it perceived as a spreading 'fashion' for sodomy.

Subsequently, after nearly a decade of silence on the issue, in 1966, the Church of Scotland convened a fresh working party in view of the progress of Lord Arran's Sexual Offences Bill in Parliament, which proposed limited homosexual law reform. In accordance with its findings, the Social and Moral Welfare Board recommended to the 1967 General Assembly that the law should be amended in accordance with the reality of Scottish legal practice and that private, consenting acts should be decriminalised. Its report emphasised the need for a more sympathetic understanding of the difficulties and handicaps of those suffering from homosexual tendencies and the need for adequate psychiatric and medical treatment. It also stressed the importance of a more charitable interpretation of biblical texts and greater regard in the counselling of homosexuals to the gospel of redemption.[65] Once again, however, the General Assembly rejected the liberalisation of the law relating to sexual offences, deploring in its deliverance 'the prevalence of homosexual practices as a source of uncleanness and deterioration in human character, and of weakness and decadence in the Nation's life'.[66]

However, throughout the period, the Free Presbyterian Church of

Scotland remained the most vitriolic at the prospect of homosexual law reform. As early as 1954, its synod had lamented that 'the voices of Sodom and Gomorrah . . . appear[ed] to be rife among us', threatening divine retribution and 'the poisoning of the moral sense'.[67] Its Religion and Morals Committee fully concurred with Adair's reservations to the Wolfenden Report and endorsed the view that homosexuals were 'dangerous men who [would] form cells of vice in the towns and villages where they live[d]'.[68] They duly forwarded their concerns in a strongly worded protest to the Home Secretary. During the 1960s, the homophobia of the Free Church remained undiminished. It was virulently opposed to the activities of the Homosexual Law Reform Society and to legislative proposals introduced from 1965 onwards.[69] Humphry Berkeley's Sexual Offences Bill, introduced into the House of Commons in December 1965, was roundly condemned for condoning a vice which was 'abominable in the sight of God, so corrupting of public morals, so perverted and so downright destructive of the social welfare and the political health of the land'.[70] The Church of England was dismissed as 'far gone in spiritual blindness' for its acceptance of law reform, and apocalyptic warnings laced the reports of the presbyteries. Thus the Southern Presbytery, meeting in Glasgow in February 1966, solemnly reminded 'all concerned':

> that the possibility of the cities of Britain being turned into ashes is by no means unnecessarily remote and there can be little doubt but that the present proposal is of the most God-provoking nature.[71]

The views of the Scottish churches, especially the deliverances of the Church of Scotland, were regularly cited, both in policy briefings and parliamentary debate, as reflecting 'the general views of the people of Scotland'.[72] In fact, hard evidence of popular attitudes to homosexual law reform in Scotland in the 1950s is meagre. However, a poll undertaken by the *Scottish Daily Record* in 1957 indicated that 85 per cent of Scottish respondents were opposed to the Wolfenden Report's central recommendations, with only 15 per cent in support. This contrasted markedly with the split of 49/51 per cent found in a poll conducted by the *Daily Mirror* south of the Border.[73] Again, this was evidence repeatedly deployed by policy makers to emphasise the strength of opposition to reform in Scotland, as was the fact that few representations for the liberalisation of sexual offences legislation had been received by the SHD and 'few proposals . . . ventilated'.[74]

The media both reflected and reinforced negative attitudes to homosexual law reform in Scotland. As Higgins has noted, while the provincial press came out 'virtually unanimously' against the Wolfenden Report, the Scottish newspapers 'were particularly repelled by any suggestion of changing the status quo; James Adair was much celebrated by them'.[75] A *Scotsman* editorial in September 1957 concluded that it was 'no solution to any public problem to legitimize a bestial offence'.[76] In a series of articles on the implications of Wolfenden for Scotland in 1959, it warned of a spreading homosexual sub-culture within Scottish cities:

> homosexuals, by the nature of their disability, owe their primary allegiance to the homosexual group before any other authority or loyalty in their lives. Hence the connection between perversion and subversion, which is one of world Communism's greatest strengths in this country.[77]

As Jeffery-Poulter observes: 'The articles zealously trotted out the old chestnuts about the self-propagating nature of homosexual groups and the serious danger of the corruption of youth, before going on to label every homosexual a potential traitor.' The media therefore concluded that, while the country awaited a convincing medical cure for such 'unnatural urges', 'an immediate campaign of police repression' was required to control the problem.[78]

By the late 1960s, *The Scotsman* had radically altered its position on homosexual law reform in line with liberal debate south of the Border and the growing medicalisation of the issue, but the editorials and correspondence columns of other regional newspapers continued their note of biblical condemnation.[79] Thus, as late as 1967, the *Scottish Daily Express* condemned the Moral Welfare Committee of the Church of Scotland for advocating the decriminalisation of homosexual acts between consenting adults:

> Sodomy is not only a sin, it is a powerful instrument for the destruction of society . . . The evil professionals who indulge in this filthy trade must continue to be punished and their misguided or diseased associates be forced to take treatment . . .[80]

The views expressed by Scottish peers and MPs in Parliament on the issue of homosexual law reform generally accorded with those of the Scottish media. In the House of Lords an influential cluster of homophobic Scottish peers sustained an unrelenting opposition to legislation. Lord Balerno emphasised the support within the Church of Scotland for James Adair's reservations to the Wolfenden Report, sharing his concerns that the decriminalisation of homosexual activities would be seen to condone licentiousness and surmising that Scotland was 'not yet ready for the more permissive society that [was] overcoming England'.[81] The Earl of Dundee also endorsed Adair's views. In particular, he questioned the medical and sociological evidence underpinning the Wolfenden Report and the ability of the medical profession to alter 'either the outlook or behaviour of homosexuals'. In his view, whether homosexuality was a 'mental disease to be pitied, or a vice to be reprobated', legal sanctions needed to be retained.[82] For Lord Ferrier, reform legislation constituted a 'queer's charter'. In his view, the homosexual was either 'mentally deranged' or a 'sinner in a sin . . . bred from self-pity out of sadism, or from lack of self-control out of lust'. Blackmail was not contingent on the law but on the widespread detestation of homosexuality in society, and he predicted that any new sexual offences bill would encourage male prostitution, endanger the sexual culture of the younger generation and serve to empower homosexuals within the structures of civil society.[83]

Meanwhile, Lord Kilmuir (formerly Sir David Maxwell Fyfe), who as Home Secretary had presided over the witch hunt of homosexuals in England in the early 1950s and the establishment of the Wolfenden Committee, criticised reformers for confusing 'a supposed candle of liberty' with the 'will-o'-the wisp of license' that 'rises only from the iridescence of decay'. He took his stand on the Old Testament condemnation of sodomy and could not countenance the legalisation of acts such as oral and anal sex, universally perceived as 'horrible, unnatural and beastly'. In his view, only a minority of men committing homosexual acts were 'genuine inverts', with the remainder guilty of wilful indulgence or predatory lust.[84]

Finally, in a series of debates, Lord Saltoun expressed two major concerns regarding homosexual law reform. First, he raised traditional eugenic concerns over the impact of homosexual (and thus non-procreative) sex on the racial health of the nation and the stability of marriage within British society. Second, he stressed what he regarded as the quintessentially evangelical and predatory nature of many homosexuals. According to Saltoun, the passions of homosexuals were 'much stronger than those of normal people, and they cast their net very wide for their satisfaction'. In particular, he feared that the decriminalisation of homosexual acts would merely present homosexual practices to young men as 'one of the enlargements and liberties of coming of age' and facilitate the efforts of aristocratic libertines to debauch 'quite young lads, when their glands [were] just developing'.[85]

Only two Scottish peers supported legislation. Lord Boothby, who as an MP had been instrumental in the establishment of the Wolfenden Committee, strongly supported its recommendations. While he advocated legal sanctions against the seduction of youth, and against acts of sexual violence or public indecency, he believed that, in a free democracy, what consenting adults did in private was merely 'a moral issue between them and their maker'. Similarly, Lord Lothian, a former member of the Committee, considered that 'the control of sexual appetites was for the average adult a personal and not a public challenge' and that the criminal law could not be based on a precise grading of moral and ethical failings.

Nevertheless, a profound sense of moral revulsion towards homosexuality informed both their arguments. Along with many of his opponents, Lord Boothby invoked the threat of a 'homosexual underground' in the great cities, menacing Britain's youth. The thrust of his objection to existing law was not that it denied basic sexual and civil liberties, but that in England and Wales it was subject to the vagaries of local police authorities, that it was vulnerable to corruption and that it often served to provide a degree of sensationalism and exhibitionism actively sought after by many homosexuals. Likewise, Lord Lothian's discussion of homosexual practices was larded with the discourse of degenerationism. He agreed that homosexuality was a graver moral offence than prostitution in that it offended 'more radically the law of nature ordained by God', and stressed that the intention of the Wolfenden Report was not to condone homosexual acts nor to effect 'a new attitude to vice itself'; it was merely intended to provide, within very defined limits, a more tolerant legal environment and eradicate the worst injustices caused by existing criminal procedures. Although Boothby regretted that successive bills did not apply to Scotland, neither peer focused on this in his contribution to parliamentary debate. Given their limited and largely legalistic agendas, Scotland, with its low incidence of prosecutions and more regularised legal processes, provided the role model rather than a suitable case for treatment.[86]

Meanwhile, there was equally little support for homosexual law reform from Scottish members in the House of Commons. Within the Scottish Liberal Party, the issue was seen as divisive and electorally damaging.[87] Even less support was forthcoming from Scottish

Labour MPs. As early as 1958, Jean Mann, MP for Coatbridge, had articulated grassroot hostility to the Wolfenden Report among the Scottish Labour movement. Criticising the lack of trade union evidence before the Committee, she reflected that:

> I cannot imagine the miners' lodges welcoming a Report which will mean that it will no longer be an offence to procure an adult male and set up a house in a mining village for a male friend. I cannot see the Co-operative women's guilds welcoming this, or the townswomen's guilds.[88]

She viewed the Wolfenden Report as part of a general homosexual conspiracy to dominate the major institutions of government and civil society – an 'evil thread' that ran 'through the theatre, through the music hall, through the Press, and through the BBC' with 'international ramifications'.[89]

It is difficult to establish how far such a conspiracy theory was shared by other MPs. Certainly, of the thirty Scottish MPs voting in 1960 on a Commons motion for the Government's implementation of the Wolfenden Report, twenty were opposed, of whom six were Labour MPs.[90] Even more Labour members, with 'a heavy concentration of Scots', voted against Leo Abse's motion in 1965 to introduce a bill to amend the law relating to homosexual offences, and it was widely acknowledged that the principal opponents of reform had been 'the Calvinist Scots, notably the Scottish miners'.[91] Indeed, on the second reading of Humphry Berkeley's Sexual Offences Bill in February 1966, Sir Cyril Osborne protested:

> It seems to me that to bring this important Measure before the House on a Friday, in the full knowledge that the good Scottish Socialist Calvinist MPs are away, is cheating . . . I believe that if on return to the House the Scottish and north-country Members were to find . . . that the Labour Party had put buggery in front of steel, there would be a revolt inside the Labour Party.[92]

As Roy Jenkins wryly reflected in July 1967 on the third reading of the Sexual Offences Bill, he could not understand the logic of omitting Scotland, 'unless the sponsors realised that if they included Scotland, all Scottish Members would descend in their wrath and vote solidly against the Bill'.[93]

From the outset, the SHD and the Scottish Office adopted a

negative posture towards the recommendations of the Wolfenden Report relating to homosexual offences. There were two central strands to their objections to the decriminalisation of private acts between consenting adults: first, that under existing criminal procedures in Scotland such acts were rarely prosecuted, and second, that there was compelling evidence, including Adair's 'minority report', the deliverances of the Church of Scotland and isolated opinion polls, that a wide spectrum of Scottish opinion was vigorously opposed to reform. Permanent officials also questioned the relevance of the Wolfenden Report's subsidiary clauses. Provisions relating to the non-prosecution of 'stale' offences and the use of oestrogen treatment already existed north of the Border, and, in their view, the incidence of blackmail in homosexual cases was not sufficiently a problem in Scotland as to require fresh legislation.[94]

During the 1960s, the policy of the Scottish Office towards homosexual law reform continued to be shaped by similar arguments in briefing papers on a succession of Sexual Offences Bills. It was urged that Scotland had never experienced the controversies surrounding certain notorious English prosecutions and that, given the more rigorous and regularised criminal process in Scotland, especially with regard to the admissibility of 'confessions' in evidence, and the continuingly low incidence of recorded prosecutions for homosexual offences in Scotland, there was no equivalent justification for legislation. Equally, the SHD and its successor, the Scottish Home and Health Department, repeatedly warned of the political dangers in alienating the more conservative strands of Scottish public opinion, and advised that the Government should adopt a neutral stance on the issue of homosexual law reform. It was, the Permanent Secretary considered, an 'area of morality' most appropriately regarded as 'a field for Private Members'.[95]

After protracted debate in Parliament, the Sexual Offences Act of 1967 finally decriminalised homosexual acts committed in private between consenting adults. As a 'progressive' measure, it had many limitations. Its clauses reflected the general tenor of debate that homosexuality remained socially objectionable and morally wrong.[96] Increased penalties were imposed on homosexual acts with males below the age of 21. Stringent definitions of 'private' were introduced to curtail homosexual acts, as were wide-ranging and ambiguous powers relating to procurement. The Act did not apply to the Merchant Navy or armed forces. Above all, in deference to the legal, cultural and political arguments rehearsed above, Scotland (along with

Northern Ireland) was excluded from its provisions. As Chapter 4 demonstrates, it was to require a further thirteen years of often bitter and divisive sexual politics north of the Border before parity was secured under the Criminal Justice (Scotland) Act of 1980.

Notes

1 The Committee's terms of reference prioritised the review of 'the law and practice relating to homosexual offences and the treatment of persons convicted of such offences by the courts' [*RWC*, 7].

2 See, for example, Higgins, *Heterosexual Dictatorship*, 2; Jivani, *A History of Lesbian and Gay Britain*, 115; Weeks, *Coming Out*, 164.

3 See, for example, Mort, 'Mapping sexual London', 94–7; Moran, *The Homosexual(ity) of Law*, 2, 22, 117.

4 See, for example, Davenport-Hines, *Sex, Death and Punishment*, 289; Newburn, *Permission and Regulation*, 61–3.

5 NRS, HH60/265, Briefing notes for House of Lords debate, 4 December 1957. Of prisoners sentenced for homosexual offences in Scotland in 1955, 7 per cent were tried in the High Court, 6 per cent in a Sheriff Court with jury, 27 per cent in a Sheriff Court without jury, 51 per cent in a court of summary jurisdiction, 0.6 per cent in a police court and 10.2 per cent by court martial [PRO, HO345/9, PWC, Evidence of SHD, 30 October 1955].

6 *RWC*, 125.

7 ECA, Burgh Court records for 1950.

8 *RWC*, 141.

9 NRS, HH57/1287, Note by SHD on Scottish Prisons and Borstal Institutions, October 1955.

10 PRO, HO345/9, PWC, Summary record of 21st Meeting, March 1956.

11 NRS, HH60/268, Evidence of SHD, October 1954.

12 See, for example, PRO, HO345/15, PWC, Evidence of K. M. Hancock, Director of the Scottish Prison and Borstal Services, 1 November 1955.

13 Ibid., PWC, Evidence of Dr W. Boyd, 1 November 1955.

14 NRS, HH60/268, Memorandum by SHD, October 1954.

15 NRS, HH57/1287, Note by Dr T. D. Inch, 13 October 1955.

16 PRO, HO345/15, PWC, Evidence of Dr W. Boyd, 1 November 1955.

17 Ibid.

18 NRS, HH57/1288, Memorandum by Dr T. D. Inch, 'Sexual Offenders: Treatment in Prisons', November 1955; PRO, HO345/15, PWC, Evidence of Dr T. D. Inch, 1 November 1955.

19 PRO, HO345/15, PWC, Evidence of Dr T. D. Inch, 1 November 1955.

20 PRO, HO345/16, PWC, Evidence of Glasgow Magistrates and ACCs for Glasgow and Edinburgh, 9 and 10 April 1956; NRS, HH60/269, Crown Agent to Secretary of Wolfenden Committee, December 1954.

21 Cited in Jeffery-Poulter, *Peers, Queers & Commons*, 55.

22 *RWC*, 50–1.

23 PRO, HO345/16, PWC, Evidence of ACC for Glasgow, 10 April 1956.

24 *RWC*, 52. On other legal contrasts, see Moran, *The Homosexual(ity) of Law*, 219–20.

25 PRO, HO345/12, PWC, Evidence of SHD, 15 October 1954.

26 Higgins, *Heterosexual Dictatorship*, 55.

27 PRO, HO345/8, PWC, Evidence of E. Abbott, June 1955.

28 Ibid., PWC, Evidence of Association of Sheriffs Substitute, March 1955.

29 NRS, HH57/1287, Note by Dr T. D. Inch, October 1955; PRO, HO345/15, PWC, Evidence of Drs T. D. Inch and W. Boyd, 1 November 1955.

30 See PRO, HO345/7 and HO345/16, PWC, Evidence of Drs W. Rushforth and W. P. Kraemer, 10 April 1956.

31 PRO, HO345/16, PWC, Evidence of Dr W. P. Kraemer, 10 April 1956.

32 British Medical Association (hereafter BMA) Archives, B/107/1/2, Memorandum by Professor J. Glaister, 30 June 1955.

33 *RWC*, 17.

34 Ibid., 141.

35 See, for example, PRO, HO345/8, PWC, Evidence of Association of Sheriffs Substitute, March 1955; HO345/16, PWC, Evidence of ACC for Glasgow, 10 April 1956.

36 See, for example, PRO, HO345/16, PWC, Evidence of Crown Agent, 9 April 1956.

37 Ibid., PWC, Evidence of Glasgow Magistrates, 9 April 1956.

38 BMA Archives, B/107/1/2, Memorandum by Professor J. Glaister, 30 June 1955.

39 PRO, HO345/16, PWC, Evidence of Drs W. Rushforth and W. P. Kraemer, 10 April 1956.

40 PRO, CAB129/966 C(54)61, Cabinet Paper on 'Sexual Offences' by Secretary of State for Scotland (hereafter SSS), 17 February 1954.

41 *RWC*, 21.

42 PRO, HO345/16, PWC, Evidence of ACC for Glasgow and Glasgow's Procurator Fiscal of Police, 9 and 10 April 1956.

43 NRS, HH60/269, Crown Agent to Secretary of Wolfenden Committee, 20 December 1954.

44 NRS, HH57/1287, Note by Dr T. D. Inch, October 1955.

45 NRS, HH60/269, Crown Agent to Secretary of Wolfenden Committee, 20 December 1954.

46 PRO, HO345/16, PWC, Evidence of Crown Agent, 9 April 1956.

47 PRO, HO345/9, PWC, Evidence of Faculty of Advocates, 1956.

48 PRO, HO345/8 and 16, PWC, Evidence of Association of Sheriffs Substitute, March 1955, 9 April 1956.

49 Ibid.

50 PRO, HO345/16, PWC, Evidence of Dr W. P. Kraemer, 10 April 1956.

51 PRO, HO345/9, PWC, Evidence of SHD, 30 October 1955.
52 PRO, HO345/15, PWC, Evidence of Drs K. M. Hancock and T. D. Inch, 1 November 1955.
53 *RWC*, 115–16.
54 PRO, HO345/4, PWC, Note by Lord Lothian, 1955. A Roman Catholic, Lord Lothian was a member of Roxburgh County Council and Commandant of Roxburgh, Selkirk and Peebles Special Constabulary.
55 PRO, HO345/10, PWC, Lord Lothian to W. C. Roberts (Secretary to the Committee), 6 April 1957.
56 Mary Cohen was a former chairman of Glasgow Union of Girls' Clubs and Scottish Association of Girls' Clubs and was a long-standing committee member of the National Vigilance Association for Scotland.
57 PRO, HO345/10, PWC, M. Cohen to Sir John Wolfenden, 12 April 1957; *RWC*, 123–4.
58 *RWC*, 117–21; PRO, HO345/12 and 16, PWC, Minutes of discussions, 15 October 1954, 10 April 1956; HO345/2, PWC, J. Adair to W. C. Roberts, 4 October 1956; HO345/10, Note on Committee discussions, 11 and 12 September 1956.
59 Adair was especially concerned to elicit from witnesses the physical damage done by sodomy and was adamant that it should be retained as a separate offence with heavy penalties. See PRO, HO345/9, PWC, Minutes of 21st Meeting of Committee, March 1956.
60 *RWC*, 118.
61 See, for example, *The Scotsman*, 5 September 1957; *Hansard* [HL], vol. 206, 4 December 1957, col. 789; *Hansard* [HC], vol. 596, 26 November 1958, cols 438, 463, 596; UFCS, *Report to General Assembly for 1958*, 18.
62 NRS, HH60/265, Cabinet memorandum on the Wolfenden Report, 15 November 1957; NRS, HH41/1748, Briefing paper for SSS, 20 May 1966.
63 GACS, *Report of Church and Nation Committee for 1956*, 373–5.
64 Ibid., 1958, 416–20. In contrast, the main recommendations of the Wolfenden Committee were accepted by the Moral Welfare Council of the Church of England. An advisory committee of the Roman Catholic Church also recommended that 'penal sanctions [were] not justified for the purpose of attempting to restrain sins against sexual morality in private by responsible adults'.
65 GACS, *Report of Social and Moral Welfare Board for 1967*, 511–15.
66 GACS, *Deliverance for 1967*, 525–6.
67 Free Presbyterian Church of Scotland (hereafter FPCS), *Proceedings of the Synod for 1954*, 51.
68 Ibid., *1958*, 54–5.
69 Ibid., *1960*, 36–7.
70 NRS, HH41/1748, Resolution of Edinburgh Presbytery to SHD, 3 March 1966.

71 NRS, HH41/1748, Report from Southern Presbytery of FPCS, February 1966.

72 See, for example, NRS, HH41/1748, Note on Home Secretary's Cabinet memorandum on homosexual offences, February 1966; *Hansard* [HL], vol. 266, 12 May 1965, col. 146.

73 NRS, HH60/265, Notes for Commons debate on Wolfenden Report, 26 November 1958.

74 NRS, HH60/268, Memorandum by SHD, October 1954; NRS, HH60/267, Notes for Commons debate, 29 June 1960.

75 Higgins, *Heterosexual Dictatorship*, 117.

76 *The Scotsman*, 5 September 1957.

77 *The Scotsman*, 23 June 1959.

78 Jeffery-Poulter, *Peers, Queers & Commons*, 48–9.

79 Ibid., 65–6; *The Scotsman*, 11 February 1966.

80 Cited in FPCS, *Proceedings of the Synod for 1967*, 22.

81 *Hansard* [HL], vol. 266, 12 May 1965, cols 145–7; vol. 284, 13 July 1967, cols 1,297–8.

82 *Hansard* [HL], vol. 266, 12 May 1965, cols 84–92; vol. 284, 13 July 1967, cols 1,287–90.

83 *Hansard* [HL], vol. 274, 10 May 1966, cols 633–5; vol. 284, 13 July 1967, cols 1,299–302.

84 *Hansard* [HL], vol. 266, 24 May 1965, col. 654; vol. 267, 21 June 1965, cols 392–6; vol. 274, 10 May 1966, cols 610–18; vol. 275, 16 June 1966, col. 156.

85 *Hansard* [HL], vol. 267, 21 June 1965, col. 306; vol. 268, 16 July 1965, cols 404–6; vol. 274, 10 May 1966, cols 624–5; vol. 274, 23 May 1966, cols 1,170–3; vol. 275, 16 June 1966, cols 159–62.

86 *Hansard* [HC], vol. 206, 4 December 1957, cols 780–7; vol. 266, 24 May 1965, cols 666–73; vol. 275, 16 June 1966, col. 169; vol. 284, 13 July 1967, cols 1,302–3.

87 Jeffery-Poulter, *Peers, Queers & Commons*, 53.

88 *Hansard* [HC], vol. 596, 26 November 1958, col. 458.

89 Ibid., cols 458–61.

90 Ibid., vol. 625, 29 June 1960, cols 1,509–14.

91 Higgins, *Heterosexual Dictatorship*, 137.

92 *Hansard* [HC], vol. 724, 11 February 1966, col. 833.

93 Ibid., vol. 749, 3 July 1967, col. 1,514.

94 NRS, HH60/265, notes on Wolfenden Report, 30 August 1957; notes for Lords Debate on Wolfenden, 4 December 1957.

95 NRS, HH41/1748, Minute Assistant Secretary to G. G. Lyall , 20 May 1966.

96 For commentaries on the Act, see especially Jeffery-Poulter, *Peers, Queers & Commons*, 81–6; Higgins, *Heterosexual Dictatorship*, 144–8.

4

HOMOSEXUAL LAW REFORM, 1967–80

INTRODUCTION

The historiography of homosexual law reform has largely neglected this subsequent campaign to decriminalise consensual homosexual acts in Scotland. For the most part, it has been treated as a coda to the central story of the 1967 Sexual Offences Act or as an incidental aspect of the continued social and legal discrimination encountered by homosexual men after 1967.[1] Where the Scottish campaign has been dealt with in more detail, it has been addressed in a somewhat tangential fashion. Some commentators have focused briefly on the parliamentary story of events.[2] Others have concentrated instead on the activities, internal politics and ideological constraints of the Scottish Minorities Group (SMG).[3] A further group of editors have recorded, in both print and sound, the evocative and moving testimonies of gay experiences in Scotland in the late 1960s and 1970s.[4]

What has been lacking is a full historical analysis of the impulses and constraints shaping policy in Scotland after 1967, and, in particular, of the interaction between the SMG and its successor, the Scottish Homosexual Rights Group (SHRG) and the machinery of Scottish governance. Using hitherto closed files of the Scottish Home and Health Department (SHHD) and Lord Advocate's Department, together with the extensive archives of the SMG and SHRG, this chapter seeks to make good this omission and to complete an important story of law reform: from the early efforts of the SMG to advance the cause of homosexual law reform in Scotland, through its abortive attempts in the mid-1970s to develop a more radical strategy in collaboration with the Campaign for Homosexual Equality (CHE) and the Union for Sexual Freedom in Ireland (USFI), to the more pragmatic and somewhat pyrrhic victory of legislation in 1980.

THE SMG'S EARLY CAMPAIGNS, 1969–74

Established in February 1969, the SMG was a largely male professional organisation, based predominantly in Edinburgh and Glasgow, but with a growing number of branches elsewhere in Scotland. It initiated a series of campaigns to expose the inconsistencies and injustices of the existing law and prosecution procedures relating to homosexual offences north of the Border. As with its English counterpart, the CHE, the SMG was essentially a moderate, reformist, predominantly middle-class, bureaucratic organisation focusing on legal processes rather than broader sexual liberation. Many of its members, reflecting the somewhat 'closeted' choice of name for the Group, were opposed to the more militant agenda and aggressive rhetoric of the Gay Liberation Front,[5] and, arguably, its ideology of sexual citizenship was very much one that sought to 'enfranchise' the respectable, privatised homosexual.

The first two years of the SMG's activities were largely devoted to establishing an effective organisation and attracting a viable membership,[6] often in the face of legal harassment and hostility from civic leaders.[7] Thereafter, in liaison with the Scottish Council for Civil Liberties (SCCL), the SMG launched a vigorous campaign, underpinned in 1972 by a draft Sexual Offences (Scotland) Bill, which targeted both Parliament and the Scottish Law Commission.[8] The SMG highlighted the weaknesses and inequities of Scots law: that, although, in practice, it was not fully enforced in respect of homosexual offences, it remained highly discriminatory and encouraged blackmail, especially of the young, isolated homosexual; that it bred 'concealment, hypocrisy and mental anguish' which worked against 'rehabilitation' and treatment; that it actively encouraged prejudice and the 'persecution of a harmless minority' and legitimated the social stigmatisation of homosexuals; that it was based on unfounded fears that homosexuality was a menace to society and family life and an incitement to paedophilia; and that there was a real danger that, if there was a backlash of public opinion against the so-called 'permissive society', it would be open to the Crown Office to rescind its previously laissez-faire policy towards private and consensual homosexual practices in Scotland.

Additional criticisms were levelled at local police and prosecution procedures. While the SMG did not condone public acts of indecency, it alleged that, in the prosecution of 'cottaging', police were often applying both the criminal law and local byelaws arbitrarily, and operating as *agents provocateurs*, and that, with the absence of legal aid and the danger of publicity, there was undue pressure on those accused of offences to plead guilty. The SMG also considered that 'petty indecencies' prosecuted in the Burgh Courts should be treated as primarily reflecting problems of mental health or social inadequacy, and that legal penalties should only be imposed on persistent offenders.

According to the SMG, its Sexual Offences (Scotland) Bill represented the first time in the history of homosexual law reform that the 'homosexual community itself' had brought forward 'its own suggestions for legal reform before the wider community'. In drafting the Bill, the SMG's Legal Reform Committee considered a range of legislative options.[9] The first was merely to extend the 1967 Sexual Offences Act to Scotland, but in the view of the Committee this would not address the fundamental issues of sexual discrimination and, while 'a useful stage on the road to . . . equality', might merely 'satisfy the public conscience that enough had been done'. A second option was to draft a wholly new Sexual Reform Bill applicable across Britain, but while viewed as desirable in the long run, the Committee felt it would require a preparatory programme of public education and much greater cooperation than had hitherto been forthcoming from homophile organisations south of the Border. A final option, and the one eventually pursued, was to introduce legislation, significantly more advanced than the 1967 Act, for Scotland alone.

The Bill sought to repeal the Criminal Law Amendment Act of 1885 and to legalise consenting homosexual acts in private between males over the age of 18 (except between members of the armed forces and merchant navy, and between mental hospital staff and their patients). It did not adhere to the age of consent of 21 designated by the 1967 Sexual Offences Act on the grounds that this had led to increased prosecutions of 18–21-year-olds and that, should the same law be enforced in Scotland, the situation of this age group would actually deteriorate. In addition, it was proposed that a homosexual act with a male between 16 and 18 should no longer be designated as sodomy but indecent assault, and that it should not be an offence if the person accused could prove ignorance of the fact that his partner was under 18. The Bill also amended the law relating to public indecency and soliciting, restricting existing offences so that homosexual behaviour (for example, public kissing) was no more an offence than similar heterosexual conduct. Furthermore, it proposed that a time limit on proceedings involving homosexual offences should be imposed. Finally, the Bill provided that advertisements for homosexual clubs, pen friend services and so on should be legalised.[10]

In the spring and summer of 1972, the SMG lobbied widely for support from organisations such as the Church of Scotland, the Scottish

Health Education Unit, the Scottish Association for Mental Health, the Socialist Medical Association and the Scottish Committee of the Howard League. However, their responses were muted and often ambivalent.[11] Thus, while the General Assembly of the Church of Scotland had finally, if reluctantly, responded in 1969 to the critic- isms of its own Social and Moral Welfare Board,[12] and recomm- ended that homosexual acts between consenting adults in private be treated as a moral and not a legal issue, it remained anxious to contain the SMG's activities within a medical strategy of selective professional counselling rather than one of social inclusion and the promotion of networks.[13]

Political reaction to the SMG's 1972 Sexual Offences (Scotland) Bill was mixed. There was predictable opposition from Scottish peers such as Lord Balerno. Less anticipated, perhaps, was the reaction of erstwhile supporters of homosexual law reform. David Steel, Liberal MP for Roxburgh, Selkirk and Peebles, was 'not convinced of the need to change the law in Scotland', given that the 'law of evidence in Scotland prevent[ed] the prosecution of consenting adults', and he considered that, in view of the recent failure of divorce law reform in Scotland, the immediate chances of a homosexual law reform bill 'were nil'.[14] In addition, Lord Arran, the sponsor of the 1967 Sexual Offences Act, while warmly supporting the repeal of the 1885 Criminal Law Amendment Act for Scotland, dismissed the proposed lowering of the age of consent to 18 in the SMG's Bill as 'just so much pie in the sky'.[15]

Clearly, as one observer remarked, Scottish politicians were increasingly 'electoral-majority-conscious and homosexual law reform [was] not high on the agenda'.[16] And this was well reflected in the reluctance of the Liberal Party to sponsor the Bill in the Lords. Thus, Lord Tanlaw, Deputy Whip, responded that: 'There is considerable stigma attached to the person and the Political Party which sponsors a Bill of this kind . . . I could not recommend the Liberal Party assoc- iating itself again with a "Sex" Bill.'[17] As a result, the quest for a Scottish peer to introduce the Bill had to continue into 1973.

In line with its previous policy, Scottish Office officials firmly resisted the need for such a bill. In briefing memoranda throughout the year, the SHHD advised that the issue of homosexual prosecu- tions had never been a problem in Scotland and that there had been no substantial pressure for reform of the law. It continued to stress the previous record of opposition to homosexual law reform from within the Church of Scotland and from Scottish MPs. In February 1972, in response to pressure in the House of Commons from Tam Dalyell, Labour MP for West Lothian, the SHHD concluded that: 'We take it that Ministers would not wish to see controversy on this subject at the present time; and that they would not wish to depart from the traditional line of government neutrality on moral questions of this kind.'[18] Thereafter, the official response to SMG initiatives continued to be that this was 'an area of morality which [was] the traditional preserve of the Private Member' and that the Conservative Government did not intend to legislate on the subject.[19] The Lord Advocate, Norman Wylie, also recorded that he was 'in no way sympathetic to the group and [would] not be of a mind to give them any support'.[20] According to *SMG News*, he considered that law reform in this area should have 'low priority' given that the 'practical legal situation was satisfactory'. More significantly, he 'carefully disclaimed any suggestion that he was "liberal" in his attitudes. If he was against the prosecution of homosexuals, this was only because he didn't want to see the legal machine clogged with unnecessary cases.'[21]

The SMG met with similar resistance in 1973. While the Lord Advocate sought to reassure the Group that Crown Office policy in Scotland continued to be to refrain from prosecution of cases involving acts between consenting adults in private, and instead to target 'the seduction and debauchery of the young',[22] the SHHD reiterated the lack of support (apart from the SMG) and justification for homosexual law reform. Indeed, in view of the fact that the SMG's Sexual Offences Bill also included provisions that sought to protect, in part, 16–18-year-olds against prosecution for homosexual acts, the Department anticipated even greater opposition than in 1967, despite the recent change of heart of the General Assembly on homosexual issues. Officials stressed that there was no evidence of prosecutions in Scotland for actions that would have been lawful under the 1967 Sexual Offences Act in England and Wales, and that the issue of homosexual law reform had accordingly not been remitted to the Scottish Law Commission for consideration.[23] To a significant extent, therefore, in resisting the SMG claims, the Department, in line with many Scottish politicians, continued to camouflage the degree of homophobia within Scottish civil society behind a constructed national identity of legal progressiveness.

As in 1972, the lobbying conducted by the SMG drew a mixed response. In its favour, the editorial policy of the *Glasgow Herald* came into line with *The Scotsman* in supporting law reform.[24] Elsewhere, however, traditional attitudes prevailed, embracing various narratives of sexual danger. Although meetings between the SMG and the Moral Welfare Committee of the Church of Scotland confirmed the latter's view that homosexual conduct was primarily an issue of private morality and not criminal justice, the Church remained badly split over the question of law reform.[25] Meanwhile, the Free Presbyterian Church of Scotland warned that 'the fire of unnatural lust [would], if unrepented of, be met with the fire of Divine judgement and retribution'. It roundly condemned 'the permissive attitude' towards homosexuality, which characterised it as an innate medical dysfunction rather than a wilful deviance.[26] The more homophobic aspects of civic governance were also reflected in the opposition of many Glasgow city councillors to a civic welcome being extended to the SMG's annual conference.[27]

Undeterred, the SMG continued to lobby Scottish MPs and organised a meeting at the House of Lords in November 1973. However, while this evoked 'useful and energetic discussions', the consensus of advice was that any Scottish bill that sought to lower the age of consent was doomed to failure.[28] No sponsor was forthcoming and the campaign organisers resigned themselves to a more protracted struggle for legislation. There was considerable disenchantment with the lack of initiative from the CHE, which, while critical of the Scottish Bill for compromising on an age of consent at 18, had not advanced any coherent proposals of its own to which the SMG might lend support.[29]

Reviewing strategy, some activists argued that, in the longer term, if legislation was ever to be effected, there needed to be 'a more widely based campaign in Scotland to change the climate of opinion'; not just of MPs and Peers, but of social workers, psychiatrists, teachers, trade unions, doctors, the churches and the media.[30] They considered that, in important respects, the campaign had focused too much on the Westminster Parliament and too little on the culture and institutions of Scottish governance. Others feared that a policy that narrowly concentrated on parity with English law might merely legitimate an ideology of legal 'tolerance' rather than a broader social enfranchisement of gay society, as in the Netherlands.

BROADENING THE AGENDA, 1974–5

Two main initiatives dominated the work of the SMG in 1974. First, in the early months of the year, it canvassed all Scottish parliamentary candidates for their views on homosexual law reform during the run-up to the general election. Forty-six replies were received of which all but six indicated general support for reform, largely on the basis of extending the 1967 Sexual Offences Act to Scotland. The overall impression gained by the Group was that opinion among prospective candidates was shifting in their favour.[31] However, there were some notable exceptions. Thus, Nicholas Fairbairn, a former Vice-President of the SMG, denied the need for a reform of Scots law, testily observing that if one took the trouble to obtain details from the Crown Office of prosecutions for homosexual acts in Scotland, one would see that they were largely related to '70 year old soldiers making improper advances to boys in streets and all of them practically . . . before 1930'.[32] In general, party organisers advised their candidates to steer clear of the issue, Michael Hirst responding that, to the best of his knowledge, 'the Conservative Party in Scotland ha[d] no policy on the subject of homosexual law reform, as this [was] considered a matter for the individual'.[33]

Second, in order to try to accelerate the process of reform by tapping into the wider movement for gay rights elsewhere in the country, the SMG also adopted a radical change in tactics in 1974, abandoning its Scottish Bill in favour of a more radical UK-wide Bill, drafted in collaboration with the CHE and USFI. Its officers succeeded in framing proposals that were more focused and radical than the rather vague aspirations previously articulated by the CHE's law reform working party.[34] The 1974 draft Sexual Offences Bill explicitly lowered the age of consent to 16 and standardised the sexual offences law for boys and girls for the age group 13–16. It also decriminalised homosexual acts between servicemen when off duty and unless such acts specifically damaged discipline. In addition, it sought to redefine the 1967 Sexual Offences Act by decriminalising the procurement of any homosexual act that was not in itself illegal, and by preventing the use of old statutes, byelaws and common law provisions to circumvent recent legislation. The Bill sought to obtain a more liberal and transparent definition of 'private' within the meaning of sexual offences legislation. More broadly, it endeavoured to revise public indecency regulations in order to ensure that homosexual and heterosexual behaviour was treated consistently, including public displays of affection and the display or distribution of magazines and newspapers containing contact advertisements.[35] A campaign in support of the Bill was launched with a rally in London in November 1974 that attracted more than 2,500 men and women.

The SHHD and Crown Office remained unimpressed by such

initiatives, continuing to advise ministers in the new Labour Government that there was no evidence of legal hardship experienced by homosexuals in Scotland under the existing law.[36] The Lord Advocate, Ronald King Murray, was insistent that, despite claims of the SMG that blackmail was prevalent, there was no evidence before him that 'this kind of extortion exist[ed]'.[37] The official response to all private and parliamentary enquiries merely repeated a now-familiar mantra: that homosexual law reform in Scotland was not an appropriate issue for government action and remained 'a field for Private Members' legislation'.

Moreover, this response remained one among many obstacles to the success of the 1975 Sexual Offences Bill (based on the 1974 draft), a bill eventually sponsored by Dr J. Dickson Mabon, Labour MP for Greenock, and the Liberal Peer, Lord Beaumont, but never successfully introduced.[38] Although there was favourable coverage in the media, the Bill encountered unanticipated hostility from MPs, notably in relation to the lowered age of consent. Their reluctance to initiate debate on the Bill was compounded by the establishment by the Home Secretary in the summer of 1975 of a policy advisory committee to advise the Criminal Law Revision Committee (CLRC) on the age of consent for homosexual sex, headed by Lord Edmund-Davies, who was 'well known for his traditional views on moral issues'.[39] The Bill's sponsors were convinced that, until the Commission had reported, there was no realistic chance of carrying through 'the wider reforms' advocated by the CHE, SMG and USFI. A further complication was the issue of Scottish devolution. On the one hand, it was feared that, if the campaign awaited a favourable report from the CLRC before introducing legislation, a Scottish Assembly might already be in existence and possibly invalidate any recommendations. On the other, it was feared that to legislate while devolution was still being debated could entangle the two issues: 'One would run up against the argument that homosexual law reform ought to be left over to the proposed assembly.'[40]

By the end of 1975, the united campaign had lost a great deal of its impetus. SMG observers felt there was a 'loss of confidence' within the CHE, an obsession with processes rather than action and a failure to go beyond the drafting of a 'model Bill' or to coordinate joint action with other groups (gay or otherwise) within the community.[41] As Weeks observes: 'The carrot dangled before the CHE lobbyists by "sympathetic" Members of Parliament was to play for minor legislative modifications as a first step, but it was essential for the unity and enthusiasm of the movement that it should have a coherent and wide-ranging campaign.'[42] The SMG and USFI were not prepared to settle for a 'short-term Bill' for Scotland and Northern Ireland on the lines of the 1967 Sexual Offences Act. Instead, it was agreed that the right strategy was to seek to secure the agreement of the House of Lords (and, if possible, of the House of Commons) for the need for equality between homosexual and heterosexual conduct in the criminal law in all parts of Britain as a matter of principle, and to sustain pressure on the CLRC to endorse appropriate legal changes.[43]

The SMG had particular reasons for advocating early action to harmonise legal rights. In August 1975, Edinburgh District Council refused permission for the SMG to put a nameplate outside its premises in Broughton Street, following protests by traders and residents that 'a homosexual colony might develop' and 'normal people' be driven out of the area. Significantly, one councillor, in opposing any advertising by the SMG, had cited the illegality of homosexual acts under existing Scots law. The SMG subsequently appealed successfully to the Secretary of State for Scotland, but the whole incident vividly demonstrated the wide-ranging effects of legal discrimination on homosexual activities and support agencies.[44]

CHALLENGE AND RESPONSE, 1976–7

The SMG's political activities in 1976 were centred on two main areas. First, in March, it sought to make representations to the Home Secretary's Policy Advisory Committee along with the CHE, whose parliamentary campaign appeared increasingly 'moribund' and distracted. The central thrust of the SMG's evidence was that Scots law remained fundamentally discriminatory and, even if interpreted narrowly by the Crown Office, still served to reinforce the social and institutional stigma suffered by homosexuals. It also compromised the legality of advisory, counselling and welfare services increasingly provided by the SMG and other voluntary agencies. In addition, the SMG stressed that both justice and common sense demanded that laws relating to issues of private morality should be uniform throughout Britain and that recent shifts in the attitude of the Church of Scotland and some areas of the Scottish press suggested that 'informed opinion' in Scotland was no longer prepared to acquiesce in inferior civil rights relating to sexual freedom.[45]

Second, in the latter half of 1976, the SMG concentrated instead on fighting the Labour Government's Sexual Offences (Scotland) Bill introduced in July to consolidate the law on sexual matters in

Scotland, and which retained Section 11 of the 1885 Criminal Law Amendment Act relating to homosexual offences. The SHHD and the Lord Advocate sought to reassure the SMG that the inclusion of the section in the Consolidation Bill did not in any way signify a more punitive policy, and that offences between consenting male adults in private would in practice continue to be normally exempt from prosecution. Permanent officials advised the Secretary of State and Lord Advocate that pressure for reform was only coming from the SMG. They affirmed, with the support of the Scottish Law Commission, that a substantive change in the existing law could not be introduced as a side effect of a Consolidation Bill and reiterated that, if legislative reform were to be sought, it would have to be by way of a Private Member's Bill.[46]

However, the policy files do reveal a softening in attitude within the Scottish administration. Significantly, in August 1976, the SHHD suggested that the Lord Advocate might encourage the SMG to promote such a bill, introduced by, for example, Robin Cook or David Steel.[47] Similarly, the Crown Agent observed to the Lord Advocate that it did 'seem pointless to retain law which [had] not been enforced for many years' and was sympathetic to the Government promising to reconsider the issue of the decriminalisation of homosexual acts in Scotland on a par with the 1967 Sexual Offences Act.[48] Nonetheless, officials also expressed the view that, with devolution pending, it might be 'inappropriate for the Government to introduce legislation at this stage on a controversial matter which was to be devolved to the Assembly'.[49]

The SMG organised a vigorous campaign in the press and Parliament for the amendment of the Consolidation Bill.[50] In the Lords, Lord Boothby, supported by Lord Wilson of Langside and Lord Byers, Liberal leader in the Lords, emphasised the dangers of discrediting the law by preserving an offence whose prosecution the Crown Office had explicitly abandoned. He managed to win a concession from Lord Kirkhill, Minister of State at the Scottish Office, that, although the Government would not alter the Bill, 'consolidation [was] often a prelude to reform'.[51] In the Commons, during the debates on the second reading and report stage of the Bill, both the Conservative MP for Edinburgh Pentlands, Malcolm Rifkind, and Labour's Robin Cook forcefully argued the SMG's case. Despite reassurances from the Lord Advocate that the Bill was not intended in any way to 'give added force to old statutory provisions' and that, on the contrary, it might well 'highlight areas needing review',

Rifkind and Cook warned that a re-statement of the law would precipitate more coercive police action and give entirely the wrong signal to the more homophobic sections of Scottish society.[52] They, along with George Reid, Scottish Nationalist Party MP for Clackmannan and East Stirling, also echoed Boothby's fear that to enact measures which the Lord Advocate had been forced to acknowledge were largely unenforceable would bring the law into disrepute. It was 'stuff', Reid expostulated, 'worthy of Alice in Wonderland'.[53]

In the event, the Scottish Office refused to yield on the clause and the vote in the Commons was 37–27 in favour of the retention of the 1885 measures in the Consolidation Bill. The SMG had, however, gained some visibility for the Scottish cause, and reduced the Labour Government's majority to only ten on what was supposed to be a non-controversial bill. The more depressing aspect of the outcome, as Robin Cook later pointed out, was that: 'The Government owed its entire majority to the Scottish Members of whom 19 voted in favour of the consolidation but only 9 for the deletion.'[54] As Leo Abse MP observed, the 'backwoodsmen of Scotland', to whose views he had in part deferred in restricting his 1967 Act, were still very much in evidence.[55]

Writing on the prospects for homosexual law reform in February 1977, Ian Dunn, a leading activist in the SMG since its inception and convener of its Legal Action Committee, was pessimistic. Citing recent contributions to the debate by leader writers in the popular Scottish Press, he detected 'a distinct chill in the air towards Gay Rights'.[56] Particularly depressing was the failure of the major political parties to adopt any clear 'sexual orientation' policy. Although the 1976 Labour Party Annual Conference had approved a draft manifesto noting the need for further homosexual law reform, the Scottish Labour Party had no policy on gay rights and was preoccupied with internal splits. While the Young Liberals had come out in favour of Gay Rights, the Liberal leadership had studiously avoided making any statements on the subject in the wake of the Jeremy Thorpe affair.[57] Meanwhile, no motions relating to homosexual law reform had ever been discussed at a Tory Party Conference. In Dunn's view, such issues were assiduously excluded from debate within the party, and anyone raising them would be 'speedily labelled "lefty" or "queer" and gradually put out on a limb, neatly and effectively neutralised'. Similarly, he considered that the SNP had 'scuttled' any attempt to acknowledge Gay Rights after deciding at their National Council in 1975 to devolve the issue to the SNP Executive:

The result? No motion has ever been debated at an SNP Annual Conference! A party which claims to treat all Scots equally can only, by this belief, reflect the *status quo*, and this means the perpetuation of that rather grey Scots attitude of mind which prefers people to be white, decent and normal and not, for Christ's sake, coloured, radical or queer.[58]

A range of options was open to the SMG in terms of further action. As in 1972, it rejected the option of settling for the extension to Scotland, with amendments, of the 1967 Sexual Offences Act. It was also reluctant to revive a more radical UK-wide Bill on the lines of the 1974–5 proposals.[59] SMG members were disillusioned with the CHE, which was in any case concentrating its efforts on amending the Government's 1977 Criminal Law Bill which proposed to remove the right of trial by jury for men accused of public importuning.[60] There was also a growing element of 'national identity' within SMG thinking. As Ian Dunn observed to Nigel Warner of the CHE:

> Our two organisations should cooperate closely at all times when UK-wide issues are at stake, but SMG should be free to follow its own policies for Scotland. A growing sense of 'scottishness' here dictates that SMG works on its own, including the exclusive lobbying of Scots MPs on Scottish legislation. Scottish political life can be worlds removed from English/London/Home Counties political life![61]

Accordingly, the SMG opted for a reform of the law applicable to Scotland alone.[62]

The content and passage of the Bill, introduced by Lord Boothby in the House of Lords on 8 March 1977, reflected the continuing weight of prejudice within British, and especially Scottish, politics and society, over the issue of homosexual law reform. Although the Bill initially proposed an age of consent of 18 for homosexual relations, many of the more radical aspects of the SMG's 1972–3 measures had to be sacrificed on the advice of the SMG's parliamentary supporters, and in the face of Boothby's repeated assertion that any attempt to press for more than the minimum provisions (effectively the simple extension of the 1967 Act to Scotland) 'would sink the Bill'.[63]

Nonetheless, debates in the Lords on Boothby's Bill once again saw Scottish peers at the forefront of opposition to reform. Addressing what he termed 'this revolting subject', Lord Ferrier condemned the

Scottish Bill as a 'charter for male prostitutes' that served merely to empower 'the compulsive lecher and decadent pervert'. He drew especially on James Adair's note of reservation to the Wolfenden Report in viewing homosexual law reform as part of a general decline in moral standards.[64] The Countess of Loudon was equally vitriolic. 'Are we,' she asked, 'to encourage the infectious growth of this filthy disease by giving the authority of Parliament to the spreading of corruption and perversion among a new generation of young men and the younger boys in contact with them?' In her view it was 'a Bill to extend the tentacles of evil' that favoured 'the pervert and the money grubbers'. While she acknowledged advances in the medical understanding of the aetiology of homosexuality, she retained a fundamentally pathological and contagionist view of homosexual behaviour:

> [Y]ou cannot be a homosexual alone, which inevitably leads to the corruption and perversion of others, which is a symptom of the disease. So although it would be wrong to condemn, just as it would be wrong to condemn the victim of an attack of cholera, such an outbreak must be contained and isolated, not given a licence to multiply.[65]

Although Lord Ferrier sought to abort Lord Boothby's Bill by deferring its consideration until after the issue of devolution had been resolved, attempts to deny the Bill a second reading were defeated by a resounding majority of 125 votes to 27.[66] Ninety-four per cent of Labour peers present effectively voted for a second reading, as did 89 per cent of the Independents, 100 per cent of the Liberals and 60 per cent of the Conservatives. 'All remaining resistance crumbled during the Committee stage' and on 7 July the Bill passed its third reading and was sent to the Commons.[67] However, when Robin Cook attempted to move a formal second reading of the Bill in the House of Commons later in the month, it failed to make progress, killed by an objection from the MP for Gainsborough.

The response of the SHHD and the Crown Office to Boothby's Bill had been unenthusiastic. They recommended that the Government's attitude should remain 'one of neutrality' and predicted that the issue of lowering the homosexual age of consent would be highly contentious and that, even if it secured widespread support, it would be unlikely to be accorded time in an already crowded parliamentary session.[68] Both the Secretary of State for Scotland and the Lord

Advocate were opposed to the lowering of the age of consent to 18, especially where one of the parties was over 21, on the grounds set out in the Wolfenden Report.[69] They were concerned that Scottish legislation should stay in line with the 1967 Sexual Offences Act. However, in May 1977, once Boothby had agreed to amend the age of consent in his Bill to 21, and to model it on the 1967 Act rather than the SMG's draft proposals, the Government was prepared to offer him the services of the Scottish parliamentary draftsmen, as long as its 'neutrality on issues raised by the Bill was not prejudiced'.[70]

THE FINAL STRUGGLE, 1978–80

Despite this assistance, when Robin Cook attempted to re-introduce Lord Boothby's Sexual Offences (Scotland) Bill into the Commons in the Winter of 1977–8, he was repeatedly frustrated by backbench MPs, including a representative of the Free Church of Scotland. After the Bill had been deferred on four separate occasions, strong representations were made by the SMG to the Scottish Office. In particular, they drew attention to the fact that, in 1967, the Government had given parliamentary time to Leo Abse's Bill, that both the Scottish Trades Union Congress and the Church of Scotland had come out unequivocally in favour of bringing Scots law into line and that there was evidence that the 1976 Sexual Offences (Scotland) Act had 'brought about increased harassment of gay people in Scotland on the part of the police and of local authorities, particularly Conservative dominated ones'.[71] Robin Cook also made direct representations to the Secretary of State for Scotland.[72] In addition, the Scottish Council for Civil Liberties pressed the Lord Advocate for reform following the case of a homosexual blackmail victim whose name and address had been made public in a Sheriff Court.[73]

The official reaction to such representations remained cool. Although some of his advisers strongly disagreed, the Lord Advocate observed to Sir Geoffrey Howe, MP for Surrey East and a member of the Shadow Cabinet, that he was not aware of any 'indication that there is any widespread or general support in Scotland for a change from the present position'.[74] For his part, the Scottish Office Solicitor's main concern was to ensure that the Bill was in line with the 1967 Act, especially with respect to the commission of homosexual acts between merchant seamen and the procurement of a homosexual act on behalf of a third party.[75] For similar reasons, the Conservative Chief Whip was determined not to allow the Bill to 'go through on the nod' and was prepared if necessary to object on the grounds that the Bill raised important issues.[76] The Secretary of State for Scotland argued that Abse's Bill had only been given parliamentary time in 1967 after a clear demonstration of support in the House of Commons. He also warned that 'it was conceivable that Westminster legislation on this subject in the year preceding devolution might provoke adverse reaction in the Assembly'.[77] An additional constraint was the Labour Government's desire to avoid anti-abortion legislation and the fear that if they gave homosexual law reform parliamentary time, they would also have to concede it to the anti-abortionists.[78] With an impending general election, controversial issues relating to morality and sexuality were increasingly avoided by political leaders in all parties.

After Robin Cook's Bill was deferred for the fifth time on 14 July 1978, it lapsed automatically at the end of the session and the Lord Advocate continued to hold out little prospect of law reform for the remainder of the year.[79] Within the SMG, the failure of the Bill led to some fundamental reassessment of strategy and of its notion of sexual citizenship.[80] Many members were unhappy with its minimalist provisions and viewed it in some respects as a reactionary measure. The difficulty for the SMG was that, in promoting such a bill, it was open to the accusation that it was 'perpetuating the "second class status" of homosexual men qua homosexual in Scotland'. Some members of the Group cautioned against over-reliance on politicians' advice – 'the "we know what's best for you" danger'. They argued that: 'The people who set the pace should be the varied members of the organised gay community', and that 'honeyed assurances from individual members of government or political party [were] no substitute for hard work by gay people united in the fight for gay rights'. In a paper for the SMG executive committee, Ian Dunn submitted that, while not abandoning Robin Cook's Bill, the SMG should return to its more radical agenda of 1975:

> This time our work will NOT be directed towards persuading a 'sympathetic' MP to introduce such a Bill in Parliament or assembly. We were mistaken in the past about this and we must see the question of Law Reform in a wider context. MPs are over-sensitive about gay rights and in fact are not really representative of researched public opinion which is well disposed towards a live-and-let-live approach on adult sexual matters. In any programme for reform, we cannot ask for less than we believe because to do

so would imply that we concede that homosexuality is indeed 'queer' or somehow a 'disability'.[81]

Dunn viewed the 'coming Scottish Assembly' as an excellent opportunity for targeting the policy committees of all parties and organised opinion in Scotland, and for re-involving the younger members of gay groups who were disillusioned with the SMG's formal meetings and 'procedural jungles'. He envisioned a more offensive strategy that challenged the '*status quo* attitudes [towards sexual discrimination] which exist[ed] in most social and political organisations'.

The new, more assertive agenda of the SMG – significantly renamed the Scottish Homosexual Rights Group in late 1978 – was reflected, first in its adoption of a Declaration of Rights of Homosexual Men and Women, and second in its vigorous espousal of the pro-devolution campaign. Its Declaration demanded a wide range of equal rights for homosexuals in matters relating to employment, health, welfare, association, publicity and sexual behaviour.[82] A central role of the document was to 'start preparing' for 'educating' a future Scottish Assembly.[83] At a press conference in February 1979, the Group stressed the potential for homosexual law reform in a devolved Assembly and urged all Scottish gays to vote in favour of the referendum.[84] Their espousal of devolution elicited some virulent protests from the anti-gay lobby. As one correspondent to *The Scotsman* declared:

> Were I tempted to vote Yes in the coming referendum, the prospect of the proposed Assembly encouraging the repugnant and depraved sexual practices which [the SHRG] regards as a basic human right would certainly dissuade me. Assembly or no Assembly, those who wish to preserve our freedom from homosexuals, paedophiles, and other perverts must fight to check the continuing threat to decent moral standards. Let those of us who seek to 'keep Scotland straight' unite . . . in the call to 'Keep the gays at bay – vote Nay!'[85]

In the event, the campaign for devolution failed in the referendum vote on 1 March 1979. Thereafter, the SHRG reverted to drafting, with the SCCL, yet another Bill to amend the Sexual Offences (Scotland) Act of 1976. Its provisions revived the more wide-ranging demands of the SMG's earlier measures, proposing an age of consent for homosexual acts of 16 years, more flexibility in the operation of the law where under-age sex had occurred and a 'defence to any charge relating to homosexual acts that such or similar conduct would not have constituted an offence had the parties been male and female respectively'.[86]

The SHRG also submitted a trenchant critique of the working paper issued in June 1979 by the Home Office's Policy Advisory Committee on Sexual Offences. In particular, it deplored the Committee's exclusion of Scotland from its remit, and criticised as 'stigmatic' the Committee's use of the term 'minimum age' instead of 'age of consent' for homosexual acts.[87] It rejected the Committee's reaffirmation of the Wolfenden Report that 'homosexual acts [were] practised by a small minority of the population and should be seen in proper perspective' and not 'given a disproportionate amount of public attention', and its assumption that homosexual relationships were intrinsically dysfunctional and less fulfilling. It was, the SHRG argued, primarily such moral and cultural prejudices surrounding homosexual lifestyles (and the associated anxiety to protect British youth at all costs from its allegedly degenerating and paedophilic influences), rather than empirical medical evidence, that had persuaded the majority of the Committee to 'err on the side of extreme caution' in locating 18 rather than 16 as the age at which sexual orientation was fixed.[88]

However, undoubtedly the most significant new initiative of the SHRG in 1979 was to submit their case to the European Court of Human Rights. Three Scottish gay activists testified that they were victims within the meaning of Article 25 of the European Convention of Human Rights in that they suffered 'prejudice by reason of fear of prosecution for the commission of homosexual acts', that they 'suffered psychological harm and distress as a result thereof' as well as 'social stigma and loss of esteem' and that they were 'open to blackmail, intimidation, and harassment'. They also claimed that they suffered discrimination as citizens of the United Kingdom 'by reason of Scottish national minority status'. Specific legal objections were raised: first, that the Sexual Offences (Scotland) Act 1976, section 7, did not provide an age of consent, contrary to the corresponding legislation in England and Wales; second, that no age of consent was provided for in the Scottish common law offence of sodomy and that there was no corresponding law regarding sodomy between male and female; third, that Scots law relating to shameless indecency rendered all overt homosexual behaviour criminal and that there was no corresponding English law that was as extensive with respect to the freedom of homosexual expression or association, and no corresponding restriction on heterosexual behaviour; and finally, that the Lord Advocate's discretionary enforcement of the law against homosexual practices, which could be rescinded by any successor in the post, had 'created a non-prosecuted criminal class who live[d] in fear of subsequent harassment at the sole discretion of one government officer'.[89]

According to Alkarim Jivani, it was this appeal to the European Court that finally persuaded the (now Conservative) Government to concede homosexual law reform for Scotland:

> [T]he British government realized that unless a concession was made, it was facing a long and expensive battle whose outcome was obvious – defeat. It decided to do the expedient thing and a tacit agreement was reached that it would not oppose law reform in Scotland. But it had to be done with a certain amount of parliamentary subterfuge. The vehicle was to be the Criminal Justice Bill of 1979 and the tactic was to propose an amendment to it late at night when it had a greater chance of getting through.[90]

In contrast, Jeffery-Poulter argues that the amendment was 'a daring and unexpected initiative' led by Robin Cook, primarily inspired by the public furore surrounding the Saunders case in the spring of 1980 which had involved the dismissal of a handyman at a residential camp for schoolchildren in Scotland, simply because his employers had discovered he was homosexual.[91] Certainly, as late as the autumn of 1979, the Scottish Office had indicated that there was little likelihood of any reform measure making progress in the near future,[92] and the official response to Cook's amendment does not suggest that any deal had been struck prior to the debate on 22 July 1980.[93] Supported by David Steel and Donald Dewar, Cook used the Saunders case to highlight the impact of the existing law in Scotland on civil liberties and employment rights, and the unacceptable legal limbo to which the gay community had been consigned. Although he personally favoured an age of consent of 18, he was prepared to concede, for the sake of securing the amendment, a legal threshold of 21, although he hoped that, where appropriate, cases involving parties between 18 and 21 would be treated leniently.[94]

There was predictable opposition from some backbenchers, either reaffirming their confidence in existing Scottish legal procedures and/or articulating more primitive fears. The Scottish Office also adopted a distinctly negative approach. In June, a Scottish Office spokesman had remarked that it was unusual to accept a major amendment on such a controversial issue so late in the process of a bill, and that a separate Private Member's Bill would have been preferable.[95] In the Commons, the Secretary of State for Scotland, George Younger, 'did his best to indicate that the Government's neutrality meant that it disapproved of the proposal', and he expressed concern that such a substantive measure had been so insufficiently considered by the House.[96] Nonetheless, the clause was adopted by a majority of 203 votes to 80. Every single Scottish Conservative MP voted against the measure, led by George Younger. According to *The Scotsman* it was 'the most significant victory in over a decade' for the Scottish gay community, and even the *Glasgow Evening News* gave its grudging approval. Predictably, the *Sun* christened it the 'McGay's Charter'.[97]

The measure drew immediate opposition from a number of quarters. Many members of the SHRG viewed the amendment, with its age of consent of 21 years, as a meagre concession to the sexual rights of gay men.[98] They shared with the Scottish Legal Action Group a view that it might well prove a 'pyrrhic victory' in that, compared with the existing laissez-faire attitude of the Crown Office, the new legislation might actually increase the legal harassment of homosexuals in the 18–21 age group.[99]

However, the real backlash came from the moral Right. Within the week, the Free Presbyterian Church of Scotland had lobbied the Lord Advocate, James Mackay, to reject the amendment when the Criminal Justice Bill was returned to the House of Lords.[100] In late August, the director of the Nationwide Festival of Light, the fundamentalist Christian organisation, had a letter published in a number of Scottish newspapers which condemned the 'sudden and unexpected' attempt to change the law and warned of the shocking repercussions that the 1967 Act had already wrought south of the Border.[101] In his view, there had emerged 'a vast sub-culture of homosexuals militantly organized to convert society', and this 'moral poison' was being deliberately targeted at the young.

Furthermore, it was precisely this familiar appeal to the myth that all homosexuals were child molesters that led to the formation of a group called Parents' Concern which bombarded the Scottish press with calls for protection for their children from the proposed new law.[102] Their opposition was clearly driven by a powerful set of fears and assumptions:

Since they cannot multiply by natural procreation, are they therefore to be permitted to do so by public display, advertising, soliciting (at least in private) and other forms of proselytising?

. . . Homosexuality is purposeless. Its practice is gratification for gratification's sake. It makes sexual satisfaction a universal right; an absolute. It produces no offspring, demands no special commitment to one's partner, or for any length of time, and is therefore especially tolerant of promiscuity, and invites venereal disease. It discolours everyday relationships in a most profound way, and for life.[103]

Above all, Parents' Concern warned Scottish readers of the quintessentially predatory nature of the homosexual 'subculture' which would increasingly batten on vulnerable youngsters if existing Scots law were to be eroded.[104]

Such views were merely reinforced by a reference in *Gay News* to Robin Cook's clause in the Criminal Justice Bill as an 'Orgy Law' on the grounds that it failed to specify that private and consensual homosexual acts were only legal between *two* men. This was also a point of contention with the Lord Advocate who had been inundated with letters opposing reform, and who insisted, despite protestations from Lord Boothby and the SHRG, that an appropriate further amendment be introduced by the Government in the House of Lords to bring the legislation in Scotland fully into line with that in England and Wales.[105]

This did little to defuse the acrimony felt by a hard core of Scottish peers towards the clause, who had waged a relentless opposition to homosexual law reform ever since the 1960s. Thus, in the Lords debate on the Criminal Justice (Scotland) Bill on 21 October 1980, Lord Ferrier once again voiced his distaste for any legal surrender to 'these wretched people [who] have turned an ancient, kindly, happy Saxon adjective into a dirty word'.[106] Lord Galpern resurrected the arguments of James Adair in his reservation to the Wolfenden Report and portrayed homosexuality as an illness that demanded government funding of medical research for a 'cure' rather than a relaxation of the law.[107] Meanwhile, the Earl of Lauderdale echoed the views of Parents' Concern in condemning homosexuality as socially and sexually 'without purpose', inherently self-gratifying, promiscuous and predatory. In his view, Robin Cook's amendment was part of a homosexual conspiracy and the views of Scotland – 'our land of Calvin, oatcakes and sulphur' – had gone unheard. The existing Act should be retained as an 'ethical pointer for the community'.[108] As a result of the efforts of the Scottish diehards in the Lords, Cook's amendment was eventually carried by only fifty-nine votes to forty-eight, a very small majority in comparison with Lord Boothby's identical Bill in 1977. The decriminalisation of private, consensual homosexual acts between males over 21 had at last been extended, albeit grudgingly, to Scotland.

AFTERMATH AND CONCLUSION

However, in important respects, it remained a very limited victory, in terms of both homosexual rights and everyday experience. Scottish gay activists continued to struggle in an increasingly hostile political and cultural environment for full legal equality for homosexuals in line with successive rulings of the European Commission and Court of Human Rights. Moreover, despite a survey by the *Sunday Mail* in October 1979 that had revealed two-thirds of the 'young Scots' interviewed as favouring homosexual law reform,[109] this was not reflected in the response of many church and civic leaders to the Criminal Justice (Scotland) Act. The report of the Committee for Social Responsibility of the Church of Scotland, established in 1981, did indicate a liberalisation of views within the Kirk. The Committee sought to moderate the biblical condemnation of homosexuality, to dissociate it from paedophilia and to caution against an over-zealous commitment to medical treatments. Nonetheless, they explicitly rejected sexual intercourse between homosexuals, as well as groups and societies that existed to promote homosexual activities.[110] Meanwhile, the Religion and Morals Committee of the Free Presbyterian Church of Scotland concluded that it was by reading the debates on Robin Cook's amendment 'that future generations will . . . come to the conclusion that our day was one of the darkest in this fallen world's history'.[111]

Evidence would suggest that the everyday exposure of Scottish homosexuals to social discrimination and legal harassment did not diminish. Homophobia remained a *leitmotiv* of the Scottish media, especially in the letter pages of the local press,[112] reflecting the moral backlash of the early 1980s. *SMG News*, and its successor, *Gay Scotland*, continued to report frequent cases of discrimination by employment and housing tribunals, of harassment by the police and customs and excise officers (who regularly seized gay literature) and of the arbitrary use of local byelaws to restrict or proscribe gay venues and advertisements.[113] Indeed, armed with newly defined powers, in some respects the surveillance of homosexual activities by the police and prosecuting authorities became more vigorous. The 1980 edition of official guidelines for police duties and procedure in Scotland still identified homosexuality with moral 'degeneration', social pollution and paedophilia and with the lewd and libidinous sexualities of the public park and lavatory, revealing just how little distance sexual politics had advanced in Scotland since 1950.[114]

Certainly, the SHRG were acutely conscious of the shortfall between the experience of Scottish homosexuals in the early 1980s and the original aims of the SMG,[115] and many activists increasingly perceived the organisation as too 'safe' and 'respectable' in its pursuit of sexual citizenship and to some extent complicit in the sexual double standards of Scottish governance.[116] Yet it can fairly be argued that the SMG had been faced with a range of often protracted and irresolvable dilemmas in the 1970s: whether to introduce legislation specific to Scotland or to associate with a broader UK-wide campaign for homosexual law reform; whether to focus purely on the issue of sexual offences or to embrace a wider agenda of sexual rights; and whether to compromise with the conservatism of Scottish public and parliamentary opinion (especially over the age of consent) in order to secure at least a modicum of legislative progress, or to hold out for a more confrontational programme of sexual equality in law and civil society. In addition, there was an urgent need to balance its political activities with its befriending and advisory roles and to ensure the financial viability of the organisation.

It is arguable that, however frustrating, given the continuing hostility of some sections of the Scottish establishment, media and public opinion to the Gay Liberation Movement, the more pragmatic stance of the SMG towards policy making was the best option. As *SMG News* had rightly reflected in 1973:

> whatever good the Gay Liberation Front might do in the South, Scotland, with its different legal position and more puritanical attitudes was not suited to Gay Lib-type protests which would [have been] counter-productive . . . A group like SMG, 'conformist' or not, was a more realistic venture.[117]

It remains to ask just how far the slow pace of homosexual law reform in Scotland can be attributed to the so-called 'democratic deficit' and the lack of constitutional autonomy in the policy-making process, an argument occasionally advanced in *The Scotsman*.[118] Certainly, as Chapter 3 indicates, such considerations do not appear to have had any significant role in the omission of Scotland from the 1967 Sexual Offences Act. Leo Abse later admitted that the principal reason for its exclusion was that the balance of opinion among Scottish MPs was more hostile than among the House as a whole and '[he] had no wish to provoke more trouble than [he] already had on [his] hands'.[119] Significantly, in the vote on whether he should be granted leave to bring in his Bill, the House divided 244 to 100, while the Scots who entered the lobbies divided almost evenly. Thereafter, for the best part of a decade, no Scottish MP sought to introduce a reform Bill for Scotland and Lord Boothby's Bill of 1977 was the first attempt to do so in the Lords. Moreover, as we have seen, the failure of Rifkind's and Cook's motion to remove the homosexual offences clause from the 1976 Consolidation Act was in large part due to the voting behaviour of Scottish MPs. Subsequently, Scottish representations in both the Lords and the Commons were instrumental in aborting the progress of Boothby's Bill in 1977–8 and in marshalling opposition to the Cook amendment of 1980.

This chapter would suggest that such opposition reflected a broader fear of sexual trends south of the Border and was part of a wider debate surrounding 'permissiveness' and national identity in this period. Evidence indicates that Scottish homosexual law reform was not significantly impeded by constitutional factors or by the minority position of Scottish MPs at Westminster. Indeed, as Robin Cook noted in 1977, voting behaviour on moral issues 'flatly rebutt[ed] the nationalist contention that there [was] a permanent and inevitable conflict of interest between Scots and English politicians, since on nearly all occasions the majority of both nations were to be found in the same division lobby'.[120] Moreover, as he concluded, with civic rights being at the mercy of local passions and prejudices, devolution would not necessarily have been consistent with a more liberal stance on homosexual issues. Another founder member of the SMG fully concurred, observing to Ian Dunn in 1979 that:

If Scotland had to carry the full responsibility for its separate nationhood, I doubt whether the law would have changed here yet. I tend to think that a truly Scottish Scotland would be a rabidly heterosexist society, and gays would not last long.[121]

Notes

1   See, for example, Weeks, *Coming Out*, 208–9, 211–12, 229, 238; Higgins, *Heterosexual Dictatorship*, 146; Jivani, *A History of Lesbian and Gay Britain*, 177–9.

2   See, for example, Jeffery-Poulter, *Peers, Queers & Commons*, 142–7.

3   Dempsey, *Thon Wey*; Orr, 'Capitalism, patriarchy and gay oppression'.

4   Cant, *Footsteps and Witnesses*; BBC Radio Scotland, *Scotland the Gay*, 15 and 22 June 2004.

5   National Library of Scotland (hereafter NLS), Ian C. Dunn Papers (hereafter IDP), Acc.11905/49, I. C. Dunn, 'SMG: organisation and progress', 25 February 1970; I. C. Dunn to David Steel, MP, 12 December 1971; *SMG News*, February 1972, 8.

6   By 1971, membership had risen to 210 (as compared with 30 in 1969).

7   NRS, GD467/2/8, 'Summary of history of SMG', 3 June 1978.

8   The following account is based on NRS, HH60/876, GD467/2/2/1, Papers relating to legislation 1971–2.

9   NLS, IDP, Acc.11905/89, Minutes of Scottish Minorities Group (hereafter SMG) Executive Committee, 14 April 1972; Acc.11905/152, SMG Annual Report for 1972, 9.

10 NRS, GD467/2/2/2, Bill papers.

11 NRS, GD467/2/2/2, Notes on SMG strategy meeting, April 1972.

12 The Board had condemned the Assembly's deliverance against homosexuality in 1967 as an 'unfeeling condemnation' which had paralysed the pastoral and rehabilitative work of the Church and impaired its relationship with the social and psychiatric services [GACS, *Report of Social and Moral Welfare Board for 1968*, 489–91, 509].

13 Orr, 'Capitalism, patriarchy and gay oppression', 25–6. As a result, although initially it was intended that the SMG and the Church of Scotland would collaborate in developing counselling services for homosexuals, they subsequently operated independently [NLS, IDP, Acc.11905/51, I. C. Dunn to A. Grey, 9 May 1970; Acc.11905/52, Minutes of SMG Executive Committee, 30 October 1970].

14 NRS, GD467/2/2/1, D. Steel to I. C. Dunn, 22 December 1971; *SMG News*, September 1972, 2.

15 NRS, GD467/2/2/2, Lord Arran to Scottish Council for Civil Liberties (hereafter SCCL), 3 February 1972.

16 Ibid., Rev. E. M. Simpson to SMG, 28 January 1972.

17 Ibid., Lord Tanlaw to SCCL, December 1972.

18 NRS, HH60/877, Briefing note by D. Dee, February 1972.

19 NRS, HH60/876, Minute by D. J. Cowperthwaite, 24 November 1972.

20 Ibid., Crown Agent to D. J. Cowperthwaite, 27 November 1972.

21 *SMG News*, December 1972, 2.

22 NRS, HH60/876, Correspondence between Crown Office and SMG, 1973; *SMG News*, February 1973, 1.

23 NRS, HH60/876, Scottish Office response to MPs on issue of Sexual

Offences (Scotland) Bill; HH60/877, SSS to Geoffrey Johnson Smith, MP, 1 November 1973.

24 *Glasgow Herald*, 10 March 1973.
25 *The Scotsman*, 9 March 1973; *Edinburgh Evening News*, 24 May 1973.
26 NRS, HH60/876, Resolution of Synod, 23 May 1973.
27 *Glasgow Herald*, 13 September 1973.
28 NLS, IDP, Acc.11905/89, Notes on meeting with Scottish MPs, 28 November 1973.
29 *SMG News*, January 1973, 7; March 1973, 7.
30 NRS, GD467/2/2/3, M. Coulson, 'Early thoughts on effectiveness', 1973.
31 NRS, GD467/2/2/4, M. Crowe, 'The General Election and us', March 1974.
32 Ibid., N. Fairbairn to Secretary, SMG, 1974.
33 Ibid., M. Hirst to D. J. Mullen, March 1974.
34 *SMG News*, July 1974, 5; NLS, IDP, Acc.11905/65, SMG Annual Report for 1975, 7; Acc.11905/144, Papers for Malvern Conference, May 1974.
35 NRS, GD467/2/2/4, Draft Bill, 18 September 1974.
36 NRS, HH60/877, Minute by A. M. Burnside, 25 July 1974.
37 NRS, HH60/876, Lord Advocate to Tam Galbraith, MP, 1 February 1974.
38 NRS, HH60/876, Crown Agent to SHHD, 1 July 1975; Lord Advocate's briefing notes, 19 November 1975.
39 Jeffery-Poulter, *Peers, Queers & Commons*, 113.
40 Ibid., 113; NLS, IDP, SMG Annual Report for 1975, 7.
41 NRS, GD467/2/2/7, I. Dunn to J. A. Barrett, 1 February 1977.
42 Weeks, *Coming Out*, 211–12.
43 NRS, GD467/2/2/5, Note of a meeting at the House of Commons, 19 November 1975.
44 NRS, GD467/2/2/5, SMG Memorandum, 'Arguments for reform', 26 September 1975. The incident also reflected the often deliberate confusion in local civic debate between adult male homosexuality and paedophilia [Cant (ed.), *Footsteps and Witnesses*, 43].
45 NRS, GD467/2/2/5, I. Dunn, 'Arguments for extending the reformed law to Scotland', 26 September 1975; Written evidence for the CLRC, 19 October 1975.
46 NRS, HH60/876 and 877, SHHD, papers and memoranda relating to Sexual Offences (Scotland) Bill, 1976; NRS, AD63/1293, Advocate Depute's papers and correspondence, 1976.
47 NRS, HH60/876, Brief for Lord Advocate's meeting with the SMG, 24 August 1976.
48 NRS, AD63/1293, Crown Agent to Lord Advocate, 19 August 1976.
49 Ibid., Note for parliamentary question on Consolidation Bill, 6 October 1976.

50 For details of the 1976 campaign, see especially NRS, GD467/2/2/6; NLS, IDP, Acc.11905/65, SMG Annual Report for 1976, 4.

51 *Hansard* [HL], vol. 375, 12 October 1976, cols 277–8.

52 *Hansard* [HC], vol. 918, 25 October 1976, cols 136–55; 3 November 1976, cols 1,570–84.

53 Ibid., vol. 918, 3 November 1976, col. 1,581.

54 NRS, GD467/2/2/7, Robin Cook, 'Personal law reform for Scotland', draft speech, 30 June 1977.

55 *Hansard* [HC], vol. 918, 25 October 1976, col. 149.

56 NRS, GD467/2/2/7, I. Dunn, 'Homosexual law reform: current position', 1 February 1977.

57 Jeremy Thorpe had resigned the leadership of the Liberal Party, as well as his seat in Parliament, after he had been accused of conspiracy to murder a man claiming to be his former lover.

58 NRS, GD467/2/2/7, I. Dunn, 'Homosexual law reform: current position', 1 February 1977.

59 Ibid., Legal Action Committee, draft introduction to the Sexual Offences (Scotland) Bill, March 1977.

60 Ibid., I. Dunn, 'Homosexual law reform: current position', 1 February 1977.

61 Ibid., I. Dunn to N. Warner, 13 October 1977.

62 NLS, IDP, Acc.11905/69, Minutes of SMG Executive Committee, 5 March 1977.

63 NRS, GD467/2/2/7, Lord Boothby to M. Crowe, 13 April 1977.

64 *Hansard* [HL], vol. 383, 10 May 1977, cols 169–74.

65 Ibid., vol. 384, 14 June 1977, cols 45–7.

66 Ibid., cols 120–1.

67 Ibid., cols 120–1.

68 NRS, AD63/1362/1, Inter-departmental correspondence on Sexual Offences (Scotland) Bill, 1977.

69 Ibid., Minute by SSS, 22 March 1977; Minute, Lord Advocate's Office to SHHD, 22 March 1977.

70 Ibid., Minute of Lord Advocate, 23 May 1977; NLS, IDP, Acc. 11905/65, SMG Annual Report for 1977, 4.

71 NRS, AD63/1427, SMG to Bruce Millan, SSS, 22 May 1978.

72 Ibid., Note of meeting between SSS, Robin Cook and Leo Abse, 28 June 1978.

73 *Glasgow Herald*, 3 July 1978.

74 NRS, AD63/1427, Lord Advocate to Sir G. Howe, May 1978.

75 Ibid., Solicitor to SSS to Lord Advocate's Office, 13 March 1978.

76 Ibid., Note by J. F. McClellan, 17 April 1978.

77 Ibid., Note of meeting with Robin Cook and Leo Abse, 28 June 1978.

78 NRS, GD467/2/2/8, Robin Cook to SMG, 6 July 1978.

79 Ibid., Lord Advocate to Councillor Brunton of Airdrie, October 1978.

80 The following overview is based on Ibid., I. Dunn, 'Law reform: discussion paper for SMG executive committee', 1 June 1978.
81 Ibid.
82 NLS, IDP, Acc.11905/71, Declaration of the Rights of Homosexual Men and Women, October 1978.
83 *SMG News*, November 1978, 14.
84 *The Scotsman*, 2 February 1979.
85 *The Scotsman*, 28 February 1979.
86 NRS, GD467/2/2/9, draft bill, 7 July 1979.
87 Ibid., Commentary on working paper, 1 September 1979.
88 Ibid.
89 Ibid., Application to European Court of Human Rights, 1979.
90 Jivani, *It's Not Unusual*, 177–8.
91 For full details, see Jeffery-Poulter, *Peers, Queers & Commons*, 141–3.
92 Ibid., 143.
93 NLS, IDC, Acc.11905/79, Scottish Office to M. O'Neill, MP, 8 July 1980.
94 *Hansard [HC]*, vol. 989, 22 July 1980, cols 284–320.
95 *Glasgow Herald*, 27 June 1980.
96 Jeffery-Poulter, *Peers, Queers & Commons*, 145.
97 Ibid.
98 NLS, IDP, Acc.11905/78, Scottish Homosexual Rights Group (hereafter SHRG) Annual Report for 1980, 3.
99 NRS, GD467/2/2/10, SHRG to Lord Boothby, 28 July 1980.
100 Jeffery-Poulter, *Peers, Queers & Commons*, 145.
101 See, for example, *The Scotsman*, 27 August 1980.
102 Jeffery-Poulter, *Peers, Queers & Commons*, 145–6.
103 NRS, GD467/2/2/10, Extract from the *Livingston Post*, 8 October 1980.
104 Similar views were expressed in the Scottish Catholic press. However, although individual priests condemned Robin Cook's amendment to the Criminal Justice (Scotland) Bill, the Roman Catholic hierarchy in Scotland adopted a broadly supportive view of the decriminalisation of homosexuality, while continuing to condemn homosexual acts as immoral in line with the Vatican Declaration of 1975 on sexual ethics [*Scottish Catholic Observer*, 7 December 1979, 1 August 1980, 19 September 1980].
105 Jeffery-Poulter, *Peers, Queers & Commons*, 146.
106 *Hansard [HL]*, vol. 413, 21 October 1980, col. 1,842.
107 Ibid., cols 1,837–40.
108 Ibid., cols 1,836–8.
109 NRS, GD467/2/2/9, extract from *Sunday Mail*, 7 October 1979.
110 GACS, *Report of Committee on Social Responsibility for 1983*, 303–8.
111 FPCS, *Proceedings of Synod for 1981*, 6.
112 See, for example, NRS, GD467/2/2/10, News cuttings, 1980.

113   NLS, IDC, Acc.11905/81, 88 and 89.
114   NRS, GD467/2/2/7, *Scottish Criminal Law: Police Duties and Procedure*, 1980; *The Scotsman*, 20 September 1980.
115   For a vivid insight into the everyday experience of gays in Scotland in the early 1980s, see Michael Wilcox's play *Rents*.
116   *Gay Scotland*, July/August 1979, 5; NLS, IDP, Acc.11905/128, I. Dunn, 'New directions for SHRG', 26 August 1980.
117   *SMG News*, May 1973, 3.
118   See, for example, *The Scotsman*, 22 January 1975.
119   *Hansard* [HC], vol. 918, 25 October 1976, col. 149.
120   NRS, GD467/2/2/7, Robin Cook, 'Personal law reform for Scotland', 30 June 1977.
121   NLS, IDP, Acc.11905/127, Donald Brooks to I. Dunn, 20 September 1979.

PART II

Reproductive Issues

5

ABORTION

INTRODUCTION

The increasing availability of safe and effective means of fertility control – abortion and contraception – arguably constitutes one of the most significant social developments of the later twentieth century, and has been viewed from a range of scholarly perspectives. Many social historians have located this trend within the general programme of so-called 'permissive' measures introduced to Britain during the 'Swinging Sixties', measures that reconfigured the role of the state in issues relating to sexual morality.[1] Other scholars have focused more specifically on the important role of the medical profession within reproductive health policy making.[2] Meanwhile, feminists have viewed policy formation with respect to abortion and birth control as a political struggle that strongly reflected the ideological prejudices of a patriarchal society.[3] In particular, they have been sharply critical of the 'medicalisation' of reproductive health, which, they have argued, left British women 'dependent on the vagaries of medical discretion and good will'.[4]

This section seeks to establish the role of Scottish policy making in the shaping of fertility control in later twentieth-century Britain. Chapter 5 considers the history of abortion law reform. It examines the greater flexibility of existing abortion law in Scotland, but the very limited extent to which Scottish doctors exploited that clinical freedom. It then highlights the sizeable input of Scottish doctors and politicians to the 1967 Abortion Act, the first piece of abortion-related legislation to cover Scotland, England and Wales collectively, and which liberalised access to abortion but placed it firmly under medical control. Thereafter, the chapter charts the initial reception and early working of the legislation, and the importance of Scottish opinion to subsequent, albeit unsuccessful, attempts to challenge and restrict access to abortion. Chapter 6 then turns to the history of contraception. It explores the social, medical and political factors that influenced family planning provision and policy in Scotland,

and the response of the policy community to a growing demand for the free and universal availability of contraceptive advice and supplies.

ABORTION LAW AND PRACTICE PRIOR TO 1966

The law surrounding abortion in Britain in the 1950s was deeply uncertain. In England, the Offences Against the Person Act of 1861 had made it unlawful to procure a miscarriage, though this legislation was qualified during the early decades of the twentieth century. The 1929 Infant Life (Preservation) Act exempted those cases where abortion was deemed necessary to save the life of the mother, and a 1938 judicial ruling, *Rex v. Bourne*, interpreted the 1929 Act as permitting abortion where 'the probable consequences of the continuance of the pregnancy [were] to make the woman a physical or mental wreck'. The latter ruling stemmed from an illegal termination of pregnancy conducted by the London obstetrician Aleck Bourne on a 14-year-old girl who had been raped by a group of soldiers. Bourne invited the law to prosecute him in an attempt to clarify English abortion law and, more specifically, to allow doctors to take a wider interpretation of 'risk' to a woman's health that incorporated mental as well as physical considerations.[5] Although the judge acquitted Bourne for his 'humane' action, English doctors appear to have remained deeply uncertain over the legalities of abortion, due in large part to the exceptional circumstances of the Bourne case.

In Scotland, abortion law followed a somewhat different course, since neither of the aforementioned Acts applied and nor did the Bourne case. North of the Border, abortion constituted a common law offence without strictly defined limits, so that it was possible to interpret it more elastically than under English statute law. In the decades before 1966, the Scottish legal establishment considered abortion a matter of medical discretion and advised that an abortion could be performed legally when certain medical criteria relating to the life and health of the mother were satisfied. In short, it was possible for a medical practitioner to terminate a pregnancy when acting in 'good faith' in the interests of the health or welfare of his patient.[6] Abortion was only a crime in mid-twentieth-century Scotland if 'criminal intent' could be proved, doctors otherwise having freedom to practise in accordance with their clinical judgement.

In addition, the mechanics of the law made prosecution more problematic in Scotland. Under English law a person could be found guilty whether or not the woman was actually pregnant, since the crime was not the abortion itself but the performing of an act with intent to procure an abortion. However, under Scots law, pregnancy had to be proven because the victim was the potential child.[7] Furthermore, a doctor who carried out an abortion in Scotland could not be charged unless a definite complaint was made against him. Thereafter, the matter would be investigated privately by doctors nominated by the Crown Office, and if they were satisfied that the operation had been carried out in good faith and in a proper manner the case would simply be closed. This contrasted with England, where a prosecution could be instituted by any local police force, even if all proper professional procedures had been followed and there appeared to be clear medical grounds for the termination. Finally, the high standard of proof called for in Scottish criminal prosecutions made it difficult to obtain sufficient evidence to prosecute an illegal abortion, since those involved – the abortionist, the pregnant woman and her family – would generally have a joint interest in concealment.

Thus, in a variety of respects, Scottish abortion law was substantially more flexible and liberal than its English counterpart. The number of prosecutions in Scotland was correspondingly small. In the two decades before 1966 not a single medical practitioner registered in Scotland was prosecuted for procuring an abortion where the defence argued that the abortion was in the interests of the life or health of the mother.[8] However, Scottish High Court records reveal that a number of cases were tried in the major Scottish cities for the crime of procuring an abortion. Prosecutions tended to result from cases where an 'amateur' person had performed an abortion for private gain, or where health had been seriously compromised through the use of improper methods, including the insertion of an instrument such as a sharpened piece of wood into the woman's body. The resulting illness or death of the pregnant woman might encourage witnesses to testify against the operator. Although these terminations were performed in a non-clinical setting, they often resulted in the hospitalisation of the pregnant woman.

Yet, in Scotland as in England, it seems that the line between criminal and non-criminal abortion continued to be perceived as uncertain. Whilst Scottish abortion law could in theory be interpreted more flexibly than could statutory provisions south of the Border, archival evidence and the oral testimony of retired Scottish medical practitioners suggest that most Scottish doctors were in fact failing to exploit this flexibility because they were unaware of their legal right to terminate a pregnancy when acting in good faith in the interests of the health or welfare of their patient.[9] The differences between English and Scots law were not made clear to medical students, so that graduates generally believed that performing an abortion was a crime unless the woman's life was in imminent danger. Indeed, textbooks such as John Glaister's *Medical Jurisprudence and Toxicology*, the 'medico-legal bible' for generations of doctors in Scotland, failed entirely to differentiate between abortion law in the two countries.[10] Thus, the services of illegal abortionists were in all likelihood used as heavily in Scotland as they were in England. Indeed, oral testimony indicates that some doctors positively valued the existence of competent local 'back-street' abortionists who were willing to help out desperate women with unwanted pregnancies at a time when doctors felt unable to assist.[11]

Only in one area of Scotland do doctors appear to have taken full advantage of the potential flexibility of Scottish abortion law in the decades before the 1967 Act, and that was in Aberdeenshire in north-east Scotland, under the guidance of the chief gynaecologist, Dugald Baird. Born in Greenock and educated in Glasgow, Baird was employed initially as a gynaecology registrar at Glasgow Royal Infirmary. It was in that city, the most Catholic in Scotland,[12] that Baird witnessed the excessive childbearing, high maternal mortality, lack of family planning information and provisions, and highly restrictive access to abortion that were to shape his whole future career in obstetrics and reproductive health. These factors, and most notably his frustration with the city's Catholic administration, propelled him towards Aberdeen, where he spent the remainder of his career.

Although both cities were plagued by similar social conditions at this time, including poverty, severe unemployment and housing shortages, Baird accepted an appointment to the Regius Chair of Midwifery at the University of Aberdeen in 1936. As he later noted, he felt that the city of Aberdeen would be ideal for researching the factors needed for 'efficient' childbearing, since it was an appropriate size for epidemiological research, and since its settled population and centralised medical service could enable the effective follow-up of women and their families.[13] Dr Ian MacQueen, the Medical Officer of Health from 1952 until the post was abolished in 1974, quickly became instrumental in helping Baird to construct his maternal healthcare policies for the city, and ensured the backing of local health authorities.[14] Moreover, Baird's wife, May, was a councillor who became Chairman of the Health Board, allowing Baird to exert significant influence upon subsequent policy and appointments. Finally, the Aberdonian community exhibited 'liberal' political attitudes and religious diversity in the post-war era, and provided an accepting environment for Baird's progressive policies. As such, Aberdeen offered promising administrative, medical and popular support.

Baird took advantage of these circumstances to implement the sort of system he could not have achieved in inter-war Glasgow. He regarded abortion as a reliable medical practice that was appropriate in many different situations, and argued that, far from producing psychological problems, it was the refusal of a termination that was likely to impair mental health.[15] Baird was conscious of the tenuous legal standing of abortion when he arrived in Aberdeen, and almost immediately sought the advice of Thomas Smith, Professor of Law at the University, for clarification on the issue. According to Baird, Smith explained that there was little likelihood of prosecution against doctors who terminated a pregnancy unless the authorities were convinced of 'criminal intent'.[16] Armed with this assurance, Baird and his colleagues adopted an active 'therapeutic abortion' policy under which they chose to recognise an increasing number of social as well as medical indications that might adversely affect a woman's health. It seems likely, as Baird later claimed, that very few abortions were performed in Aberdeenshire by 'unqualified persons' because women knew they would receive 'sympathetic and unprejudiced consideration' from the local medical profession.[17]

Legal and medical uncertainty elsewhere in Britain encouraged a series of MPs to attempt to reform abortion law in line with Aleck Bourne's interpretation. In 1952, Joseph Reeves, Labour MP for Greenwich, introduced the first of what were to be six failed parliamentary bills on abortion, all defeated largely by the delaying tactics of hostile Roman Catholic MPs. Given governmental reluctance to become embroiled in this deeply controversial subject, each reform attempt was left to the 'lottery' of the Private Member's Bill and the individual conscience of politicians. The earlier bills by Reeves and Lord Amulree (1955) were not drafted to apply to Scotland, and the exclusion of Scotland was widely welcomed north of the Border. Scottish policy makers noted that these bills were not relevant to Scotland because they were attempting to amend the Offences Against the Person Act of 1861, which did not apply north of the Border, but also because the greater flexibility of Scottish abortion law already allowed therapeutic abortion to protect a woman's physical and mental health.[18] Correspondence between the Scottish Home Department and Crown Office thus agreed: 'we might leave the English to worry about these matters'.[19]

Although subsequent bills were drafted to apply to Scotland, Scottish ministers and policy makers continued to question their applicability to Scotland. Only by the mid-1960s, in debates surrounding Lord Silkin's Abortion Bill, were occasional references beginning to be made to either the desirability or need for reform. Officials in the newly constituted Scottish Home and Health Department (SHHD) accepted the desirability of a clarification in abortion law but cautioned that 'a specific declaration that such and such is illegal' would 'harden the line between right and wrong' and potentially restrict medical discretion.[20] Meanwhile, a Home Office memorandum noted that, although there appeared to be 'little specifically Scottish controversy', the medical profession and women's organisations active in the field increasingly regarded abortion law reform 'as a Great Britain matter'. The Department therefore requested clarification of the law in Scotland as well as in England and Wales.[21]

SCOTTISH INPUT TO ABORTION LAW REFORM

The Medical Termination of Pregnancy Bill, published on 15 June 1966, was the seventh parliamentary attempt to amend and clarify the law relating to termination of pregnancy. By the mid-1960s, the Westminster climate appeared to be warming towards abortion reform, demonstrated by the favourable reception of Lord Silkin's Bill. Publicity surrounding the recent thalidomide tragedy, when a prescribed sedative was proved to have caused severe deformities in thousands of children born worldwide, had generated public sympathy for women seeking a termination. Soon after British thalidomide cases began to be publicised, a *Daily Mail* National Opinion Poll showed 73 per cent of the British public to be in favour of abortion where a child might be born deformed.[22] The Abortion Law Reform Association (ALRA) helped to orchestrate this rising tide of support through publicity and the lobbying of MPs and parliamentary candidates. Founded in 1936, this group of articulate middle-class socialist-feminists aimed to lift all restrictions on abortion, and to allow women, rather than the state or the medical profession, to judge whether or not a pregnancy should continue. The ALRA was the most notable of the women's campaign groups involved in the abortion issue.[23]

It was through their activities that David Steel became involved in the abortion issue. While fighting the general election in 1964, Steel had responded positively to an ALRA questionnaire asking whether he supported changes in abortion law. Shortly afterwards, when Steel came third in a private member's ballot, the equally sensitive subjects of homosexual and abortion law reform were suggested to him, for both of which Private Members' Bills had already been passed in the House of Lords and awaited a champion in the Commons. Steel opted for abortion because Scottish opinion was seen to be so adamantly opposed to homosexual law reform.[24] Nonetheless, when Steel put forward his Medical Termination of Pregnancy Bill, some questioned the involvement of a Scottish politician given the greater flexibility of abortion law north of the Border.

During 1966, Steel was subjected to advice and pressure from various sources whilst drafting the Bill, not least the ALRA, who assisted him with the wording of his measure, as they had his predecessor, Lord Silkin. However, there was one particular ALRA member who was arguably to prove the greatest influence upon Steel. Dugald Baird was not only busy implementing his abortion programme in Aberdeen, he was also taking an increasingly active interest in policy making. To promote the passage of Steel's Bill and to counteract anti-abortionist writings, the ALRA actively recruited such medical practitioners and publicised their support. The ability of the ALRA to cite Aberdeen as an example of a city with an active and successful abortion policy was increasingly vital for their political campaign and so, in January 1964, the year before he retired from the Regius Chair, and 'knowing of [his] support for abortion law reform', the organisation invited Baird to join their Medico-Legal Council, an invitation which Baird accepted enthusiastically.[25] He began to meet with politicians and very publicly to support the provision of abortion law reform by giving papers at fertility control forums and writing to newspapers and medical periodicals in justification of his own practice. Baird was also asked to persuade other gynaecologists to deliver statements to the local and national press in order to 'counteract [negative] publicity' engendered by opponents of reform.[26] Baird himself recognised that it was important to involve the next generation of medical practitioners in the campaign. In private correspondence to the ALRA, Baird explained that it could easily be alleged that his views were 'very exceptional in clinical circles' or even that he was 'senile'.[27] Thus, it was all the more important to the campaign for 'younger men, like [Baird's successor, Professor Ian] MacGillivray, to come out into the open on the matter'.

Steel's Bill appears to have been influenced by Dugald Baird in three key respects. First, in keeping with Baird's belief that the law should 'interfere as little as possible with clinical practice',[28] Steel opted to give doctors complete control of the decision-making process surrounding abortion, subject only to certain administrative formalities. This aspect of the legislation was supported by the major medical organisations, who all insisted that abortion must be placed in the hands of medical practitioners alone, and, more particularly, the 'judgment and skill of someone with experience in gynaecology'.[29] This element of the Bill was clearly underpinned by Scotland's strong tradition of medical autonomy, and allowed Steel to fulfil his primary stated aim: to eradicate competing and dangerous 'back-street' or 'kitchen table' abortions performed by unqualified persons.[30]

Second, Baird's views appear to have had a decisive influence in relation to the inclusion of 'social' criteria. The ALRA had been arguing strongly that the Bill should contain a specific 'social clause' in order to enable a wide range of social, economic and psychological criteria to play a role in determining access to abortion. However, Steel was acutely aware of the medical establishment's opposition to 'social' criteria that, in the view of the British Medical Association (BMA) and Royal College of Obstetricians and Gynaecologists (RCOG), lay outside the realm of medical expertise. Like his ALRA colleagues, Baird was keen to incorporate some kind of 'social' clause into the Bill, but he urged the MP not to separate social from medical factors as he did not view such a separation as good medical practice.[31] In his publications, Baird argued that social factors were inseparable from medical factors since man's 'physical and emotional health' was 'profoundly affected by his social environment'.[32] Steel himself recognised the importance of discussions with Baird on this subject, later claiming: 'I was greatly influenced by . . . Baird, who persuaded me to accept amendments creating a single socio-medical clause rather than a series of individual categories'.[33] Thus, on Baird's advice, Steel amended his Bill by burying a social clause more subtly within the grounds for termination, referring in vague terms to 'injury to the physical or mental health of the pregnant woman or any existing children of her family', and stipulating that 'account [could] be taken of the pregnant woman's actual or reasonably foreseeable environment'.[34] ALRA members reportedly felt betrayed by this development, but continued to support the Bill.

Third, Baird's role was crucial in ensuring that the Bill covered mainland Britain as a whole. Echoing debates over earlier abortion measures, there remained considerable doubt in the minds of Scottish politicians and administrators over the desirability of Scotland's inclusion in Steel's Bill. There was said to be 'no specific demand' for abortion law reform,[35] and a concern that existing Scottish medical freedom could be reduced if the grounds for termination were restricted during the Committee stage. Practical difficulties were also perceived over variances between the legal and medical systems of Scotland and England.[36] The Scottish Office questioned the wisdom of applying 'uniform standards' throughout Britain, from Orkney to Harley Street, and noted their wish to avoid being 'saddled with measures appropriate to Greater London but not to Scotland'.[37] They made particular reference to the wide variation in medical facilities between England and Scotland, and the fact that private clinics were only a problem south of the Border. However, according to Steel, Baird made him aware that the situation in Aberdeen was very different from that in the other Scottish medical centres, and that he was 'the only person' taking advantage of Scots common law at this time to 'follow his professional conscience'.[38] Accordingly, Steel successfully orchestrated opposition to a series of amendments that threatened to delete Scotland from the Bill.

Steel's Bill *was* amended to allow for variance between the Scottish and English legal systems. The conscience clause stipulated that, except in emergency circumstances, no doctor or nurse should be required to participate in abortion work where it contradicted their own personal beliefs. This clause was intended to protect the professional standing of medical and nursing staff who chose not to take part in terminations. Norman Wylie, a Conservative MP for Pentlands and a former Solicitor-General for Scotland, pointed out that the Medical Termination of Pregnancy Bill placed the burden of proof on the conscientious objector, which would conflict with Scots law, under which detailed corroborative evidence was required.[39] As Wylie argued, in a civil action it would be necessary for the doctor to prove 'not only by his own evidence but by corroborative evidence' that he had a conscientious objection, 'and this he might have great difficulty in doing', however plausible an individual he was.[40] Scottish officials recommended that this sub-section of the Bill be rewritten so that Scottish doctors and nurses would be in no worse a position than their English counterparts, and that the evidence of a single 'credible' witness would suffice.[41] Policy makers protested more generally at the 'quite unnecessary Scottish presentational and political difficulties' they were experiencing 'because of the unwillingness of English departments and draftsmen to budge from drafts which [met] English needs on purely English considerations'.[42]

Though Baird claimed to have received an 'extremely favourable' reception from general practitioners and university students,[43] policy makers noted that Scottish medical opinion 'embrace[d] all shades of attitude'.[44] Certainly, a group of gynaecologists who had worked previously under Dugald Baird in Aberdeen very publicly voiced their support for his 'liberal policy' by publishing a joint letter in the press. Labelled the 'twelve disciples' by the media, these professors and consultant obstetricians concluded that more good than harm had resulted from Baird's approach, and proposed in their own practice to operate a similar policy as far as the law would allow.[45] The 'disciples' included Ian MacGillivray, Baird's successor in Aberdeen; David Paintin, Senior Lecturer at St Mary's Hospital Medical School in London and a medical adviser to the ALRA; Alexander Turnbull, Professor of Obstetrics and Gynaecology at the Welsh National School of Medicine in Cardiff; and Malcolm Macnaughton, Senior Lecturer at the University of St Andrews and later President of the RCOG.

However, some doctors were distinctly hostile to the liberalisation of abortion law. One family doctor voiced his concern that the Medical Termination of Pregnancy Bill would enable abortion to be obtained on demand by any woman and leave the doctor in no position to refuse,[46] while another likened abortion to 'euthanasia and possibly even murder'.[47] Baird's most outspoken medical critic in Scotland was Ian Donald, an English obstetrician who had moved to Glasgow in 1954 to accept the Regius Chair of Midwifery. In the decade before 1966, Glasgow had the lowest abortion rate of any Scottish city, lying at the opposite extreme from Aberdeen. In 1966, the press claimed that 1 pregnancy in 50 was terminated in Aberdeen compared to 1 in 3,750 in Glasgow.[48] This was due in part to Glasgow's large Roman Catholic population, and in part to the influence that Donald exercised over the city's obstetrical community. An active member of the Scottish Episcopal Church, he discussed abortion within the context of the holocaust, and likened abortion for social reasons to the Nazi campaign of 'destroying the socially unacceptable Jews'.[49] Donald argued that if the profession was allowed to destroy a foetus for any reason other than to avert an immediate danger to the mother's life, it would ultimately utilise its expertise to destroy life in other situations, such as the introduction of euthanasia for old people who had become a burden to society.[50]

The vast majority of Scottish doctors appear to have been unwilling to involve themselves visibly in the politics of abortion. While the major London-based medical bodies, in particular the BMA and RCOG, actively involved themselves in the shaping of Steel's Bill, neither the Scottish Council of the BMA nor the Scottish Standing Committee of the RCOG articulated a specifically Scottish view on the issue. In marked contrast, while the Royal College of Nursing refused to formulate a policy statement on termination of pregnancy on the grounds that the abortion decision-making process was a medical one and thus beyond its remit, the Scottish Council of the Royal College of Midwives registered firm opposition to Steel's Bill on ethical grounds.[51]

The churches were rather less reticent than the medical profession. In an increasingly secular post-war society, several Scottish churches came out strongly against Steel's Bill. The General Assembly of the Free Church of Scotland, 'while recognising the dangers to society in the practice of illegal abortion', deplored the wide powers that the Bill proposed 'to terminate life in the womb'.[52] The legislation, they argued, showed 'an inadequate appreciation of the sacredness of human life', and would 'impose on doctors an intolerable burden of decision as to the cases in which such a life should be terminated'. MPs were urged 'to give earnest regard to the Christian position' and thereby to reject the Bill. Meanwhile, the Religion and Morals Committee of the Free Presbyterian Church of Scotland considered the Bill an 'affront to God' that was 'unworthy of a place in the legislation of a civilised community'.[53] It decried the 'burden' that it placed on conscientious doctors, and the fact that it subverted 'natural' maternal instincts by providing for 'the gratification of unnatural desires'. Catholic opposition to the Bill was as strong in Scotland as in England. In a series of deliverances, the Roman Catholic hierarchy in Scotland criticised the offensive presumption 'that it was better not to be born than to be born abnormal', and expressed concern over medicine's inability to diagnose foetal abnormality 'with any certainty until after the thirtieth week', by which time the child would be viable.[54]

However, it was primarily to the Church of England and Church of Scotland that Steel looked for guidance on the issue of abortion. As a church member and the son of a Church of Scotland minister, Steel later claimed to have been strongly influenced by these churches' writings on the matter. In his view, the Church of England's report *Abortion: An Ethical Discussion* (1965) 'blew to pieces a lot of the

Catholic theology on this issue', and was supported by both the Church of Scotland and the Methodist Church, which Steel described as being 'of great comfort to me in my position'.[55] The Church of Scotland 'cautiously offered Steel's Bill qualified support'.[56] In 1966, its General Assembly argued that, while the Bill 'went beyond what the Church would wish' in the breadth of its social clause, they did support wider grounds for abortion at the discretion of medical practitioners.[57] When their Working Group met again in January 1967, they were 'grateful' to find Steel's amendment of the social clause, in line with Baird's advice, and specifically that 'the deficiency of the mother, cases of rape and of the mother being under the age of sixteen' – 'the categories that the Assembly had already found unacceptable' – had all now been dropped.[58] The Church of Scotland also lamented the 'evident divergence both of interpretation and practice' in abortion law between parts of Scotland, and argued that the law 'require[d] clarification' in Scotland as well as in England.

Arguably, the most organised resistance to Steel's Bill came from the Society for the Protection of the Unborn Child (SPUC). Established in January 1967, the SPUC lobbied peers and MPs, and wrote letters to the press in vociferous opposition to the liberalisation of abortion law. The Glasgow-based obstetrician Ian Donald was a founding member of the SPUC and a leading campaigner against the Medical Termination of Pregnancy Bill. Donald's ideology did not feed into policy debates to the same extent as did Baird's, but his views were widely exploited by anti-abortion organisations and the Catholic Church, and Donald's involvement with the SPUC mirrored Baird's involvement with the ALRA. Steel later acknowledged that the SPUC could be 'a real menace', particularly through those major medical figures involved in the Society who 'really did put pressure on the MPs'.[59] In this sense, both voluntary groups were in agreement, finding that it was medical rhetoric that had the greatest potential in fighting their cause.

Donald's campaigning was perhaps most effective in combination with the medical technology with which he had become associated. During the 1950s, he had led the team of clinicians and engineers in Glasgow who developed obstetric ultrasound. Donald employed ultrasound images as a powerful anti-abortion device. In the city's Queen Mother Maternity Hospital, at a time when ultrasound was not used routinely in the management of pregnancy, Donald showed ultrasound images to women seeking an abortion in a deliberate attempt to deter them from that course of action.[60] He also made effective use of the technology more publicly, showing slides of premature babies accompanied by tape recordings of the beating heart of a six-week-old foetus as a powerful accompaniment to his anti-abortion speeches.[61] He explained that, while it was popularly believed 'that in early pregnancy there was a sort of inanimate jelly which could be scooped out', ultrasound clearly revealed the twenty-eight-day-old foetus to be 'recognizable, with head, eyes, fingers and toes'.[62] Through its depiction of the foetus's 'human' characteristics, ultrasound endowed the foetus with an identifiable individuality. The SPUC campaign made good use of such foetal images in its leaflets and colour postcards.

Yet the SPUC lacked the political skill and connections of the ALRA and formed too late to impact significantly on the immediate campaign surrounding the Medical Termination of Pregnancy Bill. Steel triumphed where his six predecessors had failed. The 1967 Abortion Act came into operation on 27 April 1968, and was the first piece of abortion-related legislation to cover Scotland, England and Wales collectively.[63] The Act legalised termination where the risk to the life of a pregnant woman, or injury to her physical or mental health or to that of her existing children, was greater than the risks from abortion, or where there was a substantial risk that a baby would be born seriously handicapped. Two doctors were required to certify that the indications for abortion existed, except in cases of medical emergency where one was deemed sufficient; and the operation was only to be performed in an NHS hospital or another officially approved location. No doctor had to administer such treatment if they conscientiously objected, except in cases of emergency.

INITIAL RECEPTION OF THE ABORTION ACT, 1968–74

Criticism of both the terms of the 1967 Abortion Act and its operation began as soon as the legislation came into force. Nowhere were its shortcomings said to be better demonstrated than in a highly disturbing case that occurred in Stobhill Hospital, Glasgow in January 1969. A doctor performed an abortion under the terms of the legislation in the belief that the foetus's period of gestation was twenty-six weeks, and therefore not viable.[64] However, as the newly aborted baby was being taken to the hospital incinerator, it was discovered to be alive and whimpering. Resuscitation was applied but the infant lived only a few hours. A fatal accident inquiry was conducted into the affair, referred to in the press as the 'foetus which cried'. A post-mortem examination judged the baby to have been aged between thirty and thirty-two weeks, and held the causes of death to be prematurity, the absence of attempts to resuscitate the child in the period immediately after its birth and subsequent exposure to cold. The jury unanimously recommended that, in all cases where an infant approaching viable age was being aborted, 'all facilities and resuscitatory [sic] measures applied in cases of ordinary birth should be adopted', and that legislation should be introduced that prohibited abortion when the foetus was approaching viability.[65]

In the summer of 1969, a brief flurry of parliamentary activity addressed the issue. Norman St John-Stevas, Conservative MP for Chelmsford, introduced a Private Member's Bill in an attempt to restrict the terms of Steel's Act. At a news conference in Glasgow he argued that the 1967 Act had created 'a climate of disregard for infant and foetal life, of which [the Stobhill case was] a dramatic example'. Given that the Stobhill abortion had in fact been performed quite legally, St John-Stevas asked 'what was intended to be done to stop something like this happening again', and suggested that the law required urgent modification through an appropriate Private Member's Bill.[66] However, given that the 1967 Act already required doctors to 'take all reasonable and proper steps to preserve the life of the child irrespective of the duration of the pregnancy', the Secretary of State for Scotland, William Ross, under advice from the Lord Advocate, argued that no further legislation was necessary on this subject.[67] The House of Commons rejected St John-Stevas's bill, albeit only by eleven votes.[68]

However, the following year, in response to continuing parliamentary, professional and public pressure, especially from West of Scotland constituencies,[69] Sir Keith Joseph, Secretary of State for Social Services, announced the Government's decision to appoint a committee to review how the Act was operating.[70] Under the chairmanship of Justice Elizabeth Lane, the Committee on the Working of the Abortion Act (Lane Committee) was assembled, consisting of fifteen senior members from the fields of education, law, medicine and welfare. Only five men were appointed to the Committee, two of whom were Scottish: Ivor Batchelor, Professor of Psychiatry at the University of Dundee, and A. M. Johnston QC, a member of the Scottish Law Commission. Johnston resigned in October 1971 on his appointment to the Court of Session, to be replaced by Ronald Ireland QC, formerly Professor of Scottish Law at the University of Aberdeen and Chairman of the Board of Management for Aberdeen

General Hospitals. Another member of the Committee was Alexander Turnbull, Professor of Obstetrics and Gynaecology in Cardiff and one of Dugald Baird's 'twelve disciples'. Thus, the 'Aberdeen perspective' appears to have been well represented.

Scottish policy makers were initially dubious about the need for the Lane Committee to review the situation in Scotland. They were sceptical for two principal reasons: because such an inquiry was considered to be 'premature', coming just a few years after the passing of the Act, and because they were 'not aware of any such pressure in Scotland' as that being experienced in England.[71] Certainly, English critics of the 1967 Act focused on rather different issues: the role of the private sector, access by foreign women to British abortion services and the advertising of British abortion services abroad.[72] None of these issues was felt to be particularly problematic within Scotland. Private abortion clinics, 'the cause of all the subsequent troubles, in the south at any rate', were rarely used north of the Border,[73] where the vast majority of abortions were performed under the NHS. In 1973, only 88 out of 7,498 abortions in Scotland were carried out in the private sector, and the number of abortions performed on foreign women in Scotland was only two in that year.[74] However, policy makers rapidly agreed that 'any enquiry should preferably be on a Great Britain basis', with the SHHD 'prepared to go along with the legislative changes proposed' for the sake of 'uniformity in the law rather than any current clamant problem in Scotland'.[75]

Between 1971 and 1974, the Lane Committee received evidence from a wide variety of organisations and private individuals on their criticisms of the Act and suggestions for its improvement. The process resulted in the publication of a three-volume report in April 1974 in which the Committee suggested a variety of administrative measures to tighten the regulations and to improve the Act's effectiveness, but in which, crucially, it also expressed unanimous confidence in Steel's legislation.[76] Its proceedings provide a range of insights into the reception and early working of the 1967 Act in Scotland.

Evidence was received from some thirty Scottish medical bodies, including the health boards, Royal Colleges and university medical faculties in Aberdeen, Edinburgh and Glasgow. A range of nursing organisations was also consulted, including the General Nursing Council for Scotland, the Central Midwives Board for Scotland and the Royal Colleges of Nursing and Midwives. Although the majority were broadly supportive of the terms of the Act, evidence reveals the dichotomy in medical opinion that Baird and Donald epitomised. As Professor McGirr, Dean of the Faculty of Medicine at the University of Glasgow, observed, there was a 'wide spectrum of opinion on the subject' which ranged from 'full agreement with the views expressed by the Committee' to the Act having constituted 'the most pagan in British parliamentary history' in its 'implied assumption of the utter disposability of life'.[77] Scottish medical criticism broadly focused upon four issues: the pressures that abortion work imposed on gynaecological services, geographical variations in provisions, the appropriateness of employing 'social' criteria and the statutory time limit for terminations.

The immediate effect of the 1967 Act was a striking increase in the number of women who attempted to obtain a legal abortion. The Scottish abortion rate rose sharply in the years immediately following its passage, from 1,492 in 1968 (2 per cent of live births) to 5,036 (5.76 per cent) in 1970.[78] The architect of the legislation, David Steel, welcomed this significant increase in women receiving safe and legal abortions rather than 'risking a back-street operation'.[79] However, the medical profession lamented the detrimental impact upon hospital facilities and staffing. As Lothian and Peebles Executive Council noted, due to their limited number of consultants, and because terminations required to be carried out 'at the earliest possible moment', many other gynaecological cases had to be deferred 'for unreasonable periods'.[80] The Matron of Bellshill Maternity Hospital, Lanarkshire, complained that the 'problem ha[d] been foisted upon [them] without the necessary resources of space, theatre time and personnel to deal with it'.[81] The Scottish Association of Executive Councils argued that 'if a choice ha[d] to be made between more terminations and a reduction in the gynaecological waiting list they would unreservedly choose the latter'.[82]

The geographical variation in abortion provision was a related concern. In the first year of the Act's operation, the Scottish abortion rate ranged from 4.9 per thousand women in the Northern Hospital Board Region to 1.6 in the Western Hospital Board Region.[83] The Scottish General Medical Services Committee claimed that facilities were 'sporadic and unevenly distributed throughout the country, due to the individual attitude of some doctors'.[84] The *Scottish Daily Record* deplored the fact that obtaining an NHS abortion was highly dependent on where you happened to live, referring to the 1967 Act as 'a giant lottery'.[85] In Glasgow, the newspaper reported, 'diehard pro and anti-abortion forces' battled over the issue; abortions in Edinburgh 'seem[ed] to be left pretty much to the consciences of individual doctors'; Aberdeen was said to be '[s]till among the leaders'; while in Dundee terminations appeared to be carried out 'almost for the asking'. As a result of this lack of uniformity in provision, and also in an attempt to protect their anonymity, significant numbers of Scottish women – upwards of 1,000 – were reported to be obtaining abortions in England and Wales.[86] This migration was especially prevalent from the West of Scotland, with the Glasgow–Liverpool train referred to as 'the Abortion Express' in recognition of this traffic south of women seeking a private abortion. As one West coast doctor noted: 'The Act might as well not have been passed as far as my patients are concerned . . . However you feel about abortions, this is not justice, not law, and not what the National Health Service is supposed to be about.'[87]

A third issue over which the medical community professed deep concern was the appropriateness of using 'social' indications to determine access to an abortion, and whether doctors were suitably qualified to make such a judgement. The question of how to distinguish between 'medical' and 'social' grounds for abortion had been one of the most contentious aspects of Steel's Bill during its passage. As one doctor complained in his submission to the Lane Committee, in too many patients wishing a termination, the 'medical' element was 'completely absent'.[88] A senior consultant surgeon from Greenock Royal Infirmary argued that psychiatric grounds for abortion were merely 'pandering to the social conscience of women who [were] not ready to accept parental responsibility'.[89] In addition, the Royal College of Physicians of Edinburgh noted that some doctors opposed abortion because it removed 'a natural barrier to promiscuity'.[90]

More broadly, many perceived a fundamental conflict between the gynaecologist's primary vocation to 'facilitate the inception of new life' and the more destructive implications of abortion, which, as the Royal College of Psychiatrists argued, 'contravene[d] his ethics, imperil[led] his relationship with nursing staff, and . . . adversely affect[ed] recruitment into his specialty'.[91] As the Scottish Council of the Royal College of Midwives similarly pointed out, abortion was 'the antithesis of Midwifery'.[92] Several commentators also complained about the 'technologically unchallenging' nature of the operation, suggesting that this was an issue of professional status as well as medical ethics.[93]

However, such concerns seem to have varied depending on the type of woman seeking a termination. The Glasgow-based psychiatrists

Evelyn Hamill and Malcolm Ingram argued that young single women who were pregnant for the first time appeared to 'provoke the most moralistic response' from the medical profession.[94] In addition to marital status and age, class prejudices appear to have been influential. The demand for abortion from the better-educated girl and her parents was said to elicit a greater degree of sympathy, with many doctors acknowledging that for educated young women who were 'anxious that their future should not be imperilled by one mistake', abortion was the least damaging solution, and one which provided such respectable girls with 'a second chance'.[95]

Finally, and receiving more comment from the Scottish medical profession than any other issue, the appropriate time limit for a termination elicited significant concern. This was an aspect of the 1967 Act that formed the basis of most subsequent reform attempts. Scottish medical commentators generally appeared to welcome the Lane Committee's recommendation that the time limit should be reduced to twenty-four weeks in order to safeguard the life of a viable foetus, and in light of the availability of 'modern support systems'.[96] However, there were pronounced differences of opinion over the issue of by how much the limit should be reduced. Most Scottish health boards favoured the proposed twenty-four-week limit, with the notable exception of Lanarkshire Health Board in the West, which argued that legal abortion after the twelfth week of pregnancy 'should only be considered in exceptional circumstances'.[97] Nursing organisations tended to be more conservative. The Royal College of Midwives (Scottish Council) and Scottish District Nursing Association urged a reduction to twenty weeks, while the Scottish Public Health Nursing Administrators and Tutors Group argued that abortion should not be performed after the twelfth week of pregnancy as morbidity rates were higher, and both patients and staff experienced increasing distress as the pregnancy progressed.[98]

Although the vast majority of organisations consulted by the Lane Committee were medical in nature, a small number of other agencies were also invited to appraise the legislation. These included governmental bodies such as the Crown Office and the General Register Office for Scotland as well as religious bodies including the Catholic Child Care Office and the Church of Scotland Moral Welfare Committee. Concerns were broadly similar to those raised by the medical profession, with a particular focus upon the appropriateness of 'social' indications and the statutory time limit for terminations.

The Scottish churches were at the forefront of criticisms of the Act.

Even before the Lane Committee was formed, the Church of Scotland's Moral Welfare Committee had begun to monitor the operation of the 1967 Act. In 1970, they wrote of their concern 'with regard to the social aspects' of the measure.[99] In subsequent reports to the General Assembly, they continued to express concern both with the terms of the Act and the way in which it was being interpreted.[100] The General Assembly of the Free Church of Scotland argued that some of those who had supported Steel's bill were now 'having second thoughts' due to the 'vast number of abortions being carried out' and the 'rogues and charlatans [making] quick and easy fortunes'.[101] This included 'many General Practitioners' who were said to be 'disturbed at the pressure being put upon hospital facilities through the operation of this evil act'. The Free Church of Scotland characterised abortion as 'at best . . . a messy business', and a 'repugnant' chore to 'many a nurse of high ideals'. Particular criticism was aimed at 'induced abortion for social or merely personal reasons, whether it be to avoid the inconvenience of having an additional child or the disgrace of an illegitimate birth'. They held such 'social' cases to be 'a quite unwarrantable destruction of life' and 'little short of legalised murder'.[102]

The Catholic Child Care Office provided a particularly lengthy submission in which they deprecated the Lane Committee's presumption that abortion was 'always a desirable thing' and its 'implicit' message that it was 'more acceptable to have an abortion than to have a baby'.[103] They reiterated the Roman Catholic Church's conviction that abortion was 'a moral and social evil and that the 1967 Abortion Act has contributed greatly to less regard being paid to the sanctity and inviolability of life'. They rebuked the Committee's disregard for life as a 'perversion of nature' which would 'actively discourage people from entering the medical and nursing professions'; and they 'fail[ed] to understand the Committee's surprise over regional disparities in the numbers of NHS abortions' given the extent to which doctors were 'allowed to exercise freedom of clinical judgement and conscience'. Finally, they noted the 'rare' need for an abortion on purely medical grounds, and the fact that 'most women' made use of the 'social clause' in the full knowledge that what they were doing was 'wrong, shameful and anti-human'.[104]

Non-medical groups tended to be more conservative than Scottish medical practitioners in their views on the desirable upper time limit for terminations. In line with nursing organisations, most strongly supported a limit of twenty weeks, including the Catholic Child Care

Office and the Society of Innocents. While the Church of Scotland Moral Welfare Committee welcomed the Lane Committee's recommendation of twenty-four weeks as 'an improvement', they voiced a preference for the recommendation of the London-based BMA – 'an authority competent to make such a judgement' – that twenty weeks was advisable.[105] Scottish policy makers noted defensively that, in 1973, 98.4 per cent of all notified abortions in Scotland had been carried out by the end of the nineteenth week, and 99.6 per cent by the end of the twenty-fourth week.[106]

CHALLENGE AND RESPONSE, 1975–80

Such pressures to reduce the time limit on terminations of pregnancy formed the cornerstone of subsequent attempts to amend the 1967 Abortion Act. Whilst nine parliamentary attempts to clarify or restrict the legislation can be charted between 1969 and 1980, all of which were unsuccessful, there is broad agreement that the two most significant measures were the Abortion Amendment Bills of 1975 and 1979.[107] Significantly, as with Steel's 1966 Medical Termination of Pregnancy Bill, the architects of both these abortion bills were MPs serving Scottish constituencies: James White, Labour MP for Glasgow Pollok, and John Corrie, Conservative MP for Bute and North Ayrshire. While the divisive and emotive issue of abortion remained one that refused to be confined to either side of the political spectrum, geography continued to play a prominent role in the politics of abortion, with Scottish politicians confronting the issue with especial vigour. West of Scotland politicians, in particular, were known to be among the most vocal of Steel's opponents. By the mid-1970s, MPs in that region were said to be 'under heavy constituency pressure to reverse the liberalising effect of the 1967 Act'.[108] Since the passing of the Abortion Act, the Roman Catholic hierarchy in Scotland had become increasingly involved with the anti-abortion campaigns of the SPUC.[109] It had even designated a day of protest by young Scottish Catholics as a 'special day of reparation' for the 'unborn dead' killed by NHS abortions under the 1967 Act.[110]

James White introduced his 1975 Abortion (Amendment) Bill in order to 'make the 1967 Abortion Act work as Parliament meant it to work, and to cut out current abuses'.[111] His Bill sought to reduce the time limit from twenty-eight to twenty weeks in most circumstances, and to allow abortion only where there was 'grave risk' to the woman's life or health.[112] SHHD consultations on White's Bill attracted comments from eleven health boards, a variety of professional organisations involved with pregnancy and its termination, and 'several hundred letters' from members of the public.[113] Reflecting the Lane Committee's recent findings, evidence suggested that most doctors were opposed to White's more restrictive measures, while nurses were 'more evenly balanced' on the subject. The balance of opinion among members of the Scottish public, based on the correspondence received, was said to be 'overwhelmingly in favour' of White's proposed amendments. However, SHHD officials noted that 'there were clear signs that support was organised', with, for example, the use of a 'standard form of letter' and 'uniform terminology'; and that the 'balance of opinion' expressed in the newspapers was 'a good deal more evenly balanced'.

Corrie's 1979 Abortion (Amendment) Bill was similarly restrictive, aiming to reduce the upper time limit to twenty weeks, to reduce the circumstances that merited a termination, to extend the 'conscience' clause so that doctors and nurses might opt out more easily and to tighten licensing procedures. Scottish responses to this Bill provide instructive insights into attitudes to abortion *circa* 1980. It is clear that pressure to amend or restrict Steel's Act did not emanate from the Scottish medical community, where doctors remained overwhelmingly in favour of retaining the status quo, as governed by the 1967 Act. As one consultant obstetrician from the Highlands and Islands commented, most doctors held the Act to be 'fundamentally correct' and to strike a good balance since there could be 'no doubt that it ha[d] been of considerable benefit' both to women who found themselves 'in a distressing position' and to doctors who were now 'protected both individually and as a group'.[114] Malcolm Macnaughton, an obstetrician based in Glasgow, exclaimed: 'I wish Parliament would stop bringing in abortion bills. The law is working fine and should be left unchanged.'[115] One of Dugald Baird's 'twelve disciples', Macnaughton argued that Corrie 'should be devoting his efforts to trying to make the facilities more evenly distributed', particularly in the West of Scotland where Corrie's constituency was located and where there were continuing inequalities in abortion provision.

The vast majority of medical respondents expressed 'profound concern' at the prospect of a reduction in the upper time limit to twenty weeks, which, it was widely felt, would 'create more problems than it would solve'[116] and which did 'not seem really tolerable on humane or economic grounds'.[117] Several medical organisations highlighted the very small number of abortions performed after twenty weeks under the existing legislation: seventy-seven in 1978, representing only 1 per cent of the total number of terminations performed in Scotland.[118] Such groups nevertheless argued that the time limit should remain higher to safeguard the mother from 'grave risk' or where the child might be born severely handicapped. Only two medical bodies – Ayrshire and Arran Health Board and Dumfries and Galloway Health Board – supported Corrie's twenty-week proposal. However, as a result of recent advances in paediatric neonatal care, a number of bodies did voice support for a reduction to twenty-four weeks, including the Scottish Executive Committee of the RCOG, the Royal College of Physicians and Surgeons of Glasgow and the Scottish Health Visitors' Association, whose General Secretary argued that this time limit 'would ensure that those women who delay[ed] attending for advice or examination for reasons of ignorance, apathy or fear' would not be disadvantaged.[119]

Corrie's attempt to restrict the qualifying criteria for a termination – for example, by adding the word 'grave' before 'risk' – met with similar medical criticism. There was wide concern that such 'imprecise' wording was 'subjective and emotive' and that it might 'inhibit a doctor from acting in the best interests of his patients' and might 'lead to attempted prosecution of practitioners acting in good faith by persons hostile to the Abortion Law'.[120] The Chairman of the Royal College of Psychiatrists expressed such reservations most forcefully when he argued that Corrie's proposed amendments were 'retrograde and would lead to considerable distress and difficulty for pregnant women', and that the 1979 Amendment Bill would 'set back the clock to the time that women seeking abortion would have to be judged as potentially suicidal or psychotic before their case could be supported on psychiatric grounds'.[121]

Scottish nurses and midwives remained the most conservative section of the Scottish medical community. Although the Central Midwives Board for Scotland argued that there was 'little evidence' that the 1967 Act was 'causing problems',[122] the Scottish Board of the Royal College of Midwives agreed with Corrie that the twenty-eight-week limit should be reduced to twenty weeks except where 'the child would be born severely handicapped'.[123] The Chief Area Nursing Officer for the Western Isles Health Board described Steel's 1967 Act as having 'verge[d] on legalised murder' and suggested that Corrie's suggested restrictions were 'not . . . going far enough'.[124]

The SHHD also consulted a small number of legal bodies over Corrie's proposed amendments. Some, including the Law Society of

Scotland, found themselves 'unable to comment on the legislative changes proposed' since they were 'matters of socio-medical policy on which it [was] impossible to take a corporate view, and which in any event [did] not interfere with the principles of the law governing abortion in Scotland'.[125] However, Solicitor-General Nicholas Fairbairn noted his opposition to 'the setting of any time limit which . . . would make a fundamental change in the law of Scotland'.[126] The Association of Scottish Police Superintendents raised a number of objections to the Bill. Their honorary secretary stressed that the small number of abortions which were performed after twenty weeks were performed by surgeons 'acting in good faith', and that the provisions of Corrie's Bill were likely to 'increase the demand for illegal abortions', thus 'creat[ing] more problems than it [sought] to solve'.[127] The Association also warned of the difficulties of interpreting degrees of risk, asking: 'How can it be proved that a risk is "grave" or "substantial"? For each expert witness prepared to support the prosecution there will be another prepared to support the defence.'

The Scottish newspapers provided widespread coverage of Corrie's proposed amendments and their reception by the public, and reflected the 'even balance' of lay opinions previously reported in relation to White's Bill, albeit often expressed in highly florid language. Some individuals wrote of their contempt for abortion, viewing it as '[a] completely innocent human being condemned to death without trial – a fate we do not reserve even for our most vicious criminals'.[128] One correspondent warned that:

> our abortion legislation will reap its reward. One day soon today's babies will be running this country, when our generation is old, vulnerable and possibly 'unwanted'. It is hardly likely that our future administrators (whose brothers and sisters we have dealt with so callously) will show the slightest concern for us. Why on earth should they?[129]

Such sentiments chimed with the Roman Catholic bishops of Scotland, England and Wales, who reaffirmed their church's opposition to abortion and called for 'basic human rights to be restored to the unborn'.[130] This was said to be the first time that the two hierarchies of Scotland and England had issued a joint statement, and their sentiments echoed those of the SPUC, whose West of Scotland branch produced posters portraying a thirteen-week foetus with the text '[s]peak out for the silent minority . . . A foetus is a baby. Don't let your MP forget.'[131] Even in the notoriously liberal north-east of Scotland, in a demonstration of inter-denominational unity, five church leaders – representing the Catholic Church, Church of Scotland, Scottish Episcopalian Church, Free Church and Free Presbyterian Church – formed a delegation to lobby their local MPs to support Corrie's Bill.[132]

However, in response, the Aberdeen Branch of the National Abortion Campaign stepped up its opposition to Corrie's proposals by holding a mass demonstration and collecting thousands of signatures in favour of the existing legislation.[133] Indeed, in early 1980, a number of groups participated in anti-Corrie demonstrations in all of the major Scottish cities. Over sixty people were reported to have joined a demonstration organised by the Dundee National Abortion Campaign, including representatives of trade unions, the Labour Party and Socialist Workers' Party, students and women's organisations such as Dundee Women's Aid and Women's Voice.[134] On a larger scale, 1,000 people were observed to have marched through the streets of Glasgow, the march ending with Margaret Wilson – the only female member of the STUC General Council – demanding that 'there should be no more amendments to the [1967] Act. No more return to the back streets and the slaughter of women. There must be a free abortion service.'[135] Further north, a group of Inverness women drew a crowd of 300 while staging a demonstration which took the form of a thirty-minute 'street theatre' in a bid to persuade their Inverness-shire MP, Russell Johnston, to vote against Corrie's Bill.[136]

Such demonstrations took place across Britain, not least outside the House of Commons, where a group of 'howling women', including some who travelled from Scotland, gathered to protest against the Bill during its report stage.[137] An unfortunate doorkeeper was reportedly 'bitten on the wrist as he helped remove protesting women' from the House, and dozens of police reinforcements had to be called when the women 'tried to sit in front of traffic in the roads'. Meanwhile, the interior of the House was described as 'crowded and emotional', with many MPs having 'delayed their weekend return to their constituencies for the occasion'.[138]

Liberal leader David Steel condemned Corrie's Bill as 'a fundamental attack on the ready availability of safe and legal abortions in Britain'.[139] At a Westminster rally in defence of his 1967 Act, once again raising the spectre of the illegal abortionist, he asked: 'Do the anti-abortion campaigners really want a return to the dark days of butchery, death, and desperately costly abortion?' Another of Corrie's main political opponents was a fellow Scot, Willie Hamilton, Labour MP for Central Fife, who fiercely attacked the tactics of some supporters of the Bill. He 'brandished pictures of aborted foetuses in an anti-abortion pamphlet and said their publicity was "a tissue of lies" which was distorting the issue'. Hamilton exclaimed: 'If I am to take advice on these matters I am prepared to accept it from world-famous doctors, not from a vociferous tribe of celibate priests, nuns, and a simple Scottish farmer [John Corrie].'[140] The Corrie Bill, like its predecessor the White Bill, received a large second reading majority, but ultimately failed through lack of parliamentary time, having being 'talked out' by opponents. However, a reduction in the time limit to twenty-four weeks was subsequently introduced in the 1990 Human Fertilisation and Embryology Act, largely in view of the increasing sophistication of medical techniques and the consequent ever-improving viability of the foetus.

Notes

1 See, for example, Weeks, *Sex, Politics and Society*; Hall, *Sex, Gender and Social Change*.
2 See, for example, Keown, *Abortion, Doctors and the Law*; Newburn, *Permission and Regulation*, ch. 6; Brookes and Roth, 'Rex v. Bourne'.
3 See, for example, Rowbotham, *A New World for Women*; Sheldon, *Beyond Control*; Latham, *Regulating Reproduction*; Hoggart, *Feminist Campaigns for Birth Control and Abortion Rights*.
4 Sheldon, *Beyond Control*, 168.
5 For further details of this case and its wider legal context, see Keown, *Abortion, Doctors and the Law*, 49–59.
6 NRS, HH41/1146, Briefing notes on Abortion Bill, 2 February 1954.
7 This was founded on a 1928 ruling by a judge in Glasgow (*HM Advocate* v. *Anderson*), who asserted that 'to attempt to do what is physically impossible can never . . . be a crime'.
8 NRS, AD63/759/1, House of Commons question, 19 July 1966.
9 Interviews with retired general practitioners, gynaecologists and psychiatrists, April 2003–April 2004.
10 Glaister, *Medical Jurisprudence and Toxicology*, 363–6.
11 Interview with retired general practitioner and gynaecologist, 12 April 2004. The recent film *Vera Drake* (2004) serves as a poignant reminder of the valuable social role that the illegal abortionist could occupy in 1950s Britain.
12 N. A. Todd ['Psychiatric experience of the Abortion Act (1967)', *British Journal of Psychiatry*, 119 (1971), 488–95, at p. 491] estimated that 30 per cent of Glasgow's population was Roman Catholic as compared

with 17 per cent for Scotland as a whole and 8 per cent for England and Wales.

13 Baird, 'Preventive medicine in obstetrics', 563.

14 For details of Aberdeen's unusually progressive approach to health services prior to Baird's arrival, and the crucial role of the medical officers of health, see Gorsky, '"Threshold of a new era"'.

15 Hindell and Simms, *Abortion Law Reformed*, 55.

16 Bhatia, 'Social obstetrics, maternal health care policies and reproductive rights', MPhil dissertation, 59.

17 Hindell and Simms, *Abortion Law Reformed*, 55.

18 NRS, HH41/1146, Briefing notes on Abortion Bill, 2 February 1954.

19 NRS, HH41/1329, D. J. Cowperthwaite to L. Gordon, 14 December 1960.

20 NRS, HH60/850, D. J. Cowperthwaite to L. C. Watson, 28 December 1965.

21 Ibid., Draft memorandum by the Home Secretary, undated.

22 *Daily Mail*, 25 July 1962.

23 Brookes, *Abortion in England*, 94–8.

24 Newburn, *Permission and Regulation*, 142. See also Chapter 3 of this volume.

25 Wellcome Library for the History and Understanding of Medicine, London (hereafter WL), SA/ALR/A.8, V. Houghton [ALRA activist] to D. Baird, 22 January 1964; D. Baird to V. Houghton, 24 January 1964.

26 WL, SA/ALR/A.61, V. Houghton to D. Baird, 4 November 1966.

27 Ibid., D. Baird to V. Houghton, 8 November 1966.

28 Ibid., D. Baird to V. Houghton, 12 March 1967.

29 Ibid.

30 *Glasgow Herald*, 2 March 1966.

31 Kandiah and Staerck (eds), *The Abortion Act*, 47.

32 Baird, 'Sterilization and therapeutic abortion', 702.

33 Steel, *Against Goliath*, 53.

34 NRS, AD63/759/13, Abortion Bill policy file, 1966–7.

35 NRS, HH60/850, M. Macdonald to W. Robertson, 14 January 1966.

36 See, for example, NRS, AD63/759/1, Note by D. J. Cowperthwaite, 5 December 1966; HH41/1821, R. A. Lawrie to G. I. Mitchell, 22 July 1967.

37 NRS, HH41/1820, W. Robertson to M. MacDonald, 2 March 1967.

38 *Observer*, 6 February 1966; Kandiah and Staerck, *The Abortion Act*, 47.

39 *Glasgow Herald*, 3 June 1967.

40 NRS, AD63/759/2, M. Macdonald to W. K. Fraser, 20 July 1967; AD63/759/10, House of Lords committee amendment, undated.

41 NRS, HH41/1821, R. Lawrie to G. Mitchell, 22 July 1967.

42 Ibid., D. Cowperthwaite to R. Lawrie, 2 October 1967.

43 WL, SA/ALR/A.61, D. Baird to V. Houghton, 8 November 1966.

44 NRS, HH41/1820, Minutes between D. J. Cowperthwaite and J. Hogarth, 28 November 1966.

45 *The Scotsman*, 14 December 1966.

46 NRS, HH41/1820, Alan Orcharton, GP, Ayrshire, to Rt. Hon. W. Ross, 3 May 1967.

47 *The Scotsman*, 31 December 1966.

48 *The Scotsman*, 23 December 1966.

49 *The Scotsman*, 26 December 1966.

50 *Daily Sketch*, 12 January 1967.

51 'Abortion law reform bill', *Midwives Chronicle*, 80 (1967), 69–70, at p. 70.

52 NRS, HH41/1820, W. J. Cameron to W. Ross, SSS, 17 November 1966.

53 NRS, HH41/1821, Rev. D. B. Macleod to SSS, 2 May 1967.

54 *Glasgow Observer*, 14 October 1966; *The Scotsman*, 28 November 1966.

55 Kandiah and Staerck (eds), *The Abortion Act*, 40.

56 *Scottish Daily Record*, 1 February 1967.

57 GACS, Church of Scotland, *Report of Social and Moral Welfare Board*, 1967, 510.

58 Ibid.

59 Kandiah and Staerck (eds), *The Abortion Act*, 42.

60 M. Nicolson, 'Ian Donald – Diagnostician and Moralist', www.rcpe. ac.uk/library/read/people/donald/donald.php, accessed 21 July 2011.

61 WL, SA/ALR/H.58, Note on a public abortion meeting, Manchester, 6 December 1966.

62 *The Times*, 12 January 1967.

63 *Public General Statutes, Abortion Act 1967, c. 87.*

64 Although the 1967 Act did not specify a time limit for abortions, a twenty-eight-week limit was effectively read into the legislation by the earlier Infant Life (Preservation) Act, as the point where the foetus was deemed to be 'viable' or capable of surviving outside the womb. Since this legislation had not applied to Scotland, there was effectively no time limit for terminations performed north of the Border, though in practice Scottish doctors appear to have considered themselves bound by the English limit.

65 NRS, HH102/1389, Note by SHHD, 1 August 1969.

66 *Glasgow Herald*, 10 June 1969.

67 NRS, HH102/1389, House of Commons written answer, 24 July 1969.

68 *The Guardian*, 16 July 1969.

69 *Scottish Catholic Observer*, 30 January 1970.

70 NRS, HH61/1315, Draft memorandum by the Secretary of State for Social Services, 1970.

71 NRS, HH61/1315, R. E. C. Johnson to J. Taylor, 21 October 1970.

72 Wivel, 'Abortion policy and politics'.
73 NRS, HH61/1315, R. M. Bell to J. Walker, 31 March 1970.
74 NRS, HH101/2877, Note by SHHD, 4 February 1975.
75 NRS, HH61/1315, W. R. Miller to R. P. S. Hughes, 16 November 1970.
76 *Report of the Committee on the Working of the Abortion Act.*
77 NRS, HH102/1232, E. M. McGirr to M. Macdonald, undated.
78 NRS, HH61/1258, Lane Committee to the BMA, Scotland, 2 August 1971.
79 WL, SA/ALR/G.69, David Steel, speech to the AGM of the Abortion Law Reform Association, 19 October 1968.
80 WL, SA/ALR/C.41, Proceedings of the Lane Committee (hereafter PLC), Evidence of Lothian and Peebles Executive Council, 2 November 1971.
81 WL, SA/ALR/C.22, PLC, Evidence of Board of Management for Coatbridge, Airdrie and District Hospitals, 1972.
82 WL, SA/ALR/C.27, PLC, Evidence of A. Smith, Scottish Association of Executive Councils, 20 December 1971.
83 I. MacGillivray, 'Correspondence', *British Medical Journal*, 1 (1969), 167–8.
84 NRS, HH102/1232, Notes of meeting between SHHD and Scottish General Medical Services Committee, 24 September 1974.
85 *Scottish Daily Record*, 16 May 1973.
86 Homans (ed.), *The Sexual Politics of Reproduction*, 84–5.
87 *Scottish Daily Record*, 16 May 1973.
88 NRS, HH102/1232, PLC, Evidence of Argyll and Clyde Area Health Board's Area Medical Committee, September 1974.
89 *Greenock Telegraph*, 3 July 1969.
90 WL, SA/ALR/C.25, PLC, Evidence of Royal College of Physicians, Edinburgh, 1972.
91 'The Royal College of Psychiatrists' memorandum on the Abortion Act in practice', *British Journal of Psychiatry*, 120 (1972), 449–51, at p. 449.
92 WL, SA/ALR/C.25, PLC, Evidence of Royal College of Midwives (Scottish Council), 28 February 1972.
93 See, for example, 'The Royal College of Psychiatrists' memorandum', 449.
94 E. Hamill and I. M. Ingram, 'Psychiatric and social factors in the abortion decision', *British Medical Journal*, 1 (1974), 229–32, at p. 231.
95 Aitken-Swan, *Fertility Control*, 11; Baird, 'The Abortion Act 1967', 293.
96 NRS, HH60/665, R. P. Fraser to G. N. Monro, 8 December 1973.
97 NRS, HH102/1232, PLC, Evidence of Lanarkshire Health Board, 23 July 1974.
98 Ibid., Evidence of Royal College of Midwives (Scottish Council), 30 July 1974.

99 NRS, HH61/1207, Secretary of the Church of Scotland's Moral Welfare Committee to Edward Taylor, MP, 23 September 1970.

100 NRS, HH102/1232, PLC, Evidence of The Church of Scotland's Moral Welfare Committee, November 1974.

101 Ibid., Copy of GAFCS, *Report of Committee on Public Questions, Religion and Morals for 1973*.

102 Ibid., *The Monthly Record*, May 1974.

103 Ibid., T. Gibbons, Catholic Child Care Office, to M. Macdonald, 18 July 1974.

104 Ibid.

105 Ibid., Evidence of Church of Scotland Moral Welfare Committee, November 1974.

106 Ibid., Draft copy of 'Lane Committee Report – Appendix B', December 1974.

107 See, for example, A. Cohan, 'Abortion as a marginal issue: the use of peripheral mechanisms in Britain and the United States', in Lovenduski and Outshoorn (eds), *The New Politics of Abortion*, 41.

108 D. McKie, 'Talking politics: the White Bill on abortion', *Lancet*, 1 (1975), 388. See also *Scottish Catholic Observer*, 15 February 1974.

109 It subsequently set up a fund for the support of agencies that could offer 'a compassionate and practical alternative to abortion', for the distribution of pro-life material to all Scottish Catholic secondary schools, and for the financing of 'anti-abortion demonstrations' [*Scottish Catholic Observer*, 24 December 1976].

110 Ibid., 4 December 1970.

111 *Glasgow Herald*, 9 June 1975.

112 *The Scotsman*, 28 November 1974.

113 NRS, HH102/1276, J. H. F. Finnie to N. J. Shanks, 20 June 1977.

114 NRS, HH102/1395, Consultant obstetrician, Western Isles Health Board, to SHHD, 18 September 1979.

115 Ibid., M. Macnaughton to W. Hamilton, MP, 12 September 1979.

116 Ibid., Forth Valley Health Board to SHHD, 1 October 1979; Royal College of Physicians and Surgeons of Glasgow to SHHD, 17 September 1979.

117 Ibid., Consultant obstetrician, Western Isles Health Board, to SHHD, 18 September 1979.

118 Ibid., Royal College of Physicians, Edinburgh, to A. Oliver, 18 September 1979.

119 Ibid., Scottish Health Visitors' Association to SHHD, 20 September 1979.

120 Ibid., Royal College of Physicians, Edinburgh, to A. Oliver, 18 September 1979; Moat Brae Nursing Home Ltd, Dumfries, to SHHD, 1 October 1979.

121 Ibid., Royal College of Psychiatrists to SHHD, 14 September 1979.

122 Ibid., Central Midwives Board for Scotland to SHHD, 21 September 1979.

123 Ibid., Royal College of Midwives Scottish Board to SHHD, 19 September 1979.
124 Ibid., Chief Area Nursing Officer to Secretary, Western Isles Health Board, 3 October 1979.
125 Ibid., D. J. NcNeil, Convener, Law Reform Committee, to A. Oliver, SHHD, 3 October 1979.
126 *The Scotsman*, 16 February 1980.
127 NRS, HH102/1395, Chief Superintendent D. Murray to D. A. Bennet, 20 September 1979.
128 *Edinburgh Evening News*, 21 November 1980.
129 Ibid.
130 *Aberdeen Press and Journal*, 24 January 1980.
131 *The Scotsman*, 8 February 1980.
132 *Aberdeen Press and Journal*, 29 January 1980.
133 Ibid., 24 January 1980.
134 *Dundee Courier and Advertiser*, 14 January 1980.
135 *The Scotsman*, 4 February 1980.
136 *Aberdeen Press and Journal*, 4 February 1980.
137 *Dundee Courier and Advertiser*, 9 February 1980.
138 *The Scotsman*, 9 February 1980.
139 *Dundee Courier and Advertiser*, 6 February 1980.
140 *The Scotsman*, 16 February 1980.

6

FAMILY PLANNING

THE ESTABLISHMENT OF BIRTH CONTROL CLINICS IN SCOTLAND

While Glasgow and Aberdeen varied greatly in their response to the issue of abortion, their involvement in the early provision of contraception displayed many similarities. The first Scottish birth control clinic was opened in Glasgow in August 1926, largely through the efforts of women associated with left-wing political activism and the Co-operative Women's Guild, such as Mary Barbour, Glasgow's first female Labour councillor, and in the face of opposition from the Scottish churches and the male leadership of the Scottish Labour Movement.[1] The Glasgow Women's Welfare and Advisory Clinic was established under the auspices of the Society for the Provision of Birth Control Clinics (SPBCC), a body founded in 1924 to campaign for municipal birth control clinics that were free and easily accessible to working-class women, and which encouraged the establishment of voluntary clinics to bridge the gap until their goals could be realised.[2] The clinic held two sessions per week and appears to have focused upon the needs of poor women, particularly those with health problems such as chronic nephritis and pulmonary tuberculosis.[3]

Further north, and with a similarly euphemistic title, the Women's Welfare Centre was opened in Aberdeen just a few months later, in November 1926, by Mrs Fenella Paton, a 'well born radical' who became involved with the birth control movement while living in London.[4] Paton was inspired by the work of the English birth control pioneer Marie Stopes, who had 'shattered the great public silence on birth control' and opened the first birth control clinic in Britain, the London Mothers' Clinic, in 1921.[5] Paton founded the Aberdeen clinic with her own money and that of friends and relatives, though the venture quickly became a financial drain.[6] The clinic was opened two days per week and the staff, consisting of a qualified nurse and a general practitioner, gave their services voluntarily; augmented by the appointment of an additional doctor after a visit in 1934 by Marie Stopes herself, which allowed the clinic to open daily, Monday to Friday.[7] The Aberdeen clinic subsequently affiliated itself with Stopes' Society for Constructive Birth Control and Racial Progress, an organisation with a similar rationale to the SPBCC but more closely associated with the eugenics movement, and seemed concerned principally with what was 'deemed best' for working-class women.[8] The doctors who staffed both this and the Glasgow clinic were trained by the SPBCC at the Walworth Clinic, founded in London in 1922.[9] The Aberdonian venture does not seem to have gained universal approval, with one doctor denouncing the initiative in the press as an affront to the city's civic morality.[10] Nonetheless, it gained widespread acceptance within the community. In 1935, Aberdeen Town Council voted to give the clinic a grant of £20, an arrangement which was to continue on an annual basis, with the amount rising to £50 by 1940.[11]

The Aberdeen clinic thus existed before the arrival of the gynaecologist Dugald Baird in 1936. As discussed more fully in Chapter 5, Baird relocated from Glasgow to Aberdeen in 1936 in order to take up the Regius Chair of Midwifery at the University of Aberdeen, whereupon he implemented an unusually active 'therapeutic abortion' policy under which 'social' as well as 'medical' indications were recognised. Even before he left Glasgow, the 'notable obstetrician' had spoken openly about the need for birth control, given his estimate that almost 50 per cent of maternal deaths occurred 'where there should not have been a pregnancy'.[12] Upon Baird's arrival, Aberdeen was already atypical in terms of both its early venture into fertility control and its progressive local health authority, which by the mid-1930s had a reputation 'for making new and useful experiments'.[13] The gynaecologist was to develop further the city's reputation in this sphere. In 1938, in contrast to practice elsewhere in Britain, Baird made post-partum sterilisation freely available to women who had completed their families, who suffered from a debilitating condition or who possessed a bad obstetric history.[14] He became an increasingly proactive champion of liberal access to contraception for the same reasons that he supported access to abortion, having witnessed the toll that excessive childbearing and restricted access to fertility control had on women.

Provision was considerably patchier across the country as a whole. In order to counter this, in 1930, the Ministry of Health issued Memorandum 153 M. C. W., which gave local authorities in England and Wales permission to apply public funds to the provision of contraceptive advice to married women for whom pregnancy would be detrimental to health. However, only a small number of local authorities actively showed enthusiasm, with, for example, gynaecological clinics set up in two public health hospitals in Manchester, and Somerset hoping to have 'a flying clinic in order to reach the villages'.[15] There was some dispute over whether this Memorandum applied to Scotland. Mildred Brown, secretary of the Glasgow Women's Welfare and Advisory clinic, held that it did not apply, and criticised the Scottish Board of Health for failing to issue anything similar.[16] In contrast, the National Birth Control Association (NBCA), formed in July 1930 to coordinate birth control provision in Britain, believed that although the application of public health legislation differed in Scotland, Scottish local authorities had the power to act under the Memorandum in the same way as their English counterparts. Accordingly, they put pressure on authorities such as Glasgow City Council to respond.[17] However, it appears that no Scottish local authority could initially be induced to take the initiative.[18]

In the mid-1930s, further support for contraceptive provision came from two official health reports, both of which recommended wider provision of contraceptive advice in Scotland as a 'definite function of the maternity services', albeit on 'purely medical and health grounds', for any woman in whom 'an unfavourable outcome' to her pregnancy 'was almost certain'.[19] The NBCA wasted no time in drawing these findings to the attention of local authorities, and in urging them to establish a birth control clinic in their area.[20] Representatives were dispatched to encourage Scottish medical officers of health to liaise with their councils. Some received these delegates very positively, such as in Falkirk, where the medical officer of health (MOH) was 'fixed with the ambition to be the first M.O.H. in Scotland to provide his own clinic'.[21] Several others declared themselves favourable to birth control but 'completely hampered' by the 'cautious attitude' or outright hostility of their council, not least the 'very vocal Roman Catholic attitudes of some councillors'.[22] However, some health officials refused to meet, owing to being 'entirely out of sympathy' with the 'ideas and principles of artificial birth control'.[23]

The NBCA encouraged Professor Dugald Baird to lead a deputation to Whitehall 'consisting of representatives from several different Scottish societies', including various women's welfare associations and mothers' welfare clinics, to meet Walter Elliot, the new Secretary of State for Scotland. Elliot, it was hoped, would urge the Department of Health for Scotland to give 'some form of encouragement' to local authorities to implement the recommendations of the two official reports.[24] However, Elliot declared himself unable to meet their request 'in view of the very heavy pressure of Parliamentary work'.[25] The NBCA lamented the fact that, by 1936, only six Scottish local authorities were providing any birth control facilities, compared to 190 in England and Wales.[26] Accordingly, in order to strengthen family planning work in Scotland, a Scottish Federation of Mother's Welfare Clinics was formed the following year.[27]

Several more Scottish clinics were founded during this decade, most notably the Edinburgh Mothers' Welfare Clinic (EMWC) in November 1933, whose remit was 'to help mothers overburdened with children or medically unfit for more'. The clinic was based in a dispensary 'kindly lent by' the Bruntsfield Women's Hospital, funded by 'a few subscribers' and staffed on a voluntary basis by several female doctors and 'one or two lay helpers to run the practical side', as well as one paid nurse.[28] By 1936, the clinic had relocated to local authority premises, on a reduced rent.[29] In the 1940s, the clinic continued to expand its activities, with most of the new patients being referred for medical reasons by general practitioners, municipal clinics and local hospitals, with a smaller number 'attending on account of housing and economic difficulties'.[30]

However, the most dramatic growth in family planning provision in Scotland occurred in the immediate post-war years to meet the escalating demand from women for contraceptive advice and prevailing fears relating to reproductive health and population growth. Aberdeen continued to be at the forefront of these changes. In 1946, Aberdeen Town Council accepted full responsibility for the birth control clinic and incorporated it into the maternity and child welfare service. This decision appears to have been influenced by Dugald Baird, and even more by his wife. May Baird studied science and medicine at the University of Glasgow, and worked in junior positions in local hospitals before marrying Dugald. Upon arriving in Aberdeen, she was elected to Aberdeen Town Council and in 1947 was elected Chairman of the North Eastern Regional Hospital Board, the first woman to hold such a post.[31] In an interview given shortly before his death, Dugald Baird claimed that May had received little support from the Town Council when she had first mooted the idea, but that she had been advised by the Chief Medical Officer to the Ministry of Health, when he visited Aberdeen, to just '[p]ut it in Other Competent Business and say nothing about it and this will just happen'.[32] Since this clinic was intended only to serve women living within the city, a second clinic was founded in 1948 for women living in the wider county, and was located in the gynaecological outpatient department of the Royal Infirmary.[33]

As well as his wife, Dugald Baird was able to rely upon the support of Dr Ian MacQueen, appointed MOH in 1952, a supporter of a comprehensive birth control service who helped Baird to implement an ambitious series of maternal healthcare policies for the city. There was, in addition, an active cooperation between the University and Hospital Board Departments of Obstetrics and Gynaecology and the Health and Welfare Department, 'a linkage so close that it was sometimes extremely difficult to explain to an overseas visitor just where the borderline between functions and responsibilities lay'.[34]

By the mid-1950s, although the arrangement had not 'received formal approval by the Scottish Office',[35] the practice had 'become established' in Scotland of allowing voluntary family planning clinics to be run in local health authority premises, and funded by local authority grants wherever the woman required contraception for medical reasons.[36] The appointment of a Scottish Area Organiser in 1955 facilitated the expansion and coordination of the service, as did the publication, from 1960 onwards, of a 'Bulletin of the Scottish Federation of the Family Planning Association' to 'knit together as one unit' the Scottish clinics.[37] Thus, by 1960, a fairly well coordinated network of voluntary clinics stretched across Scotland, albeit one that was concentrated in urban areas since in country districts there were rarely sufficient patients to justify a regular clinic.[38]

IMPULSES AND CONSTRAINTS DURING THE 'SWINGING' SIXTIES

The 1960s represented a particularly notable decade in the development of family planning services in Scotland. Upgraded clinical facilities in Edinburgh and Glasgow attracted rapidly increasing numbers of women, and the number of patients was boosted significantly when the first oral contraceptive clinic in Scotland opened in March 1962 in Dean Terrace, Edinburgh. Sessions were initially held once weekly on Wednesday mornings, but the service 'expanded rapidly' the following year to meet demand.[39]

Underlying these developments was a medicalisation of the discourse and practice of family planning. Despite the best efforts of early pioneers like Marie Stopes to present contraception as a medical issue, as in England and Wales, Scottish doctors had previously been reluctant to become involved in the question of family planning, except for a few individuals who were sufficiently motivated to volunteer at the clinics for little or no payment. However, medical reservations were overcome in large part by 'the pill', which was immediately and enthusiastically accepted by large numbers of women.[40] The pill shifted contraception from previous 'jack the lad' connotations of the condom, and from the intimate and invasive contact with the genitals associated with the diaphragm and intrauterine device, to a more detached and scientific level, available only on prescription since specific hormonal dosages required to be measured. This ensured that the pill became an integral and regulated part of medical practice, contra-indications necessitating more intensive medical supervision.[41]

Thus, the pill dramatically increased the involvement of GPs in family planning, a role increasingly endorsed by policy makers given the family doctor's greater knowledge of the patient and her family circumstances.[42] Even where patients preferred to attend clinics, given their greater anonymity, there was routine liaison with the family doctor to maintain awareness of contra-indications and adverse after-effects.[43] From the early 1960s, a series of sensational scares surrounding the adverse side effects of the pill, especially thrombo-embolic conditions, further legitimated the medical profession's formal control of this sphere.[44]

In addition to the 'revolution' in the popular and medical mindset engendered by the pill, various broader social and cultural forces at work in 1960s Scotland served to support the growth of family planning provision. One major factor was the rapid expansion in the female student population, a group more sexually active and determined to obtain access to the pill as part of a 'wider flouting of traditional conventions' and a 'permissive' shift in youth culture and moral rebellion.[45] In Aberdeen, it was noted that 'only a few single women', most of whom were 'on the eve of marriage', had attended the clinic until 1968, after which their numbers 'increased markedly'.[46] In Edinburgh, the presbytery objected vociferously to reports that the University health service, under strong encourage-ment from the Students' Representative Council, was responding to this demographic shift by prescribing oral contraceptives to students, including unmarried students.[47] Indeed, the Family Planning Association (FPA), the body known previously as the NBCA and renamed in 1939 as the term 'birth control' began to fall out of favour, had to defend itself against accusations that it was its own clinics that were the catalyst for the 'more odious excesses of the permissive society'.[48]

A related factor was the increasing awareness amongst health practitioners and policy makers of the escalation in levels amongst young women, often teenagers, of unwanted pregnancies, abortions and sexually transmitted diseases. By the later 1960s, there is evidence that, for reasons of health, social and financial savings, medical officers of health, most notably in Aberdeen and Edinburgh, were increasingly receptive to a more liberal remit for the family planning services and rejected the media's conflation of family planning and promiscuity.[49] Long-held attempts to create a distinction between worthy 'medical' reasons for fertility control and spurious 'social' reasons also gave way in the face of clients' demands for safe and effective means to plan if and when they would have children.

However, there remained various logistical, cultural and ideological constraints upon family planning provisions. First, because of lack of funding and their dependence on medical and lay volunteers to staff the clinics,[50] many clinics were only open for very restricted periods. For example, while the Aberdeen clinic opened from 10am to 6pm six days per week, the Dundee clinic could provide a mere four sessions per month. Given the size of the city, and despite the best efforts of the FPA, particular concern was expressed that the Glasgow clinic was only open two afternoons and evenings per week. In a 'vast, sprawling town of 1.25 million people', this was considered an insult to 'those dedicated and public-minded Glaswegians who had worked so hard, often in the face of bitter hostility, to build this essential service'.[51] Glasgow's relatively poor provision was attributed largely to the city's 'politico-religious climate' and the fear 'of losing the Roman Catholic vote', a fear which more prominently shaped abortion provision.[52]

Second, the FPA's overriding concern to keep family planning 'respectable' in order not to alienate public and professional opinion, and to protect the organisation's charitable status, inhibited the services that it could provide and the clientele it could serve. Until the 1960s, clinics were given euphemistic names relating to 'mother's welfare', ensuring that women 'had to be very well motivated' to find them 'even in the telephone directory'.[53] Moreover, the FPA's declared aims to help 'married people in the planning of their families', and to help with 'difficulties connected with marriage relationships',[54] encouraged the continued exclusion of unmarried women from the Scottish clinics.[55] Indeed, the Dundee clinic attempted to put married women 'at their ease' by staffing the clinic exclusively with married women, since married patients might be 'reluctant to discuss their intimate problems with someone who [was] not herself married'.[56] Although individual doctors might interpret its guidelines flexibly and extend services, for example, to stable cohabiting couples or couples about to be married,[57] the problem was complicated by the fact that single women represented a new generation with very different standards of sexual behaviour from those of their parents and, more significantly, their doctors. Thus, with FPA support, Brook Advisory Centres were founded, from 1964, specifically to serve and educate unmarried young people. The first Scottish branch was opened in Edinburgh in January 1968, targeting young people in a 'stable sexual relationship', and another was opened in Glasgow later that year.[58]

The hostile attitude of some of the Scottish churches to the provision of contraception served merely to reinforce the FPA's conservatism. Indeed, Margaret Gilmore, co-founder of the Edinburgh Brook Advisory Centre, described Scotland as struggling to emerge from 'a spiritual Ice Age' chilled by 'an anti-sexual Puritanism, shot through with overweening spiritual sadism'.[59] The Church of Scotland was broadly supportive, its Committee on Temperance and Morals holding contraception to be 'neither immoral nor unchristian', merely a logical extension of 'man's attempt to control his environment'.[60] However, this support did not extend to those motivated by 'a selfish desire to avoid the sacrifices which a family inevitably entail[ed]', or to 'young unmarried people', who should not be encouraged 'to enter into . . . illicit unions'.[61]

Rather more critically, the Roman Catholic Church adopted the view, endorsed by Pope Pius XII in 1958, that the 'deliberate intention and positive action taken by any means to deprive sexual union of its procreative potentiality' was a sin.[62] Moreover, although the pill, in mimicking the natural functions of the female body, appeared to accord with the Catholic faith's approval of 'natural' contraceptive techniques such as the rhythm method, it too was officially condemned within the Roman Catholic Church in Scotland, an attitude vigorously reaffirmed by the encyclical *Humanae Vitae* in 1968.[63] FPA correspondence with the Scottish clinics regularly lamented the difficulties of establishing and operating a clinic in more Catholic areas of Scotland.[64] To uphold their values, the Catholic Marriage Advisory Council (CMAC) founded Scottish branches in Edinburgh (1965) and Glasgow (1967), and in numerous other areas during the 1970s, funded largely by Diocesan accounts and the social work department of the Scottish Office.[65] The CMAC aimed to give matrimonial advice to Catholics and others 'to whom much of the advice given at the ordinary family planning clinic [was] unacceptable', and to teach them to space their family or avoid pregnancy by using 'natural methods'.[66]

Scattered evidence suggests that, as in England and Wales,[67] the ability of the FPA to proffer contraceptive advice and medication might also be constrained by deep-rooted cultural factors relating to masculine identity and prevailing working-class male assumptions about their responsibility for birth control. In Dumbarton, some husbands allegedly 'insisted' on their wives 'coming off the pill',[68] while in Glasgow there were reports of some working-class men burning their wife's supply of the pill.[69] Similarly, in Edinburgh, staff at the clinic noted that some husbands objected to oral contraception, and guidelines were sought from the FPA as to whose wishes the clinic should respect. The FPA responded that the patient was 'entitled to the advice she want[ed]', and that such advice was to be kept confidential even from her husband.[70]

A final constraint was the marked geographical variation in contraceptive provision, particularly in remote areas like the Highlands and Islands. As with abortion provision, in the realm of family planning Aberdeen had firmly become known as the most progressive city in Scotland, indeed Britain, and the city's clinics continued to expand. In 1967, the local health authority abolished all charges, making Aberdeen the first city in Britain to provide contraceptive advice and supplies free of charge. The removal of charges, coupled with a vigorous health education policy, resulted in an impressive rise in clinic numbers, from 653 new cases in 1966 to 1,013 in 1967,[71] and a notable increase in patients coming from social class five (defined by the census as 'unskilled'), from 6 per cent in 1965 to 14 per cent in 1969.[72] From 1968, family planning services were made available to the unmarried, though staff reported that the 'typical unmarried client' was often planning to marry in the near future, and suggested that a 'less responsible class of girl' was 'not yet being reached' but 'greatly in need of contraceptive protection'.[73] Finally, a domiciliary family planning service was made freely available to city residents from August 1970 for the 'small but important minority of patients' unable to attend a clinic and referred by their family doctor, maternity hospital consultant, health visitor or social worker.[74] The perceived successes of Aberdeen's 'pioneering' approach were advertised widely, and included a steep fall in infant and perinatal mortality rates in advance of the rest of Britain, and a fall in the ille-gitimate birth rate in contrast to the rising trend in the rest of Scotland.[75] 'Indirect' social benefits for the community were said to include an improved pupil/teacher ratio in local schools and better housing conditions.[76]

Throughout the 1960s, increased funding for Aberdeen's family planning service, and its growing inclusiveness, remained heavily dependent on the growing influence of Dugald Baird. In addition to establishing a comprehensive fertility control service, comprising abortion, birth control, and sterilisation, Baird became increasingly vocal about the merits of such a system. After his retirement in 1965, he began explicitly to discuss 'reproductive rights', his arguments couched in terms of aiding women to achieve autonomy over their bodies and greater independence in their lives. In 1965, the *British Medical Journal* published his controversial lecture, 'A Fifth Freedom', in which a notably politicised Baird proclaimed the need to achieve 'freedom from the tyranny of excessive fertility' and to allow women 'the opportunity to exercise their skills in a wider sphere than the immediate family'.[77] He also drew upon world overpopulation fears, asking: 'In a world where there are too many children should women be forced to endure this tyranny of unwanted pregnancies?' Baird quoted Julian Huxley, the English evolutionary biologist and prominent eugenicist, to the effect that scientific 'progress' must involve improving 'quality of life' and 'providing greater fulfilment' as well as merely 'accomplishing control of disease'.[78]

Baird was also active within policy-making circles. In 1958, he was invited to become a Vice-President of the FPA.[79] Baird accepted the invitation and immediately began to encourage the expansion of FPA activities in the north of Scotland, particularly in the 'capital of the Highlands', Inverness.[80] As a respected medical professional willing to go public on this sensitive subject, Baird made a powerful ally for the FPA and was used to good effect during the 1960s as the organisation was able to cite Aberdeen as a pioneering example of a successful and proactive family planning initiative.

ATTEMPTS TO REFORM POLICY, 1966–70

During the later 1960s, Scottish governance came under increasing pressure to adopt a more proactive and coordinated policy towards family planning and to incorporate this role formally into the National Health Service. Judith Hart, Labour MP for Lanark and

Joint Parliamentary Under-Secretary of State for Scotland, pressed for legislation to empower local authorities to provide family planning advice to all persons and to supply appliances and drugs on prescription, albeit while 'treading carefully and watching the way we say things'.[81] In this, she was, by her own admission, influenced by Dugald Baird's 'fifth freedom' arguments in favour of women's right to control their own fertility. Hart's proposal paralleled those of the Minister of Health, Kenneth Robinson, south of the Border.[82]

Accordingly, in June 1966, William Ross, the Secretary of State for Scotland, issued Health and Welfare Services Circular No.10/1966, which encouraged local authorities to review their existing arrangements for family planning.[83] While acknowledging the need for local variations in the content and structure of provision, Ross urged authorities, in liaison with the FPA and other voluntary agencies, to become more strategic in determining the distribution and funding of clinics.[84] The presumption was that local health authorities would accept financial responsibility for the full costs to any voluntary body of advice and supplies given to the public. The content and supportive tone of Ross's Circular were warmly received by both the FPA and the public health authorities, who viewed it as representing a progressive shift in the mindset of the Scottish Office.[85]

Further pressure was placed on Scottish policy makers by the rapid passing of the National Health Service (Family Planning) Act for England and Wales in 1967 (introduced as a Private Member's Bill by the Labour MP Edwin Brooks),[86] which gave local health authorities discretionary powers to provide contraceptive advice and treatment to all who required it, whether on medical or social grounds, and regardless of marital status. Advice and examinations were to be free, although a charge could be made for prescriptions and supplies in non-medical cases.[87] However, for a variety of reasons the Act did not apply to Scotland. Above all, Scottish ministers considered further liberalisation of family planning provisions to be too politically contentious, especially where they involved younger unmarried women. Accordingly, while the Secretary of State was broadly supportive of fresh local initiatives, he declared that he did not think Scotland 'quite ready for this legislation'.[88] He voiced a preference 'to give local authorities a chance of considering what they can do under their existing powers [Circular No.10/1966] before taking action'.

There was widespread protest from politicians and health practitioners at the exclusion of Scotland from the 1967 Act. Donald Dewar,

Labour MP for Aberdeen South, lambasted 'hidden enemies in the Scottish Office'; while Leo Abse, Labour MP for Pontypool, noted that, in view of the similar exclusion of Scotland from the 1967 Sexual Offences Act, there appeared to be a 'curious pattern . . . in relation to bills which touch[ed] on human relationships as far as Scotland [was] concerned'.[89] Abse attributed this not to a lack of demand for family planning in Scotland but to 'some prim Victorian prejudices lingering around the Scottish Office'.

In November 1967, Scottish authorities were asked to report on the current family planning arrangements in their area, including provisions by voluntary bodies. The findings of the survey were that thirty-eight of the fifty-six local health authorities were now providing a service.[90] In all but seven cases this was being conducted through the agency of the FPA. The remaining authorities, in which no family planning provision had yet been made, included remote highland areas such as Bute, Ross and Cromarty, and Sutherland, and lowland areas such as Clydebank and Kirkcudbright. In these locations, patients tended to be referred to local GPs or the nearest FPA clinic.[91]

In the following year, the 1968 Health Services and Public Health Act did introduce powers for Scotland relating to local authority family planning provisions similar to those already applying in England and Wales.[92] However, as this legislation coincided with a period of severe restraint on local authority expenditure, their operation was then suspended by the Home Affairs Committee on the grounds of manpower savings.[93] This suspension came despite widespread opposition, and gave further credence to the impression that Scottish ministers disapproved of family planning. The Director of the FPA reported the situation as 'scandalous',[94] and it was only after he had lobbied the Scottish Office, with the backing of many Scottish MPs and MOHs,[95] that restrictions were eventually lifted in September 1970. Scottish local health authorities were then finally empowered to provide, either directly or through voluntary agencies, advice on contraception and contraceptive supplies on both medical and social grounds.

The Scottish Office, however, remained committed to a limited interpretation of their family planning remit. Within the Scottish Home and Health Department (SHHD), R. M. Bell echoed the views of the Secretary of State when he observed in December 1970 that: 'In advocating an extension of Family Planning facilities in Scotland, it is not the aim to encourage the provision of contraceptives to the unmarried.' As in England, given the discretionary nature of the legislation, wide disparities remained between local authorities. By 1970, only two of the fifty-six local authorities in Scotland were providing a full and free family planning service.

FAMILY PLANNING POLICY AND PROVISION IN THE 1970S

Although Aberdeen was noted to be 'far ahead of other British local health authorities' in spending 2.5 per cent of its budget on family planning,[96] from the early 1970s a number of other local authorities in Scotland (including Renfrewshire and Glasgow) elected to use their discretionary powers to provide free contraceptive supplies.[97] Indeed, the SHHD was somewhat taken aback by the 'surprising enthusiasm' of Scottish local authorities to supply free family planning, and thus free coverage to a higher proportion of the population than in England.[98] The Chairman of the West of Scotland branch of the FPA defended this policy, particularly in areas of 'overwhelming social problems'. In response to possible criticisms, he vigorously denied that a free service increased 'promiscuity and V.D.', noting that the majority of patients attending FPA clinics were in a stable relationship and were acting responsibly by using contraception to prevent unwanted children.[99]

Nonetheless, the twin concerns of morality and public economy continued to inform and impede Scottish governance of family planning in the early 1970s, a period of dramatic change in the scope, costing and structure of family planning provisions in Britain. Policy makers remained sensitive to the likely reaction of public and religious opinion to more liberal provisions, and strove to strike a balance between those groups pressing for free contraceptive services and the opponents of 'sex on the national health'.[100]

In part, calls for free and unconditional contraceptive provisions were triggered by concern at the social and economic costs associated with escalating levels of abortion and unwanted pregnancies, especially amongst young women. The results of Aberdeen's substantial investment in family planning – benefits in health and social conditions, as well as long-term financial savings – were widely seen to justify greater expenditure upon and easier access to contraceptive advice and supplies.[101] An additional argument advanced in favour of family planning reform was the potential threat of overpopulation and its impact on the quality of life of the community.[102] While the Scottish population had been decreasing since 1971 as a result of migration,[103] there was noted to have been a 70 per cent increase in the Scottish population over the twentieth century.[104] Thus, the SHHD broadly supported attempts by Parliament to 'act to prevent the consequences of population growth becoming intolerable for the every-day conditions of life'.[105]

Although much effort had hitherto been made to dissociate the issues of abortion and contraception, the passage of the 1967 Abortion Act clearly created an alarming anomaly: easier access to termination of pregnancy than to the prevention of an unwanted pregnancy. In 1971, the Lane Committee was set up to review the operation of the 1967 Act (see Chapter 5). Although the focus of proceedings, and of the evidence received from a wide variety of organisations and private individuals, was abortion provision and the effectiveness of the legislation, the questionnaire sent to those from whom evidence was requested included a question on the relationship between abortion and family planning.[106] Thus, the evidence submitted provides useful insights into medical perceptions of the availability and comparative value of contraceptive advice and supplies in early 1970s Scotland.

The fact that therapeutic abortion was now legal, whereas local health authority provision of contraceptives remained merely optional, was seen by some to be wholly unacceptable. The Board of Management for Glasgow Royal Infirmary and Associated Hospitals considered it 'peculiar' that abortion 'should have been given approval by Parliament much more easily' and prior to 'measures for widespread contraception [being] supplied under the N.H.S.', and that this 'anomaly . . . should be corrected without delay'.[107] A number of bodies and individuals stressed the fact that more freely available contraception might stem the sharp rise in the number of women coming forward for an abortion and 'produce a more responsible attitude on the part of the community as a whole'.[108]

Medical evidence submitted to the Lane Committee advocated that a twin strategy be adopted. First, it was recommended that all obstetrics and gynaecology departments should either provide or at least facilitate the provision of 'contraceptive advice and prescriptions for all maternity and abortion patients' and for 'any other patients who [might] benefit thereby whether inpatients or outpatients'.[109] Thus, one matron based at Bellshill Maternity Hospital looked 'forward to the day' when nurses could provide free contraceptive advice and facilities directly to those many categories of patients who needed them, thereby preventing 'the unwanted pregnancy which [would become] the subject of an Abortion Act abortion'.[110]

Second, it was considered vital that education in human and sexual relations, including explicit instruction on contraception, should be provided. The SHHD noted 'massive support' for the education of both the general public and those working in the abortion field, it being hoped 'that the abortion rate could be cut by the former and the abortion service improved by the latter',[111] though a number of organisations stressed that extra 'financial and manpower resources' would be required 'in order to fulfil these desirable aims'.[112] Most organisations agreed that such education was particularly vital in the case of young people in schools and colleges, though several groups added the proviso that parental views should always 'be sought and respected' and that 'parents should have the right to withdraw their child from such instruction'.[113]

Such evidence suggests that initial Scottish health education campaigns relating to family planning had met with little success. Following the implementation of the Health Services and Public Health Act in Scotland, the Scottish Health Education Unit (SHEU), established in 1968 within the SHHD to coordinate the provision of public health education, had initiated a series of campaigns designed to raise public awareness of family planning. Working with a limited budget, the Unit's early campaigns were based upon the principles that family planning should be a right available to all, and that families should be able to plan the timing and number of children to best suit their needs and resources.[114]

The Secretary of State for Scotland and members of the SHEU's steering committee kept a close oversight of these early initiatives. They considered the issue to be highly sensitive politically and insisted on vetting all promotional materials prior to distribution. As the Secretary of State noted, it was 'just the kind of subject on which there could be – unnecessarily – a lot of fuss in the House of Commons'; and that they would come 'under fire … for religious reasons', particularly if the campaigns 'could be interpreted as directed to unmarried persons'.[115] The Unit was therefore instructed to avoid offending Roman Catholic opinion and to remain neutral when advising on planning techniques. Thus, SHEU materials tended not to emphasise any particular family planning technique, and were used mainly to convey information as to where expert advice could be obtained. Moreover, the steering committee was adamant that the Unit should devote itself to the 'easier and less controversial issue' of the married woman.[116] Failure to do so would, in the Committee's view, compromise the whole service by alienating civic and church leaders at a 'delicate stage' of the development of family planning services. Thus, although in practical terms SHEU officials considered it 'virtually impossible (even if it were desirable)' to distinguish married clients from cohabitants,[117] their first campaign was directed explicitly at married couples. Indeed, oral testimony suggests that the SHHD insisted that any figures depicted in materials promoting family planning must wear a very visible wedding ring.[118]

The second campaign, scheduled for the spring of 1971, principally took the form of advertisements appearing in the Scottish national daily and Sunday newspapers, with a parallel campaign of television commercials timed to appear the night before family planning sessions were held in individual areas. Once again, the steering committee imposed constraints. The message was to be purely factual and to be targeted at married couples, with emphasis on the spacing and limiting of births. It was to avoid raising contentious issues and was, in particular, to be 'devoid of any reference at all to Casanova or to the pregnant bride shown in publicity material circulated in England and Wales by the Health Education Council'.[119] In the event, evidence from pharmaceutical firms and condom manufacturers suggests that the campaign enjoyed considerable success. In Scotland, condom sales rose significantly in the months following the campaign, and attendances at birth control clinics rose by 25 per cent in 1971 in comparison with a 12.5 per cent increase in England and Wales.[120]

On the basis of these outcomes, in the autumn of 1972 the SHEU proceeded with a further campaign in all the mass-circulation Scottish newspapers, reinforced by television appearances by the Chief Medical Officer for Scotland and members of the Unit. Those directly approaching the Unit for information were sent a new leaflet, *The Secrets of Sharing*, together with an updated brochure, *Where to Get Family Planning Advice*, which included specific advice for Catholics. For the first time a section of this leaflet was devoted to male and female sterilisation, though not without objections from the SHHD, whose officials considered sterilisation as an option only after a couple had already fully explored all other forms of contraception, and one that should be based on health considerations rather than conscious choice.[121] The SHEU's view prevailed, that sterilisation, especially vasectomy, was being considered by an increasing number of younger couples 'in the best of health' who wished to avoid decades of contraception, a demand that needed to be addressed.[122] Other criticisms levelled at the Unit's literature were that it was too 'permissive', failed to provide a moral context and was dismissive of traditional methods such as coitus interruptus. In contrast, others considered the Unit's message to lack traction on the real problems of the unmarried and the lower socio-economic groups in Scottish society. Thus, Donald Campbell, District Medical Officer for Aberdeen, complained that publicity images were identified overly with middle-class types, and needed to be 'more like the grimy paw of an industrial workman or an agricultural labourer'.[123] The Unit's initiatives did, however, draw support from a wide spectrum of opinion, including the FPA and the Catholic Church. Success appeared to be reflected in a continuing rise in attendances at Scottish family planning clinics and an increase in the number of leaflets requested and distributed.[124] Furthermore, the Unit's new television commercial, 'Eight Ways', was awarded a 'Bronze Lion' at the 1973 Cannes Film Festival.[125]

The deliberations of the Lane Committee resulted in the publication of a three-volume report in April 1974 which predominantly focused upon abortion services but also reflected the negative tone of most witnesses regarding the availability of contraceptive services. The Committee 'strongly commend[ed] contraception as the alternative to abortion', and recommended that contraceptive facilities be improved and extended across Britain, and that 'an extension and improvement of sex education programmes' in schools and institutions of higher education was needed to better educate young people on sexual relations and the importance of contraception.[126]

The Government, whose previous failure to insist upon a free family planning service was at variance with these recommendations, endorsed the Committee's view 'that the [Abortion] Act ha[d] helped to focus attention on the paramount need for preventive action, for more education in sexual life and its responsibilities and for the widespread provision of contraceptive advice and facilities'.[127] Indeed, in anticipation of the Lane Committee's recommendations, in the final days of March 1974, Barbara Castle, Secretary of State for Social Services, announced that from 1 April, family planning would be made available under the NHS 'to all who asked for it irrespective of age or marital status', and that a prescription charge should not be imposed for this service, whether requested on medical or non-medical grounds.[128]

The SHHD duly sent out Health Care Circular 74(3) to publicise to all Scottish health boards these plans for a free and comprehensive family planning service. Under the Circular, the provision of family planning services in Scotland was to become the responsibility of the fifteen area health boards, instead of a large number of statutory and voluntary bodies.[129] Supplies were now to be provided without charge, services to the unmarried introduced, domiciliary services encouraged and provisions extended, targeting those in greatest need.[130] The Circular drew no distinction between medical and social grounds for contraceptive advice and treatment, a distinction that, according to Dugald Baird, had long bedevilled birth control policy.[131] Health boards were asked to give a 'high degree of priority' to the planning and development of these services.[132]

However, this Circular attracted various criticisms. A National Opinion Poll indicated that, within the British context, the Scottish public was the least supportive of free birth control and a more proactive role by the state in the provision of family planning.[133] The Roman Catholic Church in Scotland condemned free family planning as a 'policy of despair' and an inducement to 'promiscuity among the young',[134] while the Free Church of Scotland deplored the fact that 'drugs for serious illnesses were subject to prescription charges' but birth control would now be free, and warned that 'the flood-gates to fornication, adultery and promiscuity' were being thrown open.[135] The Free Church noted that this development would 'no doubt be welcomed by the Family Planning Association, whose views on sex and marriage [were] largely contrary to Bible ethics'.

In fact, the FPA itself did not entirely welcome Barbara Castle's announcement, fearing that their clinics would be 'thrown into confusion' by this sudden development.[136] Her 'precipitate statement' and lack of liaison with the major medical bodies 'on whom the burden must inevitably fall' also drew a sharp rebuke from the British Medical Association,[137] and meant that negotiations could not be completed in time for general practitioners to participate in the comprehensive service at the outset. While a review was conducted into how much it would cost for GPs to participate in the scheme, GPs were expected to continue to provide family planning advice and supplies without charge in medical cases, but to charge for supplies in 'social' cases. Under the headline 'GPs Fear Queues for Free Contraceptives', *The Scotsman* reported that GPs wanted £5 for each patient seen in the first year and £2 a year thereafter, but tempers were reported to be 'high' over what was 'seen as a threat' that, if GPs wanted 'too much money' for providing this service, the NHS would simply 'do so without their help'.[138] However, in July 1975, following their success in securing a 'generous' fee scale, GPs fully entered the family planning service.[139]

Arrangements for the funding of contraceptive treatment in

hospitals proved equally problematic, due largely to the 'severe difficulties' that health boards faced in financing the system. In Ayrshire, for example, the cost of family planning services in the financial year 1973/4 had been £15,000, whereas in only the first three months of 1974/5 the expenditure had run to £55,000.[140] Difficulties appear to have been particularly acute in Grampian Health Board, who declined to sanction funding for sterilisation procedures on 'social grounds' despite a growing waiting list for female laparoscopic sterilisations and for elective male vasectomies.[141] There was a growing awareness that their financial difficulties stemmed precisely from the extensive family planning provisions that Aberdeen had hitherto put in place. These had imposed a significant financial burden on the Health Board just to maintain existing levels of activity, and raised fears that the new system of remuneration 'could well mean a deterioration in the services provided'.[142] Elsewhere, a number of other health boards continued to complain that they were simply unable to finance a free family planning service.

The result of Circular 74(3) was expected to be a substantial expansion in the involvement of the NHS in family planning, particularly geared towards those in greatest need. The SHHD and FPA agreed that the existing clinic arrangements should continue for a limited period, after which these activities should be systematically transferred to the NHS. A phased programme for the transfer of Scottish clinics was drawn up, ranging from March 1975 (Grampian, Highland and Lothian) to September 1976 (Greater Glasgow and Lanarkshire).[143] In total, 178 Scottish FPA clinics were transferred to the NHS,[144] reflecting government recognition that the NHS had to include family planning in order to be fully comprehensive.[145] By the late 1970s, it was estimated that up to 80 per cent of contraceptive services to women in Scotland was now provided by GPs,[146] suggesting that women had quickly accepted the 'medicalisation' of family planning.

Historians have been quick to credit oral contraception as a 'key factor' in bringing the medical profession into family planning,[147] despite the fact that GPs do not appear, in Scotland at least, to have provided a significant proportion of family planning services until the later 1970s. Less historiographical attention has been devoted to the significance of the payment of doctors for providing this service. The rising demand for free contraceptive advice and treatment, and its integration into the formal responsibilities of the NHS, raised the contentious issue of remuneration, not least as this coincided with a period of severe cutbacks in government expenditure. Moreover, not all doctors were enthusiastic about this boost to their earning potential. Ian Donald, the Glasgow-based obstetrician and leading campaigner against medical termination of pregnancy, was highly critical that remuneration allowed doctors to add thousands to their pay packets by treating birth control like 'pest control'.[148] However, oral testimony suggests that it was the additional, in fact fairly substantial, income that could be made from family planning that ultimately encouraged most Scottish family doctors to enter this sphere.[149]

Indeed, once Scottish doctors embraced family planning as a legitimate and lucrative part of their activities, they immediately began to press for increasing autonomy within the sphere. Evidence suggests that they more proactively encouraged patients to come to them rather than their local clinic.[150] Tensions also arose when health promotion campaigns failed to accord at least equal status to the GP as a source of family planning advice and supplies. In 1977, a group of Grampian GPs objected to the fact that family planning posters did not give due prominence to GPs, who appeared as a mere 'footnote', implying that they provided some kind of 'secondary service'.[151] They even suggested that GPs should be consulted about the design of future posters.

After 1975, as well as a shift in those providing family planning, there was a significant, albeit gradual, shift in the centre of gravity of Scottish health education initiatives towards the targeting of family planning information at the young. In 1975, a Chief Scientist Organisation working party was established, which included representatives of the SHEU and the Scottish Education Department (SED), to examine family planning and related services in Scotland, and to identify research priorities.[152] Two groups of clients emerged as priorities – the young and the socially disadvantaged – because they were seen to lack the necessary knowledge that would enable them to plan their families. Figures published in *The Scotsman* reinforced concerns about young people. In particular, the data suggested that earlier physical maturation combined with sexual experience at a younger age was placing young people at much greater risk of conception than previous generations. It was estimated, for example, that annually there were 29,000 illegitimate births among teenagers in Scotland, and that half of the 40,000 teenage brides were pregnant, with a majority of first conceptions occurring outside marriage.[153]

As a result, by the late 1970s, a new target group had emerged at the top of the Scottish health education agenda: 16–20-year-olds. In 1980, the Scottish Health Education Group (SHEG), established to replace the SHEU, proposed an ambitious family planning publicity campaign using the press and radio to reach this age group. The campaign was intended to provide information on where advice and condoms could be obtained, and to use fictional case histories to demonstrate the consequences of unwanted pregnancy.[154] The response of the SED, SHHD and Scottish ministers to the proposal clearly reveals the political and cultural constraints on sex education policy still operating in Scotland on the eve of the AIDS epidemic. First and foremost, the campaign was viewed as politically highly sensitive. The SHHD advised that, while the publicity material had 'no basically objectionable features', it could easily be construed as 'anti-baby, devoid of a family context', and as offering 'no positive advice on the benefits of <u>planned</u> pregnancies'.[155] In advancing such objections, the SHHD was no doubt sensitive to similar warnings being administered by the Department of Health and Social Security south of the Border, prompted in part by a resurgence of parliamentary pressure for the closer regulation of sex education materials and for the curtailment of contraceptive advice to young girls.[156] Certainly, a need to place 'more emphasis on abstinence and less on contraception' continued to inform the SHHD's critique of SHEG sex education initiatives well into the 1980s.[157]

CONCLUSION

The need to frame policy with respect to family planning presented Scottish governance with a continuing dilemma. The issue was politically highly contentious and there was an overriding need to strike a balance between those groups agitating for free and comprehensive services and those who complained vigorously about 'sex on the national health'. As in so many other areas of policy making where sexual morality was involved, the Scottish Office was constrained by a range of social and ideological factors. The fear of alienating the Scottish churches, and particularly the Church of Scotland and the Roman Catholic Church in Scotland, was an enduring concern of officials, not least because church leaders retained disproportionate influence within civic government and municipal politics.

More broadly, policy makers were sensitive to the moral conservatism of Scottish society in general and to the need to formulate legislation that respected public opinion north of the Border rather than indulge metropolitan values. As a result, the Scottish health and education departments continued to boundary the more liberated ventures of agencies such as the SHEU, and insisted on the ethos of family planning remaining attached as far as possible to traditional values of premarital chastity.

The reluctance of the policy community to engage with reproductive issues was duly reflected in the degree of devolvement that characterised the development of the family planning services in Scotland. Scottish departments of state continued to delegate responsibility for family planning to the FPA and local authorities, and it was from local health committees, pre-eminently Aberdeen's Public Health Committee, that the major initiatives and stimulus to the more coordinated, state-sponsored provisions after 1974 stemmed.

The relationship of the medical profession to the shaping of family planning policy in the period 1950–80 was highly ambivalent but nonetheless decisive. In the early years the development of individual family planning clinics was strongly dependent on the support and cooperation of individual doctors (particularly female doctors), for whom the work was neither lucrative nor a boost to their status. Yet oral evidence suggests that, before GPs came to dominate the provision of contraceptive advice and supplies in the later 1970s, the clinics were run mainly by voluntary lay workers who provided the 'backbone' of the service. It was the lay socialist-feminist activists within the ALRA and FPA who recognised the critical importance of doctors and medical rhetoric in fighting their cause, and who recruited figures such as Dugald Baird who became so central to the shaping of policy on reproductive issues.

Thereafter, the medical profession moved increasingly, if hesitatingly, to the centre stage of the story and were crucial for translating policy into practice. Initially, because of moral, legal and technical concerns, the Scottish medical establishment was reluctant to engage with the debates over abortion and family planning. At the same time, however, the small coterie of gynaecologists who were prepared to press for legislation became pivotal in the policy-making process. Finally, once the medical profession had been pressured (in abortion) or enticed (in family planning) into becoming involved in reproductive issues, it very quickly sought and secured domination of the new NHS fertility services after 1974.

Notes

1 Hughes, *Gender and Political Identities in Scotland*, 118–25.
2 WL, SA/FPA/A11/73C, Note '1930–48, Glasgow S.B.', undated. See also Debenham, 'Grassroots feminism', PhD dissertation.
3 Elliott, 'Birth control clinics in Scotland', MSc dissertation.
4 C. Debenham, 'Aberdeen's birth control pioneer', *Leopard Magazine*, October 2007, www.leopardmag.co.uk/feats/169/fenella-paton-aberdeens-birth-control-pioneer, accessed 21 July 2011.
5 Leathard, *The Fight for Family Planning*, 11.
6 Debenham, 'Aberdeen's birth control pioneer'.
7 *Evening Express (Aberdeen)*, 13 September 1934; Baird, 'The changing pattern of human reproduction', 84.
8 Elliott, 'Birth control clinics in Scotland', 26–7.
9 Ibid., 28.
10 *Aberdeen Press and Journal*, 13 December 1926.
11 NHSA, Minutes of Aberdeen Public Health Committee, 12 June 1935, 12 March 1940.
12 *The Bulletin and Scots Pictorial*, 11 October 1933.
13 WL, SA/FPA/A11/73E, Handwritten note, unsigned, Stirling, 27 April 1936.
14 D. Baird, *Proceedings of the Royal Society*, 65 (1972), 6–8, at p. 7.
15 WL, SA/FPA/A11/73C, Secretary, NBCA, to Miss Pirie, 20 October 1931.
16 M. K. Brown, 'Diary of the Glasgow Women's Welfare and Advisory Clinic, 28 June 1934', cited in Elliott, 'Birth control clinics in Scotland', 9–10.
17 WL, SA/FPA/A11/73C, Secretary, NBCA, to W. H. MacEwan, 17 March 1932.
18 WL, SA/FPA/A11/74, Secretary, NBCA, to K. W. L. Dobie, 23 March 1932.
19 Douglas and McKinlay, *Report on Maternal Morbidity and Mortality in Scotland*; *Report of the Committee on Scottish Health Services*.
20 WL, SA/FPA/A11/74, H. Holland, Headquarters' Organiser, NBCA, London, to all County Councillors, 1936.
21 WL, SA/FPA/A11/73B, Note 'Falkirk L.A.', 17 May 1936.
22 WL, SA/FPA/A11/73C, Note by H. Holland, Glasgow, 5 May 1936.
23 WL, SA/FPA/A11/73, C. Slorach, MOH, Dumbarton, to Miss Holland, Headquarters' Organiser, NBCA, Edinburgh, 19 April 1937.
24 WL, SA/FPA/A8/25, President, NBCA, London, to W. Elliot, 13 March 1937.
25 WL, SA/FPA/A8/25, W. Elliot to The Lord Horder, President, NBCA, 30 April 1937.
26 WL, SA/FPA/A8/25, Headquarters' Organiser, NBCA, to D. Baird, 18 December 1936.
27 Elliott, 'Birth control clinics in Scotland', 20–1.

28   WL, SA/FPA/A4/A5.1, J. Cairns, Honorary Secretary, Edinburgh Mothers' Welfare Clinic (EMWC), to Mrs Wintersgill, 26 May 1947.

29   WL, SA/FPA/A11/73A, Note '1931–43 Edinburgh S.B.', undated.

30   WL, SA/FPA/A4/A5.1, *EMWC 17th Annual Report, 1949–50*; *The Scotsman*, 29 November 1948.

31   www.universitystory.gla.ac.uk/biography/?id=WH3040&type=P, accessed 21 July 2011.

32   Special Libraries and Archives, University of Aberdeen, MS3620/1/21 and 22, Interview with D. Baird, 3 April 1985.

33   WL, SA/ALR/C.115, Note by D. Baird, undated.

34   NHSA, GRHB E1/7/9, *Health and Welfare*, 28 (October 1965), 3.

35   WL, SA/FPA/A8/38, Secretary, Clinics' Sub-Committees, to Mrs Craig, 30 March 1955.

36   WL, SA/FPA/A8/38, Branch Organisation Secretary, FPA, to Mrs Moodie, EMWC, 14 June 1955.

37   WL, SA/FPA/A4/G1, 'Bulletin of the Scottish Federation of the Family Planning Association', Summer 1960.

38   Ibid.

39   WL, SA/FPA/A4/G1, 'Bulletin of the Scottish Federation of the Family Planning Association', Summer 1962, 20; WL, SA/FPA/A4/A5.5, *EMWC 30th Annual Report*, 1963.

40   Oral contraception was introduced to Aberdeen in 1964, and within four years was the favoured contraceptive method of 90 per cent of those attending the clinic [NHSA, GRHB E1/7/9, *Health and Welfare*, 40 (October 1968), 5].

41   Marks, *Sexual Chemistry*, 116–37.

42   NRS, HH98/136, National Medical Consultative Committee (NMCC) position paper, October 1980.

43   NRS, HH61/1434, SHHD Minutes of Consultative Committee of Medical Officers of Health, 19 January 1971; Marks, *Sexual Chemistry*, 143.

44   Marks, *Sexual Chemistry*, 138–57. Although the consensus of opinion amongst Scottish family planning experts was that the benefits of the pill far outweighed the risks involved, some concerned Scottish gynaecologists promoted sterilisation as a safer option for married couples who had completed their families, with a significant rise in the demand for sterilisation documented from 1972. See Bone, *Family Planning in Scotland in 1982*, 35–9.

45   Marks, *Sexual Chemistry*, 202.

46   WL, SA/ALR/C.8, B. Thompson, 'Summary of preliminary analysis on the epidemiology of pregnancy, sterilisation and oral contraception in the City of Aberdeen since 1961', undated.

47   *Glasgow Herald*, 7 February 1967, 24 November 1967; *The Scotsman*, 16 January 1968.

48 NHS Greater Glasgow and Clyde Archives (GGCA), HH77/3/13, Untitled newspaper clipping, undated.

49 *Scottish Daily Express*, 9 December 1969; *Glasgow Herald*, 14 October 1970.

50 Exceptions included the Glasgow clinic, 'run in a somewhat extravagant way in that the voluntary principle ha[d] been practically abandoned'. By 1959, doctors there were paid £1.1.-, the nurses 15/- and the lay workers 10/-. See WL, SA/FPA/A4/A6.2, Report of an Advisory Visit to Glasgow Branch by Mrs Bedford and Mrs Raphael, 16 April 1962; WL, SA/FPA/A4/A6.1, Report of Mrs N. Raphael's visit to Glasgow, 22 October 1959.

51 *Glasgow Herald*, 21 June 1966.

52 WL, SA/FPA/A4/A6.1, Report of Mrs N. Raphael's visit to Glasgow, 22 October 1959; WL, SA/FPA/A4/A5.2, M. Marwick to Mrs Pyke, Honorary Secretary of FPA, London, 3 March 1954.

53 GGCA, HH77/1/5, FPA leaflet, 1975. Most Scottish clinics were only renamed 'family planning' clinics in the mid-1960s.

54 WL, SA/FPA/A4/A5.5, *EMWC 24th Annual Report, 1957*.

55 For medical debates on the subject, see WL, SA/FPA/A16/24.62a, *Family Planning for Scotland: Conference Proceedings* (Bristol, 1969).

56 GGCA, HH77/3/4, Untitled newspaper clipping, 17 May 1956.

57 See, for example, the EMWC, which provided special 'pre-marriage' clinics on Thursdays from 6 to 7pm, and which required a letter of introduction from the couple's minister, family doctor or parents. See WL, SA/FPA/A4/A5.2, Leaflet, 'The Special Clinic', 1956.

58 *The Scotsman*, 22 January 1968; WL, SA/FPA/A16/24.62a, *Family Planning for Scotland: Conference Proceedings* (Bristol, 1969).

59 *The Scotsman*, 2 February 1968.

60 WL, SA/FPA/A4/G1, 'Bulletin of the Scottish Federation of the Family Planning Association', Summer 1960, 19.

61 *The Times*, 5 May 1960; *The Scotsman*, 10 May 1968.

62 Leathard, *The Fight for Family Planning*, 113.

63 *Glasgow Observer and Scottish Catholic Herald*, 5 October 1962; Marks, *Sexual Chemistry*, 218.

64 See, for example, WL, SA/FPA/A4/H35, C. G. McLachlan, Scottish Federation Area Organiser, to Mrs Parker, Branch Organisation Secretary, FPA, London, 22 July 1966.

65 NRS, HH61/1434, Note by P. Millington, Tutor and Honorary Treasurer to CMAC, 1974.

66 *Glasgow Observer and Scottish Catholic Herald*, 12 March 1965.

67 Fisher, *Birth Control, Sex and Marriage*.

68 WL, SA/FPA/A4/H35, FPA Note on Dumbarton, 30 September 1965.

69 Wilson, *Sex on the Rates*, 157; Interview with retired general practitioner, August 2004.

70 WL, SA/FPA/A4/A5.3, Dr E. Mears, Medical Secretary, FPA, to Dr N. Loudon, EMWC, 30 April 1963.

71 NHSA, GRHBE1/1/68, City of Aberdeen, *Medical Officer of Health Report*, 1967.

72 *The Benefits of Birth Control: Aberdeen's Experience, 1946–1970* (London: Birth Control Campaign, 1973), 18.

73 Ibid., 18–19.

74 Ibid., 20.

75 Ibid., 1–9.

76 Ibid., 10.

77 D. Baird, 'A fifth freedom?', *British Medical Journal*, 2 (1965), 1,141–8, at pp. 1,141, 1,148.

78 Ibid., 1,148.

79 WL, SA/FPA/A14/101, FPA to D. Baird, 26 June 1958.

80 WL, SA/FPA/A4/A6/2, Branch Organisation Secretary, FPA, to Mrs Stark-Brown, 20 July 1960.

81 NRS, HH61/1005, W. G. Robertson, Private Secretary, Scottish Office, to M. MacDonald, SHHD, 15 December 1965.

82 Webster, *The Health Services Since the War*, 246–7.

83 NRS, HH61/1005, SHHD, Health and Welfare Services Circular No.10/1966, 1 June 1966.

84 *Glasgow Herald*, 3 June 1966.

85 *Scottish Daily Record*, 3 June 1966.

86 Parliamentary opposition was focused instead on the highly contentious Medical Termination of Pregnancy Bill, introduced by David Steel. See Chapter 5 of this volume.

87 Leathard, *The Fight for Family Planning*, 158.

88 NRS, HH61/1005, W. Ross, SSS, to K. Robinson, Minister of Health, 28 June 1966.

89 *The Sun*, 18 February 1967.

90 NRS, HH61/1208, SHHD background notes, 16 April 1971.

91 NRS, HH61/1391, Miscellaneous Family Planning.

92 Public and General Statutes, *Health Services and Public Health Act, 1968*, c. 46.

93 NRS, HH61/1208, E. Taylor to T. Galbraith, MP, 7 August 1970.

94 *Scottish Sunday Express*, 14 October 1968.

95 See, for example, *Glasgow Herald*, 30 November 1968; *Scottish Daily Mail*, 24 July 1969.

96 *The Benefits of Birth Control*, 23.

97 NRS, HH102/1616, Dr M. Barron to Scottish Office, 9 May 1973.

98 NRS, HH61/1355, J. Walker to Sharp, Ogilvie and Macdonald, 24 October 1972.

99 NRS, HH102/1616, Dr M. Barron to Scottish Office, 9 May 1973.

100 NRS, HH61/1211, R. M. Bell to Mr E. Redmond, November 1975.

101 *The Benefits of Birth Control*.

102 *The Scotsman*, 18 January 1973; Leathard, *The Fight for Family Planning*, 177–89.
103 Bone, *Family Planning in Scotland in 1982*, 1.
104 *Glasgow Herald*, 30 November 1968.
105 NRS, HH102/1294, Memorandum by SHHD on 'Conclusions and recommendations of the Population Panel', 31 January 1973.
106 NRS, HH61/1258, Committee agenda and minutes, 15 June 1971.
107 WL, SA/ALR/C.35, Proceedings of the Lane Committee (PLC), Submission of Board of Management for Glasgow Royal Infirmary and Associated Hospitals, December 1971.
108 NRS, HH102/1232, F. N. Mitchell, Honorary Secretary of the Scottish Association of Nurse Administrators, to M. Macdonald, SHHD, 3 July 1974.
109 NRS, HH102/1232, Professor E. McGirr, University of Glasgow, to M. Macdonald, 1974.
110 WL, SA/ALR/C.22, PLC, Submission of Board of Management for Coatbridge, Airdrie and District Hospitals, 1972.
111 NRS, HH102/1232, E. U. E. Elliott-Binns to G. G. Hulme, 10 December 1974.
112 Ibid., PLC, Submission of Scottish Public Health Nursing Administrators and Tutors, 25 July 1974; Submission of Royal College of Physicians and Surgeons of Glasgow, 25 July 1974.
113 NRS, HH102/1232, Miss J. Main, Registrar of The General Nursing Council for Scotland, to M. Macdonald, 28 May 1974; R. Stewart, Secretary of Highland Health Board, to M. Macdonald, 22 July 1974.
114 NRS, HH61/970, Memorandum by Dr A. Yarrow, SHEU, 13 October 1970. In 1970, the total budget for the Unit's family planning campaign was only £2,500.
115 NRS, HH61/970, Memorandum by SHHD on 'Family planning and health education', November 1970.
116 NRS, HH61/970, Dr A. Yarrow to R. M. Bell, 3 November 1970.
117 NRS, HH61/970, Memorandum by SHHD on 'Family Planning and Health Education', November 1970.
118 Interview with retired gynaecologists, July 2004.
119 NRS, HH61/970, D. Dee to N. Shipman, 23 February 1971.
120 NRS, HH61/1208, Draft reply to SSS, undated.
121 NRS, HH61/1208, J. Walker to Dr A. Yarrow, 9 May 1972.
122 Ibid., Dr A. Yarrow to J. Walker, 11 May 1972.
123 NHSA, GRHBA4, D. Campbell, District Medical Officer, West District, to Grampian Health Board, 3 June 1974.
124 NRS, HH61/1020, SHEU Steering Committee, Minutes of meeting, 10 January 1973.
125 NRS, HH61/1020, SHEU Steering Committee, Minutes of meeting, 24 July 1973.
126 NRS, HH60/665, R. P. Fraser to G. N. Monro, 8 December 1973.

127 NRS, HH101/2877, Draft home affairs/social services paper, undated.
128 BMA archive, B/455/1/7, Memorandum by Scottish Committee for Hospital Medical Services, 1973–4. It was estimated that the cost of not imposing a charge would be around £1,000,000 per year.
129 NRS, HH61/1188, Report by Dr A. Laurie, 'Health Services Research Committee – Family Planning in Scotland', 1974.
130 NRS, HH98/298, NMCC Specialty Sub-Committee for Obstetrics and Gynaecology discussion paper, January 1978.
131 Baird, 'Sterilization and therapeutic abortion', 702.
132 BMA, B/455/1/7, Health Circular (74)3 issued to all health boards by the SHHD, 28 March 1974.
133 *The Scotsman*, 18 January 1973.
134 *The Scotsman*, 8 April 1974.
135 *The Scotsman*, 16 May 1974.
136 *The Scotsman*, 1 April 1974.
137 BMA, B/455/1/7, Memorandum by Scottish Committee for Hospital Medical Services, 1973–4.
138 *The Scotsman*, 1 April 1974.
139 Webster, *The National Health Service*, 135.
140 NHSA, GRHBA4, R. McCrorie, Secretary, Ayrshire and Arran Health Board, to SHHD, 14 August 1974.
141 NHSA, GRHBA4, D. Galloway, Hospital Junior Staff Committee, to Dr J. Petrie, Secretary, South District Medical Committee, Aberdeen University, 26 June 1974.
142 NHSA, GRHBA4, Scottish Trades Union Congress General Council to the SSS, 4 November 1976.
143 NRS, HH61/1286, J. Walker, SHHD, to Health Boards, 28 March 1974.
144 NRS, HH98/135, NMCC discussion paper, September 1979. Only one FPA centre remained – in Glasgow – to provide training and contraceptive provision.
145 Leathard, *The Fight for Family Planning*, 229.
146 NRS, HH98/298, NMCC discussion paper, January 1978.
147 See, for example, Anderson, 'The most important place in the history of British birth control', 25; Marks, *Sexual Chemistry*, ch. 5.
148 Ian Donald, 'Superfecundity – Simpson oration: his problem and ours', *British Medical Journal*, 1 (1977), 555–60, at p. 558.
149 Interviews with retired general practitioners and gynaecologists, March 2004–August 2004.
150 Interview with retired general practitioner, August 2004.
151 NHSA, GRHBA4, Memorandum by Grampian Health Board, 26 April 1977.
152 NRS, HH61/1188, Memorandum by SHHD, 16 April 1975.
153 *The Scotsman*, 6 July 1977.
154 NRS, HH61/1018, Note 'Family Planning – General Questions, 1980–82'.

155 Ibid. (original emphasis).

156 See, for example, *Hansard [HC]*, vol. 982, 1 April 1980, cols 162–3; vol. 990, 8 August 1980, cols 367–8.

157 NRS, HH61/1265, Minutes of SHEG Family Planning Advisory Group, 22 January 1985. Official inhibitions may have also been affirmed by the findings of SHEG that, when questioned about the content of sex education publicity materials, many young people themselves requested the inclusion of 'abstinence' as an option [NRS, HH61/1018, Note by G. McHugh, SHEG, 'Proposed publicity campaign on contraceptive advice to 16–19 Year Olds', 1 December 1981].

PART III

Disease and Enlightenment

7

SEXUAL HEALTH

INTRODUCTION

Society's response to venereal disease (VD) has been shown to be a central strand in that whole web of discourses that has constructed and regulated sexuality in modern society. During the first half of the twentieth century, VD became in many countries a metaphor for physical and moral decay, and for the forces of pollution and contamination that appeared to threaten the institutions of social order and racial progress. Alarm over the issue of VD therefore offered an opportunity to express concern about the moral direction of society and changing standards of conduct. Given the supposedly wilful nature of its diffusion and its threat to 'social hygiene', it also provided a powerful justification for the social construction and proscription of dangerous sexualities.[1]

In post-war Scotland, the incidence and impact of VD (officially redesignated as sexually transmitted diseases (STDs) after 1972) continued to underpin debate over shifts in sexual mores and their implications for public order, public health and public morality. Concerns over VD/STDs continued to provide a peg upon which to hang broader social anxieties. This chapter explores those concerns and examines the range of policy options considered and/or implemented by Scottish government in a period of radical change in patterns of social intercourse and sexual behaviour.

THE SCALE OF THE PROBLEM

Scottish health statistics for the period 1950–80 reveal a dramatic and sustained decline in the number of cases of syphilis from the peaks associated with wartime and post-war demobilisation.[2] Some 80 per cent of this decline occurred prior to 1956, and the Scottish trend clearly paralleled that experienced in England and Wales. Scottish gonorrhoea figures also reveal a sharp decline in the immediate post-war years. Thereafter, the most significant feature was their relative stability until the mid-1960s. This was in marked contrast to the sharply rising trend in the incidence of gonorrhoea elsewhere in Britain and overseas from the mid-1950s onwards. Indeed, this aspect of the Scottish health experience was one that the Scottish Office was at pains to stress,[3] and it was to have a decisive impact on the shaping of VD/STD policy. Between 1968 and 1974, Scotland did experience a significant upswing in the number of gonorrhoea cases (some 58 per cent) but they then levelled off for the remainder of the decade and, although some convergence took place, new cases remained well below the level for England.

However, as in England, there was a dramatic rise in the incidence of the 'newer' venereal infections in Scotland after 1965, with a 156 per cent rise in the number of cases of male non-specific urethritis (NSU) over the following decade, along with significant increases of 63 per cent in other sexually transmitted diseases, including chancroid, genital candidosis, genital scabies, pubic lice, genital warts and genital herpes. As a result, the 'classical' venereal infections of syphilis, gonorrhoea and soft chancre came to occupy only about one-quarter of the caseload of the special clinics by 1980 compared with three-quarters prior to the Second World War.

A breakdown by sex of VD/STD cases attending the Scottish clinics between 1950 and 1980 reveals a slow but steady rise in the male share of syphilis cases from an annual average of 57 per cent for the 1950s to 63 per cent in the 1960s and 68 per cent in the 1970s, which clinicians attributed largely to an emerging pattern of 'homosexually acquired infections'.[4] In contrast, statistics for gonor-rhoea show that, although in absolute numbers male cases continued to far exceed female cases, there was a significant convergence in their respective shares after the mid-1960s. By the 1970s, female cases in Scotland represented over one-third of the total workload for gonorrhoea in the clinics, a trend that was to figure prominently in contemporary debate on the state of public health and morality. The age-specificity of much of the rising incidence of VD/STDs also tapped into a deep well of concern over the moral decadence and sexual promiscuity of youth culture, and in particular of girls and young women. Contemporary health statistics revealed that a growing proportion of VD/STDs was contracted by the 15–24 age group and that female teenagers represented the fastest growth area for infec-tions such as gonorrhoea.[5]

CONTEMPORARY CONCERNS AND PERCEPTIONS

Many strands of pre-war discourse surrounding VD survived well into later twentieth-century Scottish society. There is a notable similarity between the language and assumptions of the social hygiene and purity literature of the inter-war period and those articulated in the reports of public health departments in the 1950s and 1960s. In particular, there was a continuing identity in the media and professional journals between VD/STDs and moral degeneration. As in the 1920s, it was widely believed in the 1950s that war had seriously eroded family and community controls and that its disinhibiting effects on patterns of sexual behaviour had profoundly 'demoralised' the nation.[6] Scottish venereologists were always sceptical of the more sensational claims of moral decadence, but they continued to view VD as a symptom of a more general debasement of sexual standards and of a decline in the influence of religious values and commitment to the sanctity of marriage.[7]

The long-established association between alcohol and promiscuity also resurfaced in post-war attempts by public health and church authorities to explain the incidence of VD/STDs. Thus, in the view of the Church of Scotland, VD was one of many social problems arising from the influence of drink upon 'the censor of the conscience'.[8] Evidence suggested that the overwhelming majority of VD patients had frequented a public house prior to infective intercourse and that seasonal fluctuations in the incidence of disease were in part related to 'drunken parties at the festive season'.[9]

Meanwhile, concerns were emerging about the impact of new penicillin-based chemotherapies on sexual behaviour. Health practitioners and administrators were increasingly aware of the moral dilemma posed by the widespread application of antibiotics. The myth of a miracle drug with the prospect of a cure at state expense 'without discomfort or inconvenience', and with a much reduced opportunity for the clinician to regulate behaviour as part of therapy, was seen to have trivialised venereal infection in the minds of patients and undermined the impact of social hygiene propaganda.[10] This association between VD, promiscuity and over-confidence in antibiotics was to be frequently asserted in both the Scottish press and official circles throughout the 1950s and early 1960s.[11]

However, as in other countries, from the late 1950s, venereologists and public health officials in Scotland increasingly adopted a more sociological approach to the issue of VD. Its incidence was explained less in terms of individual moral deficiencies and more in terms of the impact of a range of cultural, institutional and economic factors upon general patterns of sexual morality and behaviour. In the view of many social commentators, it was 'the price of the Permissive Society'.[12] Indeed, the central explanatory concepts informing medical and public debate over the rise of VD/STDs in late twentieth-century Scotland were to become 'sexual promiscuity' and 'permissiveness'. The role of prostitution, with its epidemiological mindset of a small cluster of feckless and vicious vectors, remained a *leitmotiv* of public health reports, but it was steadily superseded by the spectre of widespread casual sex and an endless chain of infection.

In particular, certain 'high risk' groups were identified who were socially isolated due to marital or family disharmony and who were alienated from traditional values and prey to a range of disinhibitors including alcohol, drugs such as cannabis and LSD, new forms of contraception and a media 'obsessed with sexual permissiveness and gratification'.[13] Although attitude surveys on sexual issues continued to reveal a younger generation in Scotland that was 'conformist rather than permissive or hedonistic',[14] the burden of blame was commonly attached to teenage promiscuity. The rising incidence of VD was widely interpreted as part of a wider social pathology of youth culture that involved violence, drug taking, illegitimacy and sexual deviancy, and Scottish public health and church reports frequently identified the increase in teenage cases with adolescent alienation from a morally bankrupt, acquisitive society.[15]

In addition, the casual attitude of teenagers towards venereal infection and medical therapy was identified as a major factor in the increase in the number of carriers and penicillin-resistant strains in the community. While it was reluctantly conceded that there was little evidence 'that the teddy boy cult . . . or Rock 'n' Roll' had any significant influence on the incidence of VD/STDs, its addicts were typified as 'uncooperative in treatment' and lacking in 'the self-discipline necessary for cure'.[16] Such non-compliance with medical authority was often viewed as part of a broader breakdown in civic and moral discipline amongst Scottish youth.[17]

However, as previously, post-war moral panic surrounding the sexual hygiene of the young centred on the sexual promiscuity of teenage girls and young women. The potent image of asymptomatic, promiscuous girls as 'reservoirs of infection' haunting cafés, pubs, cinemas and dance halls was widely projected in the media and public health literature.[18] It was female adolescent promiscuity that was presented as 'the real danger' and significantly, when recording the sources of venereal infection in male patients, Edinburgh's Public Health Department continued to categorise sexually active single women as 'amateur types', retaining by implication their association with prostitution.[19] This asymmetry in perceptions of sexual behaviour and disease was powerfully reflected in contemporary analyses of the sources of infection, which enshrined the concept of women as the proactive polluters well into the 1960s.

Moreover, the emergence of a more social scientific interpretation of sexual behaviour and disease in the 1960s and 1970s served in many ways to reinforce this pathological view of female adolescent sexuality. Sexual promiscuity and VD/STDs among teenage girls became increasingly identified with a syndrome of distinctively female juvenile delinquency.[20] Girls were deemed to manifest their 'anti-social urges' primarily through promiscuity, with 'the ever-willing teenage girl' being 'the female equivalent of the skinhead in his bovver boots'.[21] Social psychologists also resurrected the linkages between VD, sexual permissiveness and mental instability that had so powerfully shaped inter-war responses to 'problem girls'.[22]

Inevitably, the debate surrounding female sexuality and the incidence of VD/STDs gave prominence to the increasing use by girls and young women of the 'pill'. The broad consensus amongst social commentators and medical practitioners was that the pill had radically altered patterns of female sexual behaviour, thus promoting sexual promiscuity and disease. This was a view shared by officials within the Scottish Office, and the Scottish Home and Health Department (SHHD) acknowledged it to be a contributory factor in the rising incidence of venereal infection.[23]

In Scotland, the linkage between the pill and the rise in VD/STDs was central to the broader campaign of the churches against the extension of family planning provisions for single women and girls. According to the Free Church of Scotland, increasing sexual disease was due to the Government 'throwing open the flood-gates to fornication, adultery and promiscuity, making them risk-free on the NHS'.[24] It maintained that the ready availability of the contraceptive pill had 'violated the sanctity and beauty of sex' and, in the crisis of escalating STD rates, 'reaped the whirlwind for having sown to the wind'.[25] Such views were shared, albeit somewhat less stridently, not only by the other Scottish churches but also by the 'Moral Right' within Scottish public health debates of the early 1970s.[26] The Chairman of Edinburgh's Public Health Committee used similar arguments in her campaign to frustrate the extension of family planning provisions, as did the Scottish Tory Conference in endorsing a motion denouncing what it perceived to be a general breakdown of public order and public morality.[27]

The 'homosexual' failed to surface within the post-war demonology surrounding VD/STDs in Scotland in the same way as it did in the early 1960s in England and in European countries such as Holland,[28] and the prominence accorded by the Ministry of Health to 'homosexual practices' in explaining their rising incidence was never matched in the reports of the SHHD. Nonetheless, discussion of sexual health issues often reflected broader social concerns and moral outrage surrounding homosexual behaviour. Moreover, medical opinion did little to dispel lay prejudices surrounding the issue. In the 1950s and 1960s, leading Scottish venereologists continued to view homosexuality as a deviant and dangerous perversion, driven by an 'aberrant instinct'.[29] The subsequent report in 1973 of the Gilloran Committee on Sexually Transmitted Diseases in Scotland served to reinforce prevailing prejudices when it identified 'passive homosexuals' as 'reservoirs of infection',[30] thus stigmatising their sexuality as a source of pollution and disease in a fashion traditionally reserved for female prostitutes and 'good-time girls'.

A distinctive feature of the debate surrounding VD/STDs in post-war Scotland was the notable absence within Scottish health publications of allusions to immigration. This reflected the absence in Scotland of 'coloured, West Indian immigrants' who were viewed south of the Border as major vectors of disease, especially gonorrhoea.[31] Yet, although it lacked the racial imagery of sexual politics in London and the industrial cities of the Midlands and north of England, the discussion of VD/STDs in Scotland was not entirely free of racial prejudice. During the immediate post-war decades, public health reports sustained the long tradition of stigmatising 'foreign infections'. Thus, in the 1950s, Edinburgh's VD Department attributed the survival of syphilis in the city largely to the importation of infection from countries 'where Mars, Bacchus and Venus [were] still a formidable trio'.[32] Moreover, there were powerful xenophobic, if not racial, overtones in the condemnation by Scottish venereologists of the impact on the sexual mores of the younger generation of 'the worst type of American and negro films, booklets, music and dancing'.[33] They surfaced also in several diplomatic incidents when local clinicians and politicians publicly linked the spread of casual prostitution and VD to the presence of American servicemen at the Polaris base at Holy Loch and at airbases in

Midlothian.[34] The blame attached by some commentators to the 'hospitality schemes' of American oil multinationals in north-east Scotland and to the sexual behaviour of Irish navvies employed on platform construction sites such as Ardyne during the oil boom of the 1970s had similar connotations.[35]

The social politics surrounding VD/STDs in Scotland between the Second World War and the onset of HIV/AIDS continued to be shaped by a powerful set of moral fears, assumptions and stereotypes. Gradually there was, as in other countries, a shift in emphasis from diseased 'types' to patterns of individual sexual behaviour and their associated risk, but it was only a partial shift. Traditional patterns of scapegoating persisted within contemporary sociological analyses of public health and the 'permissive society', and in some areas of Scotland, long-entrenched church attitudes and admonitions on sexual issues remained highly influential. These powerful strands of continuity were duly reflected in the shaping of sexual health policy.

THE FRAMING AND IMPLEMENTATION OF POLICY

Compulsory notification and treatment

The issue of legal controls for regulating sexual contacts and those defaulting from treatment, which Scottish health authorities had campaigned for since 1918,[36] continued to surface in the late 1940s and early 1950s, with active support from the Scottish Council for Health Education (SCHE).[37] In the 1960s, prompted by the rising incidence of gonorrhoea and non-specific STDs, the debate was reopened in the *Lancet* and in the House of Commons.[38] As late as 1968, Sir Myer Galpern, MP for Glasgow Shettleston, sought to introduce a bill 'to provide for the compulsory examination and treatment of persons suspected of suffering from venereal diseases'.[39]

During the debate on the Bill particular attention was drawn to the variety of VD controls operating in other European and Commonwealth countries.[40] In post-war Sweden, the transmission of VD or sexual behaviour likely to expose others to a venereal infection was an offence, and treatment was compulsory for all patients. In Italy, all contagious cases of VD were notifiable. In France, persons suspected of communicating VD were compelled by health authorities to undergo medical examination. In New Zealand, those infected were by law required to undergo treatment, while in Canada, it was the duty of medical practitioners to notify VD cases and to secure their isolation and appropriate treatment if contagious.

However, in line with the Ministry of Health, the DHS remained opposed to new legislation. In their view, the traditional arguments against legal controls still held good. They considered that the operation of VD controls under Defence Regulation 33B during the Second World War had not demonstrated the value of compulsion and that the reintroduction of similar powers would merely undermine the confidence of patients and contacts in existing voluntary treatment and tracing procedures. It was feared that patients, especially homosexual patients already in fear of the law, would be deterred from obtaining prompt and professional treatment. Concern was also expressed that it would revive an informer system with the danger of blackmail and with 'totalitarian' implications that were inimical to civil liberties, especially those of young women.[41] Moreover, there was a growing belief in official circles that compulsory measures would prove inoperable in a society where casual sex was increasingly prevalent and a target group of culpable vectors no longer so clearly identifiable.[42]

Yet, significant strands of socio-medical control did persist in postwar Scottish VD administration. During the 1950s, Scottish venereologists campaigned for comprehensive screening for VD on lines analogous to contemporary mass radiography for TB. They argued that the application of penicillin to a wide variety of non-syphilitic conditions had masked significant pools of hidden infection and that routine serological testing should be undertaken of hospital in-patients and out-patients, of candidates for insurance and of personnel demobilised from the armed services.[43] As in England,[44] such proposals encountered opposition on the grounds that they would infringe civil liberties and the medical confidentiality so central to public confidence in any VD service.

At the same time, there were particular groups of female vectors within Scottish society whom venereologists and health officials sought to regulate in the interests of public health: namely infected pregnant women, convicted prostitutes and so-called 'moral delinquents'. In order to combat the stubborn persistence of congenital syphilis in the community, the major Scottish health authorities had all introduced routine antenatal VD testing by the 1960s, with long-term surveillance of women found to be infected.[45] In addition, there is evidence that, in Edinburgh at least, with the encouragement of epidemiologists, wider screening and prevalence testing were undertaken from the late 1950s employing information from the Blood Transfusion Service, a procedure rejected in England.

There was also a continuing anxiety to ensure that prostitutes submitted to adequate treatment. Dr R. C. L. Batchelor had considerable sympathy with the prophylactoria of inter-war Russia in which prostitutes were institutionalised for treatment and moral rehabilitation.[46] Along with other clinicians whose ideology was shaped by pre-war eugenics and the social hygiene movement, he continued to identify promiscuity and prostitution with mental deficiency and to advocate the notification and confinement of 'moral defectives' for the purposes of reducing the reservoir of infection within the community.[47] His successor as Physician-in-Charge of Edinburgh's VD services, Robert Lees, who was an influential policy adviser, also advocated a more vigorous policy towards prostitution in the interests of social hygiene, observing that, if only the problem was 'tackled as a public health problem and every painted street-corner wench [was] recognised as a carrier of disease rather than an unfortunate victim of society, then the "racket" [could] be broken'.[48]

In fact, it was already common practice in Scotland for 'habitual prostitutes' appearing before the courts to be remanded in custody for medical examination under Section 26 of the 1949 Criminal Justice (Scotland) Act. Although Scottish law officers subsequently ruled that such powers had been intended as an aid to sentencing and not infectious disease prevention, and could not be used purely as a public health measure, in some Scottish cities all women convicted of prostitution continued to be referred to the VD clinics irrespective of whether or not they had any symptoms.[49] However, as the focus of debate surrounding VD/STDs shifted in the 1960s and 1970s from prostitution to the effects of greater sexual permissiveness within society, calls for the closer regulation of prostitution on public health grounds (as distinct from concerns over public order and morality) became less strident.

Meanwhile, the regulation of the sexual behaviour of so-called 'problem girls' that had so exercised health officials and clinicians in inter-war Scotland remained an integral part of VD/STD administration. Prior to the 1970s, girls (but not boys) committed to remand homes and approved schools under the Children and Young Persons (Scotland) Act of 1937 were routinely examined for venereal infections on their first admission and on any readmission after absconding or after returning from a holiday or home visit.[50] Whereas young persons of either sex might be brought to the juvenile courts for suspected promiscuity, in practice it was girls 'deemed to be promiscuous' or 'exposed to moral danger' who were targeted and referred to the clinics.[51] In the late 1960s, some 56 per cent of female patients under 18 years of age attending the Edinburgh clinic were referred by approved schools and remand homes, and about 9 per cent of the work of the clinic was devoted to ensuring 'that adolescent girls committed to custodial institutions [were] free from sexually transmitted infections'.[52] While physical compulsion was never contemplated, formal permission was rarely sought from the girls for vaginal examinations as they were perceived as 'rebellious and uncooperative' and 'impervious to argument' as to the medical risks of their sexual behaviour.[53]

However, by the late 1960s, there was growing unease amongst Scottish venereologists; first, that it was 'possible for a group of girls to be continuously segregated because of sexual behaviour which [was] not in itself punishable in other persons', and second, that medical expertise was being deployed as part of coercive procedures of social work departments designed to control juvenile promiscuity.[54] The recommendation of the Latey Committee on the Age of Majority that the age of consent for medical treatment should be lowered to 16, coupled with the introduction of Children's Panels under the Social Work (Scotland) Act 1968, altered the situation. Girls might still be subject to supervision orders and residential care for moral offences and sexual promiscuity but the VD services were no longer an integral part of such procedures.[55] For the most part, therefore, post-war Scottish VD administration did not rely on compulsion but on the traditional strategies of voluntary medical treatment and health education, together with a developing system of contact tracing.

The funding of VD/STD treatment services

While the specific content of treatment for VD/STDs in Scotland after 1950 was largely determined by medical authorities, its availability and delivery were heavily influenced by policy decisions within the Scottish Office relating to the funding and status of sexual health as a specialty. The first circular issued to regional hospital boards on the development of specialist services under the National Health Service (Scotland) Act of 1947 had stipulated that 'the diagnosis and treatment of venereal diseases constitute[d] a separate clinical specialty and should not be left to become a minor interest of specialists in other fields'.[56] However, from the start, in part as a result of dramatic changes in the treatment of VD associated with the introduction and refinement of penicillin therapies,[57] the boards failed to recognise the specialist status of venereology in their staffing of VD clinics.

As the reported incidence of VD declined in the 1950s, and the moral panic over wartime sexual behaviour dissipated, venereology was, as in the inter-war period, relegated to 'Cinderella' status among the specialist health services. Venereologists continued to lack influence on the advisory committees shaping Scottish and regional health policies and resource allocations. Whereas in England and Wales, a Special Adviser in VD represented the interests of the specialty within the Ministry of Health, no such post existed at the DHS/SHHD, where issues relating to VD were administered as part of a wider remit by the Infectious Diseases Unit.

The low status and priority accorded to the specialty by the regional hospital boards mainly stemmed from the view of medical administrators that VD no longer presented a serious health problem, given the lack of any dramatic upswing in Scottish VD rates, and the common belief that new forms of chemotherapy, often within the competence of general practitioners, rendered a large specialist clinical establishment redundant.[58] This was a view shared by many officials within the DHS. R. J. Peters, Deputy Chief Medical Officer, agreed with the view of the Ministry of Health in 1958 that 'there was no longer the same justification for VD specialists and that the number of consultants required would decline'.[59] In 1960, W. D. Hood, Principal Medical Officer, questioned whether health authorities would 'ever deliberately try to raise another crop of specialists in the treatment of VD'.[60] Similarly, in 1964, I. M. Macgregor, Senior Medical Officer in the newly constituted Scottish Home and Health Department, opposed the recommendation of the BMA report entitled *VD and Young People* that the staffing and resources of venereology should be substantially upgraded. 'I would not,' he minuted, 'encourage any young doctor to take up this work as the report suggests – it is not a field which could give very much satisfaction to any physician except as a part-time interest.'[61]

As a result, Scottish venereology became chronically under-resourced in the 1950s and early 1960s. As in England and Wales, there was little, if any, increase in the number of consultants despite a steady rise in the workload of the clinics. Increasingly, senior posts were left unfilled, and VD sessions farmed out on a part-time basis to non-specialists and general practitioners. The problem of staffing was further compounded by the lack of adequate training provisions for venereology. As VD slipped down the agenda of Scottish health politics in the 1950s, it was increasingly marginalised within both undergraduate and postgraduate medical curricula and, outwith

Edinburgh, the exposure of students to lectures and clinical training in sexual health issues was meagre and inadequate.[62]

Working conditions represented an added constraint upon recruitment to the specialty in the 1950s and 1960s. Many of the Scottish VD clinics dated back to the early 'cloak and dagger days of VD' in the 1920s, 'when people slunk in basement bolt-holes to get the unspeakable disease dealt with'.[63] Their location and facilities generated an aura of moral censure. Although the BMA's 1964 report, *VD and Young People*, stressed the urgent need for the modernisation of VD clinics in order to improve professional morale and to create a less stigmatic ambience for patients, little progress was achieved. Given the prevailing budgetary constraints facing health authorities and their already hard-pressed building programmes, the SHHD was unwilling to put pressure on regional hospital boards to reallocate their resources.[64]

However, by 1970, there was a growing crisis of public confidence, widely articulated in the national press, in the ability of the VD services to cope with the rising incidence of VD and in particular the 'newer generation' of sexually transmitted diseases.[65] Clinical workloads were rising dramatically, especially as an increasing amount of time had to be spent on patients with non-specific infections. At the same time, the laboratory service was compromised by a lack of funding, seriously limiting the range and frequency of serological testing. The pressure of events was making the comparatively laissez-faire stance of the SHHD towards VD policy increasingly difficult to sustain. The media campaign surrounding VD, coupled with the upward convergence of Scottish VD trends with those south of the Border, precipitated a renewed demand for a fresh appraisal of VD services and procedures in Scotland. As a result, a Joint Sub-Committee on Sexually Transmitted Diseases (the Gilloran Committee) was appointed in 1971 to advise on a wide range of issues relating to the epidemiology, treatment and control of VD in Scotland.

In its subsequent report in 1973, the Committee recommended 'the expansion of all services concerned with the management of sexually transmitted diseases'. It considered that the specialist establishment was inadequate to provide a comprehensive venereology service in Scotland. In the light of the dramatic upswing in the incidence of sexually transmitted diseases in Scotland since 1965, it identified an urgent need 'for a new consultant establishment to be defined' to supervise the 'special clinics'. The Gilloran Committee also made wide-ranging proposals with regard to staff training. It recommended that instruction in sexual problems and STDs should be provided for all medical undergraduates. In addition to postgraduate courses in STDs for all general practitioners, especially those undertaking sessional work in the clinics, it stressed the urgent need for improved training for nurses and contact tracers. An upgrading of the equipment, premises and diagnostic facilities of the STD clinics was also recommended.[66]

The Gilloran Report, coming as it did in the middle of a period of severe financial restraint and a major reorganisation of the National Health Service, received a dismissive response from the new area health boards. They were neither prepared to commit new resources to the STD services nor to reallocate their existing health budgets. While they acknowledged that a shortage of specialists existed, they remained unconvinced of the case for comprehensive consultant cover. Moreover, given the continuing need for public expenditure cuts, the SHHD was not prepared to issue directives on the issue.[67] Despite public concern at the rising incidence of STDs, and determined lobbying by Scottish venereologists, senior advisers within the SHHD continued to question the need for STD work to be staffed as a separate specialty, and to accord it low priority in the allocation of NHS resources.[68]

Health education

Meanwhile, in the immediate aftermath of the Second World War, the rising incidence of VD occasioned by demobilisation had led to a renewed propaganda campaign. Under the aegis of the SCHE, health authorities launched a series of press and poster campaigns in the late 1940s, supplemented with public film shows and exhibitions devoted to social hygiene and VD.[69] In addition, a cluster of new posters was issued by the DHS and the SCHE from 1950 to 1953 that stressed the disastrous effects of untreated VD on fertility, parenthood and family life, and the importance of early treatment.

The VD posters and literature distributed in the late 1940s and 1950s continued to enshrine many of the assumptions and stereotypes that had shaped inter-war propaganda. There was a less overt moralistic tone to VD posters, but a continuing stress on VD as a racial pollutant, a disease undermining the virtue and efficiency of the nation and the mental and physical health of future generations.[70] Likewise, VD continued to be identified in propaganda materials with dysfunctional extramarital sex in which moral and physical degeneracy was intimately related. As before, infidelity and infection were conflated, with syphilis and gonorrhoea the 'homebreakers, bringing suspicion and danger to family life'.[71]

Moreover, the language of VD propaganda still remained strongly gendered, representing young women as the primary protectors/ destroyers of the moral health and efficiency of the nation. Thus, central to the plot of *The People at No. 19*, which was frequently screened in Scotland, was the infidelity of a young wife leading to syphilitic infection. Even the natural sexual attraction of a chaste girl had the 'power' to pollute, for, according to the SCHE:

> She should remember that a man whose desires have been excited without being satisfied may be driven to that type of woman who merely gratifies the man's physical sex hunger which has been so unfairly aroused [and who] too often give him venereal disease.[72]

Similarly, again echoing inter-war representations, while male VD was depicted as a 'shadow on health', female VD was a 'shadow on happiness', a lasting degradation of social reputation and domestic fulfilment with wide-ranging moral overtones.[73]

Although less acute than in England, the rising incidence of gonorrhoea in Scotland in the late 1950s prompted fresh initiatives in the field of social hygiene education. A DHS Circular in 1960 urged local health authorities to review their publicity arrangements and to 'intensify their efforts'.[74] In addition, new posters were produced for the department. The SCHE also upgraded its materials on VD and sexual relationships, and films relating to VD rose from under 5 per cent to 15 per cent of its public screenings by 1968. Posters and leaflets continued to stress the importance of early treatment where 'a sexual risk' had been taken. Although their tone was less censorious and intimidating than that of earlier VD propaganda, they continued to imply a model of infection that located blame within the female body. Thus, a leaflet issued in 1962 warned that the 'sexual adventurer' was:

> sooner or later . . . bound to come into contact with the infectious, and so runs a continuing risk. Many a man has said: 'But she was a clean girl!'. Such a belief is worthless, since a girl may be perfectly clean in the ordinary sense of the word and yet have in her body millions of the invisible germs of gonorrhoea or syphilis, or perhaps both.[75]

Meanwhile, local initiatives were also being undertaken. In Edinburgh, Robert Lees persuaded the Public Health Committee to introduce a new propaganda campaign to counter the widespread ignorance of 'doctors, nurses and laymen' surrounding VD, and the prevailing belief that gonorrhoea was 'a trivial infection easily cured'.[76] In particular, he advocated a new set of VD notices targeted at public houses, dance halls and washrooms.[77] In addition, in response to the recommendations of the Cohen Committee on Health Education in 1964 that more priority be given to education in human relationships, including sex education, other Scottish cities introduced a range of courses incorporating sexual health issues.[78]

Despite such initiatives, only limited progress in raising public awareness of VD and in affecting patterns of sexual behaviour appears to have been achieved. The issue of VD became increasingly overshadowed in local health education programmes by other issues such as mass radiography for TB, polio immunisation and air pollution and was starved of funding. In addition, there was resistance from publicans and ballroom owners to displaying literature and posters relating to VD, on the grounds that it was offensive to their clientele and would attract obscene graffiti. As a result, both spatially and symbolically, VD continued to be 'thought of and dealt with' mainly 'on a lavatorial level'.[79]

However, in the late 1960s, rising public concern with sexual promiscuity and sexually related diseases led Scottish health administrators to adopt a more proactive stance. The Scottish Health Education Unit (SHEU), established in 1968, issued a new set of posters and information leaflets focusing on the dangers of casual sex and targeted at the venues of youth culture.[80] The main poster depicted youngsters in a dance hall setting with the wording: 'It's the first time they've met, but any casual sex encounter is a risk'. Significantly, it was the first time that the word 'sex' had appeared in VD posters in Scotland. It reflected the shift in epidemiology from a preoccupation with a few critical vector groups, such as prostitutes, radiating disease, to the endless chain of infection created by the casual sex of a promiscuous generation.

The central message of the new materials was that 'people who [were] too easy [were] too dangerous' because of their previous sexual contacts. There was more gender symmetry in their wording. However, the posters still depicted the female contact in red, the traditional colour coding for pollution and moral danger employed in VD propaganda since the 1920s. Moreover, the hidden threat of vaginal infection was still deployed to pathologise female sexuality. Thus, a poster designed for male lavatories in public houses read:

Sex – and her. Is she easy? – Then she's dangerous. Women often don't know when they have VD – but they can give it to you during intimacy. You don't know who she was with last.[81]

There were also fresh local initiatives in the late 1960s and early 1970s. For example, Edinburgh and Glasgow facilitated greater public access to information on sexual health issues, including a telephone advice line. Meanwhile, a shift in public awareness of the health hazards of VD/STDs elicited a more receptive response to the display of publicity materials. Public lavatories remained the main venue for posters but increasingly they were also displayed in dance halls, libraries, colleges, hostels, public houses and voluntary welfare agencies, as well as on municipal information boards and vehicles (although predictably only those of the cleansing department).[82]

Nonetheless, although health education was viewed by many health administrators as the best hope of halting the increase in STDs, its funding was constrained and its content open to criticism. Health education budgets were under intense pressure in a period of public expenditure cuts and the SHHD was reluctant to put pressure on the Scottish area health boards to expand their education provisions. For much of the 1970s, VD/STDs were not accorded high priority by the SHEU in comparison with issues such as smoking, alcoholism, immunisation and family planning.[83]

Meanwhile, health education materials were increasingly criticised as inappropriate and ineffective. Evidence suggested that posters and leaflets had a limited success in educating the general public, and that the main points of referral to the clinics continued to be general practitioners and friends, and, in the case of women, contact tracing.[84] It was claimed that much of the material was unsuitable for social groups who were often semi-illiterate and resistant to health messages that were frequently 'coded' both to avoid public offence and to secure ministerial approval.[85]

Resistance may also have been due to the moral conservatism that continued to inform VD posters and information leaflets in post-war Scotland. As in the inter-war period, moral issues and taxonomies significantly shaped post-war VD literature, with its concern for the social costs of casual sex, and endorsed a highly normative view of sexuality and sexual behaviour. Thus, the information leaflets of the 1970s focused as much on social behaviour as on medical symptoms, with the key vectors identified as those who 'had intercourse without the *normal* courtship'.[86] Concepts of 'virtue', 'vice' and 'deviance' still figured prominently in the warnings that venereologists sought to convey in public health reports.[87] As Weeks has noted: 'Even the most liberal texts tended to endorse a "stages" view of sexual development, which was either to be happily resolved in heterosexual monogamy or unhappily resolved in sadness and isolation.'[88] This ideology was very much at the heart of the operational philosophy of the Scottish Education Department (SED) and SHHD in their handling of health education,[89] as was the view that, despite the more 'permissive' social trends of the 1960s, 'safe' female sexual activity remained primarily a procreational duty rather than a recreational pleasure.

Meanwhile, health education materials did little to dispel the ignorance and stigma that continued to surround the role of homosexual behaviour in the spread of STDs. SHEU circulars were clearly worded for an exclusively heterosexual audience. From the mid-1970s, Scottish venereologists made increasing efforts to publicise the risks of casual gay sex in liaison with the SMG, but it is significant that, when writing or lecturing on the subject, they often felt compelled to use a pseudonym for fear of attracting adverse publicity or offending the medical establishment.[90]

Perhaps the most revealing testimony to the lasting moral agenda underpinning later twentieth-century VD health education in Scotland was the absence of any reference to the use of condoms for protective purposes. In the late 1940s and 1950s, in accord with the views of the Scottish churches and many local authority venereologists, the DHS believed that state-sponsored prophylactic measures beyond the conventional appeal to moral restraint would prove highly contentious, and would be seen to legitimise 'irregular' sex and promote immorality.[91] The Department did reconsider the issue of contraceptive advice in its VD publicity in the early 1960s, but decided that such an initiative would provoke widespread opposition and might render health education even more of a sectarian issue in the West of Scotland. Some officials doubted the protective value of sheaths and concurred with the Ministry of Health's view that physical barriers to infection or inunction with chemicals before or after intercourse, through misuse or for other reasons, had not proved to be reliable safeguards.[92] Others, such as I. N. Sutherland, Head of the Infectious Diseases Section, were adamant that the use of mechanical contraceptives would 'in general reduce the risk of acquiring VD'. However, he felt compelled to warn the Chief Medical Officer that: 'Objections to publicising such information have in the past been based on the supposition that Health Departments must not "encourage promiscuity" and I shall be surprised if these objections do not still hold.'[93]

They did indeed, and were to become increasingly strident as the whole issue of contraceptive advice and facilities for single girls and women moved to the forefront of Scottish civic debate in the early 1970s.[94] As a result, health education continued to rely on moral prophylaxis in its approach to STDs. The concept of 'safe sex' as articulated in official posters and literature remained firmly associated with concepts of courtship and marriage and sexual fidelity rather than with the use of 'precautions'. As many clinicians and health administrators increasingly recognised, given this ideology of prevention and the evident shift in the pattern of sexual behaviour within British society, there were severe limits to the degree to which health education might contain the rising incidence of STDs. Any real success in disease control would have also to depend on tracing the chain of infection and identifying infected contacts for treatment.

Contact tracing

A limited system of contact tracing had been introduced during the inter-war period and subsequently expanded during the Second World War with emergency powers under Defence Regulation 33B.[95] However, until the 1960s, little further progress was made. During the 1950s, tracing was primarily restricted to female contacts identified by the armed forces or by police or child welfare authorities. It was conducted in a very *ad hoc* and uncoordinated fashion and, during the period 1948–60, only about 10 per cent of the contacts of men diagnosed with acute VD in the major cities were followed up.[96]

A range of constraints operated upon contact-tracing provisions. Concern over the legal status of contact tracing under Scots law continued to inhibit the VD policy of the DHS and SHHD. Law officers advised that existing legislation would not protect health authorities from action for damages under Scots law for slander or for 'injury done to feelings', should information be divulged for the purposes of contact tracing. As a result, while senior officials advised VD medical officers in confidence that 'contact tracing should be conducted as vigorously as ever', they felt unable to issue formal guidelines analogous to those of the Ministry of Health in England and Wales.[97]

In addition, the division of responsibilities for VD under the National Health Service (Scotland) Act 1947, with diagnosis and treatment the responsibility of the regional hospital boards and issues of epidemiology and prevention remaining within the remit of the local authority health departments, served to disrupt existing contact-tracing services. For their part, not only did the regional hospital boards accord venereology low status as a specialty, they also took the view that the availability of fast-acting antibiotics had reduced the urgency for 'follow up' procedures.[98] Many health administrators continued to adopt a 'Calvinistic' attitude towards those infected with VD and considered the issue of venereal infection control to be the responsibility of local health authorities. The latter were keen to upgrade contact tracing but were concerned at the ability of their tracers to obtain medical information from hospital authorities and at the lack of legal protection for their activities.[99]

Despite continuing legal concerns, by late 1959 senior medical advisers within Scottish government were conceding the need for a Scottish circular. Faced by new publicity releases from the Ministry of Health, several television exposés of the worsening problem of gonorrhoea and mounting pressure from Scottish venereologists, the DHS felt compelled to act. Officials were also concerned that, unless they took the initiative, the SCHE and Scottish local authority associations might revive their inter-war campaign for the compulsory notification and treatment of VD. Accordingly, after further protracted discussions with medical officers of health, with the hospital boards and with its legal advisers, the Department eventually issued a circular to health authorities in September 1960.[100]

Compared with its English counterpart, the Scottish circular was extremely tentative. Priority was given to vague exhortations to local health authorities to 'intensify their efforts' to reduce the incidence of VD and to upgrade their publicity arrangements. Reference to contact tracing was limited to stressing the value of gaining information from patients as to the likely source of their infection. The more advanced tracing procedures being implemented in the major urban centres of Scotland were neither mentioned nor endorsed.

This rather reactive approach of Scottish departments continued for the remainder of the 1960s. The SHHD responded cautiously to the stress placed by the Standing Medical Advisory Committee for England and Wales upon an efficient system of contract tracing as the vital control strategy for VD in its 1962 report. It had particular reservations about the use of official circulars to expound matters of clinical care and treatment to the medical profession.[101] Similarly, given the low priority accorded to the VD services by the regional hospital boards and their assurances that VD provisions were adequate, the

SHHD was also reluctant to endorse the recommendation of the BMA report *VD and Young People* that contact tracing should be allocated increased resources.[102]

In the latter half of the 1960s the Department came under renewed pressure to review Scottish contact-tracing policy. In 1965, a Scottish Medical Advisory Committee working party on the incidence, epidemiology and control of gonorrhoea in Scotland urged the need for more intensive contact tracing by social workers, especially among younger age groups. According to its report, contact tracing was not being pursued systematically in Scotland outside Edinburgh and Glasgow, because of a lack of resources, poor liaison between medical social workers and the VD clinics, and the failure of regional hospital boards to make full use of local authority health visitors.[103] In addition, in 1968, the Ministry of Health issued fresh regulations and guidelines designed to facilitate contact tracing by extending statutory protection for the disclosure of information in the further-ance of the prevention of the spread of VD. Local health authorities and hospital boards were exhorted to improve their tracing procedures and facilities as a means of 'breaking the chain of infection', and provided with a set of detailed guidelines on interviewing patients, identifying and locating contacts, and monitoring success rates, along with a summary of the legal issues involved.[104]

The SHHD remained resistant to following the example of the Ministry of Health. In the light of the more favourable VD figures for Scotland, repeated assurances from the hospital boards as to the adequacy of existing clinical arrangements and continuing doubts as to the wisdom of openly promoting procedures vulnerable to action for damages under Scots law, its medical officers remained of the view that no new regulations should be issued in Scotland.[105] However, despite this reluctance on the part of the Scottish Office to issue directives, local initiatives *were* undertaken within the major Scottish cities during the 1960s, primarily in response to the rising incidence of gonorrhoea in women and teenage girls. More systematic interroga-tion of infected patients was instituted and additional staff dedicated to contact tracing. The focus of 'social work' in the clinics shifted from the traditional preoccupation with 'defaulters' to tracking down the 'hidden pool of infection within the community'.[106] This continued to be represented as primarily a female phenomenon and particular attention was paid to identifying the 'inmates' of the more notorious brothels and to tracing prostitutes operating in the docks.[107] As a result, by 1970 nearly 50 per cent of primary contacts named in male

VD clinics in Edinburgh and Glasgow were being traced and over 40 per cent of all first-time female patients attended clinics in response to contact tracing, as compared with 16 per cent in 1951.[108]

Yet such advances continued to be frustrated until the early 1980s by an enduring lack of funding and staff resources, reflecting the broader struggle of venereology to maintain its professional identity and status as a specialty within the Scottish health services. The report of the Gilloran Committee in 1973 stressed the importance of improved contact tracing in controlling the spread of STDs and, in particular, in securing medical treatment for the 'promiscuous females' and 'passive homosexuals' who, it argued, constituted the major 'reservoirs of infection'. It noted the lack of uniformity within Scotland in contact-tracing facilities and procedures, and recommended as a matter of urgency that adequate provisions and standardised procedures should be available at all special clinics and that appropriate recruitment and in-service training be introduced, along with a proper career structure for contact tracers.[109]

In response, the SHHD eventually issued a guidance booklet on VD in 1975 that stressed the importance of contact tracing, and some form of practical training for contact tracers was gradually introduced, but the SHHD remained opposed to issuing any major directive to health authorities.[110] Quite apart from continuing concerns over the legal issues associated with tracing in Scotland, its officials were preoccupied with the reorganisation of the health services and reluctant to sanction additional resources in a period of severe financial restraint.[111] As a result, although the SHHD conducted a more focused review of contact-tracing facilities in the mid-1980s, as Scotland entered the era of HIV and AIDS, provisions for contact tracing remained extremely variable and chronically under-resourced.

CONCLUSION

The history of sexual health policy making in Scotland during the period 1950–80 is as much a story of moral regulation as it is of public health. Public and professional attitudes towards sexually acquired diseases continued to be influenced by broader concerns to regulate sexual behaviour and public morality. Despite the impact of new chemotherapies and sociological insights, debate over VD and STDs was still informed, and indeed triggered, as much by anxieties over the erosion of community and family values as by the medical dimensions of the problem, and taxonomies of guilt and moral culpability continued to circumscribe the social response to such diseases.

To some extent, there was a 'democratisation' of the discourses shaping policy towards VD and STDs in post-war Scotland. The association of class, 'wantonness' and unhygienic sexual behaviour that had characterised inter-war debate largely disappeared from the rhetoric of public health reports and health education literature, partly in response to the broadening social distribution of patients attending the special clinics. However, in Scotland, as in many other countries, the process of moral regulation, in which VD had played such a central role, continued to be heavily gendered. As previously, while legitimate medical arguments might be advanced for viewing women as 'reservoirs' of infection, it was also very much a social construction built upon long-standing cultural beliefs of 'woman as polluter'. Although, after the 1950s, the social epidemiology of VD shifted, at least in part, from the rhetoric of 'prostitution' to 'promiscuity' and 'high-risk behaviour' and the concept of a few core vectors was succeeded by that of a chain or network of infection, female sexuality and sexual behaviour remained the focus of public concern over the incidence of VD and STDs. New theories of sexual delinquency merely added a patina of scientific respectability to traditional fears identifying female sexual 'precocity' with pollution. Thus, despite 'the permissive movement', the processes by which medical, sociological and legal discourses surrounding VD in late nineteenth- and early twentieth-century society had criminalised and pathologised sexually active single women clearly remained operative, albeit in more coded forms.

Another clear strand of continuity lay in the determination of post-war health educationalists and VD administrators to regulate the sexual urges of the young. Throughout the early twentieth century, public health debate surrounding VD had been informed by acute concern at the apparent breakdown of family and community controls upon the sexual behaviour of adolescents. Shifts in the lifestyle of juveniles, occasioned by changes in income and consumption patterns and by the onset of new forms of leisure and entertainment, were perceived as a threat to the rational, sober, responsible sexuality expressed within marriage that was necessary for social stability and racial health. Again in the 1960s and 1970s, contemporary debate over VD policy was used to articulate such anxieties and VD figures were widely presented as part of a wider 'social pathology' of youth culture. Although, as Weeks has argued, this was not just a simple resurrection of old themes and a new moral authoritarianism had emerged by the late 1970s,[112] there remained a substantial legacy from the socio-medical discourses that had for so long surrounded VD.

In addition, many of the logistical and ideological constraints upon VD control strategies prior to the Second World War continued to operate. As for much of the inter-war period, the VD services in post-war Scotland were marginalised both in health politics and within the medical profession itself. The enduring problem of resourcing control strategies such as health education and contact tracing reflected this ongoing struggle of venereology to maintain its professional identity and status as a specialty within the Scottish health services. However, the slow and often erratic development of control procedures in late twentieth-century Scotland was also a function of broader ideological concern over medico-legal issues of personal liberty, confidentiality and the inquisitorial role of the state in protecting public health. Once again, even within the sexual politics of the so-called 'permissive society', the terms of the debate had shifted very little. They remained anchored within a traditional dialogue between libertarianism and public health imperatives over the governance of dangerous sexualities.

Notes

1 Davidson and Hall (eds), *Sex, Sin and Suffering*, 1–14.
2 DHS/SHHD, *Scottish Health Statistics, 1950–80*.
3 See, for example, SHHD, *Report on Health and Welfare Services in Scotland* (hereafter *RHWSS*), PP, 1962–3 (Cmnd 1996) XIX, 14; PP, 1968–9 (Cmnd 4012) 63, 9.
4 Davidson, *Dangerous Liaisons*, 239.
5 See, for example, Schofield, *Sexually Transmitted Diseases*, second edition, 39.
6 Haste, *Rules of Desire*, 143.
7 See, for example, *Edinburgh Public Health Department* (hereafter *EPHD*) *Annual Report for 1958*, 196.
8 GACS, *Report of Committee on Temperance and Morals for 1960*, 419–20.
9 *EPHD Annual Report for 1957*, 152; Davidson, *Dangerous Liaisons*, 246.
10 Davidson, *Dangerous Liaisons*, 247.
11 See, for example, NRS, HH58/66, DHS memorandum on venereal disease, 1961.
12 See, for example, *Glasgow Herald*, 3 October 1972.
13 *Report of Joint Sub-Committee on Sexually Transmitted Diseases*, 14.
14 *The Scotsman*, 28 April 1976.
15 See, for example, *EPHD Annual Report for 1959*, 142–3; Schofield, *Sexually Transmitted Diseases*, third edition, 35–7.
16 *EPHD Annual Report for 1956*, 157; *1962*, 156.

17 See, for example, *Glasgow Herald*, 15 May 1971.
18 See, for example, *Edinburgh Health and Social Services Department* (hereafter *EHSSD*) *Annual Report for 1969*, 71.
19 *EPHD Annual Reports for 1958–65*.
20 See, for example, *EHSSD Annual Report for 1968*, 66–7; *1969*, 71.
21 Schofield, *Sexually Transmitted Diseases*, second edition, 43–4.
22 Ibid., 44–6.
23 SHHD, *RHWSS*, PP, 1970–71 (Cmnd 4392), 38, 9.
24 GAFCS, *Report of Committee on Public Questions, Religion and Morals for 1974*, 146.
25 Ibid., *1975*, 155.
26 See, for example, GACS, *Report of Social and Moral Welfare Board for 1968*, 491–2; *1969*, 503–8; *Glasgow Herald*, 14 April 1971, 13 May 1971.
27 *Glasgow Herald*, 3 and 10 February 1971, 15 May 1971, 28 September 1971.
28 Mooij, *Out of Otherness*, 181–3, 185–8.
29 See, for example, *EPHD Annual Report for 1961*, 144.
30 *Report of Joint Sub-Committee on Sexually Transmitted Diseases*, 2.
31 Schofield and McNeil, 'Venereal disease in Scotland', 20.
32 *EPHD Annual Report for 1952*, 99.
33 *EPHD Annual Report for 1959*, 142–3.
34 NRS, HH58/66, Memorandum by I. N. Sutherland, 31 October 1960; HH104/35, papers relating to parliamentary questions, 17 July 1963; Giarchi, *Between McAlpine and Polaris*, 188–92.
35 *Glasgow Herald*, 6 June 1975; Giarchi, *Between McAlpine and Polaris*, 209.
36 Davidson, *Dangerous Liaisons*, chs 8–9.
37 The Scottish Council for Health Education (hereafter SCHE) had been established in 1942, inheriting much of the agenda, personnel and mindset of the former Scottish Committee of the British Social Hygiene Council.
38 *Lancet*, vol. II (1966), 1,289; vol. I (1967), 159, 221, 328–9, 384, 510; *Hansard [HC]*, vol. 662, 3 July 1962, cols 291–4; vol. 679, 28 June 1963, cols 1,920–36.
39 *Hansard [HC]*, vol. 774, 27 November 1968, col. 511; vol. 780, 21 March 1969, cols 944–76.
40 Ibid., vol. 780, 21 March 1969, col. 950.
41 NRS, HH58/66/93, DHS memorandum on control of venereal diseases: compulsory examination and treatment, 20 June 1962.
42 Davidson, *Dangerous Liaisons*, 274.
43 See, for example, *EHPD Annual Report for 1956*, 155; *1957*, 153.
44 Towers, 'Politics and policy', 55–73.
45 See, for example, *Annual Report of Medical Officer of Health* (hereafter

MOH) *for Aberdeen, 1959*, 5; *EPHD Annual Report for 1957*, 153; *Annual Report of Medical Officer of Health for Glasgow, 1958*, 164.

46 R. C. L. Batchelor papers, 'Changing concepts and changing patterns in venereology', 21 October 1963.

47 Batchelor and Murrell, *Venereal Diseases*, 196, 202–3.

48 Lees, 'VD – some random reflections', 160.

49 NRS, HH57/568, 'Treatment of venereal diseases in prison: general questions', minutes by Dr I. D. Inch, 10 January and 18 April 1961.

50 *EPHD Annual Report for 1961*, 143; *1964*, 99; Robertson and George, 'Medical and legal problems', II, 46–51.

51 Robertson, 'Medical and legal problems', I, 135.

52 Hunter and Neilson, 'Sexually transmitted diseases in Edinburgh', 24; *EHSSD Annual Report for 1968*, 69.

53 Medical Society for the Study of Venereal Diseases Scottish Branch, correspondence and papers.

54 Robertson, 'Medical and legal problems', 135–6.

55 Ibid., 132–5.

56 NRS, HH48/65/7, DHS circulars, 1947.

57 For a survey of these changes, see Davidson, *Dangerous Liaisons*, 277–82.

58 See especially NRS, HH65/128/9, Minutes of Senior Administrative Medical Officers Committee (SAMOC), 20 March 1958.

59 Ibid.

60 NRS, HH58/66, Minute by W. D. Hood, 6 October 1960.

61 NRS, HH104/35/39, Minute by I. M. Macgregor, 14 July 1964.

62 *Lancet*, vol. I (1958), 656.

63 Davidson, *Dangerous Liaisons*, 262.

64 NRS, HH104/35/39, Minute by A. F. Reid, 2 June 1964.

65 See, for example, *Glasgow Herald*, 3 October 1972.

66 *Report of Joint Sub-Committee on Sexually Transmitted Diseases*.

67 NRS, HH104/36, Correspondence and papers relating to the Gilloran Report.

68 Ibid., Memorandum by D. H. H. Robertson, June 1977; Memorandum by G. Gilray, 25 April 1979.

69 DHS, *Annual Report for 1949*, PP, 1950 (Cmd 7921) XI, 27; NRS, HH58/108, SCHE minutes, 28 October and 31 December 1947.

70 See, for example, NRS, HH48/65/6, DHS circulars.

71 See, for example, NRS, HH58/66/74b, DHS poster: *Syphilis and Gonorrhoea are Homebreakers*, 1952.

72 SCHE, *Women in War and Peace*.

73 NRS, HH58/66, Official VD posters.

74 NRS, HH48/65/19, *DHS Circular 64/1960*.

75 NRS, HH58/112/11, Draft of leaflet: *A Personal Word*, March 1962.

76 *EPHD Annual Report for 1959*, 15, 144.

77 *EPHD Annual Report for 1961*, 16; *1962*, 158.
78 *Annual Report of MOH for Dundee, 1965*, 25; *1966*, 27–8; *Annual Report of MOH for Aberdeen for 1966*, 32; *1967*, 35.
79 Anon., 'Publicity material on VD', *Health Bulletin*, XXVIII, no. 1 (1970), 6; G. D. Rees, 'The menace of venereal disease and the need for education', *Health Education Journal*, XXVIII (1969), 209–10.
80 Davidson, *Dangerous Liaisons*, 290–1.
81 *Health Bulletin*, XXVIII, no. 1 (1970), 6.
82 *EHSSD Annual Report for 1970*, x, 60; *Glasgow MOH Annual Report for 1971*, 173; *1972*, 178.
83 NRS, HH61/970/3, SHEU, Current and proposed programmes, 1970–5.
84 See, for example, City of Edinburgh Health Department, *Annual Report for 1972*, 72.
85 C. B. S. Schofield, 'The knowledge of patients about sexually transmitted diseases', in Billington and Bell (eds), *Research in Health Education*, 26; NRS, HH61/1020/6, SHEU, Minutes of Steering Committee, 24 July 1973.
86 See, for example, SHEU, *Circular No. 1, 5 January 1970* (authors' emphasis).
87 See, for example, *EHSSD Annual Report for 1968*, 66.
88 Weeks, *Sex, Politics and Society*, 256.
89 See, for example, SHHD, *Annual Report for 1970*, PP, 1970–1 (Cmnd 4667) 48, 11.
90 Mcmillan and Robertson, 'Sexually-transmitted diseases', 270; Interview with former consultant venereologist, 2 June 1998.
91 Davidson, *Dangerous Liaisons*, 295–6. Brief references to 'early preventive treatment' were, however, retained in leaflets distributed to seamen and lorry drivers.
92 NRS, HH58/112/11, Papers of SCHE Medical Advisory Committee, March 1962; HH104/55/12, Papers relating to *Ministry of Health, Circular 84*, November 1968.
93 NRS, HH58/66, Minute by I. N. Sutherland, 17 October 1961.
94 See, for example, *Glasgow Herald*, editorial, 3 February 1971; NRS, HH61/970/29, SHHD, Family planning and health education: aide memoire for discussion, November 1970.
95 For details, see Davidson, 'Searching for "Mary, Glasgow"', 196–206.
96 *EPHD Annual Reports for 1948–60*; *MOH for Glasgow Annual Reports for 1948–60*.
97 NRS, HH58/66, Minutes and correspondence on contact tracing, 1948–62.
98 See, for example, BMA Archives, Venereologists Group Committee, Memorandum by Robert Lees, 26 February 1953.
99 NRS, HH58/66, Minutes and correspondence on contact tracing, 1948–62.

100 Ibid.; *DHS Circular 64/1960, Venereal disease in Scotland: increase in incidence of gonorrhoea*, 2 September 1960.

101 NRS, HH104/35/21a, Note by SHHD, May 1963.

102 NRS, HH104/35/37, Minute by I. M. Macgregor, 14 July 1964.

103 NRS, HH104/35/75, Report of working party, October 1965.

104 *National Health Service (Venereal Diseases) Regulations, 1968, S. I. 1968 No. 1624; Ministry of Health, National Health Service: Control of Venereal Disease HM (68) 84, November 1968.*

105 NRS, HH104/35/49, 75, 79; HH104/55/7, 92, Papers on venereal disease: incidence and control, 1963–71.

106 *EHPD Annual Report for 1962*, 144; *EHSSD Annual Report for 1967*, 77.

107 *EHSSD Annual Report for 1966*, 133.

108 *EHSSD Annual Report for 1970*, 58.

109 *Report of Joint Sub-Committee on Sexually Transmitted Diseases*, 2, 6, 14–15.

110 NRS, HH104/36, Correspondence relating to sexually transmitted diseases: Gilloran report, 1975–80.

111 Ibid.

112 Weeks, *Sex, Politics and Society*, 277–8.

8

SCHOOL SEX EDUCATION

INTRODUCTION

Since the early twentieth century, one of the more contentious issues facing policy makers in their efforts to combat venereal disease (VD) had been the sexual enlightenment of the young. After 1950, the provision of sex education in schools continued to represent an area of social contest between those with a vested interest in children, including the central and local state, the churches, moral welfare agencies, doctors, teachers and parents. As has been rightly observed, the issues of sex and education combined to generate a 'discourse of conflict' reflecting competing moral ideologies.[1] Moreover, not only did sex education – its existence, timing, content and delivery – form the target for wider social anxieties over sexuality and childhood; it also fell, as Lesley Hall observes, in 'the delicate liminal zone between the public and private' and 'between medical and educational concerns'.[2]

This chapter seeks to chart the impact of such concerns and contestations on the dynamics of sex education policy making in Scotland from the early initiatives of wartime to those of the late 1970s, during a period of rapid social change. First, it examines the nature of the debate surrounding the issue prior to the Second World War. Second, it charts the reappraisal of policy in wartime and the immediate post-war years in response to the perceived breakdown in moral and sexual standards among the young. Thereafter, it examines the devolvement of responsibility for school sex education in the 1950s and 1960s to traditional purity and social hygiene organisations – the Alliance-Scottish Council and the Scottish Council for Health Education (SCHE). Finally, the demise of such organisations and the often conflicting and ineffectual efforts of the Scottish Education Department (SED) and Scottish Home and Health Department (SHHD) to address the sex educational needs of a more 'permissive' youth culture in the late 1960s and 1970s are explored.

Prior to the Second World War, a range of pressure groups lobbied the Department of Health for Scotland and the SED on the issue of social hygiene education for children. The Scottish Committee of the British Social Hygiene Council campaigned for it to be an integral part of the curriculum, as a means of reducing the incidence of VD, and established local committees to liaise with educational leaders. Various purity organisations, such as the National Vigilance Association and the Alliance of Honour, as well as women's organisations, such as the Edinburgh Women Citizens' Association, also advocated the introduction of additional moral hygiene and biological instruction in schools. In addition, health officials and clinicians, often inspired by eugenics, canvassed the need for sexual issues to be addressed in schools, as part of a quest for 'racial health'.[3]

However, as in England,[4] the issue of sex education became a sharp focus for disagreement both within and between the social hygiene and social purity movements. A considerable body of Scottish public and professional opinion remained fearful of a policy of sexual enlightenment and a Scottish Office committee encountered a widely held belief that, unless closely regulated, sex education would merely lead 'to the very precocity and malpractice which it [was] designed to prevent'.[5] At a local level, there was often tension between medical practitioners, purity groups and educationists over the control and content of hygiene education. Purity groups, along with church leaders, were concerned that moral issues and ideals should remain to the fore. For their part, many teachers and education authorities in working-class areas of Scotland feared that such instruction might disrupt pupils and offend religious sensibilities.

As a result, there was very little sex education in Scottish schools beyond a scatter of *ad hoc* local initiatives, predominantly involving girls.[6] Some school medical officers gave incidental instruction in sex to older pupils on an informal basis. Some talks were also given in a few schools on hygiene, including anatomy and physiology, as part of the physical training lesson. In addition, lady specialists and nurses took advantage of PE lessons and medical examinations to give advice on intimate matters of sex hygiene to girls. Only in Aberdeen was sex education given separately, outside the normal curriculum, to all girls who were leaving school by, it was affirmed, 'a responsible nurse, a widow with an understanding, tactful turn of mind', the girls receiving instruction in matters of 'cleanliness at menstrual times, sex dangers and their future responsibilities in life'.[7]

The SED remained unreceptive to the varied pressures for wider provision. A departmental circular in 1929 had stressed the lack of public and professional consensus on the issue of sex education and opted to leave the matter to the discretion of individual education authorities rather than issue directives.[8] Officials were strongly resistant to sex education being accorded a separate status within the curriculum, considering that, if at all appropriate, it should be imparted solely as 'an incident of biology'. They feared that guidelines would merely entangle the Department in a contentious and potentially compromising public debate.[9]

However, wartime concerns at the apparent erosion of the moral fabric of British society and citizenship, especially as reflected in the sexual behaviour of the young, presented significant challenges to this laissez-faire policy. A succession of reports in the period 1943–5 by the Scottish Medical Advisory Committee, the Scottish Advisory Council on Education and the Scottish Youth Advisory Committee urged the introduction or development of sex education in order to direct 'the natural urges of human nature', to instil 'a more informed and responsible attitude to sex' and to stem the rising tide of promiscuity and VD.[10] The Church of Scotland also advocated the need for a new moral and sexual code for young people.[11] In addition, a major challenge to the SED's passive stance came from the issue, in late 1943, of an advisory circular on sex education by the English Board of Education.[12] Although the circular did not advance explicit guidelines, it clearly favoured a graduated scheme of sex instruction, focusing in the early years on the physiology of sex, and in senior classes on its more contentious social aspects, where the central aim would be to channel what were perceived as potentially disruptive sexual instincts into the acceptable realms of marriage and parenthood. To the consternation of the SED, some leading Scottish education authorities, including Moray and Nairn and Edinburgh, immediately began to formulate proposals on the lines of the circular.[13]

While acknowledging the demoralising impact of the war upon youth culture, the SED remained resistant to any explicit engagement with the issue of sex education and was not persuaded of the desirability of a Scottish circular on sex education. Undoubtedly, the Department was heavily influenced by the likely reaction of the Roman Catholic Church in Scotland.[14] The Scottish Roman Catholic bishops issued a public statement in 1944 voicing 'their instinctive distrust of all talk of sex instruction and sex teaching'. They feared that secular proposals would not adhere to a 'moral and spiritual approach' or to a 'clear matrimonial doctrine and practice', and that 'positive training in purity' would be sacrificed to mere factual instruction in sex anatomy, thus aggravating rather than curing the moral evils of contemporary youth culture.[15]

Moreover, within the SED itself, there was a marked lack of consensus on the issue. While receptive to the teaching of basic sexual anatomy and physiology as part of the biology or domestic science curriculum, Dr G. W. Simpson, the Department's Medical Officer, considered the presentation of what he called 'the social desiderata of sex' to be fraught with difficulties, not least the enduring public and professional debate over its appropriate timing, content and delivery.[16] In contrast, W. F. Arbuckle, the Assistant Secretary, was firmly opposed to any scheme of sex education that separated its physical and social aspects. As he reflected:

> The sex relation is after all primarily a matter of conduct, and the amount of factual knowledge necessary to provide a basis for right conduct is quite limited. I doubt very much whether all the physiological studies . . . have really much practical value . . . The transition in the [Edinburgh] scheme of instruction from the rabbit to the human, with the phrase 'human reproduction similar', completely ignores the fact that the change is also one from the instinctive to the conscious level of experience. It is rather like confining instruction in the use of TNT to information about its chemical composition . . . and omitting to mention its explosive qualities.[17]

In the event, while the SED was now prepared, on an *ad hoc* basis, to encourage education authorities to experiment with the use of special lecturers in their schools, it continued to withhold approval for the inclusion of 'human reproduction' in the standard biology curriculum. Moreover, the Department's response to all requests for a more proactive policy was that 'officially their attitude was the same as it had been in 1929'.[18]

Instead, as the issue of sex education in schools became subsumed within a wider post-war reconstruction debate over health education in general, the initiative shifted to the recently established Scottish Council for Health Education. Over the period from 1946 to 1950, it organised a series of national conferences on the future of health education in Scotland, attended by representatives of the medical and educational professions along with delegates from government

departments.[19] Their proceedings revealed that, with the exception of
Aberdeen, no long-standing 'direct instruction on sex' was given in
Scottish schools. Many areas reported that some indirect instruction
was given during biology lessons, but with a very limited bearing on
human physiology and relationships. Indeed, some education authorities claimed that sex education was primarily an urban problem
and that it was unnecessary in rural areas, where there was 'a close
contact with farm life'. There was a similar lack of sex education
within the teacher training colleges, with only one institution providing
explicit instruction on the physiology of human reproduction.

The proceedings also highlighted how acutely divided the educational and medical professions were over the content and delivery of
sex education in schools. Thus, while medical officers of health were
agreed that adolescents should receive some guidance on 'sex hygiene
and the allied problems of social hygiene', they differed over its
delivery, some favouring the role being performed by school medical
officers and nurses, while others viewed it as primarily the remit of
the teacher. For their part, while recommending the greater use of
nurses to monitor female adolescent hygiene, school medical officers
in Scotland were sceptical of the benefits of the type of sex education
syllabus outlined in the English Board of Education's advisory
circular, fearing adverse effects on the mental and emotional stability
of schoolchildren. In contrast, many venereologists, advancing a
medicalised view of sex education inherited from the pre-war social
hygiene movement, advocated the greater use of medical expertise in
the delivery of home-craft and parent-craft classes, with more explicit
focus on the social repercussions of sexual promiscuity.

The views of educationists at the conferences were equally mixed.
While directors of education and headteachers in the East of Scotland
were generally supportive of additional provisions for sex education,
many in the West of Scotland were resistant. Not untypical was the
view of one headmaster of a Roman Catholic school that class
instruction in sexual issues would 'merely encourage the inherent
weakness and wickedness of man, and possibly develop sensualists'.
Other teachers voiced their concern that, as a profession, they were
being asked to address contentious issues that intruded on parental
rights and which rendered them vulnerable to attack, both in the
media and local politics.

Nonetheless, the weight of opinion did favour pupils, outwith the
Roman Catholic schools, being given sex instruction as an integral
part of health education, and the proceedings did inspire several

experiments in Edinburgh and Aberdeenshire schools. Those in girls' schools (the overwhelming majority) involved short courses in the physiology and social aspects of sex undertaken by a member of the Alliance of Honour, a long-established purity organisation, after consultation with both staff and parents. Each set of courses consisted of three forty-minute periods every week. During the first week, the instruction dealt with personal hygiene, the care of the body, the importance of mental and physical purity, and character formation. In the second week, each class was given talks on the reproduction of fish, birds and animals, 'including the human subject', illustrated by a filmstrip. The third week was devoted to answering a wide range of questions submitted anonymously in writing by the girls. In addition, a similar course, with the emphasis on 'clean living', 'chivalry' and 'moral purity' as the 'only real safe-guard' of personal and racial health, was conducted in a boys' secondary school in Edinburgh, drawn up by the school medical officer and conducted by the headmaster and selected male teachers. Throughout the syllabus, 'sex desire' was conveyed as 'normal' but 'a powerful force' that needed to be controlled and channelled, rather than expressed.

The favourable feedback on such courses led the conferences' so-called Continuing Committee to recommend that the pilot schemes should form the basis of official guidelines and specimen curricula for use in Scottish schools. However, the Educational Institute of Scotland (EIS) vociferously opposed such a move. Its president stressed that, although some teachers were already doing innovative work in this field, the bulk of the profession felt inadequate to cope with the sensitive issues involved and that sex education was primarily the responsibility of the parents and/or school medical officer.[20] Such concerns were duly reflected in the resolution of the final conference in 1950 that 'in regard to sex education, the guiding note should be cautious advance', and in the fact that the model syllabuses on health education drawn up by the Continuing Committee, and circu-lated by the SCHE in December 1950, explicitly excluded the sex education syllabus '*along with all other reference to the subject*'.[21]

For their part, the Department of Health for Scotland and the SED sustained a detached and often evasive stance on the issue. While broadly supporting the SCHE's report on health education, they were emphatic that it was purely advisory and not a directive, and that such support should not convey 'any impression that the Secretary of State for Scotland was explicitly advocating the giving of sex education

in schools'.[22] In the event, the Scottish health and education departments were broadly content over the next decade to devolve responsibility for such a contentious issue to other agencies.

SEX EDUCATION POLICY IN THE 1950S

Throughout the 1950s, such sex education as was provided within
Scottish schools was primarily furnished by two, often competing,
organisations, both heavily dependent on government funding – the
Alliance-Scottish Council and the SCHE. The Alliance of Honour
had been established in London as part of the Edwardian purity
movement, originally for men, in 1903. A Scottish branch had been
formed in 1926 and continued until the outbreak of war in 1939. In
1946, the Alliance in London sent one of its lecturers, Annabelle P.
Duncan, a qualified midwife with wide-ranging experience of social
work and teaching in physiology and anatomy, to investigate the
state of public opinion on sex education in Scotland. Subsequently,
she became involved in the pilot schemes mentioned earlier and the
Alliance-Scottish Council was established as a 'Society for education
in personal relations and family life', with Duncan as its secretary
and sole lecturer.[23] After protracted negotiations, the SED cautiously
agreed to partially fund her efforts. However, the Department
declined to have a representative on the Council on the grounds that
'in this particular respect [sex education]', it had 'to walk warily'.[24]

   During the 1950s, Duncan attended a growing range of secondary
girls' schools across Scotland controlled by some twelve education
authorities.[25] Some of the schools were very large with as many as
500–600 girls, while others were small country schools. Visits were
always preceded by extensive consultations with the director of
education and education committee, and by talks with parents and
staff. Duncan deliberately incorporated information on sex within
more generic talks such as that entitled 'Growing Up', usually
accompanied by biological films. She initially attracted support from
many directors of education who agreed with her view that, given
the reluctance of parents to undertake the task of sex education and
resistance to its integration within the school curriculum, talks by a
visiting expert were essential. Duncan's visits always ended with an
open discussion of anonymous questions submitted by the girls, with
parents and staff excluded.

   The construction of sexual information and sexuality within the
Alliance's talks and literature reflected its origins as an explicitly

religious purity organisation. Underlying its discourse was a concern to restore the social and moral controls fractured by the impact of the war. Outside the context of Christian marriage, sexual experience was depicted as inherently pathological and polluting. Thus, the development of the sex glands in boys was conveyed as a defining moment in the building of character rather than sexual self-awareness, which was inherently dangerous. While nocturnal emissions were biologically normal, the Alliance was clearly uncomfortable with their implications. They were, the literature claimed, often 'accompanied by rather unpleasant dreams' and 'the loss of this fluid' should not 'as a rule, be more often than once a week'. If it was more frequent, the child was advised 'to speak to your father or mother, as you may need a tonic'.[26] While boys were exhorted to attend to the hygiene of their 'sex glands', 'careless handling was deplored' on the grounds, reminiscent of Baden Powell's more repressive exhortations, that 'it may sometimes force some of the semen from the storehouses before nature is ready'.[27] Deliberate masturbation – or in the terminology of the Alliance's literature, 'self-abuse' – was strongly condemned as a 'waste of vital energy' and a negation of the opportunities of Christian manhood.

Such warnings reflected the continuing ambivalence within the Alliance, shared by many other governmental and professional bodies, about the possible effects of sex education. On the one hand, there was the felt need for the young to be exposed to 'correct knowledge' about sex rather than furtive or evasive misinformation from their peer group or parents. On the other, there was acute concern to avoid sexual precocity. Thus, having stressed the importance of sexual hygiene, Alliance literature immediately recommended that boys spare no further thought to the issue.

For physiological reasons, advice to girls about reproduction was more explicit, but the overriding stress was again on the association of sexual intercourse with marriage and motherhood. The knowledge of 'intimacy' was conveyed as a preventative in order to instil 'chastity' and 'self-control'. In particular, as with the social hygiene literature of the inter-war period, girls were exhorted not to excite the more uncontrollable urges of boys, the explicit assumption being that the sexual appetites of boys and girls were fundamentally different.[28] Again, the rhetoric of hygiene and pollution informed much of the detailed advice, with menstruation conveyed as essentially a cleansing process keeping 'the nest as fresh and pure as possible'.[29] The message for older girls was that female sexual health was contingent on sexual relationships being within marriage and that other sexual experiences would produce both physical and mental damage:

> In the case of a woman, this sex experience is wedded to the instinct to make a home and have children and look after the man she loves . . . It is linked with all that; and all that is the normal and true consequence of sexual experience. When a woman is sexually awakened, and when the process stops at mere intercourse so that she is not led on to all these self-fulfilling experiences, the harmonies of her nature are spoilt. Her hunger has been aroused and she will never be the same again.[30]

The Alliance's literature on sex education reflected its long-standing broader involvement in moral vigilance. It conducted a vigorous campaign against the permissive and debasing influence of cafés, cinemas, dance halls and the media upon the sexual behaviour of the young. It inveighed especially against magazines targeted at teenagers, such as *The Boy Friend*, and by the early 1960s was actively collaborating with the police, the Scottish presbyteries and the Moral Law Defence Association to suppress their distribution in schools.[31]

Meanwhile, the SCHE attempted to advance the provision of sex education by *ad hoc* lectures in schools, by the training of teachers and by its efforts to establish health education as a recognised part of the school curriculum. Dr Alex G. Mearns, Medical Adviser to the Council and Senior Lecturer in Hygiene at the University of Glasgow, responded to regular invitations to address schoolboys on 'sex hygiene'. As he reported: 'A Sex talk – "the Gift of Life" – was delivered to boys in groups by ages. A simple and straightforward exposition of the facts of human reproduction was given' with blackboard illustrations and film displays. To the senior boys of monitor grade, assembled in the Chaplain's study, he gave 'a man-to-man talk on "Decent Living"'.[32]

The Council's message echoed that of the inter-war social hygiene movement.[33] The fundamental aim of sex education was seen to be 'clean living' and the 'control of racial instinct', with medical risk conflated with the moral culpability of casual sex. As with Annabelle Duncan, Mearns was concerned to limit the sexual explicitness of instruction and for sexual knowledge, once delivered, to be 'stored away in the memory like history and geography, and not made a frequent subject of thought'. He also conveyed a gendered view of sexual responsibility and pollution. A fervent supporter, as indeed was Duncan, of the National Vigilance Association and women police in their surveillance of so-called 'problem girls', his talks and writings sustained the traditional ambivalence of policy makers and purity activists towards young female sexuality – as quintessentially chaste but, in practice, potentially corrupting. Thus, he argued that even the natural sexual attraction of a chaste girl had the 'power' to pollute and 'girls should not behave in any way which might cause a normally-passioned boy to forget himself'.[34]

The SCHE also organised regular vacation courses for teachers and student teachers in health education (including sex education), directed by Mearns, as a means of 'educating the educators'. Again, however, there was a strong emphasis on the dysgenic aspects of sexual activity. Sex was treated primarily as a 'problem' and the courses devoted to 'social pathology' – marital breakdown, infertility, abortion, divorce and sexual 'delinquency' – delivered from a perspective of racial health and social hygiene.[35] Educationists and health officials were increasingly concerned at the lack of focus in the courses on contemporary shifts in the sexual behaviour and concerns of the young and the need for a broader, more positive, behavioural approach to sexual issues.

Another central objective of the Council was to introduce human biology into the school curriculum as a certificated subject within a more general programme of health education. On this issue, however, it continued to encounter resistance from the SED on a variety of grounds: that some aspects of biology teaching were already devoted to mammalian biology; that it was undesirable to 'elevate human biology' from its scientific context, thus provoking an unhealthy and precocious approach to the subject; and that it would hold little attraction as a qualification except for girls intending to enter the nursing profession.[36] Mearns lamented that, in the introduction of 'personal relationships' into the Scottish curriculum, 'the whole situation remain[ed] depressingly non-progressive' and that the SED had signally 'failed' the education system 'in this respect'.[37]

Meanwhile, the Department was facing pressures from other directions. First, the Royal Commission on Marriage and Divorce, backed by evidence from Scottish women's organisations and the Scottish Marriage Guidance Council, strongly recommended that there should be a 'carefully graded system of education for young people as they [grew] up in order to fit them for marriage and family living' and that there should be a review of existing arrangements 'for pre-marital education and training'.[38] Second, the English Ministry of

Education issued an updated version of its handbook on health education which gave unprecedented priority and space to the issue of sex education and, while refraining from any central directive, emphasised that instruction on the sexual and reproductive functions of the human body should be central to any health education curriculum.[39]

Again, the SED remained unmoved. It argued that the Royal Commission's recommendations ignored the existing work of the Alliance-Scottish Council and the existing provision of home-craft and mother-craft classes for girls, and that premarital education for young people should be left to teachers and youth leaders.[40] Despite the Ministry of Education's more proactive policy, given the continuing lack of consensus within the Scottish medical and education professions over the issue of sex education and the enduring need to placate religious sensitivities, the Department was still not disposed to formulate specific guidelines. Thus, the annual report of the Secretary of State for Scotland on education for 1958 stressed that opinions remained divided as to whether the advantages of sex education talks were 'outweighed by their drawing attention to sexual matters which might best be dealt with informally and perhaps individually'.[41] While acknowledging that, even in non-Catholic schools, 'comparatively few lessons in sex [were] given', and those 'almost entirely to girls', the SED remained content to leave it 'to the education authorities to decide, what, if anything, they should do'.[42]

SEX EDUCATION POLICY IN THE 1960S

By the mid-1960s, it was becoming increasingly evident that the *ad hoc* efforts of the Alliance-Scottish Council and the SCHE in the field of sex education were inadequate to address rising concerns over the sexual permissiveness of the young.[43] The Alliance's activities involved only about 3 per cent of the secondary school girl population in Scotland. It had begun to innovate by doing experimental work in boys' schools and holding mixed-sex sessions on issues such as contraception, abortion and homosexuality. It also modified its mission statement to embrace value systems other than those of Christian morality. Nonetheless, both logistically and ideologically, the Alliance was increasingly seen by education authorities and government departments as unsuited to the needs of the time. In effect, its activities were still conducted single-handedly by Annabelle Duncan, now in her seventies, and its local authority funding had declined markedly.

Moreover, Duncan's approach was increasingly viewed by educationists as overly moralistic and out of touch with the realities of youth culture and sexual experience, a view reinforced by the involvement of the Alliance in purity campaigns reminiscent of the early twentieth century.

There was also growing criticism of the sex education provided by the SCHE. By the 1960s, it was visiting more schools than the Alliance, and the reports of its medical lecturer testified to a rising demand for its services. Nonetheless, its scattergun approach, involving a very small proportion of Scottish schoolchildren, was regarded as cost-ineffective. In addition, although it had extended its use of film materials, its syllabuses and literature were seen as little altered in tone and content from the late 1940s. Mearns himself was viewed as a powerful force for conservatism, his approach reflecting the narrow focus on reproductive hygiene of the old social hygiene movement and ignoring more recent developments in the behavioural sciences.

Moreover, during the early 1960s, Scottish health and education departments came under increasing pressure from public and professional opinion to address the deficiencies in the provision of sex education, driven by what was perceived as a degeneration in the sexual proclivities and health of the young. Scottish medical officers of health lobbied for a more formal recognition of human biology within the curriculum.[44] The Scottish branches of the BMA and the Medical Society for the Study of Venereal Diseases, alarmed at the upswing in Scottish VD figures (especially for gonorrhoea), also pressed for better instruction of the young in 'the perils of promiscuous sex'.[45] In addition, despite continuing disagreement on the precise content and delivery of sex education, a series of high-profile conferences on youth and sexuality, sponsored by the Church of Scotland and the Scottish Marriage Guidance Council, and bringing together medical, educational and moral welfare practitioners, recommended that the SED should support a graduated syllabus of instruction throughout the education system.[46] The Church of Scotland increasingly endorsed such initiatives as a means of counteracting the rising incidence of teenage pregnancies, the increasing exposure of the young to pornographic images and literature, and the moral relativism purveyed by prominent figures within the media relating to sex which threatened to 'make sordid, suggestive and degrading this gift of God'.[47]

Meanwhile, working groups within the Department itself were exerting additional pressure. Thus, the Sub-Committee on Growth and Development was 'surprised that the case for sex education in primary schools should have to be argued'. While it recognised the need to respect religious beliefs, and the concerns of some parents to 'safeguard against incest', it advocated that, provided that issues of physiology were treated within the context of human relationships, sex education 'should be the normal and ongoing part of the primary school teacher's responsibilities'.[48] In the Sub-Committee's view: 'Sex values [were] the job of all teachers and non-commitment [was] impossible.' Similarly, the Physical Education and Health Education Panel pressed for more integrated sex instruction that balanced the anatomical, social and moral aspects of the subject, as a means of enabling pupils to cope with the 'stresses of puberty and the problems of sex' in a period of growing sensationalism within the media and the breakdown of traditional religious and community controls.[49]

Publicly, the SED's response to such pressures was to reiterate that the responsibility for the extent and content of sex education rested with individual education authorities and school managers, 'in the light of local opinion'.[50] Privately, throughout the early 1960s, it sought to explore with the SHHD possible solutions to 'this vexed question'.[51] A succession of inter-departmental working groups highlighted the need for greater coordination of sex education initiatives, but differed over their delivery; some officials envisaged a central role for appropriately trained teachers, others (predominantly within the SHHD) favoured the use of medical experts. They also differed over the most suitable coordinating agency. There was strong resistance to expanding the roles of either the Alliance-Scottish Council or the SCHE. Instead, discussions increasingly focused on the possible use of the Scottish Marriage Guidance Council, which had begun to provide talks and counselling to both sexes in some of the grant-aided and independent schools and to train student teachers, and which was perceived by many officials as by far the most relevant agency for addressing the adolescent problems of a 'permissive society'.

However, perhaps the most powerful constraint on official sex education policy in the early 1960s was the social politics surrounding the Cohen Committee on Health Education. In advance of its report, the Scottish education and health departments remained acutely concerned that, in introducing contentious measures relating to sex education, any restructuring of health education in general would be compromised, especially in view of the sensitivities of the Roman Catholic and Free Church communities.[52] In the event, although the Cohen Committee did identify as a 'special health problem' the need for 'education about the relationship of the sexes in all its human and social implications', including the 'physical basis of procreation' and the 'risks involved in promiscuity', it took very limited evidence from Scottish medical and educational experts and failed to confront the central issues of the timing, content and delivery of such education and the appropriate role of the state.[53] Above all, its highly contentious recommendations for separate and equal status for health education in the curriculum, taught by specialist health educationists, and for a new Central Board for Health Education in Scotland to absorb the existing health education functions of the SHHD and SCHE, immediately overshadowed any existing departmental review of sex education provisions.[54] As an SED minute indicated in December 1964, any such initiatives were speedily put on the back burner:

> As you know, SED have not taken any active part in sex education in schools in the past; their role has been to support a body which was willing to help education authorities who applied for it. Even following on Cohen, it seems doubtful whether we would wish to do much more than issue some general exhortation and perhaps increase our support to the Alliance or its successor.[55]

In the event, the Alliance-Scottish Council was persuaded to close in 1967 on the grounds that the future lay with sex education as a public responsibility, implemented directly by the education authorities.[56] At the same time, the SCHE's visits to schools were gradually phased out and its activities restricted to the in-service training of teachers and health educators. Its more general health education functions were subsumed in 1968 within a newly established Scottish Health Education Unit (SHEU), funded and closely monitored by the SHHD. Initially, it had been contemplated that the Unit should also have school sex education within its remit but the SED quickly scotched this idea, preferring instead to explore the option of involving the Scottish Marriage Guidance Council.[57]

Meanwhile, however, by the late 1960s, in the absence of clear guidance from the SED, the initiative in sex education had shifted to the education authorities. In 1968, the *Scottish Educational Journal* reported that a number of authorities were 'bestirring themselves in an effort to meet the manifest need of adolescents to be armed against the blandishments of the permissive-acquisitive society'.[58] The major pioneer, as in so many other aspects of sexual health policy, was Aberdeenshire, where from 1965 a systematic scheme of sex instruction in primary and secondary schools had been developed. The scheme was on a voluntary basis with provision for parental opt-out. Teachers were advised not to give any formal instruction to children before they had reached the Primary VI stage but to answer truthfully any questions arising naturally in the younger classes or asked privately by individual pupils. The scheme for the top two primary classes was designed to impart a vocabulary using the correct anatomical and physiological terms and knowledge of parts of the body and changes at puberty, of the function of the reproductive organs (intercourse to be dealt with only 'on an elementary level') and the process of conception. This instruction was always to be part of health education with a close relation to nature study and with an understanding of the simpler forms of reproduction prefacing the study of human reproduction. The schemes for the first two years of the secondary school covered the same ground in much more detail and put the 'problems of growing up' into their moral context. At this stage, it was recommended that the study of human reproduction should form part of a general science course, taught where possible in mixed groups, with the science teacher assisted by the parent-craft teacher and the health visitor. More senior pupils were to attend a social studies course which would include the 'social aspects of sexual behaviour', while other disciplines such as English literature and religious education were employed to explore the more 'sociological' aspects of sexual relationships.[59]

A number of other authorities adopted a variety of schemes. Moray and Nairn used the Aberdeenshire scheme as a template, as did the EIS in its major campaign in 1968 for improved sex education provision in preparation for the raising of the school-leaving age.[60] Dundee operated a syllabus devised by the staff of its health and welfare department.[61] Edinburgh appointed an adviser in so-called 'social education' to train housemasters in the larger secondary schools to give instruction in 'personal relationships'.[62] Glasgow also began to make provision for social education in its comprehensive schools and collaborated with the local marriage guidance council in training and selecting suitable teachers.[63]

In some schools there was a significant shift to the use of television programmes to underpin sex education. Schools in Aberdeen, Inverness and Fife successfully employed Grampian TV's series *Living and Growing*, a course on human reproduction transmitted during the day and repeated in the evening for adults. Designed for

10–13-year-olds, it provided a simple explanation of issues such as 'wet dreams', the physical changes of puberty, menstruation and sexual intercourse. The response from pupils, teachers and parents suggested that the films facilitated a more relaxed discussion of sexual issues within both the school and the home.[64]

Yet, evidence clearly suggested that, despite these initiatives, there was still, by 1970, no systematic provision for the teaching of sex in Scottish schools or for the training of teachers in sex instruction. Apart from the formal schemes described above, what was done was 'of a desultory nature' and largely dependent on the whim and sexual enlightenment of the head teacher.[65] In 90 per cent of Scottish primary schools surveyed, sex education was not included in the syllabus, while information on menstruation was included in the syllabus for girls in only 7 per cent of primary schools. Only 5 per cent of such schools reported even an occasional use of broadcasts, and several authorities, most notably Glasgow Education Committee, refused to sanction the use of sex education films, such as *Living and Growing*, in their primary curriculum.[66] Of Scottish secondary schools, 57 per cent did not include any sex education for boys in the syllabus and 48 per cent did not provide any for girls.[67]

The EIS and the Scottish Marriage Guidance Council laid the blame squarely on the SED for 'dragging their feet' on the issue.[68] The only reference to sex education in the Department's annual reports throughout the 1960s had been a somewhat defeatist observation in 1961 that: 'The sphere of personal relationships may be one in which it is not easy for the schools to provide much direct help.'[69] Subsequently, the implications for sex education of improved guidance provisions in secondary schools and the raising of the school-leaving age were left largely unexplored by officials.[70] The SED's response to a revised edition of the Department of Education and Science's handbook on health education in 1968, with its more explicit reference to human reproduction and recent developments such as oral contraception, was similarly unresponsive. Officials were primarily concerned to reassure the Secretary of State for Scotland that references to sexual morality within the handbook would be 'cautious' and that it 'would preserve the Minister's neutral position'.[71] Predictably, when the Curriculum Committee on Moral and Religious Education threatened in 1968 to address the issue of sex education, the SED advised it to confine its terms of reference to the broader questions of morality and to avoid 'this thorniest of problems'.[72] Accordingly, in its subsequent report, while furnishing ample proof of the lack of sex education in Scottish schools, the committee failed to make any specific recommendations on the issue.[73]

SEX EDUCATION POLICY IN THE 1970S

In many ways, the story of Scottish sex education policy in the 1970s replicates that of the 1960s. Among policy makers, the shift in focus from long-term eugenic concerns for racial health to the immediate health risks of a more permissive generation, and to issues such as abortion and contraception, continued. Again, the discussion of sex education in Scottish schools became embedded in the social politics of health education in general and the competing agendas, not only of the Scottish health and education departments, but also of pressure groups such as the Family Planning Association (FPA) and the Moral Welfare Committee of the Church of Scotland. However, initiatives were increasingly constrained by the politicisation of the issue, the more so as a 'New Morality', hostile to the sexual law reforms of the 1960s, gained increasing influence within central and local government debate.

Scottish policy making in the early 1970s was dominated by the proceedings of the SED's Working Party on Health Education, culminating in the Cunningham Report of 1974.[74] The deliberations of the working party and its sub-committee on sex education reflected the continuing lack of consensus over the appropriate content of sex education, especially where it related to contentious issues such as contraception, to the extent that Roman Catholic members 'seriously considered issuing a separate report'.[75] Others were exercised by the 'difficulty of guiding young people from innocence or ignorance to knowledge without giving the impression that they were expected to use the information', in direct contrast to usual teaching practice. In the event, while stressing that sex education was a joint responsibility that had to be shared with parents, that it should not be treated in isolation and that the view of the churches and society must be respected, the Cunningham Report concluded that it was an essential part of any health education programme at all stages from nursery to higher education. In particular, it recommended that, in order to cope with peer-group and media pressures, secondary schools needed to provide opportunities for the discussion of a wide spectrum of sexual issues, including masturbation, homosexuality and lesbianism, as well as information for school-leavers on contraception and family planning, as long as it was conveyed as an 'aid to family limitation and not promiscuity'.

The reaction of the SED's influential Consultative Committee on the Curriculum (CCC) to the Cunningham Report was hostile. It considered that the working party had unwisely wandered into controversial areas beyond its remit, and that its recommendations on sex education would serve to alienate teachers and public opinion against the reform of health education in general.[76] The CCC's view, shared by senior officials within the Scottish Office, was in part determined by growing political controversy at Westminster over sex education materials, with increasing calls for their greater regulation and for the right of parents to withdraw their children from lessons involving sex instruction. Scottish peers were especially vociferous in condemning what they alleged was 'ill-disguised pornography' designed to 'undermine our civilisation based on inherited morality and family life by teaching children to behave like cats and dogs'.[77] While not wishing to publicise the more explicit sex education films by prosecuting them, the Scottish Office also condemned material whose 'ethos shifted from the usual view of sex as something which takes place within marriage to the view that sex experience is <u>essential</u> to development'.[78]

Despite the CCC's reservations, many of the central recommendations on sex education of the working party were incorporated in Curriculum Paper 14, published in 1974.[79] Much of the detail relating to content and delivery (especially the role of teachers) had been excised and more prominence given to the rising incidence of teenage VD, pregnancy and abortions in an effort to mollify anti-sex educationists. However, the central thrust of the draft report – the need for more systematic school provision of sex education not only on human anatomy and physiology but also on sexual relationships, sexually transmitted diseases, abortion and family planning – was retained. Yet, once again, as with the Cohen Report in the 1960s, specific proposals for the reform of sex education were negated by official hostility to the general recommendations of the report on the future of health education. Thus, the SED published the report of the Cunningham Committee purely as a discussion paper, with an accompanying circular highlighting the opposition of the CCC to health education becoming a prescribed element of the curriculum underpinned by a specialist qualification. This lack of official endorsement inevitably, by association, also encompassed sex education.[80]

Medical advisers within the SHHD and SHEU were increasingly dismayed at the lack of action, especially in the light of the degree of sexual ignorance of the young in Scotland highlighted in the Gilloran

Report on Sexually Transmitted Diseases,[81] and the growing evidence of the lag in the growth of Scottish sex education provisions compared with those in England and many European countries.[82] Health officials felt constrained in a whole range of areas by the SED's timidity. Given the medical aspects of sex education and its close association with family planning, the SHHD was keen for the SHEU, in liaison with the health boards, to expand its work in the training of teachers and the provision of appropriate materials to schools, but the SED and its inspectorate remained adamantly opposed to any such incursions into its official territory. The Chief Medical Officer to the SHHD was deeply concerned at the consequent lack of coordination on the issue of sex education. As he warned in December 1974: 'We still have some way to go in showing the world outside that the natural differences in emphasis between health and education services do not amount to the Secretary of State adopting conflicting policies.'[83] For like reasons, the SHHD felt unable to respond to the recommendations of the Finer Report that there should be educational support for pregnant school-girls and other 'casualties of sex'.[84] Similarly, it encountered protracted resistance from the SED to its attempts to sponsor research into the extent of sex education in Scottish schools; the SED argued that it would offend local sensibilities, that it would politicise the issue and that it would be based on the false assumption that the SED had failed in some way to provide a national policy for sex education – for which, it was claimed, the Secretary of State had neither the power nor indeed the proclivity.[85]

Once again, in the absence of a proactive lead from the SED, other agencies attempted to take the initiative. Thus, the FPA in Scotland was making inroads into the field, albeit mainly to support teachers rather than to deliver instruction. Since the early 1970s, it had been invited into some schools on an *ad hoc* basis, although often requested not to address the issue of contraception.[86] In 1974, it opened a training centre in Glasgow for schoolteachers. Thereafter, it campaigned for a greater role in sex education provision, in part to compensate for the takeover of its clinics and services by the NHS in 1975.[87]

Meanwhile, the Scottish churches were developing their own initiatives. The Moral Welfare Committee of the Church of Scotland was critical of the lack of official action on sex education. Subject to personal relationships being taught within 'a Christian framework', it recommended that all children should be informed about reproduction before they were involved physically or emotionally, that sex education should form an integral part of a health education programme in the upper stages of primary schools and that, in secondary schools, all 'young people should be given the opportunity to have all the information they want[ed] regarding the psycho-sexual aspects of sex'.[88] In 1977, the Church introduced its own pilot schemes of moral education for 14–16-year-olds, 'reflective of Christian values', in several Glasgow schools, in the hope of developing a set of guidelines that might underpin SED curriculum development policy.[89]

In addition, the Roman Catholic Church in Scotland was slowly establishing its own national syllabus for sex education. Schemes had been introduced during the early 1970s in the West of Scotland to support Catholic parents in instructing young children of primary school age on sexual matters. Subsequently, while stressing the continued importance of parents in the process, an advisory committee of the hierarchy recommended in 1973 that a systematic programme of instruction be instituted for older pupils in Catholic schools, focused especially on early leavers. Such instruction was designed to form part of the social education syllabus and to place sexual issues within a framework of moral and ethical enlightenment.[90] Significantly, at a conference in 1976, Cardinal Winning, Roman Catholic Archbishop of Glasgow, emphasised the need for 'positive' sex education that addressed more than just the dysfunctional and dysgenic effects of the sexual instinct, in a speech viewed by the Scottish Office as a breakthrough in Catholic policy.[91]

Despite renewed pressure for government action in the mid-1970s, the SED's policy on sex education remained largely unchanged. It continued to brief ministers that responsibility rested with education authorities and headteachers.[92] Significantly, its annual reports made no reference to sex education, and references to sex instruction in its health education guidelines to primary schools in 1976 were openly acknowledged to be more cautious than a previous memorandum of 1965.[93] The Department continued to view the activities of the SHEU with deep suspicion, fearing that its activities would conflict with its Curriculum Committee and the inspectorate, alienate the teaching profession and antagonise religious groups.[94]

Similarly, although talks were conducted with the FPA in the mid-1970s, the SED 'took fright' after a vigorous attack in the House of Lords in January 1976 on the Association's work and materials, and its scheme of school peer-counselling, Grapevine.[95] The attack, again led by Scottish peers, alleged that the Association's permissive message was a function of commercial links with the London Rubber Industries and the sale of contraceptives. Citing, with relish, extracts from alleged FPA-recommended reading on female masturbation, lesbianism, and oral and anal intercourse, the Earl of Lauderdale and Lord Macleod of Fuinary condemned the FPA for undermining family values and pandering to 'the sickness of society'.[96] For his part, the Marquess of Lothian viewed the integration of the FPA within the NHS as 'the infiltration of extreme ideologies' and regarded its sex education materials as a form of sexual entrapment, luring children into a vicious cycle of promiscuity, pregnancy and abortion.[97] Both the SED and the SHHD were at one in wishing to avoid entanglement in the increasingly polarised Westminster debate over sex education and declined to follow up on earlier overtures to the FPA in Scotland.[98]

The only concession made by the SED to its critics had been the appointment of yet another investigation in 1975 into health education in Scotland – an HMI panel – that did not report until 1979.[99] It provided a depressing picture of the progress achieved. Of the 100 primary schools investigated, only 40 per cent taught any sex education relating to birth, reproduction and menstruation. It found that teachers in many primary schools were reluctant to address the issue of sex education and to 'broach the physical aspects of human relationships in groups of children of very different sensitivity and maturity'.[100] In secondary schools, the panel found a continuing unwillingness and/or inability of teachers to undertake sex education in any depth and a widespread failure to address controversial issues such as family planning, contraception and STDs with early school-leavers. However, its most stringent criticism was levelled at the lack of coordination between medical, educational and moral authorities in the design and delivery of sex education and the absence of clear advisory guidelines.[101]

Other surveys conducted by the SHHD, by individual health boards and by the Scottish Branch of the Society for the Study of Venereal Diseases came to similar conclusions. In Grampian and Dundee, there was a reported lack of coordination between health and education authorities and ignorance of 'how, or even if, any sexuality content of any health education programme [was] being carried out'. In the West of Scotland, provisions varied enormously. In some schools, medical officers and health visitors were regularly integrated into the curriculum to undertake sex education, while in many others, staff were explicitly banned from involvement in the subject. In Edinburgh, provisions varied from: 'Biology taught but reproduction not mentioned' to 'occasional discussions at a senior level by a guidance teacher'. One survey reported in 1977 that one in four Scottish children aged 16 were receiving no sex instruction compared with one in thirty in the south of England.[102]

In an effort to address the problem, while still seeking to distance itself from the increasing politicisation of the issue, the SED sought to embed sex education in new curriculum developments in 'social education', with less focus on the more sensational dysfunctional aspects and repercussions of sexual behaviour and more attention devoted to its cultural determinants and social context. However, within the Curriculum Committee, opinion remained divided as to the most suitable allocation of responsibility for moral education between subject and guidance teachers and outside professionals.[103] Moreover, various investigations in the early 1980s revealed the continuing lack of coordinated and consistent provision of school sex education in Scotland and the enduring resistance of many parents, teachers, education authorities and civic leaders.[104] Thus, sadly, as one Scottish witness before the Social Services Committee on AIDS was to testify in 1987, more than half a century after the issue had first engaged the attention of policy makers, there was still 'no real infrastructure of health and social education in Scottish schools which carrie[d] a sex education programme to which AIDS [could] be added'.[105]

Notes

1 Wallis, 'Some ideological issues', unpublished thesis, 6–7; Meredith, *Sex Education*, ch. 4.
2 Hall, 'Birds, bees and general embarrassment', 98.
3 For details of such lobbying, see Davidson, *Dangerous Liaisons*, 142–4.
4 For an overview of sex education policy making in England and Wales, see especially Hall, 'In ignorance and knowledge: reflections on the history of sex education in Britain', in Sauerteig and Davidson (eds), *Shaping Sexual Knowledge*, ch. 2; Pilcher, 'School sex education', 153–70.
5 *Report of Departmental Committee on Sexual Offences against Children and Young Persons in Scotland*, 44–6.
6 NRS, ED48/181/1, Minute by G. W. Simpson, 10 July 1933.
7 Ibid., Minute by G. W. Simpson, 6 July 1933.
8 NRS, HH60/278, Scottish Education Department (hereafter SED), *Circular no. 79*, 16 January 1929.
9 NRS, ED48/181/1, Minute by H. W. Cornish, 18 February 1934.
10 *Report of Medical Advisory Committee (Scotland) on Venereal Diseases*, 9; *Training for Citizenship: A Report of the Advisory*

Council on Education in Scotland, 12; *The Needs of Youth in These Times: A Report of the Scottish Youth Advisory Committee*, 91–2.

11 GACS, *Report of Committee on Church and Nation, 1943*, 246; *1944*, 280–1.

12 *Pamphlet no. 119, Sex Education in Schools and Youth Organisations.*

13 NRS, ED48/181/1, Minutes of Moray and Nairn Education Authority, 6 October 1943; ED48/773, Sex education: schemes of work in Edinburgh Corporation secondary schools, 17 October 1944.

14 See, for example, NRS, ED48/1364, J. Mackay Thomson to J. Jardine, 4 May 1944.

15 Ibid., Memorandum on sex education, May 1944.

16 Ibid., Evidence of Dr G. W. Simpson to Scottish Advisory Council on Education, 1943.

17 NRS, ED48/773, Minute by W. F. Arbuckle, 27 October 1944.

18 Ibid., Notes of meetings between the SED and Edinburgh Education Committee, 6 December 1944, 13 June 1945.

19 Unless otherwise stated, the following is based on the reports of the conferences' proceedings and enquiries in NRS, HH61/585.

20 Ibid. See also *Scottish Educational Journal* (hereafter *SEJ*), 33 (1950), 796.

21 NRS, ED48/178, Scottish Council for Health Education (hereafter SCHE) to Secretary, SED, 22 December 1950 (original emphasis).

22 Ibid., Minute by K. E. Miller, 3 May 1950.

23 NRS, ED48/1850, *The Alliance-Scottish Council* (hereafter A-SC) *Annual Report for 1957–8*, 5; *1966–7*, 3–5.

24 NRS, ED35/16, Sir J. M. Thomson to A. Duncan, 26 June 1948.

25 Unless otherwise stated, the following account is based on A-SC materials deposited in NRS, ED35/16; ED48/181/1; ED48/1850.

26 NRS, ED35/16, Alliance of Honour, *How you Grow* (n.d.), 22.

27 Ibid., 25.

28 Ibid., Alliance of Honour, *Telling Your Children* (n.d.), 3.

29 Ibid., Alliance of Honour, *How you Grow*, 20.

30 Ibid., Alliance of Honour, Dr A. H. Gray, *Are Sex Relations Without Marriage Wrong?* (n.d.), 4–5.

31 NRS, ED48/181/1; ED48/1850, *A-SC Annual Report for 1953–4*, 4; *1954–5*, 7; *1958–9*, 8–9; *1961–2*, 17.

32 NRS, HH58/108, SCHE, Medical Adviser's annual report for 1953–4; HH58/111, SCHE, minutes of Executive Committee, 15 December 1958.

33 The following is based upon Mearns, *Teaching Health*, 25; Currie and Mearns, *Manual of Public Health Hygiene*, 60; NLS, P.la.689, SCHE pamphlets, especially *Yourself and Your Body*, 15–16; *The Approach to Womanhood*, 10–13, 16; *From Boyhood to Manhood*, 17–21.

34 Mearns, *Teaching Health*, 25.

35 NRS, HH58/111, SCHE, minutes of Executive Committee, 22 April 1958; HH61/573, SCHE, Medical Adviser's report for 1958–9.

36 NRS, HH61/848, SCHE, minutes of Medical Advisory Committee, 30 June 1959; ED48/181/2, 'Note for record', n.d. 1960.

37 NRS, HH61/573, SCHE, Medical Adviser's reports for 1954–5, 1955–6; Mearns, *The Whole Child*, 78.

38 *Report of Royal Commission on Marriage and Divorce*, 93, 313; NRS, ED48/185, Correspondence and papers on the curriculum.

39 Ministry of Education, *Pamphlet no. 31, Health Education, 1957*.

40 NRS, ED48/185, Correspondence and papers on the curriculum.

41 *Annual Report of the Secretary of State for Scotland on Education in Scotland in 1958*, 45.

42 NRS, ED48/185, S. C. Aldridge to J. Kidd, 26 November 1956; Memorandum on 'Sex education in schools', 10 April 1957.

43 The following account is based on NRS, ED48/181/1–2; ED48/1638, 1850; HH58/108; HH61/1099.

44 NRS, ED48/1638, J. Kidd to H. H. Donnelly, 24 May 1960.

45 MSSVDSB, Minutes and correspondence.

46 NRS, ED48/181/2, Extract from *The Scotsman*, 22 May 1962; Minute Dr A. Law to F. M. M. Gray, 8 May 1963.

47 GACS, *Report of Committee on Temperance and Morals for 1961*, 455; *1962*, 442; *1963*, 419. Particular objection was taken to the 1962 Reith Lecture, delivered by G. M. Carstairs, Professor of Psychiatry at the University of Edinburgh, which was seen to endorse premarital sex.

48 NRS, ED48/1785, Draft report on 'The growth and development of the child', January 1963.

49 NRS, ED48/1638, Submission from PE and HE panel, June 1963.

50 See, for example, NRS, ED48/181/1, SED to Scottish Council of Women Citizens' Associations, 1 December 1960.

51 The following account is based on NRS, ED48/1638, Note for record, n.d. 1960; ED48/181/2, Note for record, 12 July 1963.

52 NRS, HH61/589, Scottish evidence to Cohen Committee.

53 Ibid.; *Health Education – Report of a Joint Committee of the Central and Scottish Health Services Councils*, 3, 42, 74.

54 NRS, HH61/1002, F. A. Adams to J. P. Dodds, 28 May 1964; ED48/1638, J. F. McClennan to R. Allan, 3 July 1964.

55 NRS, ED48/181/2, Minute I. W. Inglis to J. J. Farrell, 18 December 1964.

56 NRS, ED48/1850, *A-SC Annual Report for 1966-67*, 10–11.

57 NRS, HH61/1099, Health education in schools, note of meeting, 29 March 1966.

58 *SEJ*, 51, 9 February 1968, 134.

59 NRS, ED48/181/1, Minute T. Haig to J. J. Farrell, 15 June 1965; *Annual Report of MOH for Aberdeen for 1966*, 32; *1967*, 35.

60 NRS, ED48/1338, EIS report on sex and health education, May 1968, 2–4.
61 *Annual Report of MOH for Dundee for 1966*, 27–8.
62 *Annual Report of MOH for Edinburgh for 1967*, xii.
63 *SEJ*, 51, 8 March 1968, 243.
64 Ibid., 51, 5 July 1968, 664–5; 12 July 1968, 683. Initially, 60 per cent of schools arranged for the viewing to be single-sex.
65 NRS, ED48/1338, EIS report on health and sex education, May 1968.
66 GCA, C1/3/160, Minutes of Glasgow Corporation Education Committee, 19 November and 17 December 1969; *Glasgow Herald*, 9 January 1970. This decision was vigorously supported by the Roman Catholic hierarchy in Scotland. They criticised the films for failing to locate sex within the broader moral and spiritual context of marriage and family life, for encouraging a precocious and potentially harmful interest in sexual issues, for usurping a vital parental responsibility and for marginalising the call of the Church for 'education in chastity' [*Scottish Catholic Observer*, 28 November 1969, 6 February 1970].
67 NRS, ED48/1337, 1338, Papers and minutes of Curriculum Committee on Moral and Religious Education.
68 *SEJ*, 51, 8 March 1968, 243.
69 *A Report of the Secretary of State for Scotland: Education in Scotland in 1961*, PP, 1961–2 (Cmnd 1673), XIII, 52.
70 *Guidance in Scottish Secondary Schools* (HMSO, 1968), paras 18–20, merely identified a need for improved social and moral education, including 'frank and open-ended' group discussion of personal relationships. *Raising the School Leaving Age: Suggestions for Courses* (HMSO, 1966), paras 6 and 18–21, referred vaguely to the responsibility of schools to give pupils 'the opportunity to look at moral problems' including 'questions of sex morality'.
71 NRS, ED48/181/2, Minutes on DES handbook, 16 February 1965.
72 NRS, ED48/1337, 1338, Papers and minutes of Curriculum Committee on Moral and Religious Education.
73 *Moral and Religious Education in Scottish Schools.*
74 For the proceedings of the working party and its sub-committee on sex education, see NRS, ED48/1954.
75 Ibid., Minutes of working party, 16 October 1970.
76 NRS, ED48/1463, Consultative Committee on the Curriculum (hereafter CCC) minutes, 9 January and 28 February 1973.
77 See, for example, *Hansard* [*HL*], vol. 318, 12 May 1971, cols 1,064–5.
78 NRS, HH61/1021, Minutes on film, *Growing Up*, May–June 1971 (original emphasis).
79 SED, *Curriculum Paper 14: Health Education in Schools.*
80 NRS, HH61/1019, Covering letter and *Circular 896*, 16 April 1974.
81 Ibid., Minute by G. N. Munro, October 1974.

82 *SEJ*, 57, 19 April 1974, 406; 58, 29 August 1975, 787.

83 NRS, HH61/1019, Chief Medical Officer to J. M. Fearn, 11 December 1974.

84 Ibid., E. Redmond to J. A. M. Mitchell, 30 April 1976.

85 NRS, ED48/2341, H. Robertson to E. Redmond, 24 December 1975, 3 February 1976; HH61/1019, Robertson to Redmond, 2 July 1976.

86 *SEJ*, 57, 19 April 1974, 406, 458.

87 NRS, HH61/1021, Extract from *Glasgow Herald*, 5 April 1976; D. Player to M. Maclean, 4 May 1976; Scottish Family Planning Association (hereafter SFPA) to Secretary CCC, 18 October 1977.

88 GACS, *Report of Moral Welfare Committee, 1975*, 344.

89 Ibid., *1977*, 305–6.

90 For an overview of Catholic initiatives, see SED, *Health Education in Primary, Secondary and Special Schools in Scotland. A Report by HM Inspectors of Schools*, 37–8.

91 NRS, HH61/1019, Extract from *Scotsman*, 18 September 1976; Note of steering group, 24 November 1976; *Scottish Catholic Observer*, 24 September 1976. However, according to the *Scottish Catholic Observer*, 11 November 1977, there remained a 'tremendous variation' in the width and depth of sex education in Catholic schools, reflecting 'a profound uncertainty in many Catholic teaching circles about the correct organisational, psychological and theological framework within which the subject should be taught'.

92 See, for example, NRS, HH61/1019, Briefing note for House of Lords debate, January 1976.

93 NRS, ED48/2341, Minutes on *Health Education in Primary Schools*, 16 September 1976.

94 NRS, HH61/970, H. Robertson to W. A. McNeill, 5 March 1975.

95 NRS, HH61/1019, E. Redmond to A. Mitchell, 5 May 1976. On the broader implications of the 1976 debate, see also Meredith, *Sex Education*, 19–25.

96 *Hansard [HL]*, vol. 367, 14 January 1976, cols 134–50, 241–7.

97 Ibid., cols 196–200. For a similar transition in the USA in the discourse of anti-sex educationists from a focus on the fear of arousal to allegations of emotional abuse, see Irvine, *Talk About Sex*, 135–7.

98 NRS, HH61/1019, I. M. Robertson to E. Redmond, 11 May 1976; HH61/1021, Memorandum by R. S. Johnston, 'Links Between SED and FPA', 26 October 1977; Minutes of meeting with FPA, 22 November 1977. For a similar distancing of government from the FPA south of the Border, see Meredith, *Sex Education*, 85–6.

99 SED, *Health Education in Primary, Secondary and Special Schools in Scotland. A Report by HM Inspectors of Schools*.

100 Ibid., 10. For a comparable picture of sex education provision in schools in England and Wales in the late 1970s, revealing similar deficiencies, see Farrell and Kellaher, *My Mother Said*, ch. 8.

101 SED, *Health Education in Primary, Secondary and Special Schools in Scotland*, 17–19.

102 NRS, ED48/234; HH61/1021, C. B. S. Schofield and F. M. Martin, 'Health education in schools, with particular reference to sexually transmitted diseases'; HH104/36, Memorandum by Dr D. H. Robertson, June 1977.

103 NRS, ED48/1725, 48/1736, Minutes of CCC, 2 December 1980, 3 February 1981.

104 NRS, HH61/1018, F. M. Martin, 'Health education in secondary schools with particular reference to sex education: a survey of professional and parental attitudes', September 1981; MSSVDSB minutes, 7 April 1984, 5 October 1985, 10 May 1986.

105 *House of Commons Social Services Committee, Problems Associated with AIDS*, 174.

PART IV
Sex and Censorship

9

MORAL CENSORSHIP AND THE STATE
IN THE 1950s

INTRODUCTION

In addition to confronting issues of sexual criminality, education, health and reproduction, during the period 1950–80 the Scottish state also sought to regulate public access to sexually explicit material. The history of censorship has in recent years been the subject of considerable revisionism. Conventional approaches that interpreted censorship primarily as a function of unilaterally imposed institutional practices and proscriptions have been increasingly challenged. Instead, censorship has come to be seen more as an ongoing, interactive process reflecting complex and sometimes contradictory relations of power, especially in relation to sexuality.[1] In addition, the theories of both Michel Foucault and Jacques Lacan have been deployed to view censorship as part of broader discursive practices that impart societal norms, with linguistic structures playing a vital role.[2]

However, whatever the conceptual framework adopted, as with other areas of sexual policy making after 1950, the main focus of historical research on moral censorship has been on England: on the moral panics, police campaigns, sensational trials and policy debates south of the Border.[3] Records of the Home Office and the Lord Chamberlain, and of English pressure groups and cultural organisations, have primarily shaped the historical narrative. The aim of this section is to explore for the first time the Scottish dimension to the story, dealing in turn with the censorship of literature, theatre, broadcasting and film, and examining the dynamics of policy making at both a national and a local level.

In Chapter 9, a survey of developments in the 1950s will first trace the response of Scottish governance to post-war moral panics surrounding obscene publications. The nature of Scots law and legal processes will be reviewed, along with the pattern of criminal proceedings and key legal judgements. In addition, the approach of the policy community in Scotland to legislative proposals culminating in the 1959 Obscene Publications Act will be examined in detail. Second, the chapter will discuss the contribution of the Scottish Office to the debate surrounding the future of theatre censorship under the Lord Chamberlain, and its unease at possible measures that might run counter to the moral concerns of Scottish public opinion. Finally, the nature and extent of film censorship will be addressed, focusing on the social politics surrounding the regulation of children's cinema attendances, on the process of local licensing and on the types of film whose public exhibition was prohibited or restricted because of their sexual content.

Chapter 10 extends our story into the so-called 'permissive sixties'. First, given the absence of Scotland's involvement in the Obscene Publications Acts of 1959 and 1964, it concentrates instead on the imposition of censorship by the local state, both by magistrates and by librarians, using Edinburgh as a case study. Second, the chapter explores the impulses and constraints shaping the Scottish response to the repeal in 1968 of the 1843 Theatres Act, and investigates the degree to which existing local powers relating to indecency and obscenity continued to be exercised in Edinburgh and Glasgow to ban experimental and avant-garde theatrical performances. Third, the growing concern in Scotland at the cultural impact of broadcasting is documented. Particular attention is paid to the efforts of both the Scottish Office and the Broadcasting Council for Scotland to protect the moral identity of Scottish society. Finally, the chapter surveys the extent of locally imposed film censorship in Edinburgh and Glasgow in the 1960s, and the increasing resistance within both the council chambers and the press to local magistrates determining the viewing habits of the public.

Chapter 11 addresses developments in the 1970s. The issue of obscene publications and pornography dominates the narrative. The impact in Scotland in the early years of the decade of a moral backlash against the permissive values of the 1960s, akin to that experienced in England, is reviewed. Thereafter, the chapter investigates the response of Scottish departments of state and law officers to a series of reports and legislative initiatives relating to pornography in the 1970s, including the Longford Report of 1972, the Cinematograph and Indecent Displays Bill of 1973, the 1978 Protection of Children Act and the reports on obscenity of the Williams Committee and the Church of Scotland in 1979. In addition, the pattern of ongoing local enforcement, and efforts to modernise local powers and to introduce a more proactive and consistent policy of prosecution, are also examined. The censorship of theatre, broadcasting and film in Scotland in the 1970s is then surveyed, revealing the relatively passive role of the Scottish Office, the continuing importance of church proceedings in the policy-making process and the increasing challenge within public debate to the moral surveillance and censorship traditionally exercised by local councillors and magistrates. Some concluding remarks seek to identify the main fears and assumptions that underpinned moral censorship by the state in Scotland over the entire period 1950–80, and to tease out some of the central aims that policy makers sought to achieve.

OBSCENE PUBLICATIONS

Scots law and legal procedures

Under common law in Scotland, it was an offence 'to publish, circulate or expose for sale any obscene work – book, picture, photograph, print or writing – devised and intended to corrupt the morals of the community and to create inordinate and lustful desires'.[4] In terms of statute law, the 1857 Obscene Publications Act, which empowered magistrates in England and Wales to initiate destruction orders for publications adjudged to be obscene, did not apply in Scotland. However, other measures applied both sides of the Border. Thus, clauses of the 1824 Vagrancy Act relating to the public exhibition of obscene materials had been applied to Scotland under the 1871 Prevention of Crime Act. Under the 1889 Indecent Advertisement Act, it was an offence to exhibit in the window of any shop, any picture or printed or written matter of an indecent nature. In addition, the Judicial Proceedings (Regulation of Reports) Act of 1926 had made it an offence 'to print or publish in relation to any judicial proceedings any indecent matter or indecent medical, surgical or physiological details calculated to injure public morals'. Meanwhile, the importation and transmission of indecent or obscene articles was a punishable offence under the Customs Consolidation Act of 1876 and the 1953 Post Office Act.

Yet, as in so many other areas of moral regulation in post-war Scotland, in practice, the most important powers were those enacted under the Burgh Police (Scotland) Act 1892, and the corresponding provisions of local acts and corporation orders. Under Section 380 (3) of the 1892 Act, it was an offence within a burgh 'to publish, print, offer for sale, distribute, or exhibit to view, any indecent picture, print, text, or other object, or to send any printed or written paper of an indecent nature through the post', on penalty of a fine of up to £10 or a maximum of sixty days' imprisonment. While a very few of the most serious cases might be heard in a Sheriff Court, the over-whelming majority of cases relating to obscene publications during the 1950s were heard summarily as contraventions of the Police Act or corporation orders before a magistrate in a Burgh Court.[5]

Enforcement of the law sometimes commenced with a complaint by one or more members of the public to the police. At other times, cases appear to have stemmed from contemporary moral panics surrounding juvenile sexual delinquency. Thus, in 1953, the prose-cution of eighteen newsagents in Methil and Buckhaven followed a decision of the Town Council to stamp out the 'sale of trashy and pornographic literature' on display in shops adjacent to the local school, whose 'sexy titles and cover illustrations' were viewed as harmful to 'youthful minds'.[6] Finally, although there does not appear to have been in Scotland anything approaching the witch hunt against obscene literature conducted by the Metropolitan Police in the early 1950s,[7] some proceedings in Scotland do appear to have been initiated as part of a more coordinated campaign by the police. For example, in Glasgow, a rise in prosecutions for offences relating to indecent advertisements and obscene publications in 1951 resulted from a deliberate campaign by the police authorities.[8]

Consolidated lists of titles of novels and magazines that had been the subject of destruction orders by various courts across Britain were circulated annually to Chief Constables in Scotland,[9] and plain-clothes police cadets and clerks were regularly used to entrap book-sellers alleged to be handling material on these lists. Thus, in 1954, Edward Duncan Haig was charged with having sold a 'Boy Clerk of the Edinburgh City Police' an indecent book entitled *London Models*.[10] The Burgh Prosecutor for Aberdeen reported in 1955 that he did 'not recollect a single case where proceedings were instituted because of complaints by members of the public. Instead, police action [had] been taken because publications mentioned in the Home Office lists of forfeited publications [had] been seen in the shops.'[11] Moreover, while there was no equivalent to London's 'Vice Squad' within the Scottish police, evidence suggests that individual forces increasingly designated officers to vice-related duties. In Edinburgh, police duties relating to pornography were reviewed, and by the end of the decade formally integrated with those relating to the suppression of prosti-tution, brothel-keeping and 'unnatural sexual offences'.[12]

Penalties for conviction varied. Except where there existed a string of previous convictions, imprisonment was rare and the usual sentence was a fine, typically varying from £3 to £5 for a first offence. However, the real penalty often lay in an accompanying forfeiture and destruction order that, in some instances, involved large amounts of material. In the case against William Irving, a bookseller in Kilmarnock, while the fine was only £5, the magistrate ordered the forfeiture of 853 books and magazines.[13] Similarly, in the case of William Gamble, charged before Glasgow Central Police Court in 1951 with possessing indecent publications, a fine of £10 was imposed and some 918 publications ordered to be destroyed.[14]

Two judgements were central in shaping the legal response to obscene publications in Scotland in the 1950s.[15] First, in *McGowan* v. *Langmuir* in 1931 the High Court had held that the magistrate, in considering whether the offending materials were indecent, was entitled to take into account the circumstances in which they were kept. Whether or not any particular work was obscene might therefore depend on 'extrinsic circumstances'. Second, the appeal judgement in *Gellatly* v. *Laird* in 1953 not only stipulated that it was the magistrate's duty alone to examine the publications, and 'to decide for himself whether or not they were indecent or obscene', but also provided guidelines as to what constituted an obscene publication. According to the Lord Justice General, Lord Cooper, to justify a conviction, the Crown had to be satisfied on two grounds, that:

(1) The book or picture was of such a nature as to be calculated to produce a pernicious effect in depraving and corrupting those who were open to such influences.
(2) Such a book or picture was being indiscriminately exhibited or circulated or offered for sale in such circumstances as to justify the inference that it was likely to fall (and perhaps intended to fall) into the hands of persons liable to be corrupted.

In his judgement, the second of these seemed the more important, given that a book or picture, however obscene, would 'create no social evil of the type sought to be repressed so long as it [was] kept in proper custody and under responsible control'. In Lord Cooper's view, the

mischief reside[d] not so much in the book or picture as in the use to which it [was] put usually deliberately and for gain by the trafficker in pornography who [made] a business of inspiring and catering for depraved and perverted tastes.

Moreover, as intention to pervert was clearly the critical issue, he held that evidence for the defence that similar materials circulated freely elsewhere should not be admitted: 'The character of other books [was] a collateral issue, the exploration of which would be endless and futile.'

At the same time, Lord Cooper was at pains to emphasise that the penal provisions were not aimed at 'a setting-up in each locality of a *censor morum* with the duty of compiling on the principles of Mrs Grundy an *index expurgatorium* of the literary and artistic productions of all the ages, and with the power of imprisoning reputable dealers'. Given that, in his view, the legal process in Scotland took account of the context in which material was displayed and distributed, he remained unpersuaded by those who argued that the liberty of dealers was threatened by the possibility of their being in possession of a work – 'perhaps a celebrated classic – which might offend the susceptibilities of the type of magistrate described as "the morose puritan"'.

These judgements were a constant source of reference in Scottish obscenity trials in the following decades. In particular, they were deployed to deny the defence the right to cross-question prosecution witnesses (pre-eminently the police and civic dignitaries) on their definition of obscenity, or to introduce comparative examples of allegedly indecent material circulating freely elsewhere, including local public libraries.

The 1959 Obscene Publications Act

These judgements were also to figure prominently in the deliberations of Scottish policy makers confronting the issue as to how far, if at all, Scotland should be affected by a new Obscene Publications Act. In the mid-1950s, the Conservative Government was faced with growing pressure to reform the law relating to indecent and obscene literature led by the Society of Authors and articulated in a series of Private Members' Bills that proved highly contentious.[16] There were five central aims of the proposed measures: first, to replace the existing definition of obscenity with one more explicitly related to intent and effect; second, to permit expert evidence to be led on the artistic and literary merit of a work; third, to centralise the prosecution process so as to produce more consistency and to curb witch hunts driven by the moral agendas of individual police chiefs and magistrates; fourth, to secure a fairer and more transparent process for the issue of destruction orders; and finally, at the same time, to ensure that the courts had adequate powers to punish and deter those who were producing or distributing pornographic material.

Scottish law officers and senior policy advisers were agreed that existing Scots law and legal procedures were adequate on most counts and that there was no need for Scotland to be included in new legislation. They argued that, under the 1892 Burgh Police (Scotland) Act and equivalent corporation orders, penalties were substantially higher than those operating in England and that, except in Edinburgh, Scottish police authorities were generally content with the powers at their disposal.[17] According to official statistics, although there had been a rise in convictions relating to obscene publications immediately after the Second World War, the recent trend was downwards.[18] Moreover, whereas in England magistrates could issue a destruction order without court proceedings, leading in some notorious instances to the forfeiture of literary classics, in Scotland, the forfeiture and destruction of material only followed the legal conviction of an individual. As a result, the list of books and magazines scheduled for destruction was, it was claimed, more closely scrutinised and the process had not fallen into disrepute.[19]

Scottish officials were also opposed to the authorisation of prosecutions being coordinated by the Lord Advocate. In their view, this was both impractical and, in view of the role of the procurators fiscal in Scotland, unjustified. They were acutely aware that such a move would be viewed as inferring the incompetence of the Burgh Courts, and that north of the Border, public opinion, often led by the churches, expected the enforcement of moral issues to conform to local values and not some set of statutory norms laid down in Westminster or even Edinburgh.[20] In addition, the Scottish Office considered that legal decisions in Scotland had already created considerable flexibility in the interpretation of obscenity, and that issues relating to the intention of the accused and the likely impact of material were already being taken into account in Scottish courts.[21]

These arguments were advanced in response to a succession of Private Members' Bills over the period 1955–8, with a final decision to exclude Scotland from legislation being taken in December 1958. Although it was acknowledged that it might appear anomalous to have different definitions of obscenity north and south of the Border, based on statute in England and common law in Scotland, few problems were anticipated. Hitherto, publishers, librarians, booksellers and writers had not encountered difficulties with there being two legal systems, and it was emphasised that, in many respects, the Scottish interpretation of obscenity, and specifically that laid down in *Gellatly* v. *Laird*, was very similar to that sought by the proponents of law reform in England.[22]

Furthermore, Scottish law officers were reluctant to be associated with any bill that afforded a defence of literary or artistic merit in proceedings relating to obscene publications. They adhered to the opinion of Lord Cooper that the evaluation as to whether a specific work was obscene rested solely with the individual magistrate and not with the testimony of expert witnesses seeking to contextualise it within a broader cultural debate.[23] In addition, the legal technicalities involved in any attempt to conflate English and Scottish legal procedures relating to obscenity were legion; whether it was the process of initiating legal proceedings, the conduct of any trial or the implementation of penalties. Above all, officials did not relish the prospect of having to redraft a myriad of local acts and byelaws that had hitherto defined the response of the local state in Scotland to issues involving indecent material.[24]

Officials noted that there was 'no pressure from the press or the public to change the Scottish position'[25] and, with only one very minor exception,[26] the issue of bringing Scotland into line with English proposals was not raised in Parliament. As the Scottish Legal Secretary and Parliamentary Draftsman concluded in December 1958:

> The alleged position in England is that their present law enables what is not obscene on a reasonable view to be prosecuted as obscene and that therefore their law should be amended. There is no complaint or suggestion that the present law in Scotland fails in its purpose, or, with our system of public prosecutors, is directed capriciously against persons who ought not be prosecuted, and there seems no ground for altering it.[27]

Accordingly, Scotland did not figure in the Obscene Publications Acts of 1959 and 1964 or in the prolonged debates surrounding them.

THEATRE

As in England and Wales, theatrical performances in Scotland were subject to censorship by the Lord Chamberlain under the Theatres Act of 1843. He was empowered by the Act to forbid the presentation of any play or part thereof if, in his opinion, 'it [was] fitting for the preservation of good manners, decorum, or of the public peace so to do'. The 1950s witnessed a protracted debate in England over the future of theatre censorship, largely initiated by the Lord Chamberlain, the Earl of Scarborough, in 1957.[28] In his view, there was an urgent need to introduce more flexibility into the licensing of plays in order to allow for shifting social attitudes towards the discussion of issues such as homosexuality, especially in view of the widespread publicity accorded to the proceedings of the Wolfenden Committee. This would, he argued, reduce the growing evasion of existing censorship procedures by private theatre clubs and restore some measure of credibility to the Lord Chamberlain's role. However, at the same time, in order to protect the young, he proposed that he be empowered to restrict certain plays to adult audiences over the age of 18, and that local licensing authorities be required to implement such restrictions.[29]

Initially, the Home Office was broadly supportive of updating the Theatres Act and introducing a more graduated system of theatre licensing in line with film censorship that would liberalise the censorship of controversial issues. However, it was concerned that the measure might prove controversial and open up for debate the whole issue of censorship. Accordingly, officials recommended that, in the first instance, encouragement should only be given to a Private Member's Bill.[30]

For a range of, sometimes contradictory, reasons, the Scottish Home Department (SHD) was lukewarm towards the idea of fresh legislation. Although a recent showing of Arthur Miller's *A View from the Bridge* at a private club organised by the Glasgow Citizens Theatre had attracted publicity, the Department did not think theatre censorship was a problem north of the Border.[31] Moreover, officials were mindful of the conservatism of Scottish attitudes towards sexual issues and of the growing concerns of Scottish church assemblies at the immorality of modern plays. As Assistant Secretary N. D. Walker reported to the Home Office, the Secretary of State for Scotland would inevitably take a cautious stance and would have 'to take into account the body of public opinion which would take a puritanical attitude towards plays dealing with perversion'.[32]

Finally, the Scottish Office foresaw major problems in implementing a measure that merely grafted additional powers onto the existing Theatres Act, especially with respect to the responsibilities of local licensing authorities to restrict the access of children to so-called A [Adult] plays. Under the Local Government (Scotland) Act of 1947, in cities and towns (where most of the theatres were located) 'order and decency' in theatres was ensured by byelaws and local acts. Any amendment to existing powers would therefore involve the revision of a mass of local regulations and byelaws. Instead, the SHD favoured entirely fresh legislation that devolved responsibility for regulating audiences to theatre managers.[33]

Throughout 1958, the Home Secretary continued to discuss the issue with the Lord Chamberlain and the Home Affairs Committee. However, the Home Office was increasingly reluctant to proceed with a substantive measure of reform. It was feared that to enhance the Lord Chamberlain's powers to classify the age-appropriateness of plays would serve only to emphasise the anachronism of his post as censor and add further public and political controversy to that already surrounding the issue of obscene publications. At the same time, it was anticipated that any erosion of the existing process of theatre censorship might provoke the forces of moral conservatism in society, and leave theatre managements at the mercy of possibly more arbitrary and coercive local licensing bodies.[34]

The Scottish Office remained sceptical of the need for legislation. Perhaps mindful of the contemporary opposition to homosexual law reform in Scotland, it did not share the Lord Chamberlain's desire to introduce age restrictions on plays as a precursor to the licensing of performances that addressed issues relating to homosexuality. In the view of the Joint Parliamentary Under-Secretary of State, if greater permissiveness was '*really thought necessary*', all that was needed was a change of view by the Lord Chamberlain as to what was 'fitting for the preservation of good manners, decorum, and the public peace'.[35] The Secretary of State for Scotland, John Scott Maclay, shared his reservations, and feared that new measures would be criticised in Scotland as 'being halfway to Wolfenden'.[36]

In the event, having explored and subsequently discounted the possibility of an informal, non-statutory arrangement between the Lord Chamberlain and theatre managers that involved conditional licensing, and 'alarmed at the prospect of the pre-censorship system being submitted to parliamentary and press scrutiny', Conservative ministers declined to take further action.[37]

CINEMA

Children's films

Prior to the 1950s, as in England, the powers of Scottish licensing authorities to control cinema exhibitions were conferred by the 1909

Cinematograph Act.[38] However, the interpretation of the Act had varied. In England, the courts had ruled that, in addition to conditions relating to safety, it was lawful for local authorities to attach to a licence conditions 'with respect to the character of the films being shown'. In addition, in 1929, the Home Office had issued a set of model conditions suggested for inclusion in cinematographic licences. These proposed that no film should be shown which was 'likely to be injurious to morality', that no film which had not been passed by the British Board of Film Censors (BBFC) should be exhibited without the express consent of the licensing authority, and that no film that was not passed by the BBFC for 'universal exhibition' could be shown while a child under (or appearing to be under) the age of 16 was present. The model conditions also incorporated the so-called A rule, which stipulated that, while an A film was being exhibited, no person under 16 could be admitted to or allowed to remain in the cinema unless accompanied by a parent or *bona fide* guardian. Subsequently, the overwhelming majority of licensing authorities in England and Wales had adopted these conditions and made regular use of the BBFC's classifications to regulate the films that children might see.

In contrast, in Scotland, successive Lords Advocate had advised that the Scottish courts were unlikely to adopt such a flexible interpretation of the 1909 Act, and that, legally, Scottish licensing authorities had 'power only to impose "safety" and not "moral" conditions'. However, in the 1930s, there was strong pressure from various bodies, including women's organisations, purity groups, such as the National Vigilance Association, and social welfare agencies, for Scottish practice to be brought into line with that in England. Separate legislation for Scotland was rejected, but following meetings between the Secretary of State for Scotland and the Scottish Branch of the Cinema Exhibitors' Association (SBCEA), the Association agreed to recommend its members to observe voluntarily all the Home Office model conditions except the A film rule.[39] Subsequently, in 1938, the Association also undertook not to display A films at children's matinées, but as the general practice in Scotland was not to hold special matinées but simply to admit children to cinemas at reduced rates to afternoon and early evening performances, Scottish children were routinely exposed to unsuitable programmes.

The possible impact of the cinema on the moral values and behaviour of children and young people produced widespread public and professional concern in Scotland in the immediate post-war years.

As in the 1930s,[40] middle-class religious, educational and social welfare groups viewed the film-going habits of the young as a likely cause of moral degeneration. Information on the incidence of cinema attendance north of the Border only served to reinforce such anxieties. It was estimated that some 56 per cent of Scottish children went to the cinema at least once a week as compared with 36 per cent of children in England and Wales. Moreover, as many as 47 per cent of Scottish children in the age group 10 to 15 years went to the cinema at least twice a week as compared with 22 per cent in London and the south-east.

Evidence to the Wheare Committee on Children and the Cinema (1947–50) clearly reflected contemporary anxieties. In Scotland, apart from the representatives of the film distributors and exhibitors, the Committee canvassed opinion from a wide range of organisations including the civil service, the police, the judiciary, the juvenile probation and remand system, the churches, welfare and education departments, women's pressure groups and the licensing authorities. Much of their testimony criticised the lack of a clear legal framework in Scotland for the regulation of children's attendance at the cinema, and viewed their exposure to inappropriate images as erosive of character and moral fibre. In general, most witnesses favoured the remit of Scottish licensing authorities being extended from safety to 'child welfare' issues. Continuing reservations were, however, expressed by some commentators about the adoption of the A film rule in Scotland, partly on the grounds that, in encouraging children to solicit strangers in order to gain entry to adult films, it facilitated child molestation.[41]

While acknowledging the lack of hard data on the correlation between cinema attendance and the incidence of moral laxity and delinquency in the young, the Wheare Committee was persuaded of the adverse effects of films that glorified 'sexual licence'. Evidence presented to the Committee had highlighted the 'low standard of sexual morality in many films' ranging from 'particular immodesties of gesture, dress and appearance in the characters, and in their physical relationships, to a thoroughly licentious purport in the whole plot and presentation of the film'.[42] In order to address this threat of moral degeneration, the Committee recommended that, even if accompanied, children should be banned from any films 'whose episodes or general tenor [was] licentious or suggestive'. More broadly, it recommended that throughout Britain there should be one system of film classification, and clear and uniform powers for licensing authorities to regulate the attendance of children in the interests of their moral welfare.[43]

The Government's response was the Cinematograph Bill of 1952. It provided that the powers of the Secretary of State to issue regulations under the 1909 Act should be extended to 'the health and welfare of children in relation to attendance at cinematograph exhibitions'. In addition, it empowered licensing authorities to attach to their licences conditions relating to attendance at films, and imposed upon them the duty not only of ensuring that children did not have access to exhibitions deemed unsuitable by the licensing authority or the BBFC, but also of considering what conditions, if any, should be applied to the admission of children to all other films.[44]

During the debates on the Bill in the House of Commons, strong opposition was voiced on behalf of the Scottish film exhibitors. Their association protested that, since 1934, they had adhered voluntarily to the English guidelines except for the condition that required the exhibitor to exclude unaccompanied children from A films. It considered that this voluntary agreement had operated very successfully, in contrast to that of the A rule in England that had proved ineffective and highly contentious. The Association opposed any licensing condition that involved the exhibitor in having to recognise the age of children seeking to gain admission to the cinema.[45]

Some MPs also opposed the Bill on grounds relating to national identity and cultural differences. Thus, A. Woodburn, Labour MP for Clackmannan and East Stirlingshire, objected that the number of unaccompanied children in Scottish cinemas was primarily a function of overcrowded housing and that it was safer for young children to be with their siblings in the cinema than soliciting strangers in order to gain admittance. In his view, excluding them might merely expose them to the moral hazard of the streets.[46] He also claimed that, in Scotland, there was no demand for the 'highly intellectual problem film' that might contain inappropriate material, and that Scottish children were unresponsive to films depicting intimate behaviour of any sort.[47] Meanwhile, Patrick Maitland, Conservative MP for Lanark, protested that the recognition and preservation of Scots law, enshrined in the Act of Union, was in danger of being undermined and that in Scotland 'an effective system [was] already operating to keep children from the greater of two evils, namely, undesirable company being something worse than undesirable film shows'.[48]

However, the SHD was disposed to support the Bill.[49] In line with the recommendations of the Wheare Committee, with the views of

Scottish educational and youth organisations, and with representations from Scottish local authority associations, it argued that, in the
interests of the moral welfare of children, licensing authorities in
Scotland should have powers to regulate their access to film exhibitions. The previous dependence on voluntary agreements with the
cinema industry was regarded as insufficient and anomalous. Indeed,
the SHD pointed out that, although strictly *ultra vires*, in Scotland,
three cities, seven counties and nine burghs had already passed local
regulations widening the powers of their licensing authorities to
include the regulation of children's admission.

At the same time, the Department was not persuaded that Scottish
audiences were sufficiently culturally distinct to merit a separate
process of licensing. In its view, Scottish children shared the same
vulnerability to immoral material as those in England and Wales and
were similarly liable to be corrupted by sexually explicit and salacious
films. Nor was it convinced that the evidence of indecency offences
against children in cinemas in England and Scotland supported the
view that the more liberal conditions of access for children to A films
in Scotland reduced their risk of molestation. In an attempt to
placate Scottish film exhibitors, the Department emphasised that,
while the Bill imposed a *duty* to exclude children from X rated films,
it only required licensing authorities to *consider* what exclusions
they might impose on access to A films. Scottish cinema owners and
managers were also assured that any future regulations under the
Act relating to contravention of the A film rule would allow for a
competent defence that a child 'appeared' to be over 16 or to be
accompanied by a parent or guardian.

Following the enactment of the 1952 Cinematograph Bill, policy
making centred around protracted negotiations with local authorities,
with the cinema industry, and with church and welfare agencies over
the specific content of regulations and model licensing conditions to
be issued by the Secretary of State for Scotland. Film exhibitors in
Scotland continued to oppose any standardisation of regulations that
disregarded the cultural differences in cinema attendance between
London and 'Scottish country towns and villages'. In particular, they
stressed that, in Scotland, children under 5 were very often sent to
the cinema with their older siblings to relieve 'parental pressures' and
overcrowding, and that children attending evening performances
were, in fact, less liable to sexual molestation, as the cinemas were
generally full.[50] In contrast, the Scottish churches and women's
organisations continued to press for more stringent regulations on

the grounds that, in their view, there was a clear link between the exposure of children to inappropriate material and the decline in moral standards of Scottish youth.[51] Local education and magistrates' committees approved of the imposition of a minimum age for un-accompanied children (although differing in opinion as to whether it should be 5 or 7). In addition, they supported the proposal that an accompanying person should be at least 16, and that the attendance of children at evening performances should be closely regulated.[52]

After extensive consultations with interested parties, the Secretary of State finally announced in August 1955 that the 1952 Act would come into operation in Scotland as from 1 January 1956. The circular re-emphasised the power of licensing authorities to take the moral welfare of children into consideration in laying down conditions of access to films 'designated as unsuitable' and, in addition, to keep under review the need for restrictions on the admission of children to all other films.[53] The subsequent statutory instrument stipulated that no child apparently under the age of 5 was to be admitted to a cinematograph exhibition unless in the charge of a person who appeared to have attained the age of 16 years, and that no child apparently under the age of 12 was to be admitted after 7pm to an exhibition where there was an earlier showing unless accompanied by someone who appeared to be 16.[54]

In implementing the 1952 Act, the SHD was at pains to conciliate Scottish interests. In particular, in the light of evidence submitted to the Wheare Committee and the view of the Cinema Consultative Committee that it would be 'undesirable' to impose the A film rule on Scotland, reference to the rule was explicitly excluded from the model guidelines attached to the circular and from the statutory instrument. In the event, very few, if any, local authorities in Scotland adopted the rule and, in the absence of any strong representations on the issue, the SHD was content to let the matter drop.[55]

Adult films

Meanwhile, in accordance with the voluntary agreements established between the Scottish Office and the SBCEA in the inter-war period, most local licensing authorities in Scotland normally adhered to the classifications awarded by the BBFC in their treatment of adult films. The 1952 Cinematograph Act, underpinned by widespread pressure from church and moral welfare organisations, served to homologate this agreement in law.

The requirement of cuts or amendments to the content of films as the condition of a specific classification for public exhibition remained the only means of censorship in the power of the BBFC. Scottish licensing authorities (commonly the Magistrates' Committee) were generally content to rely on this degree of regulation, despite the fact that the Board lacked any clear yardstick for evaluating the moral calibre of cinematic material. However, the ultimate power continued to reside at the local level, and it remained possible for a film, whether or not certificated by the Board, to be refused a licence in one part of Scotland and given a licence in another. As a later report by a committee of the Church of Scotland observed, 'this might not only reflect substantial regional differences of taste and life-style' – for example, as between Glasgow and the Highlands and Islands – but also eccentric local variations such as between Edinburgh and Musselburgh.[56]

Generally, all the films that were 'uncensored' and that either lacked or had been refused certification from the BBFC were previewed by representatives of the Magistrates' Committee. The Committee might then refuse permission for exhibition or impose restrictions. In the case of Edinburgh,[57] some twenty-two 'uncensored' films were previewed during the period 1950–9, of which four were refused permission for public exhibition. Nine of the remainder were only licensed for exhibition subject to age restrictions. Some refusals and restrictions related to films that were considered blasphemous, such as *The Miracle*, or, as in the case of *The Wild One*, depicted juvenile violence and the breakdown of social order, but the majority related to issues of sexual morality.

First, there was a range of largely foreign-produced films that were deemed risqué and provocative, and that portrayed transgressive sexual behaviour such as adultery, abortion, promiscuity and prostitution.[58] Such films included *Street Corner*, *Keep Your Eyes on Amelia*, *Manon*, *We Want a Child*, *Trois Femmes*, *Stain in the Snow*, *Wicked Woman* and *Femmes de Paris*. This type of film appears to have generated the most disagreement within the Magistrates' Committee. Thus, the over 16 restriction imposed on *Manon*, a graphic depiction of Paris and its *demi-monde* society after the war,[59] which had been awarded the Grand Prix at the Venice Film Festival, was only arrived at after two previews and a majority decision.[60] Similarly, *Femmes de Paris*, another film addressing the more salacious aspects of Parisian nightlife, was refused a licence for exhibition on the casting vote of the Lord Provost.[61]

A second group of films, such as *Garden of Eden* and the documentaries *Isle of Levant* and *Elysia, Valley of the Nude*, raised concerns surrounding the depiction of nudity. With respect to *Garden of Eden*, the plot of which focused on a nudist camp with shots 'of shapely female nudes in colour', while the BBFC had declined to certificate the film, more than 180 local authorities had passed it under categories ranging from U to X.[62] In this instance, the Edinburgh magistrates appear to have erred on the side of liberal-mindedness, passing it for 'universal exhibition'.[63]

A third film genre, of concern to the BBFC as well as to licensing authorities across the country, were 'educational' films with a sexual content containing images and/or script relating to reproduction, family planning and venereal disease.[64] In Edinburgh's case, a predictably cautious line was adopted. *Should Parents Tell*, submitted for exhibition by the National Baby Welfare Council, was refused permission. In addition, an age restriction of 16 and over was imposed on *A Family Story* in which the plot, informed by a social hygiene agenda, centred round the repercussions of sexual ignorance and venereal disease. A similar restriction was placed upon the 'informational Canadian docudrama' *Sins of the Fathers*, which also focused on VD and the medical hazards of promiscuity, and on the semi-documentary *The Birth of a Baby*.[65] Such decisions by the Edinburgh magistrates represented but one part of a broader apparatus of moral censorship that was to face an increasing challenge as a more permissive culture invaded Scotland in the 1960s.

Notes

1   See especially Kuhn, *Cinema, Censorship and Sexuality*, ch. 1.
2   See, for example, Freshwater, *Theatre Censorship in Britain*.
3   See, for example, Aldgate and Robertson, *Censorship in Theatre and Cinema*; Newburn, *Permission and Regulation*; Sutherland, *Offensive Literature*; Travis, *Bound and Gagged*.
4   Unless otherwise stated, the following account is based upon NRS, AD63/291, Summary of the law on obscenity, February 1955.
5   NRS, HH41/455, Summary of proceedings relating to obscene publications.
6   *Leven Mail*, 17 June 1953.
7   Travis, *Bound and Gagged*, 94.
8   GCA, D-TC7/19/2, *Report of the Chief Constable of the City of Glasgow for the year 1951*, 55; 1952, 53.
9   NRS, HH48/64, Scottish Police circulars.
10   ECA, Burgh Court papers, 23 November 1954.

11 NRS, HH41/455, L. I. Gordon to C. G. R. H. Jacques, 5 March 1955.

12 ECA, ED6/1/14, *City Police Annual Report for 1959*, 15.

13 *Kilmarnock Standard*, 25 August 1951.

14 *Glasgow Herald*, 15 May 1951.

15 For a detailed analysis of these judgements, see NRS, AD63/291, Summary of the law on obscenity.

16 Travis, *Bound and Gagged*, ch. 5; Jarvis, *Conservative Governments, Morality and Social Change*, ch. 6.

17 NRS, HH41/455, Minutes of the Working Party on the law of obscenity, 17 February 1955.

18 Ibid., Working Party draft report, 5 August 1955.

19 Ibid., N. J. P. Hutchison to C. G. R. H. Jacques, 21 February 1955; AD63/335, Comments by SHD on Obscene Publications Bill, 26 March 1957.

20 NRS, HH41/455, Report of the Working Party on the law of obscenity, November 1955.

21 NRS, AD63/335, N. J. P. Hutchison to E. U. Elliot-Binns, 16 December 1958; CAB134/2015/A, Minutes of Cabinet Home Affairs Committee, Sub-Committee on Obscene Publications, 28 November 1958.

22 NRS, AD63/335, N. J. P. Hutchison to A. F. C. Clark, 19 March 1957; AD63/335, Comments by SHD on Obscene Publications Bill, 26 March 1957.

23 NRS, CAB134/2015/A, Minutes of Cabinet Sub-Committee, 10 December 1958.

24 NRS, HH41/455, Report of Working Party, November 1955.

25 Ibid., Draft submission by E. U. Elliot-Binns, 19 December 1958.

26 In 1957, on the second reading of Viscount Lambton's Private Member's Bill, Emrys Hughes, Labour MP for South Ayrshire, had pressed for the Bill to be extended to Scotland on the grounds that Gretna Green was 'just as interested in pornography' as was Carlisle, and that 'it should not be thought that Scotland [was] still in the days of John Knox' [*Hansard* [HC], vol. 158, 29 March 1957, cols 1,543–6].

27 NRS, AD63/335, Sir Andrew Innes to E. U. Elliot-Binns, 24 December 1958.

28 For a full account of the debates over theatre censorship in the 1950s, see Johnston, *The Lord Chamberlain's Blue Pencil*, chs 12–13; Holden, *Makers and Manners*, 87–91; Thomas, Carlton and Etienne, *Theatre Censorship*, ch. 6.

29 NRS, HH41/1315, Amendment of the Theatres Act, 1843, Memorandum by the Secretary of State for the Home Department and Lord Privy Seal, October 1957.

30 Ibid., Bill papers.

31 Ibid., A. B. Hume to N. D. Walker, 10 October 1957.

32 NRS, HH41/1315, N. D. Walker to H. W. Stotesbury, 11 October 1957.

33 Ibid., Minute N. D. Walker to A. B. Hume, 10 October 1957.

34 Johnston, *The Lord Chamberlain's Blue Pencil*, 159–61; NRS, HH41/1315, Minutes of Cabinet Home Affairs Committee.

35 NRS, HH41/1315, SHD memorandum, 18 June 1958 (original emphasis).

36 Ibid., Minute by Secretary of State for Scotland, 25 June 1958.

37 Holden, *Makers and Manners*, 89.

38 Unless otherwise stated, the following survey is based upon the *Report of Departmental (Wheare) Committee on Children and the Cinema*, 6, 54–5, 100; NRS, HH41/567, Cinematograph Bill, 1952: Scottish notes.

39 This agreement with the trade was homologated in a Scottish Office *Circular no. 2833*, January 1934.

40 For earlier moral panics, see Smith, *Children, Cinema and Censorship*.

41 *Report of Wheare Committee*, 1–3, 12–17; NRS, CO1/4/200, Wheare Committee, Evidence of Association of Scottish County Councils, 1948; ECA, SL119/3/18, Minutes of Edinburgh Magistrates' Committee, 5 May and 2 June 1948.

42 *Report of Wheare Committee*, 45–7.

43 Ibid., 80–4.

44 See NRS, HH41/566; HH41/567, Papers relating to Cinematograph Bill, 1952.

45 *Hansard [HC]*, vol. 505, 24 October 1952, col. 871.

46 Ibid., cols 901–2.

47 Ibid., cols 902–3. Woodburn noted: 'These mass cinemas to which children go simply give it the "bird". I am told that in Inverness, whenever the characters in a film start kissing, the film is actually booed off the screen.'

48 Ibid., col. 1,447.

49 Unless otherwise stated, the following account is based upon NRS, HH41/567, Cinematograph Bill, 1952, Commons – Second Reading, Scottish notes, 13 June 1952; Commons Committee, notes on amendments; *Hansard [HC]*, vol. 505, 24 October 1952, cols 924–5.

50 NRS, HH41/958, Memorandum by the SBCEA to Royal Commission on Scottish Affairs, 27 December 1952.

51 NRS, HH41/754, 1952 Cinematograph Act, consultation papers.

52 See, for example, ECA, SL164/1/26, Minutes of Edinburgh Education Committee, 16 November 1953; SL119/3/23, Minutes of Edinburgh Magistrates' Committee, 6 April 1954.

53 NRS, HH41/1165, *Circular 8656*, 5 August 1955.

54 Ibid., *The Cinematograph (Children) (Scotland) (No. 2) Regulations, 1955*.

55 Ibid., Cinematograph Acts: The 'A' film rule, note by the Scottish Home and Health Department, March 1964.

56 Social Responsibility Committee, *Obscenity and Community Standards*, 17–18.

57 The following is based upon ECA, SL119/3/18–29, Minutes of Edinburgh Magistrates' Committee, 1950–9.

58 Unless otherwise stated, details of individual films are based upon www.imdb.com/ and www.bfi.org.uk/filmtvinfo/ftvdb/, accessed 21 July 2011.

59 http://movies.nytimes.com/, accessed 21 July 2011.

60 ECA, SL119/3/20, Minutes of Edinburgh Magistrates' Committee, 7 and 27 September 1950, 23 November 1950.

61 *The Scotsman*, 27 February 1958. For a similarly hostile response to foreign films from the Catholic press in Glasgow, see *Glasgow Observer and Scottish Catholic Herald*, 21 August 1959: 'Of Bardotlatry, Love and Guilt'. In a few instances, it appears to have been film posters that provoked most concern. For example, in the case of *Chained for Life*, while the film centred on the ethical issues involved in punishing a Siamese twin for murdering her husband, the posters focused on more prurient aspects of the story such as 'Joined Together How Can They Make Love?' and 'What Happens in Their Intimate Moments?'.

62 Trevelyan, *What the Censor Saw*, 95.

63 ECA, SL119/3/27, Minutes of Edinburgh Magistrates' Committee, 1 August 1957.

64 Trevelyan, *What the Censor Saw*, 119.

65 ECA, SL119/3/20, Minutes of Edinburgh Magistrates' Committee, 5 July and 5 November 1950; SL119/3/21, 5 and 25 June 1951; SL119/3/22, 2 July 1952; SL119/3/26, 6 March 1957; http://movies. nytimes.com/movie/110377/Sins-of-the-Fathers/overview, accessed 21 July 2011. Likewise, in Glasgow, a thirty-minute documentary, *Birth Without Fear*, that had received a special award at the Venice Film Festival, was only exhibited as part of an X-certificate programme at the Grand Central Cinema [*Glasgow Herald*, 15 December 1958].

10

SEX, CENSORSHIP AND SCOTTISH GOVERNANCE IN THE 1960s

OBSCENE PUBLICATIONS

National policymaking

As a consequence of Scotland's omission from the 1959 Obscene Publications Act, Scottish departments of state were marginalised in the 1960s from much of the political debate at Westminster surrounding issues of obscenity.[1] In particular, representatives of the Scottish Office were absent from the policy discussions that shaped the 1964 Obscene Publications Act, designed to ensure greater control of a growing market in pornography that was exploiting loopholes in the 1959 Act.

There *were* pressures on Scottish governance to strengthen its regulation of obscene materials, especially from the Free Presbyterian Church. Its synod condemned contemporary literature as one of 'the most potent sources of immorality' – a 'foul stream pour[ing] into the hearts and homes of young and old, demoralising society and ruining family life'.[2] It blamed the circulation of obscene books and magazines for the increase in juvenile delinquency and sexual promiscuity,[3] and viewed the influx of American pornography as reflecting 'the old morality of paganism' which, 'having sown to the flesh', was 'now reaping corruption'.[4] The Church criticised the failure of the Government to convict the publishers of *Lady Chatterley's Lover*, and called for a strengthening of the law. It pressed for Scottish law officers to take more decisive action against 'dirty little bookshop[s]' that 'screamed lechery from each and every filthy book jacket', and against works such as *Last Exit to Brooklyn*.[5]

The Church of Scotland and Roman Catholic Church in Scotland also addressed the issue of censorship, albeit in more muted language. While not wanting to denigrate modern literature, the Social and Moral Welfare Board of the Church of Scotland did express concern at the impact of obscene materials on sexual behaviour, especially in the young. It received a constant stream of complaints from the district presbytery courts, some of which were forwarded to the Scottish Home and Health Department (SHHD).[6] Indeed, as with other issues relating to sexual morality, on the issue of censorship, Church of Scotland policy would appear to have been heavily influenced by the moral fears of its local congregations. Meanwhile, the Roman Catholic hierarchy in Scotland was equally exercised by the apparent proliferation of obscene literature, and supported efforts to lobby Westminster for more legal controls. However, as with the issue of sexual content in films and the tabloid press, it viewed the power of Catholic consumers to boycott immoral material as the most effective sanction.[7]

A group of Scottish Labour backbench MPs also argued for a more vigorous prosecution of obscene literature in the early 1960s. In a series of parliamentary questions, they pressed the Lord Advocate to prosecute booksellers who sold copies of *Lady Chatterley's Lover* and called for the application of the 1959 Obscene Publications Act to Scotland.[8] However, the Lord Advocate, William Grant, and the Secretary of State for Scotland, J. S. Maclay, were opposed to any such measure. In their opinion, *Lady Chatterley's Lover* did not 'offend' the conditions for obscenity under Scottish common and statute law – that it 'was of such a nature as to be calculated to produce a pernicious effect in depraving and corrupting those who [were] open to such influences'.[9] Along with most Scottish legal authorities, they continued to regard existing Scottish provisions as adequately defending public morality while respecting works of literary merit.[10] In addition, the Lord Advocate pre-empted any attempt on the part of burgh prosecutors unilaterally to prosecute booksellers for offering unexpurgated versions of *Lady Chatterley's Lover* by directing that all alleged offences had to be reported to the procurator fiscal of a Sheriff Court and thence to the Crown Office.[11]

Nonetheless, as in the 1950s, it was at the local level that the issue of obscene literature was mainly addressed in the 1960s. Two main strands of censorship operated: first, by means of formal prosecutions brought under the Burgh Police Acts and the corresponding provisions of local acts and corporation orders; and second, by means of the informal screening of literature by public librarians. Although practices often varied across the country, both processes are perhaps best illustrated by events in Edinburgh.

Local case study

In November 1960, it was widely reported that, in the aftermath of the Penguin trial, having bought a copy of *Lady Chatterley's Lover* from the Paperback Bookshop in Edinburgh, a Mrs Agnes Cooper, 62, a former missionary in the Belgian Congo, had carried it outside with a pair of tongs and set fire to it on the pavement with a jar of kerosene, convinced 'it was evil'.[12] Although Mrs Cooper's pyrotechnics represented but one extreme of local public opinion, it could be argued that her response to the book was symptomatic of a broadly conservative and Calvinistic attitude to sexually explicit literature in Edinburgh in the early 1960s, an attitude shared by many booksellers within the city.[13]

Certainly, James Heatly, the City Prosecutor, was active in enforcing the obscene publications clauses of the Edinburgh Corporation Order Confirmation Acts of 1933 and 1961.[14] Thus, in January 1960, Edward Haig received twenty days' imprisonment for selling and exhibiting for sale a range of indecent publications, the proceedings having been initiated by the sale of a copy of *Lovelies Special* magazine to a police constable.[15] The publications included copies of titles such as *Bamboo Summer Special, Follies at St Freda's, Jem, Pose, Scanties, Sensations, Silky, Sir, Sprite, Velvet* and *X for Men*. More significantly, in 1964, Edinburgh magistrates successfully prosecuted four booksellers in the Leith Walk area for stocking *Fanny Hill, The Perfumed Garden* and the *Kama Sutra*.[16] Edinburgh was the only city to have brought proceedings against the sale of the *Kama Sutra*, more than three-quarters of a million copies of which had been sold without challenge and a copy of which was allegedly available to the public in Edinburgh Central Library. Moreover, the edition of *Fanny Hill* involved was an expurgated one with about a quarter of the original omitted, and was said to be on sale at one of Edinburgh's most reputable bookshops.

These cases aroused disquiet in the correspondence and editorial pages of the Scottish press. There was considerable sympathy with the view of the defence counsel in the case relating to *Fanny Hill* that it was 'intolerable' that a prosecution could be initiated under a local Act by a City Prosecutor who was not answerable to the Lord Advocate, and that a conviction could be based purely upon the personal views of a magistrate rather than upon reasoned argument, including a proper evaluation of literary merit, in a higher court. Fears were expressed that such a process was creating a literary *cordon sanitaire* around Edinburgh and that it threatened the recrudescence of a 'narrow, morose, restrictive' puritanism that was culturally damaging.

In addition, there were concerns that, in placing emphasis on the social context in which a work was displayed, Scottish legal principles in cases involving obscene publications were discriminatory. Strong suspicions were voiced that such prosecutions would not have proceeded had the booksellers been located in the more socially exclusive New Town of Edinburgh.[17] A poem in the local press lampooning recent cases well captured the perception of double standards operating in the City:

The Librarian and the Prosecutor
A Tale of Two City's [sic]

You can talk of R. L. S. and praise Sir Walter Scott.
But it's quite a feat,
In this 'darling seat',
To know what to read – and what not

Though Bailie McQueen declared it obscene.
And it might be to youth detrimental,
This book so exotic, on matters erotic,
May be seen in the 'Ref' at the 'Central'

Lacking McQueen's pardon, 'The Perfumed Garden'
Is banished from shops in Elm Row;
But on shelves elevated, for minds cultivated,
Its rare blooms are always on show

The City Librarian is a fine libertarian
Whose duties are discharged discreetly;
Does he now have to ask, when performing his task,
'Have you read any good books lately, Heatly?' [The City Prosecutor][18]

In fact, evidence would suggest that the Librarian was far from being 'libertarian'. Indeed, in the late 1960s, an increasing focus of public disquiet was the informal system of moral censorship operated by librarians in the acquisition and location of books. As early as 1954, it had been admitted that Edinburgh public libraries operated special annexe sections, closed to the public, which included 'books of recognised literary merit that contained passages which might prove offensive to many readers or harmful if they fell into the wrong hands'.[19] This was also a system operated by the County Librarian for Midlothian who, in 1964, refused to stock Mary McCarthy's *The Group*, on the grounds that it typified all the worst aspects of 'the modern type of fiction', which indulged the 'psychological, sex-obsessed outpourings of angry or simply neurotic novelists'. The Librarian readily conceded that he was 'more concerned with whether a work of fiction [would] give offence to readers than with the alleged reputation of the author'.[20] In this instance, the book was, in fact, freely available at Edinburgh Central Library, illustrating how dependent on personal preference and prejudice such informal censorship could be.

In July 1967, a vigorous attack on the process was launched in the pages of *The Scotsman* and *Edinburgh Evening News*, triggered by the removal to the annexe of Edinburgh Central Library of Alan Sharp's *A Green Tree in Gedde*, a recent winner of a £1,000 award from the Scottish Arts Council.[21] Although the ban on open access was defended by some correspondents, others saw the episode as just one more example of 'the ghastly Calvinist hangover' constraining Scottish literary culture.[22] In response, the City Librarian justified his use of an 'annexe' on the grounds that all libraries required some facility for making books only available on request, mainly for 'the protection of stock from theft, defacement or mutilation' and to respond to 'seasonal or other fluctuations of demand'.[23] As far as fiction was concerned, he admitted that:

> The annexe included novels which have been proceeded against in the Courts but not banned, as well as novels of a 'strong meat' character. There were also included novels which had been accepted on the basis of favourable review of literary merit but which might later be complained about by the public.

Some members of the Library Sub-Committee proposed that 'no work of fiction should in future be "annexed" because it had been the object of subjective criticism by members of the public'. However, on a casting vote, their motion was defeated in favour of retaining existing procedures.[24]

Thereafter, a letter to *The Scotsman* from a former librarian added fresh fuel to the debate. The writer argued that Edinburgh was exceptional for the range of modern fiction annexed in its public libraries.

He claimed that apart from *A Green Tree in Gedde*, such works included Edna O'Brien's *August is a Wicked Month* and *Casualties of Peace*, Walter Baxter's *The Image and the Search*, three novels by James Jones including *From Here to Eternity*, Norman Mailer's *The Naked and the Dead* and Radcliffe Hall's *The Well of Loneliness*. Moreover, he alleged that, in many instances, books were annexed even before they were added to stock and were never available on the open shelves, further empowering the role of librarian as moral gatekeeper.[25] Subsequently, a proposal to exclude moral considerations from any process of 'annexing' works in public libraries was submitted to Edinburgh City Council, but defeated by thirty-six votes to nineteen.[26]

THEATRE

By the mid-1960s the issue of theatre censorship had resurfaced within the Scottish Office. In 1962, the Government had rejected a Censorship of Plays (Abolition) Bill introduced by Dingle Foot. In January 1963, the Conservative Home Secretary, Henry Brooke, had reaffirmed his support for the existing system of censorship, and as late as May 1964, a ministerial response in the House of Lords, while conceding that the role of the Lord Chamberlain might appear archaic, concluded that it had worked well in practice and that no alternative system was likely to be found which would command general support.[27]

However, during the winter of 1965–6, the Labour Home Secretary, Sir Frank Soskice, and his successor, Roy Jenkins, submitted proposals for a thorough review of existing procedures for theatre censorship.[28] The Home Office argued that the system of compulsory censorship by the Lord Chamberlain had long been 'regarded as anomalous' and subject to enduring criticism. Various arguments were advanced in favour of reform: that it was inconsistent that a play performed in front of a theatre audience of a few hundred people could be prohibited by the Lord Chamberlain, while it could be broadcast to millions of television viewers; that no other country censored stage plays; that the rules applied by the Lord Chamberlain were 'inflexible' and appeared to some people as 'absurd'; that censorship inhibited free expression by requiring strict adherence to the approved script; and that, in a growing number of instances, the existing censorship was evaded by presenting plays in 'theatre clubs' which anyone might join.

The response of the Lord Advocate and SHHD to Home Office proposals was largely negative. In their view, the implication of the proposed inquiry – that theatre censorship should be relaxed – ran counter to the prevailing mood of public opinion in Scotland which was deeply concerned with the demoralising impact of the arts and media on contemporary society and which viewed '*more* control of theatrical productions [as] desirable rather than *less*'. The Department warned that, on the basis of Scottish evidence, any committee 'might feel driven to suggest something even more restrictive than the existing censorship'.[29]

Scottish officials were sensitive to the degree of opposition in Scotland to the more explicit and sexually charged genre of plays emerging, mainly in London, in the early 1960s. The Scottish churches were voicing increasing concern at the role of theatrical performances in promoting an 'insidious decadence' that threatened to undermine society.[30] The more sexually explicit plays were depicted in church reports as 'morally subversive',[31] and, according to the Free Presbyterian Church, part of a deliberate plot by the literary world to soften the moral backbone of the British people.[32] This concern was reflected in their growing reluctance to house innovative and experimental productions in church premises, such as the Assembly Halls in Edinburgh, especially during the Festival.[33] Thus, in 1960, the Edinburgh Gateway Theatre Company had been forced to abandon its production of Aristophanes' *Lysistrata*, centred round the threat of the women of Athens to withdraw sexual favours, because of opposition from members of the Home Board of the Church of Scotland, who owned the theatre premises.[34]

In addition, in many cities, civic dignitaries and magistrates, often inspired by the lurid, sensationalist reports of the *Scottish Daily Express*, and by the puritanical campaigning of the Moral Rearmament Movement, with its mantra of 'Godliness and Dirt', were also on the offensive against theatrical events and productions.[35] In Edinburgh, the police department was routinely monitoring theatre scripts scheduled for performances during the Festival and Fringe Festival in the early 1960s.[36] Plays and 'happenings' that involved nudity or appeared to challenge Christian morality received a hostile response both in the press and council chambers.[37] Especial disquiet was expressed at the activities of 'theatre clubs', such as the Close Theatre in Glasgow and the Traverse Theatre Club in Edinburgh, which were not subject to official censorship and whose artistic policy favoured experimental and radical plays.[38] Thus, in briefing the Secretary of

State for Scotland in late 1965, R. E. C. Johnson, Secretary of the SHHD, accurately captured the mood of Scottish opinion when he cautioned that it was doubtful if, in Scotland, the public at large, or even the general theatre-going public, felt 'itself imposed upon by the censoring activities of the Lord Chamberlain'.[39]

The second major objection advanced by the SHHD against the Home Office proposals related to their scope. Mindful of the growing unease in Scotland at the moral calibre of broadcasting (see below), the Department warned that any inquiry limited to theatre censorship would be viewed as leaving 'the most sensitive problems untouched'. A failure to widen its remit would, it intimated, be seen as ignoring Scottish concerns as expressed through the General Assembly of the Church of Scotland. In the view of the SHHD, public attitudes to morality and decency had 'so much changed in recent years', and so many new forms of entertainment had been developed, that there might well be a case for a comprehensive inquiry into what forms of control over entertainment in general were needed, or would be acceptable.[40] Certainly, it anticipated that, should the issue of theatre censorship be raised at Westminster, Scottish representatives would be likely to push for a wide-ranging review in the hope of more rather than less stringent controls.[41] The Scottish Education Department concurred. In its view, while the Arts Council and English dramatists might view the issue as simply a choice between the complete abolition of censorship and the substitution for the Lord Chamberlain of a system of voluntary censorship, Scottish interests would 'be more inclined to press for the extension of theatre censorship to plays on Television'.[42]

However, the Home Secretary, Roy Jenkins, continued to adhere to the view that an inquiry could appropriately be confined to theatre censorship. In January 1966, he initiated the appointment of a Joint Committee, with a restricted remit, chaired by Lord Annan, and predominantly composed of members who favoured the abolition of the existing system.[43] Its report, issued in June 1967, recommended that the pre-censorship role of the Lord Chamberlain be abolished, that the theatre should come under the same legal constraints as literature (that is, the Obscene Publications Acts), where the test of obscenity was the sole basis of censorship, and that local authorities should no longer exercise powers relating to censorship. In addition, the Committee recommended certain desiderata that should attach to the future operation of the law, namely the prevention of frivolous prosecutions, the right of trial by jury, the admissibility of expert evidence, the effective control of obscene plays and the uniform application of the law.[44] The following month, Roy Jenkins, conscious of mounting public pressure in England, announced that the Government intended to introduce appropriate legislation to give effect to the Committee's findings.[45]

The Committee's report met with considerable consternation within the Scottish Office. Although Lords Tweedsmuir and Kilmuir (until his death in 1967) had been members of the Committee, it had taken no evidence from Scottish officials or law officers, made no mention of Scotland in its report and taken no account of the many disparities between legal processes north and south of the Border, not least the exclusion of Scotland from the 1959 and 1964 Obscene Publications Acts.[46] As a result, the proposals presented a range of intractable legal issues that were to preoccupy the SHHD and Lord Advocate over the following months. A key issue was whether, if the 1843 Act was repealed, given the lack of any Obscene Publications Act in Scots law, Scotland could rely on the application of existing common law, the Burgh Police Acts and miscellaneous local acts to regulate theatrical performances. After much discussion it was generally agreed that such reliance was untenable. Not only did burgh and police courts lack powers to impose sufficient penalties, it was argued that, in the absence of the 1843 Act, 'the presentation of stage plays would be subject . . . to criminal proceedings in the burgh court at the whim of local magistrates and this would lead to wide variations in practice, would tend to put the law in disrepute and infuriate all those concerned with the theatre'.[47]

Reliance on burgh and police courts, which only held summary proceedings, would inhibit the ability of the Scottish legal system to meet the aims of the Joint Committee in other ways. In order to prevent 'frivolous prosecutions', to enable a body of coordinated case law to be built up using authoritative witnesses and to achieve uniform application of the law, it was recognised that cases needed to be held in a Sheriff Court or High Court.[48] Furthermore, burgh and police courts were inappropriate if, in line with the report of the Annan Committee, cases were to involve trial by jury and the admissibility of expert evidence.

By the summer of 1967, after protracted consultation within and between the SHHD, Crown Office and Lord Advocate's Department, it was generally, if reluctantly, agreed that the best solution was for an entirely new statutory offence relating to theatre productions to be created applying to the whole country, with powers to initiate legal proceedings in Scotland residing with the Lord Advocate rather than local magistrates.[49] However, there was one issue upon which Scottish ministers were not prepared to compromise. Under Scots law there was no right to a jury trial, and it was the Lord Advocate who determined whether an offence should be tried summarily or by indictment. The Secretary of State for Scotland, William Ross, was adamant that there should be 'no departure from Scots tradition', a view endorsed by the Lord Advocate and the Crown Agent.[50] SHHD officials recognised that there might be 'powerful voices in the theatre lobby' who considered a jury would be more likely to reflect public opinion. They were also aware that to introduce legislation without a right to trial by jury might not 'satisfy Parliament' and might bring Scottish legal principles 'under hostile scrutiny'.[51] Nevertheless, they did not consider that the issue of theatre censorship was 'important enough' to justify a departure from Scottish legal process.[52] Their compromise suggestion was that, as with the Obscene Publications Act, a Theatre Censorship Act might merely allow for the alternatives of summary conviction or conviction on indictment, leaving it for the Lord Advocate to direct when a case justified solemn procedure before a jury.[53]

The Theatres Act was subsequently passed in July 1968.[54] Its principal effect was to abolish the functions of the Lord Chamberlain as a censor of plays and to substitute a criminal offence of presenting obscene performances of plays, whether in public or private. Significantly, the definition of obscenity in a play closely followed that of Lord Justice Cooper in his 1953 appeal judgement in *Gellatly* v. *Laird* (see above pp. 219–20), namely, 'the tendency of the performance of the play as a whole to deprave and corrupt those persons likely, having regard to all the circumstances, to attend it'. A complementary provision removed from local licensing authorities any pre-existing powers under public general statute to impose conditions on the content of theatre performances.[55] The Act explicitly allowed for a defence of 'the public good' on the grounds that a play was in the interests of the arts, literature or learning, and provision was made for the submission of expert evidence on the 'artistic, literary, or other merits' of a theatre performance. In deference to the Scottish legal system, there was no reference to any right to trial by jury.

The Act provided that proceedings in Scotland could only be instituted in the Sheriff Court or High Court. Concerns had been expressed by the Scottish Arts Council that this might still leave theatre managers at the mercy of an 'unsympathetic' and independent-minded procurator fiscal. However, the Scottish Education Department and SHHD were quick to reassure the Council and the Federation of Scottish Repertory Theatres that the Crown Agent would be issuing instructions to all fiscals that proceedings under the Act could only be initiated with the permission of the Crown Office, which acted under the direction of the Lord Advocate.[56]

Other concerns had centred round the role of the police. Officials within the SHHD anticipated that the police would find it very difficult to enforce the legislation, given that, in the first instance, they were required to form an opinion on whether or not an offence had been committed.[57] Accordingly, the Department endeavoured to establish a clear set of guidelines. Chief Constables were advised that the offence of obscenity under the Act related not only to the formal content of a play but also to the manner in which it was performed, including the publicity material put out by the presenters and the likely presence of children.[58]

Despite the best efforts of policy makers to centralise the process of theatre censorship, local powers relating to indecency and obscenity had continued to be invoked by Scottish civic authorities in an effort to regulate the moral content of performances.[59] In Edinburgh, the vitriol of some magistrates and the surveillance operations of the police remained focused on performances at the Traverse Theatre, especially during the Edinburgh Festival.[60] Thus, in 1967, the Edinburgh police closely monitored the admissions policy of the Traverse Theatre Club following complaints from the public and several magistrates over the performance of *Fuzz* in the Festival Fringe by an experimental theatre company from New York, alleged by one reviewer to consist of 'an orgy of bestiality, incest and indecency'.[61] Again, in February 1968, Councillor John Kidd called for the withdrawal of funding from the theatre in protest at a performance of *Mass in F* by an Edinburgh student group, in which 'a girl, naked to the waist, related her experiences of sex'.[62] The following month, Nicholas Fairbairn QC, Chairman of the Traverse, was forced to defend (successfully) the Theatre Club's right to produce unlicensed plays.[63] Undeterred, in May 1968, Councillor Kidd urged the Secretary of State for Scotland to address the issue of the use of club status to evade prosecution for obscenity, arguing that it was 'about time this place [the Traverse Theatre] was closed once and for all' as it constituted 'a smear on our city'.[64]

Meanwhile, similar controversy surrounded the more innovative plays being performed by the Glasgow Citizens Theatre and the associated Close Theatre Club. In 1965, there had been protests from the audience at the immorality of some of the scenes in John Arden's play *Live Like Pigs* at the Citizens Theatre.[65] Subsequently, a succession of artistic directors resigned over what they perceived as the 'ageing prudery' of the Board of Directors, who had objected to the inclusion in the programme of Harold Pinter's *The Homecoming*, along with a range of other plays.[66] A lively correspondence appeared in the *Glasgow Herald* in the spring of 1969, contesting the artistic merits of the theatre, with a number of civic leaders condemning recent productions. Not untypical was the view of Baillie Wood that, in funding the Citizens and Close theatres, ratepayers were effectively subsidising 'pornographic filth'.[67]

BROADCASTING

Pressures

Scattered references to the moral dangers of broadcasting had already surfaced in Scottish church proceedings in the 1950s. In 1951, a committee of the United Free Church had deplored many of the programmes produced by the BBC on the grounds that 'unnatural sexual relationships' were 'too frequently presented as attractive and natural behaviour'.[68] In 1954, the Moderator of the Church of Scotland had publicly criticised the immorality of certain TV plays produced by the BBC.[69] Subsequently, the Free Presbyterian Church had expressed similar concerns and warned that the content of broadcasting was contributing to the rise of moral delinquency in the young.[70] The Roman Catholic press in Scotland had also endorsed a Papal Encyclical warning of the potential for TV and radio to be 'perverted to evil uses'.[71]

In the 1960s, with the rapid increase in ownership of television sets,[72] the onset of more sexually explicit programmes and a greater moral relativism in the ideology of the BBC and the newly established Independent Television Authority (ITA), such fears moved to the forefront of church debate on the state of society. In 1961, in evidence to the Pilkington Committee on Broadcasting, the Church and Nation Committee of the Church of Scotland stressed the cultural impact of TV and the duty of broadcasters to maintain 'moral standards in the community' and not to undermine the sanctity of marriage and family life,[73] a view subsequently endorsed in the Pilkington report.[74]

In 1965, the Church and Nation Committee returned to the issue in a major report to the General Assembly on what it termed: 'The New Impuritanism'.[75] Referring to a spate of protests from public bodies, private associations and individuals 'about an alleged deterioration in the moral standards of television', the Committee heavily criticised the policy of the new Director-General of the BBC, Sir Hugh Carlton Greene, and the lack of moral safeguards built into the BBC's renewed charter. Particular criticism was levelled at a speech delivered by Greene in February 1965 in which he had claimed that a primary duty of any broadcasting authority was to secure 'the maximum liberty of expression' and to resist attempts at censorship by 'the new puritans'. The Committee disputed that the BBC had the right to take advantage of their freedom from censorship to foist 'advanced' and 'shocking' material on the general public in the privacy of their homes. In their view, British democracy could be 'damaged just as much by a decadent morality as by subversive politics', and the line between 'protecting the public – particularly young people – from corruption, and inhibiting literary and dramatic talent' had to be even more strictly drawn in broadcasting than for other forms of entertainment.

The Committee's report was duly endorsed by the General Assembly of the Church of Scotland, which called upon the Chairman and Governors of the BBC to reverse the policy of Carlton Greene in order that its 'high moral standards might be restored'.[76] However, despite discussions in Edinburgh between the heads of the BBC and the Committee in October 1965, the continuing flow of complaints from local presbyteries suggested that little change in programming policy had been effected, and that the permissiveness of 'certain London-based writers and thinkers' had also infected the output of the ITA's channels.[77] Thereafter, while acknowledging the need, in part, for the Church of Scotland to come to terms with a more morally ambivalent society, the Committee continued to campaign on a range of advisory committees, including the Broadcasting Council for Scotland, for more stringent controls on the content of programmes,[78] maintaining its 'strong offensive' against what it perceived as 'a deliberate strategy of cultivated immorality' by the broadcasting companies.[79]

Meanwhile, the Free Presbyterian Church of Scotland was equally vocal on the issue of censorship and broadcasting. In the early 1960s its synod passed a series of resolutions condemning the portrayal of sexual issues on radio and TV and calling upon the Government to 'exercise more constraint' upon programmes as a means of countering the rising immorality of the younger generation.[80] In 1963, the main target of criticism was the Reith Lectures delivered by the psychiatrist Professor G. M. Carstairs, in which he rejected any form of moral absolutism and suggested that 'unchastity' was 'a better preparation for marriage than the exercise of self-restraint'.[81] Thereafter, the Free Presbyterian Church increasingly blamed TV for the rising incidence of teenage pregnancies and VD in the young.[82] It commended the efforts of the newly formed National Viewers' and Listeners' Association, criticised the Postmaster General for declining to intervene in protecting moral standards in broadcasting and welcomed the arrival of Charles Curran as Director-General of the BBC in the hope that he would reverse the moral permissiveness of the previous regime.[83]

Throughout the 1960s, some elements within the Kirk were attempting to review its relationship to the arts in terms of its moral agenda. In the late 1960s, a series of colloquia were held by the Scottish Council of Churches in Dunblane to discuss the impact of broadcasting on society and the most appropriate policy for reconciling the aims of creativity and control.[84] As with other areas of censorship, attitudes to broadcasting varied considerably between the different churches and, at times, within the same church. Some more progressive members, while pressing for greater regulation of radio and TV output, acknowledged its immense cultural and educational value to British society, and recognised the need for censorship to be a 'responsible rather than a repressive use of power'.[85] In particular, Church of Scotland officials were at pains to distance themselves from the efforts of Mary Whitehouse and the Clean Up TV Campaign south of the Border. While commending the 'vigilance' of such organisations, the Church and Nation Committee was concerned that, as the 'moral guardian' of Scottish society, the Church of Scotland should be seen to address the issue of censorship from a broad and contemporary perspective and not as just another 'negative viewing group'.[86] However, evidence from the proceedings of the general assemblies and synods would suggest that the main body of the Kirk remained intolerant to any erosion of Christian ethics and viewed the intrusion of immorality into public broadcasting as a greater threat to civil liberties than any regulatory system.

The Roman Catholic Church in Scotland also displayed increasing concern with the moral impact of broadcasting. Through its press and through organisations such as the Union of Catholic Mothers and the League of Catholic Women, it campaigned for a system of classification of radio and television programmes analogous to that operated by the British Board of Film Censors.[87] Church leaders welcomed the efforts of Mary Whitehouse to regulate the output of the BBC and ITA and gave her campaigns generous publicity in the Scottish Catholic press.[88]

A range of secular bodies in Scotland was also pressing the Government to introduce greater regulation for broadcasting in the 1960s. Women's organisations, such as the Scottish Council of Women Citizens' Associations, regularly collated and forwarded complaints relating to TV programmes and subsequently supported the formation of local branches in Scotland of the National Viewers' and Listeners' Association.[89] Educational agencies were also expressing concern at the moral content of broadcast material. Submitting evidence to the Pilkington Committee, the Educational Institute of Scotland condemned a minority of programmes for disregarding the 'principles of morality' and contributing to the general lowering of standards and conduct. It was especially critical of the tendency to elevate the 'eternal triangle' theme, with its implication that 'marital fidelity was an outworn convention', and recommended the establishment of an independent council to address complaints relating to material that offended public morality.[90]

In addition, education committees in the Scottish cities frequently pressed for broadcasting standards to be raised. For example, in 1965–6, the Education Committee of Glasgow Corporation urged the BBC and ITA to review the 'content and display of programmes in order to reduce the emphasis on subjects of sex and immoral behaviour' and called for a concerted campaign from Scottish local authorities on the issue.[91] More generally, reports and correspondence in the Scottish press revealed a growing support from civic leaders for Mary Whitehouse, and disaffection with what one writer dismissed as the 'feverish perverted imaginings of our intellectual mentors on television'.[92]

Policy response

The Conservative Government from 1960 to 1964, led by Edward Heath, was ambivalent on the issue of censorship in broadcasting.[93] On the one hand, it was sensitive to the growing concerns of backbenchers and grassroots supporters at the impact of TV programmes on sexual crime and deviancy, and on the erosion of Christian moral values. It was aware of the criticisms levelled at broadcasting standards by the Pilkington Committee and, in particular, the demoralising potential of TV programmes. It was also feared by some that the subsequent Clean Up TV Campaign, led by Mary Whitehouse, threatened to transform the issue into one of major political and electoral significance. On the other hand, many Conservative leaders believed that the state should not undermine personal responsibility by directly interfering in the content of programmes, and that standards would be best maintained by free competition unfettered by any formal processes of censorship. A major reason for breaking the BBC's monopoly in the first place had been to dilute its power to shape public values. Moreover, while there was a significant amount of support for Mary Whitehouse within the parliamentary party, her campaign was viewed by most ministers within the Cabinet as attracting puritanical extremists, and the whole issue as too contentious to justify government intervention.

In the early 1960s, the issue of censorship in relation to broadcasting does not appear to have engaged Scottish departments of state to any significant extent, and they did not become involved in the debates in Whitehall and Cabinet. The Scottish Education Department did give evidence to the Pilkington Committee but no concerns over moral and ethical standards were raised. However, Scottish officials were monitoring church opinion on the issue, and in late 1965, they reacted robustly to the decision of the Home Secretary not to widen an inquiry into theatre censorship to include broadcasting. In the view of the SHHD, the strengthening of controls on broadcasting was regarded within Scotland as of far greater importance than any review and probable liberalisation of theatre censorship. It was not convinced that the BBC and ITA were sufficiently regulated, and did not regard the proposal of the Postmaster General for a National Broadcasting Advisory Council as adequately meeting public concerns relating to programme content. Instead, it favoured the establishment of a Watchdog Committee, and a comprehensive inquiry into the role and appropriateness of censorship in a mass-media society.[94]

In its negotiations with the Home Office, the SHHD stressed the strength of feeling on the issue within Scotland. It warned that Scottish peers were likely to oppose any inquiry into censorship that excluded broadcasting. It also forwarded a copy of the Church and Nation Committee's report entitled 'The New Impuritanism' that focused on the demoralising aspects of TV. The Department was at pains to emphasise the importance of the proceedings of the General Assembly as a reflection of Scottish public and professional opinion. It was angered by the fact that, while acknowledging the views of 'a body initiated by some Harlow housewives' [Mary Whitehouse's National Viewers' and Listeners' Association], government ministers did not see fit to recognise the deliverances of the Church of Scotland.[95] As G. F. Belfour, the Assistant Secretary to the SHHD, concluded:

> It will have to be got into them that people in this part of the world attach importance to what the Assembly says, and that if ministers give the impression that what they have communicated simply has not been read, there will fairly certainly be trouble.[96]

In the event, Scottish opinion was marginalised and separate legislation on theatre censorship went ahead.

The Broadcasting Council for Scotland

Meanwhile, although Scottish departments were playing a very minor role within the legislative process, within the BBC a limited degree of moral censorship was being imposed on Scottish radio and television output by the Broadcasting Council for Scotland. Founded under Royal Charter in 1952, the Council's remit was extended to include television broadcasts in 1962. It was responsible for monitoring all programmes produced and/or broadcast in Scotland other than those on the national networks, and for representing to the BBC's Controllers and Board of Governors the views of the listening and viewing public in Scotland. Evidence would suggest that the Council was selected to 'represent the establishment' and that 'it tended to concur with an equally conservative local executive'.[97]

Throughout the 1960s, the Council provided a conduit for public concerns relating to the moral content of broadcasting output, including those voiced by the General Assembly and presbyteries of the Church of Scotland, and by women's organisations such as the Scottish Women's Guild and Scottish Housewives' Association.[98] Council members strove to reduce the incidence of sexually explicit material (broadly defined) in radio and television programmes, especially in plays scheduled at family viewing times or on Sundays. More broadly, the Council was anxious to ensure that the moral integrity and identity of Scottish society was not eroded by metropolitan permissiveness. It strove to convince BBC management that, while the Corporation might defend the need to commission plays that reflected contemporary society, British society was not monolithic and there was a need to take into account differing cultural values across Britain. In the view of the Council, there were fundamental 'differences in atmosphere and interests' between London and Scotland that needed to be acknowledged by programme producers, and that, if programmes 'of bad taste' were networked in London, they should be 'blacked out in Scotland' and alternative programmes scheduled instead.[99]

It is difficult to gauge the impact of such representations. Senior executives of the BBC were unmoved by accusations that programmes were morally subversive and firmly resistant to calls for any formal process of regional censorship involving the pre-production scrutiny of schedules.[100] The minutes of the Council therefore convey the same tone of frustration and the same marginalisation of Scottish opinion as do the policy files relating to broadcasting.

CINEMA

There were no substantive legislative changes affecting cinema censorship in Scotland in the 1960s. In 1964, the SHHD consulted Scottish local authorities over the operation of the A film rule. Responses from the major cities indicated that the rule was not applied and that, in the absence of any difficulties with existing admission procedures, there was no real pressure to alter arrangements north of the Border.[101] In addition, in 1969, the views of Scottish local authorities were canvassed on the revision of the BBFC classification system, incorporating a new X certificate for films restricted to audiences over 18, a system endorsed by the Scottish Office.[102] However, the primary interface between the state and cinema in 1960s Scotland continued to be through the licensing role of local magistrates.

As in the 1950s, all films that were uncensored by the BBFC, and which distributors wished to exhibit, had to be submitted to local magistrates for previewing and licensing, and evidence would suggest that this role was performed with continuing, if not increasing, vigour, again with encouragement from the Scottish church assemblies.[103] As Aldgate has noted, the process of liberalisation of British cinema 'was slow, complex, and fraught', and a range of issues relating to sexual indulgence, deviance and reproduction continued to be viewed as unfit 'entertainment to put before the British cinema-going public in undiluted or unsanitized form', if at all.[104] However, as in England, there was often wide variation across Scotland in the treatment of particular films.

Edinburgh

In the case of Edinburgh, some seventeen uncensored films were previewed by members of the Magistrates' Committee during the period 1960–9, of which twelve were refused permission for public exhibition and five licensed only for exhibition to audiences over the age of 16.[105] Some bans and restrictions related to films, such as *The Rape*, *Lady in a Cage* and *Onibaba*, that contained underlying themes of sexual violence and sadism. Other films were banned for their vacuous exploitation of nudity, such as *How I Lived as Eve*, *Her Bikini Never Got Wet*, *The Naked World of Harrison Marks* and *Nude Camera*. A genre of voyeuristic feature films relating to prostitution and vice in post-Wolfenden London, such as *Soho Striptease* and *West End Jungle*, were also refused a licence. Finally, there were films that could, in the view of the magistrates, be construed as either endorsing sexual deviance, or as containing images and language that were pornographic and obscene. These included *Fanny Hill*, *The Pornographer*, *Ulysses* and *The Killing of Sister George*, all of which were banned from public exhibition in Edinburgh.

Two features stand out from the process of cinema censorship in Edinburgh in the 1960s. First, there was evidently a growing polarisation on the Committee between conservative and more progressive councillors. Voting was split in a third of the cases, with the Lord Provost consistently opposed to the showing of more explicit or avant-garde films.

Second, the process of local censorship became an increasingly controversial issue in the local and national (Scottish) media. Thus, one journalist later recalled the 'furious controversy' surrounding the banning of *Fanny Hill* in 1965 in a 'sexually repressed' Edinburgh, when the 'determined seekers of soft porn could go and see the film in [the neighbouring town of] Musselburgh'.[106] The banning of the film *Ulysses*, based on the novel by James Joyce, provoked even greater furore in the summer of 1967. Two separate applications from the Edinburgh International Film Festival to show the film were rejected by a large majority of magistrates who attended the preview, led by the Lord Provost, Herbert Brechin, who dismissed it as 'the most disgusting film I have ever seen'.[107] His comments precipitated a spate of correspondence in the press and public protests that criticised his puritanical 'philistinism' and his denigration of an author of outstanding literary merit. However, Brechin was unrepentant, declaring that the film 'should be publicly burned' and describing the Molly Bloom soliloquy as 'like the product of a warped mind'.[108] The incident led the press to question the whole process of local film censorship and the competency and desirability of a small group of magistrates taking responsibility for maintaining the 'moral fibre and public taste' of the city. According to the *Edinburgh Evening News*, the system bordered on the farcical given that the magistrates involved were:

> [G]enerally well on in years, often fixed in their attitudes, frequently unable to make any artistic judgement, and notably infrequent cinemagoers . . . If we must have the offensive weapon of local censorship, then the people who make the decisions should be hand-picked for the job – a psychiatrist, a film-maker, a film distributor, a social worker, representatives of filmgoers' organisations, and even a few sensible house-wives.[109]

Ridicule was also levelled at the response of Edinburgh magistrates to *The Killing of Sister George*, Robert Aldrich's film about an ageing lesbian actress whose life unravels when she is axed from a TV series. On 17 November 1969, the Magistrates' Committee voted by five votes to four in favour of refusing a licence.[110] The following day *The Scotsman* printed a spoof play entitled 'Magistrates' Meeting: The Epic That Eclipsed Sister George' along with the magistrates' photos as *dramatis personae*.[111] Their proceedings were presented as ignorant and bigoted and as bringing into disrepute the existing system of censorship. Although Edinburgh was in line with St Andrews and Helensburgh in banning the film, it was licensed for exhibition in Aberdeen, Dundee and Glasgow. It was also licensed in Dumfries, Falkirk and Perth without even being previewed. However, when faced with a renewed application from the distributors in 1970, the Edinburgh Magistrates' Committee continued to adhere to the ban, forcing its citizens to commute the short distance to Musselburgh, where the film was permitted to be shown.[112]

Edinburgh magistrates were also increasingly concerned at the exhibition of uncertificated, avant-garde films by film societies such as the Edinburgh Film Guild. In 1968, after public complaints, the National Film Theatre was warned by the police that, if it showed

Jean-Luc Godard's *Weekend*, which contained a mélange of sex, sadism and violence, during the Edinburgh International Film Festival, the film would be seized and the names of the audience recorded. Subsequently, the police were forced to concede that, as long as the audience was restricted to 'members only', there was no requirement to obtain a licence from the magistrates. However, while the Licensing Inspector maintained that the police 'never intended – and never would intend – to act as the censors of any film shows', he reaffirmed that they remained duty bound to report to the burgh prosecutor should any complaints of obscenity be lodged by members of the audience.[113]

Glasgow

Throughout the 1960s, civic leaders in Glasgow were also exercised about the effect of films in producing moral delinquency in the young. As in Edinburgh, Glasgow magistrates banned films such as *Soho Striptease: Time of Desire* and *How to Undress in Public Without Undue Embarrassment* which they perceived as depicting gratuitous nudity and/or sexual deviance and immorality.[114] They also banned *Ulysses* in 1967.[115] However, in contrast to Edinburgh, they decided, on a split vote, to permit *West End Jungle* to be exhibited on the grounds that it served as a powerful critique of metropolitan vice.[116] After a special preview and long deliberations, they also granted a local licence to *Fanny Hill* in 1965 and to *Lady in a Cage* in 1968 (subject to an X certificate). In addition, the uncut version of *The Killing of Sister George* was granted an X certificate.

Although evidence suggests that Glasgow magistrates prohibited fewer films than their counterparts in Edinburgh, they were more proactive in campaigning for more stringent controls on the content of X-certificated films. In 1960–1, they made strong representations to the BBFC and met with John Trevelyan, the Chief Film Censor, and with Lord Morrison of Lambeth, President of the Board. The Magistrates' Committee also protested to cinema owners and the Scottish branch of the Cinematograph Exhibitors' Association over the moral calibre of their programmes and the indecency displayed in cinema posters.[117]

As in Edinburgh, the banning of *Ulysses* precipitated a lively public debate in Glasgow over the licensing powers of magistrates. The senior magistrate observed that 'it was difficult to act in the role of censor, but he felt the city fathers did have a measure of responsibility'. An editorial in the *Glasgow Herald* defended the ban and argued that, given that the BBFC had declined to certificate the film, the magistrates had performed 'their appropriate democratic duties' in protecting the 'majority of cinema goers who [were] not highly cultured persons . . . impervious to obscenity'. Unsurprisingly, the editorial attracted vigorous criticism and the episode left a strong residue of disquiet in cultural circles at the continuing ability of the magistrates to determine the viewing habits of the public.[118] Such concerns surfaced again in 1969, when the Glasgow Chamber of Commerce urged that decisions with respect to the public showing of a film should only be taken by magistrates who had actually viewed it and only after half of all magistrates had attended a showing. On the casting vote of the Senior Magistrate, under pressure from church leaders, the proposal was rejected and the existing procedures homologated.[119] Meanwhile, in line with their Edinburgh counterparts, Glasgow Magistrates' Committee was exploring ways of regulating the exhibition of uncensored films in private cinema clubs.[120] Thus, evidence would suggest that, as the 1960s drew to a close, while liberals in the Scottish churches may have been 'engaging with the radical promoter-entrepreneurs of art and drama',[121] in Scotland's two major cities an 'illiberal Presbyterian theocracy' continued to operate within local government to regulate the cultural agenda of the community.

Notes

1 For an overview of this debate, see especially Travis, *Bound and Gagged*, ch. 7; Newburn, *Permission and Regulation*, ch. 4.
2 FPCS, *Proceedings of Synod for 1960*, 14.
3 FPCS, *Proceedings of Synod for 1962*, 8.
4 FPCS, *Proceedings of Synod for 1964*, 15–16.
5 FPCS, *Proceedings of Synod for 1961*, 9; *Report of Religion and Morals Committee for 1961*, 44; *1966*, 50; *1968*, 66.
6 GACS, *Report of Social and Moral Welfare Board for 1964*, 343; *1967*, 515; *1969*, 513.
7 *Glasgow Observer and Scottish Catholic Herald*, 7 September 1962, 19 July 1963.
8 *Hansard* [HC], vol. 629, 10 November 1960, cols 81–2; vol. 630, 22 November 1960, cols 959–62; vol. 631, 29 November 1960, cols 35–6.
9 *Hansard* [HC], vol. 630, 22 November 1960, cols 960–1; vol. 631, 29 November 1960, cols 35–6. Subsequently, the Scottish Office was

equally reluctant to initiate proceedings against *Last Exit to Brooklyn* [*Glasgow Herald*, 16 July 1966].

10   *Glasgow Herald*, 5 November 1960.
11   Ibid., 8 November 1960.
12   Haste, *Rules of Desire*, 182.
13   Calder, *Pursuit*, 150, 183–4.
14   Similar prosecutions, involving the seizure and forfeiture of materials, were taking place in Glasgow, using local powers [*Glasgow Herald*, 12 November 1965].
15   ECA, Burgh Court papers for 1960.
16   The following account is based upon ECA, ED6/1/15, *Edinburgh City Police Annual Report for 1964*, 29; *Evening News and Dispatch*, 9 October 1964; *The Scotsman*, 9 October 1964, 11 and 17 December 1964; *Glasgow Herald*, 9 and 23 October 1964, 20 November 1964, 8 December 1964. Three of the cases were initiated by 'anonymous tip-offs' to the police. In the remaining case, a police constable initiated proceedings by purchasing copies of the books, 'after being asked to watch out for them' [*Glasgow Herald*, 20 November 1964].
17   *The Scotsman*, 17 December 1964.
18   Edinburgh Central Library (hereafter ECL), YHV6727, Banned books, press cuttings, 1964.
19   ECA, SL24/1/1, Minutes of Edinburgh Library and Museums Committee, 16 December 1954.
20   *Evening News and Dispatch*, 8 February 1964.
21   The work followed the fortunes of four young people, including an incestuous brother and sister.
22   *The Scotsman*, 5 August 1967; *Evening News*, 2 September 1967.
23   ECA, SL24/1/8, Minutes of Libraries Sub-Committee, 7 September 1967.
24   Ibid., 16 November 1967.
25   *The Scotsman*, 24 November 1967.
26   Ibid., 8 December 1967.
27   For detailed accounts of the debates surrounding theatre censorship in the 1960s, see especially Travis, *Bound and Gagged*, ch. 8; Holden, *Makers and Manners*, ch. 4; Thomas, Carlton and Etienne, *Theatre Censorship*, ch. 7.
28   NRS, HH41/2355, Home Secretary to SSS, 24 November 1965; SHHD minute, 'Theatre censorship', 26 January 1966.
29   Ibid., A. T. F. Ogilvie to A. P. Reid, 30 November 1965 (original emphasis).
30   See, for example, GACS, *Report of Committee on Temperance and Morals for 1962*, 430; *Report of Social and Moral Welfare Board for 1964*, 343; FPCS, *Report of Religion and Morals Committee for 1964*, 42–3.

31 Church of Scotland, *Kirk and Theatre* (1961), cited in GACS, *Report of Church and Nation Committee for 1967*, 163.

32 FPCS, *Proceedings of Synod for 1965*, 9.

33 Bartie, 'Festival city', PhD dissertation, 112, 234, 237–8.

34 *Glasgow Herald*, 26 October 1960.

35 For a detailed account, see Bartie, 'Festival city', ch. 5.

36 Ibid., 113.

37 Calder, *Pursuit*, 197, 246–63. Edinburgh's Lord Provost claimed that such events were part of a 'conspiracy of decadence' [*Glasgow Herald*, 16 October 1963].

38 NRS, HH41/2355, Minute on 'Theatre Censorship' by SHHD, 30 December 1965.

39 Ibid., Memorandum by R. E. C. Johnson, 30 November 1965.

40 Ibid.

41 Ibid., Briefing note for SSS, 1 December 1965.

42 Ibid., I. M. Robertson to R. H. Law, 20 April 1966.

43 Ibid., Note by SHHD, 'H(66)8 Theatre Censorship', 26 January 1966; Travis, *Bound and Gagged*, 221.

44 *Report of Joint Committee on Censorship of the Theatre*, xiv–xix.

45 NRS, HH41/1707, Note from Home Secretary, 10 July 1967.

46 Ibid., Minute by J. Inglis, 23 June 1967; Minute I. L. Sharp to Solicitor, 6 July 1967. Significantly, Roy Jenkins had initially suggested that the inquiry be limited to the London theatre as a means of avoiding the necessity of having 'hostile Scottish representation' on the Committee [Holden, *Makers and Manners*, 150].

47 NRS, HH41/1707, Minute I. L. Sharp to D. J. Cowperthwaite, 6 July 1967. London theatre managers had warned that any system of decentralised censorship that gave more powers to local magistrates would almost certainly inhibit West End plays touring Scotland [*Proceedings of Joint Committee on Censorship of the Theatre*, 88].

48 NRS, HH41/1707, Minute I. L. Sharp to D. J. Cowperthwaite, 6 July 1967.

49 Ibid., Minute I. L. Sharp to J. M. Fearn, 11 July 1967; Briefing note by R. E. C. Johnson, 14 July 1967.

50 Ibid., I. L. Sharp to W. Kerr Fraser, 17 July 1967; Crown Agent to D. J. Cowperthwaite, 15 September 1967.

51 Ibid., J. M. Fearn to I. L. Sharp, 25 July 1967; D. J. Cowperthwaite to Crown Agent, 11 September 1967.

52 Ibid., Memorandum by R. E. C. Johnson, 23 October 1967.

53 Ibid., I. L. Sharp to D. J. Cowperthwaite, 28 August 1967.

54 *Public and General Statutes, Theatres Act 1968 c. 54*.

55 However, Scottish local authorities retained other powers to prosecute obscene performances under local statute and byelaws [NRS, AD63/852/2, Theatres Bill, notes on clauses, 1968].

56 NRS, HH41/1709, J. Kidd to I. L. Sharp, 28 May 1968; I. L. Sharp to J. Kidd, 23 May 1968.
57 Ibid., N. E. Sharp to W. Hutchison, 26 January and 2 February 1968.
58 Ibid., SHHD, *Police (Chief Constables) Circular No. 36/1968*.
59 For an insight into the challenges faced by the more innovative theatre companies in Scotland in the 1960s, see especially McMillan, *Traverse Theatre Story*, 39–40; Coveney, *The Citz*, 56–63.
60 According to McMillan [*Traverse Theatre Story*, 40], 'the Traverse was a powerful focus for respectable Edinburgh's fantasies and fears about the new "permissive" age'.
61 *Glasgow Herald*, 24, 25 and 31 August 1967.
62 Ibid., 5 February 1968.
63 Ibid., 9 April 1968.
64 Ibid., 31 May 1968.
65 Ibid., 26 October 1965.
66 Ibid., 11 and 15 April 1969.
67 Ibid., 24 April 1969.
68 United Free Church of Scotland (hereafter UFCS), *Report of Committee on Public Questions for 1951*, 44.
69 *Glasgow Herald*, 13 December 1954.
70 FPCS, *Report of Religion and Morals Report Committee for 1957*, 49.
71 *Glasgow Observer and Scottish Catholic Herald*, 13 September 1957.
72 In 1962, there were 111,900 TV sets in Scotland compared with 41,000 in 1952 [Harvie, *No Gods and Precious Few Heroes*, 140–1].
73 *Report of the Committee on Broadcasting*, Appendix E, 892.
74 Ibid., 301.
75 GACS, *Report of Church and Nation Committee for 1965*, 245–7.
76 GACS, *Deliverances of the General Assembly for 1965*, 300.
77 GACS, *Report of Church and Nation Committee for 1966*, 130.
78 Ibid., *Report for 1967*, 162; *1968*, 138.
79 *Pornography: The Longford Report*, 388.
80 FPCS, *Proceedings of Synod for 1960*, 14; *1961*, 9; *1962*, 8.
81 FPCS, *Report of the Religion and Morals Committee for 1963*, 42.
82 Ibid., *Report for 1965*, 48; *1966*, 50–1; *1968*, 67. The BBC's programmes on sex education attracted particular criticism as empowering medics and psychiatrists to propound 'pagan views on morals', thus ruining 'not only the souls but also the bodies' of the young [FPCS, *Proceedings of Synod for 1964*, 11–12, 16].
83 FPCS, *Report of the Religion and Morals Committee for 1967*, 51; *1969*, 73; *Glasgow Herald*, 18 November 1965.
84 General Assembly of the UFCS, *Report of Committee on Public Questions for 1966*, 21; *1967*, 22; *1969*, 22.
85 *Glasgow Herald*, 2 December 1965.
86 GACS, *Report of Church and Nation Committee for 1966*, 130.

87 See, for example, *Glasgow Observer and Scottish Catholic Record*, 3 April 1961.

88 Ibid., 24 December 1965.

89 NRS, GD333/14, Papers of the Edinburgh Women Citizen's Association, Minutes of Executive Committee, 2 December 1960, 22 March 1967.

90 *Report of Committee on Broadcasting*, appendix E, 828.

91 GCA, C/1/3/152, Minutes of Glasgow Education Committee, 26 November 1965, 4 March 1966.

92 *Glasgow Herald*, 10 October 1969.

93 The following overview is based on Jarvis, *Conservative Governments, Morality and Social Change*, 137–40.

94 NRS, HH41/2355, Memorandum by R. E. C. Johnson, 30 November 1965; Briefing note and draft response for Secretary of State for Scotland, 1 December 1965.

95 Ibid., G. F. Belfour to R. H. Law, 23 February 1966.

96 Ibid., G. F. Belfour to C. T. Hole, 24 February 1966.

97 Harvie, *No Gods and Precious Few Heroes*, 128.

98 See, for example, Edinburgh University Library (hereafter EUL), GB0237 E95.25, Minutes of Broadcasting Council for Scotland (hereafter BCS), 4 January 1960, 15 May 1961, 7 May 1962, 29 November 1963, 29 May 1964, 26 February 1965, 4 February 1966.

99 Bartie, 'Festival city', 184.

100 EUL, GB0237 E95.25, Minutes of BCS, 4 November 1960, 12 May 1961, 26 November 1965, 21 October 1966.

101 ECA, SL119/3/33, Minutes of Edinburgh Magistrates' Committee (hereafter EMC), 12 February 1964.

102 Ibid., SL119/3/39, Minutes of EMC, 10 October 1969.

103 GACS, *Report of Committee on Temperance and Morals for 1962*, 430; FPCS, *Report of Religion and Morals Committee for 1962*, 29; *1968*, 67.

104 Aldgate, *Censorship and the Permissive Society*, 151–2.

105 The following is based upon ECA, SL119/3/31–9, Minutes of EMC, 1960–9; www.imdb.com/ and www.bfi.org.uk/filmtvinfo/ftvdb/, accessed 21 July 2011.

106 *The Scotsman*, 1 August 1996.

107 ECA, SL119/3/37, Minutes of EMC, 14 June 1967, 11 August 1967. By contrast, the film was exhibited in Dundee.

108 *Edinburgh Evening News*, 30 June 1967; *The Scotsman*, 3, 5 and 24 July 1967; *Evening News and Dispatch*, 15 July 1967.

109 *Edinburgh Evening News*, 17 July 1967.

110 ECA, SL119/3/39, Minutes of EMC, 17 November 1969.

111 *The Scotsman*, 18 November 1969.

112 ECA, SL119/3/39, Minutes of EMC, 11 February 1970; *Edinburgh Evening News*, 24 March 1970.

113 *Glasgow Herald*, 27 and 28 November 1968, 2 and 5 December 1968.

114 Ibid., 2 January 1960, 1 September 1965.

115 Ibid., 28 June 1967.

116 Ibid., 27 June 1962.

117 Ibid., 3 February 1960, 30 November 1960, 11 January 1961. These representations were closely monitored and actively supported by the Scottish Catholic Film Institute. The Institute had been established in 1952, partly to coordinate the efforts of the Roman Catholic Church in Scotland to provide an informal system of film classification and review (published in the Catholic press) by which to protect Catholic values. See especially *Glasgow Observer and Scottish Catholic Herald*, 20 November 1959, 11 March 1960, 2 December 1960, 3 February 1961.

118 *Glasgow Herald*, 7 and 28 June 1967, 1 July 1967.

119 Ibid., 5 March 1969.

120 Ibid., 30 April 1969.

121 Bartie, 'Festival city', 231.

11

POLICING PORNOGRAPHY AND OBSCENITY
IN THE 1970s

PORNOGRAPHY

A new moral crusade

Historians of sexuality have rightly identified the early 1970s as a watershed in the relationship of the state to moral censorship, characterised by a sustained and increasingly coordinated backlash against the permissive values and cultural ethics of the 1960s.[1] A new moral authoritarianism, advanced by a powerful coalition of puritanical groups, such as the National Viewers' and Listeners' Association (NVLA), the Festival of Light and the Responsible Society, sought, increasingly by recourse to the law, to reassert a Christian-based moral order/rearmament that would relocate sex within the framework of conjugal love and faithfulness and protect the innocence and moral fibre of the nation's youth. At the centre of their campaign was a desire to strengthen the law against pornography and to ensure its rigorous enforcement.[2]

This backlash was also experienced in Scotland where the puritan lobby south of the Border attracted significant support from both church and civic leaders. The Free Churches in Scotland actively supported the views of the NVLA and the Festival of Light. They viewed the intrusion of pornographic material into bookshops and magazine stands as a conspiracy of publishers to undermine 'the morality of the nation' and welcomed the prosecution of the *Little Red Schoolbook*. They commended the moral evangelicalism of Lord Longford's inquiry into pornography and pressed for more stringent laws to contain the problem.[3]

The Church of Scotland was conducting its own moral crusade against pornography, inspired by a Scottish Festival of Light, attended by more than 2,000 people in George Square, Glasgow, in January 1972.[4] In February, it launched the Scottish Petition for Public Decency, protesting at the 'increasing commercial exploitation of sex' and 'the public portrayal of intimate or unnatural sexual behaviour', and calling upon the Government to review the law on obscenity. The petition, presented to the Secretary of State for Scotland in June 1972, was signed by over 200,000 adults and attracted support from nearly all the Scottish churches and from more than half of all Scottish MPs.[5]

The degree of moral outrage in Scotland at the spread of pornography was clearly reflected in the response to the opening of a so-called 'sex supermarket' in St George's Cross, Glasgow, in 1971, selling pornography and sexual appliances.[6] Protests were made by all the voluntary youth organisations in Glasgow to the Corporation and to the Secretary of State for Scotland. An 'Anti-Smut' march was organised and a former councillor forwarded a petition with over 6,000 signatures protesting that such shops would corrupt the young and attract 'undesirable elements', and pressing for their suppression.[7] The 'sex supermarket' in question was raided by the police, its customers' names recorded and contents seized, and its owner and manager charged with obscenity under local legislation. However, public outrage was further fuelled by the owner's subsequent abortive attempts to open up shops in other Scottish cities, and his final gesture of giving away his stock in Glasgow and setting off in a gaily coloured bus to sell 'kinky underwear, contraceptives and sexual appliances' in the Highlands. The whole episode left a legacy of local discontent with the inefficacy of the law relating to obscenity in Scotland, and the enduring commitment of many civic and church leaders to the call for more rigorous controls.

The Scottish Home and Health Department (SHHD) adopted a cautious response to the moral panic surrounding pornography. In their view, local legislation, if rigorously applied, appeared sufficient to meet the problem of 'sex supermarkets', insofar as it existed in Scottish towns and cities. The existing laws on obscenity could be applied to sexual appliances as well as publications and videos. Officials also warned that more coercive measures against sex shops would necessarily involve addressing intractable issues of legal definition.[8] Accordingly, petitioners were advised that the Secretary of State viewed national legislation on the issue as premature, although the Scottish Office would continue to monitor the situation.[9]

The Longford Report – the Scottish dimension

By the autumn of 1972, the focus of official attention had shifted to the issue of how best to respond to the Longford Report on Pornography, the product of a self-funded and widely publicised sixteen-month inquiry by the Labour peer, the seventh Earl of Longford, a leading figure in the Festival of Light. The Secretary and Vice-Convener of the Church of Scotland's Moral Welfare Committee were members of Lord Longford's unofficial inquiry and contributed a report on the Scottish experience along with recommendations and a draft bill.[10] Their report acknowledged that the problem of pornography was not as great in Scotland as in other parts of Britain and that there was no area that might be considered 'a minor Soho' in any of the Scottish cities or towns. At the same time, it stressed the degree of 'genuine public concern' over the increasing prevalence of pornographic materials, not least because of the 'strongly moralistic' cultural heritage of the Scot, as reflected in the Scottish Petition for Public Decency. Three main defects in the law in Scotland relating to obscenity were identified.[11] First, it was regarded as too fragmentary. Offences at common law were too vague and statute law, such as the Burgh Police (Scotland) Act of 1892, did not apply to vast areas of the country. Second, the penalties were viewed as 'derisory' and as having no deterrent effect. Finally, the lack of uniformity in obscenity laws north and south of the Border was considered inappropriate and an open invitation for pornographers to view Scotland as a safe haven for their activities. Accordingly, Scotland needed to be included under any new legislation.

In accordance with the main recommendations of the Longford Committee, the Scottish report recommended that the 'basic test of obscenity be that the offending material outrages contemporary standards of decency or humanity accepted by the public at large'.[12] Again, in line with English proposals, it was suggested that a defence for the 'public good', introduced in the 1959 Obscene Publications Act, should no longer be retained. In addition, the Obscenity (Scotland) Bill, drafted as an attachment to the Scottish report, proposed that the penalties for publishing obscene material should be substantially increased, and that there should be additional penalties where the material was supplied to someone under the age of 18. Heavy penalties were also proposed for those who sexually exploited others in the production of pornography. The report was endorsed by Cardinal Gordon Gray, Archbishop of St Andrews and Edinburgh, and by all the Roman Catholic bishops in Scotland.[13]

In response to the Longford Report and to growing public and parliamentary pressure for action, the SHHD conducted a series of consultations in the autumn of 1972; first, with the Home Office and its policy advisers, and second, with the Crown Agent and Chief Constables in Scotland. The Department was ambivalent towards the prospect of new legislation. On the one hand, it was aware of the strength of public support in Scotland for more rigorous measures to control the spread of pornography, and of the likely criticism that would arise if the Church of Scotland's representations were ignored.[14] On the other, it was equally aware that there were many in the media, the police and the legal profession in Scotland who doubted many of the assumptions and assertions of the Longford Report, especially with respect to the social impact of pornography and the likely effect of redefining obscenity.[15] In particular, the SHHD sympathised with the view of the Crown Office and Scottish Chief Constables that the definition of 'obscene' in the Longford Report was unenforceable as its interpretation would inevitably vary depending on which magistrate or sheriff was sitting.[16] Moreover, the SHHD shared the concerns of Home Office officials that any attempt to amend the Obscene Publications Acts would run the risk of reviving the whole controversy surrounding censorship and civil liberties.[17] It agreed with the Home Secretary, Robert Carr, that policy should focus instead on controlling the display of indecent material – such as on posters outside cinemas and clubs, and the covers of books and magazines in shop windows and easily accessible shelves – rather than attempt to address broader issues of content.[18]

Officials perceived the issue of pornography as analogous to that of prostitution, and, as with the Street Offences Act of 1959, sought not to prohibit the private consumption of pornography, but its public display, as a form of 'environmental pollution'.[19] Accordingly, the Home Office suggested that the issue be remitted to a working party that was currently reviewing the law on vagrancy and street offences, to which a representative of the SHHD was added. During October and November 1972 the working party gradually formulated some policy guidelines.[20] First, it reaffirmed the need to focus on the public display of offensive material rather than attempt any revision of the law of obscenity. Second, it recommended that new legislation be introduced rather than merely amending antiquated powers contained in the 1824 Vagrancy Act and the 1889 Indecent Advertisement Act, which the courts were reluctant to use. Third, it stressed the need to provide a more supportive legal and cultural environment within which the police might operate, along with clearer policy directives. It was felt that, by emphasising that legislation was an attempt not to impose a form of censorship or to regulate private morals, but to deal with a 'public nuisance', it would create 'a climate in which the police could take a firmer line with some assurance of public support and backing also from the courts'. Fourth, in defining the location of an offence, the working party favoured limiting restrictions to the street, shop windows and displays within shops visible to children. It was aware that, in targeting retail outlets, it would risk being seen as sanctioning sex shops, but felt that the immediate need was to deal with the problem on the high street rather than go up against the entire commercial trade in pornography. Finally, while initially it proposed the seizure of materials for evidence purposes alone, on the grounds that the offence lay in 'displaying' and not 'stocking' materials, under pressure from the SHHD the working party agreed to recommend that, in order to placate public opinion, courts should be given discretionary powers of forfeiture.

However, SHHD officials remained ambivalent about the need for new legislation. Its Under-Secretary, W. K. Fraser, saw the immediate issue as one of enforcement. He was keen to explore why existing statutes and the patchwork of local legislation in Scotland were proving ineffective in regulating the display of offensive material.[21] He was especially concerned by the apparent failure of the Crown Office to proceed against larger retailers such as Menzies, thus leaving the police to continue raiding back-street 'peddlers of porn' to little effect, as they had 'neither reputations nor shareholders to protect'. The Department realised that the police and the prosecution service in Scotland were reluctant to be seen to play the role of 'censors' in initiating legal proceedings.[22] It was also aware that the low level of penalties, the absence of a precise legal definition of 'indecent' and 'obscene', and the need to defer to English legal processes in cases involving material originating south of the Border acted as further disincentives.[23]

Nonetheless, the SHHD considered that existing legislation – especially the powers contained in the 1892 Burgh Police Act and local legislation – was adequate to address the issue of pornographic display in Scotland, albeit that such powers needed to be consolidated and applied uniformly. The Department anticipated that this would eventually be effected as part of local government reorganisation but rightly predicted that the Conservative Government would be forced, well before then, to introduce fresh measures.

Meanwhile, during the autumn and winter of 1972, the Church of Scotland launched a fresh campaign to gain the support of Scottish

MPs for its proposed amendments to the obscenity laws. A new petition was submitted to the Secretary of State for Scotland.[24] In addition, the Scottish Office was repeatedly pressed in Parliament to introduce new legislation on the lines of the Longford Report. The campaign was led by Lord Ferrier and the Earl of Lauderdale. In his usual apocalyptic style, Lord Ferrier viewed pornographers as the 'out-riders of anti-Christ' funded by the 'resources of world revolution' and intimately linked to a lethal cocktail of violence, drugs, vice and venereal disease. In his view, liberal intellectuals were leading the nation into a 'moral Spaghetti Junction' in denying the links between pornography and the decline in moral standards. The problem, he asserted, was 'a straightforward crossroads, and the sooner a revised law repaint[ed] the signpost the better for all of us'.[25] The Earl of Lauderdale, another lay leader within the Kirk, was adamant that pornography affronted family values, debased women, sullied men and corrupted adolescents. He explicitly rejected libertarian claims that the private perusal of sexually explicit materials was outside the purview of the state.[26]

In response, the Scottish Office reiterated its view that it was an undesirable and 'unprofitable exercise' to seek to redefine the legal meaning of obscenity as recommended in the Longford Report. It continued to regard the existing test of obscenity in Scotland as defined by Lord Cooper as the most effective test, in that it balanced 'in a reasonable way the two conflicting considerations – the right to freedom of expression to the greatest extent possible and the desirability of protecting the community from corrupting influences'.[27] However, in order to placate public opinion, it was conceded that the Secretary of State for Scotland would press for Scotland to be included in any new provisions relating to indecent displays.

Indecent displays

New provisions relating to indecent displays were subsequently introduced by the Conservative Government in the autumn of 1973 as the second section of its Cinematograph and Indecent Displays Bill. The Bill sought to rectify the limitations and anachronisms of existing law relating to the public display of indecent materials. By extending the offence, increasing the penalties involved and modernising the language employed in legal proceedings, it was hoped to simplify the task of the police and to encourage the courts to adopt a more proactive attitude to the issue of pornography. The Bill was not intended to affect the operation of the Official Publications Acts in dealing with the publication and distribution of obscene material but merely to protect the public from unintentional exposure to its display. The Bill proposed that courts should have powers of forfeiture and that penalties for conviction should be significantly increased – to a maximum of £400 or three months' imprisonment for a summary conviction and an unlimited fine or two years' imprisonment on indictment. It was also hoped to penalise shop window signs that advertised indecent materials, such as '*Adult Mags*' or '*The Best Stock of Skin Flicks in Town*', as well as salacious cinema posters. In addition, unsolicited circulars for books containing indecent photographs or for strip clubs, and the free distribution of indecent leaflets in public (including the distribution of leaflets on contraception to schoolgirls) were to be proscribed.[28]

The response of Scottish officials to the Bill was broadly favourable. While, in theory, existing statute and common law in Scotland provided similar powers, it was readily acknowledged that they had proved ineffective in addressing the issue of pornography and had led to a lack of consistency in the application of the law. Scottish law officers conceded that new legislation was desirable in order to give greater priority to pornography in the work of the local prosecutors. However, the perennial problem remained of how to ensure consistency given the existing array of powers under the Burgh Police Acts and corresponding local acts in the Scottish cities. It was recommended that the best solution was for the Crown Office to oversee all prosecutions relating to indecent displays through the procurators fiscal rather than leaving the initiative to City Prosecutors and the Burgh Courts.[29]

An additional complication was the fact that the Bill left the concept of 'indecency' undefined. As the Lord Advocate warned, although Lord Reid had recently argued in a case before the House of Lords that it included 'anything which an ordinary decent man or woman would find to be shocking, disgusting and revolting, a member of a Scottish jury might well take a different view from an English jury man of what is shocking, disgusting and revolting!'[30] Scottish newsagents were especially concerned that this lack of definition would lead to a 'lack of transparency and equity in prosecutions', and make it impossible for their National Federation to issue guidelines with respect to 'girlie magazines'.[31]

The Bill received a mixed response from Scottish MPs. David Steel welcomed the measure as long as it was restricted to curbing 'visual pollution' and was not designed to extend censorship. Drawing on the Swedish experience, he recommended that the regulation of displays should be confined to the type of 'girlie magazines' on public display and should not encompass material out of sight in smaller back-street shops specialising in explicit material, which could more appropriately be dealt with under the laws relating to obscenity. In contrast, W. H. K. Baker, Conservative MP for Banff, did not feel the Bill went far enough to halt the 'slither towards moral decadence'. In particular, he wanted sex shops to come within its ambit.[32]

In the event, after its Second Reading and Committee stages, consideration of the Bill was adjourned, and progress was halted by the dissolution of Parliament and general election in February 1974. In May 1974, the Interdepartmental Working Party on Vagrancy and Street Offences recommended legislation along similar lines.[33] Although Scottish officials were frustrated by the failure of the Working Party's report to take account of legal differences north and south of the Border, they pressed for Scotland to be included in any legislation relating to indecent displays.[34] However, Roy Jenkins, as Home Secretary, was not prepared to reintroduce the Bill, and over the following years the Labour Government withheld official support for a series of Private Members' Bills that sought to revive the measure.

Pornography and the Sexual Offences (Scotland) Act 1976

Nonetheless, against a backdrop of moral panic orchestrated by Mary Whitehouse, articulated by Conservative backbenchers, sensationalised in the press and manifested in a series of highly publicised prosecutions and police campaigns,[35] the issue of pornography and obscenity continued to generate public concern in Scotland. The major source of pressure continued to come from the churches. Citing the social philosopher David Holbrook, the Free Church of Scotland emphasised that pornography was essentially a regressive sexual perversion imposed by 'diseased imaginations on the unsuspecting public'. It liaised with the Church of Scotland, the Nationwide Festival of Light and the Order of Christian Unity in an effort to secure government action against displays of offensive material in bookshops. It also encouraged congregations to support the formation of Community Standards Associations as a means of ensuring moral vigilance across Scottish society.[36] Meanwhile, in 1976, the Church of Scotland's Social Responsibility Committee, frustrated at the failure of Scottish governance to respond to the Longford Report and the Petition for Public Decency, established a working party to undertake a wide-ranging review of obscenity in Scottish society.[37]

In view of resistance from the Home Secretary to the revival of any new legislation relating to indecent displays, the SHHD was content just to maintain a watching brief. No Scottish view was advanced during the House of Lords' debate on obscenity and the law in March 1976, and when pressed in the House of Commons in April 1976 by the Scottish Nationalist Ian MacCormick as to how the Scottish Office planned to inhibit the display of salacious books and magazines, the Secretary of State for Scotland, William Ross, merely responded that, although the issue was 'under review', 'no immediate plans for legal changes' were contemplated.[38]

Scottish officials and law officers did explore the possibility of modernising the content and language of Scots law relating to the production, distribution and display of indecent materials in the course of drafting the Sexual Offences (Scotland) Act of 1976, designed to consolidate enactments relating to sexual offences in Scotland.[39] Those working within the Scottish Office on the reform of civic governance were keen to see what they regarded as the 'most sensitive and politically controversial' part of the Burgh Police Acts – that is, their 'sexual provisions' – recast and uniformly applied across Scotland prior to a more general reorganisation of local powers.[40] However, the issue was problematic. Merely to impose a slightly modified version of the 1892 Burgh Police Act across the country would have been seen as retrogressive in those cities such as Edinburgh and Glasgow that had already taken steps to modernise their local provisions relating to indecency and obscenity. At the same time, any attempt to introduce more radical changes would have breached constitutional rules governing Consolidation Acts. As a result, the 1976 Act did not attempt to address existing powers relating to obscene publications and displays in Scotland.

Challenge and response, 1977–80

The social politics surrounding censorship in Britain in the late 1970s were dominated by the proceedings and report of the Williams Committee, appointed in 1977 by the Labour Government to investigate 'obscenity, indecency and violence in publications, entertainments and displays'. In Scotland, the Social Responsibility Committee of the Church of Scotland was already undertaking its inquiry into 'Obscenity and Community Standards' and endeavoured unsuccessfully to concatenate its work with that of the Williams Committee.[41] It lobbied the Secretary of State for Scotland and Scottish MPs for Scottish interests and views to be represented on and to the Williams Committee so as to ensure that future legislation on issues of censorship and pornography – issues that affected the whole of Britain – did not ignore legal and cultural variances north of the Border. As most of the obscene material in Scotland was imported from or through England, it was argued that Scottish society had 'a crucial concern with the law in England, notwithstanding differences in the legal systems'.

However, the Home Office was resistant to the terms of reference of the Williams Committee embracing the Scottish experience and even denied the Church of Scotland observer status. Significantly, the Scottish Office did not press the issue. The Secretary of State, Bruce Millan, agreed that the Committee should not stray into the intricacies of Scots law, and that it was inappropriate to 'invite a committee to tackle such disparate laws and social circumstances as exist[ed] in the two jurisdictions'. In his opinion, a separate review of Scottish legislation should appropriately await the outcome of the Working Party on Civic Government in Scotland and be the responsibility of a future devolved Scottish Assembly that was currently anticipated in government circles.[42] Spurred on by what it viewed as the 'cavalier attitude' of the Williams Committee to its overtures, the Church of Scotland's Social Responsibility Committee continued to conduct its own independent inquiry and declined to give evidence.

Scotland was also excluded from the 1978 Protection of Children Act, a 'panic' measure aimed at the criminalisation of child pornography and promoted by a powerful alliance of moral conservatives led by Margaret Thatcher and Mary Whitehouse with widespread all-party support from backbench MPs, educationists and the media.[43] In Scotland, the Free Churches and local presbyteries were especially vocal in support of the Bill and pressed the Secretary of State to tighten Scots law on child pornography.[44] During its Second Reading, several MPs, in many instances responding to the concerns of constituents, pressed for Scotland to be included in its provisions, on the grounds that its exclusion might lead to Scotland becoming 'some form of pornographic haven'.[45] The Nationwide Festival of Life also campaigned for the Bill to extend to the whole of the United Kingdom, arguing that child pornography was readily available in Scotland and not being prosecuted.[46]

In the view of the SHHD, such representations were merely 'a backwash of the concern that ha[d] been expressed in England and Wales rather than a reflection that there [was] any problem at all in Scotland'.[47] Moreover, in their view, shared by the Crown Office and Lord Advocate, there were no circumstances relating to the production and distribution of child pornography that could not be prosecuted under existing laws in Scotland. Officials also pointed out that not only would the new bill represent a needless duplication of powers, it would in fact contain lighter penalties than those already available under common law in Scotland.[48] However, the Secretary of State for Scotland, Bruce Millan, was adamant that the Scottish Office should not be made to appear complacent about the problem of pornography and that it should concede the argument for inclusion if there was any further pressure in Parliament. He stressed that, in defending Scotland's exclusion, 'in no circumstances' should it be argued that there was not a problem of pornography north of the Border and that the argument should be 'purely the adequacy of the existing Scottish criminal law'.[49] In the event, reassurances from Scottish officials on this point persuaded the Bill's sponsor, Cyril Townsend MP, not to extend it to cover Scotland.[50]

Scottish officials did give support to an Indecent Displays (Control) Bill, introduced as a Private Member's Bill and modelled on part two of the 1973 Cinematograph and Indecent Displays Bill. As previously, the Scottish Office was broadly in agreement with a strategy of addressing the issue of obscenity by focusing on its display rather than its definition, and concentrated its efforts on trying to reconcile new powers with those enshrined in Scots law. As before, after securing a Second Reading, the Bill fell on the dissolution of Parliament in the spring of 1979.[51]

Meanwhile, in May 1979, the Social Responsibility Committee of the Church of Scotland published its long-awaited report entitled *Obscenity and Community Standards*. The Committee hoped its report would not be viewed as just 'another rearguard action with outmoded tactics on behalf of an ageing religious community on the run' and acknowledged the argument that censorship might constitute a 'pesticide which [might] easily destroy too much blossom with the caterpillars'.[52] At the same time, underpinning its recommendations was a concern to affirm moral absolutes and the right of the law to intervene in the private sphere in order to contain the insidious effects on society at large of obscene materials and behaviours.[53] While according a central role to the 'constructive vigilance' of local presbyteries and churches in maintaining community standards, the report high-lighted the need for legislative changes at a national level.[54] It advanced a range of criticisms on the state of the law relating to obscenity in Scotland. In the view of the committee, the law was too complex and fragmented to cope with a rising problem of pornographic materials that constituted a 'continuous, graded incitement to degradation'. It appeared to be too random and inequitable and too dependent on the chance 'initiative of some vigilant or over-zealous member of the public'. As a result of this lack of clarity and uniformity, it lacked the confidence of both the public and prosecuting services and gave 'inadequate protection to society', failing in particular to address child sex exploitation, to protect citizens offended by the display of obscene materials and to provide a predictable legal framework within which artists, publishers and retailers might operate.[55]

The report recommended that, in view of the fact that the Williams Committee had not included Scotland within its remit, immediate action should be taken to amend the laws relating to obscenity in Scotland. It was feared that, otherwise, English law might be strengthened, leaving Scotland as a 'soft option' for the distributors of pornography.[56] In amending Scots law, the Social Responsibility Committee was concerned to ensure as much social consensus as possible and to maintain a balance between freedom and licence. It opposed the reduction of legal sanctions and proposed that the main emphasis of legislation should be on making the operation of existing powers more consistent and effective.[57] It recommended that all existing statutes be repealed and consolidated within three new statutory provisions: the extension of the 1978 Protection of Children Act to Scotland, a new Indecent Displays Act on the lines of previous Private Members' Bills, and a new Obscene Publications Act covering the whole of the United Kingdom and incorporating a definition of obscenity in line with the Church of Scotland's contribution to the Longford Report, namely, material that 'when, taken as a whole . . . would outrage contemporary community standards of decency'. In addition, it advocated that the legal penalties laid down in new legis-lation should be sufficiently severe as to represent a real deterrent, and that the police should be encouraged to take a more proactive stance against pornography, with greater support from the Crown Office and additional resources, including the appointment of specialist officers devoted to the problem.[58]

Later in the same year, the report of the Williams Committee on Obscenity and Film Censorship was also issued, receiving a hostile reception from Margaret Thatcher and her newly elected Conservative administration.[59] The Committee recommended that the existing Official Publications Acts be repealed and that there should be no censorship for the written word. It proposed that the legal terms 'obscene' and 'indecent' should be discontinued and concepts of 'deprave and corrupt' be superseded by more utilitarian concepts of harm. In the view of the Williams Committee, material should be restricted as a public nuisance if offensive to reasonable people but banned only if liable to cause harm in the course of its production or circulation, such as material involving children or sexual violence. There was to be no 'public good defence'. The aim therefore was to limit the availability and display of pornography but to make all but a small class of hard-core porn available in restricted circumstances – that is, in designated adult-only cinemas and sex shops.[60]

While some areas of the Scottish media were broadly supportive of these proposals,[61] in private, Scottish Office officials were highly sceptical about the more libertarian aspects of the Williams Report.[62] They shared the view of Scottish peers and church leaders, and of moral pressure groups such as the Glasgow Branch of the NVLA, that, rather than a reduction in legal controls, there needed to be greater recognition of the link between pornography and sexual crime and greater vigilance and legal protection against material that threatened to demoralise children, offend the sensibilities of many citizens and undermine Christian family values.[63] However, in public, the Scottish Office remained evasive and non-committal about the Report, merely stressing the differences in Scots law and the lower incidence of pornography north of the Border.[64]

Scottish officials were equally reticent in their response to the Church of Scotland's report. In the view of Malcolm Rifkind, Minister of Home Affairs and the Environment at the Scottish Office, apart from concerns surrounding child pornography and indecent displays, there was not a 'broad groundswell of public opinion' in favour of new wide-ranging legislation on obscenity. He argued that, given the lower incidence of obscene material in Scotland, the existing law in Scotland was regarded as adequate and did not suffer from the same deficiencies as that operating in England and Wales. He pointed in particular to the recent increase in the use of common law to prosecute offenders in Scotland, which did not involve the same problems of definition as were entailed in the use of statute and was therefore better able to reflect variations in the moral attitudes and tolerances of the Scottish community.[65]

Malcolm Rifkind held to this position despite continuing pressure from the Church of Scotland for the Scottish Office to be more proactive on the issue of pornography.[66] However, Scottish departments did collaborate with the Home Office in finally securing an Indecent Displays (Control) Act in 1981.[67] In addition, Rifkind pressed, albeit unsuccessfully, for sex shops to be included under the planning clauses of the 1981 Local Government (Miscellaneous Provisions) (Scotland) Bill.[68] Subsequently, in response to rising complaints about their proliferation, an amendment to the Civic Government (Scotland) Bill of 1982 was tabled introducing a licensing scheme similar to that already operating in England and Wales, and empowering local authorities to determine the number (if any) and location of sex shops in their area. Under the same Bill, provisions relating to indecency and obscenity in the Burgh Police (Scotland) Act of 1892 and associated local acts were also consolidated and modernised, and heavier penalties introduced.[69] In addition, powers similar to those under the 1978 Protection of Children Act were extended to Scotland. However, in accord with the advice of the Crown Office and Lord Advocate, the Scottish Office resisted any attempt to define 'obscenity' in the Bill in line with the 1959 Obscene Publications Act in England, electing, as before, to leave it to the courts to interpret in the light of 'the prevailing moral consensus'.[70] As the Scottish Office continued to hold out against any major review of the obscenity laws in Scotland,[71] the legal framework concerning obscene publications was therefore left very much as it had been in 1950.

Local enforcement

It is difficult to ascertain the level of Scottish prosecutions in the 1970s relating to indecent or obscene publications. The figures cited in official evidence are not consistent with annual police reports and parliamentary answers. The disruption and/or subsequent destruction of records consequent on local government reorganisation in 1974 further compound the problem. Evidence submitted to the Longford Committee suggested that many cases went unrecorded in the criminal statistics and that there were probably in the region of 100 prosecutions per annum in Scotland.[72]

In contrast to developments in England, there were no private prosecutions in Scotland after *McBain* v. *Crichton* in 1961, when the High Court refused a petition to prosecute a bookseller who had sold a copy of *Lady Chatterley's Lover*, on the grounds that the petitioner could not show that he had suffered a personal wrong of a criminal nature.[73] In the early 1970s, there were also very few cases brought under the common law, although a successful case – *Skeen v. Palumbo* – was brought in Paisley Sheriff Court in 1971.[74]

As in the 1960s, the bulk of prosecutions in Scotland during the 1970s relating to obscene publications were brought under the Burgh Police (Scotland) Act of 1892 and a variety of comparable local statutes and provisions. The overwhelming majority of cases were brought by City Prosecutors and took place in the Burgh Courts (or District Courts as they became known in 1975), and only a small proportion was heard in the Sheriff Courts.[75] Thus, the penalties imposed remained modest. Although the burgh/district courts could order the seizure and destruction of sizeable amounts of obscene material, their sentencing powers were limited and the fines imposed in Scottish courts were said to average only £37 in 1976.[76]

In theory, the Lord Advocate could have ordered the police to report specific cases directly to the procurator fiscal, thus shifting hearings to more senior courts, but in the first half of the 1970s this power does not appear to have been exercised in cases relating to pornography. The Crown Office, which directed the procurators fiscal, was reluctant to get involved, given the ambiguities of the law, the contentious nature of censorship and the uncertainty of securing a conviction. Moreover, this reactive rather than proactive approach to offences involving pornography appears to have informed police procedures, in that they remained very reluctant to initiate action unless a specific complaint was lodged by a member of the public. This inevitably led to random prosecutions rather than any systematic operation of the law.[77]

Nonetheless, some of the local powers had recently been strengthened and modernised. For example, under the 1960 Glasgow Consolidation (General Powers) Order Confirmation Act, a court could impose six months' imprisonment without option of a fine for repeat offenders,[78] powers homologated in the Glasgow Order Confirmation Act of 1971.[79] Similarly, the 1967 Edinburgh Corporation Order Confirmation Act had consolidated the law from previous statutes and incorporated clearer and more flexible criteria for proof of obscenity, in line with Lord Cooper's High Court appeal judgement in *Gellatly v. Laird* (1953).[80] Both Acts also empowered the burgh/district courts to order the forfeiture and destruction of obscene materials. Moreover, evidence suggests that these powers were being more vigorously exercised. Thus, in 1973, the publishers of the

Edinburgh underground magazine *Cracker* were successfully prosecuted under the Edinburgh Corporation Act for publishing an indecent cartoon.[81] Under the same powers, legal action was also taken that year against the proprietor of a small magazine shop frequented by students for displaying copies of *Oz*.[82]

There are other indications that, by the mid-1970s, law officers in Scotland were going onto the offensive against obscene literature and pornographers. More cases were being taken in the Sheriff Courts under common law, with heavier penalties,[83] and a series of successful prosecutions was launched against the proprietors of sex shops in all the major Scottish cities, using powers contained in local statutes.[84] In addition, in 1978, the Crown Office undertook a review of its prosecution policy on pornography with a view to establishing more uniformity. As a result, the Lord Advocate ordered that all police reports and productions relating to offences involving pornography should be sent to the Crown Office for a decision as to whether, and at what level, a prosecution should take place.[85]

Meanwhile, scattered evidence would suggest that, to varying degrees, informal systems of censorship continued to be operated by librarians and their committees during the 1970s. Edinburgh's Chief Librarian claimed that, in 1974, it 'was decided to have a clean sweep and to put books like *Lady Chatterley's Lover* . . . on the public shelves'.[86] Nonetheless, in the same year, Edinburgh Library and Museums Committee banned *Gay News* from the reading room of Edinburgh Central Library, on the grounds that the library should not be seen to condone illegal behaviour.[87] Moreover, although what might be termed 'blue books' formed a small proportion of books kept off open shelves, other librarians in the region regularly 'annexed' books that offended readers. For example, in 1977, Borders Regional Council withdrew Lesley Thomas's *Tropic of Ruislip* from open access after complaints from ratepayers.[88] It also appears that, even where a librarian wished to adopt a more permissive attitude, fear of prosecution could still impose a form of censorship. Thus, in late 1976, the Chief Librarian for Edinburgh public libraries purchased multiple copies of George Macbeth's *The Samurai*, 'a sexy, extravagant and very elegant spoof on the Bond genre', one of which was deposited in the Morningside branch. However, after a complaint from the public, the police warned the Librarian that he might be liable to prosecution if the volume remained on display. As a result, it had to be kept 'under the counter' and only made available on demand.[89]

THEATRE

The 1968 Theatres Bill, which terminated the censorship role of the Lord Chamberlain's office, had met with a cautious, if not hostile, response from Scottish policy makers, attuned to the somewhat heightened moral sensitivities of Scottish public opinion. These sensitivities were to persist into the 1970s, and local church and civic leaders continued to press the police and politicians to impose stricter controls on the content of theatrical performances. John Calder recalled the atmosphere of 'deeply ingrained Calvinist Puritanism' within which Scottish theatre companies had to operate.[90]

In the early 1970s, there was a fear amongst some members of the Scottish public that the 'moral decadence' of the London theatre would spread north across the Border. In particular, it was alleged that the more avant-garde plays performed at the Edinburgh Festival – a major site of cultural conflict – were increasingly aping sexually explicit London productions such as *Oh! Calcutta!* and *Hair*.[91] In 1971, Scottish politicians, backed by Teddy Taylor, the Scottish Under-Secretary for Health and Education, supported the campaign of the Paymaster General to withhold funding from publicly subsidised theatre companies that put on plays that could be deemed pornographic. They also welcomed the Arts Council's warning of the need to avoid 'obscene productions' and to demonstrate that subsidies had been 'spent for valid artistic purposes'.[92] The following year, Scottish peers, such as Lord Ferrier, used the debate on the Longford Report to highlight the moral decline of British theatre,[93] a concern echoed later in the 1970s at the annual synods of the Free Presbyterian Church of Scotland, in the light of what they viewed as an invasion of the type of plays that had made the West End a 'cesspit of iniquity'.[94] Once again, performances at the Edinburgh Festival proved the most frequent cause for complaint from the Scottish presbyteries.[95]

However, whereas in the 1960s, the Edinburgh Traverse Theatre had been the focus of concern, in the 1970s, it was the programme of plays performed at the Glasgow Citizens Theatre that attracted most controversy. In 1970, the performance of what was claimed to be a 'tasteless' avant-garde production of *Hamlet* triggered a flurry of protests in the correspondence columns of the *Glasgow Herald* at the moral decadence of the theatre, and a call from one Labour councillor for the local authority to impose greater controls, given that the theatre was subsidised from public funds.[96] Strathclyde Regional Council again considered the issue in 1975, although an editorial in the *Herald* strongly opposed any suggestion that funding should determine the moral content of theatre programmes.[97] Finally, in 1977, Glasgow's Lord Provost called for the resignation of the management of the Citizens Theatre over nude scenes in a performance of *Dracula*, claiming that he had been 'inundated' with complaints and had the backing of the Glasgow Presbytery and Roman Catholic Archdiocese.[98] Although other councillors refused to support his recommendation, the Licensing Committee determined that no visiting company could perform a play likely to be attended by school-children before it had been vetted by Strathclyde Regional Education Department.[99]

During the 1970s, theatre censorship remained for the most part an issue for the local media and magistrates, and did not figure prominently in the deliberations of Scottish departments of state. This largely reflected the lack of pressure on the issue from the Church of Scotland. In its report to the Longford Inquiry, the Church's Moral Welfare Committee did not highlight theatre as an area of real concern in Scotland. It emphasised that, although a degree of 'liberalisation' had occurred in the content of Scottish productions, this was not 'entirely unwelcome' given that it had never approached the excesses of the London theatre.[100] In its 1979 report entitled *Obscenity and Community Standards*, the Social Responsibility Committee reaffirmed this position. In its view, the theatre was a minority interest in Scotland and there was no evidence that the majority of theatregoers would be attracted 'by any attempt to repeat in Scotland the commercial exploitation of pornography and obscenity which [had] affected the London theatre'. The report emphasised that professional theatre was inaccessible to much of the Scottish population, and that evidence suggested that those who did frequent the theatre were morally discerning and effectively imposed their own self-censorship based on notices in the serious newspapers.[101] The Committee did recommend that the Theatres Act be amended to incorporate a new definition of obscenity – that a work, when taken as a whole, 'would outrage contemporary community standards of decency'.[102] However, it did not support the introduction of any more stringent powers of censorship in the theatre. Indeed, it warned that to attempt to prevent by law occasional lapses in taste in the Scottish theatre would merely divert attention from other areas of civil society more seriously contaminated by obscenity and pornography.[103]

BROADCASTING

As in the 1960s, it was the views of the churches that dominated debate in Scotland surrounding the moral content of broadcasting in the 1970s. While acknowledging the cultural benefits of radio and television, the Church of Scotland sustained its 'strong offensive against what it considered to be a deliberate strategy of cultivated immorality and conscious abdication of ethical responsibility' by the broadcasting companies.[104] Such concerns, which typically blamed metropolitan playwrights and producers for exporting their moral turpitude north of the Border, were echoed in Westminster by leading lay members of the Church,[105] and in editorials in the Scottish press. Thus, a leader in the *Glasgow Herald* warned: 'That which is leading us close to an abyss of immorality is being piped up from London where the power of the Kirk is diluted in direct proportion to the distance of the English Capital from St Giles'.[106] Similar views were also expressed at the Broadcasting Council for Scotland, where, as in the 1960s, church representatives emphasised the importance of programmes reflecting the 'distinctive' moral identity of Scottish society.[107]

By the late 1970s, the position of the Church of Scotland had, if anything, hardened. Its working party on obscenity questioned the moral relativism of broadcasting output and considered it an 'inappropriate medium in which to experiment with explosives in taste or morals or to probe across the boundaries of public sensitivity'.[108] In particular, it was exercised by the 'seepage through the fictional programmes of loose moral assumptions' that condoned infidelity and promiscuity.[109] In an attempt to counter the impact of such programmes upon the young, it recommended that there should be some form of classification for films shown on TV, for the purposes of parental guidance.[110] The working party also proposed that the Obscene Publication Acts should be extended to include radio and television material.[111] However, at the same time, it strongly recommended the establishment of viewing panels by Kirk sessions in order to exercise 'constructive vigilance' at a local level, a process viewed as a 'much healthier and more positive intervention' than any system of institutionalised censorship.[112]

Throughout the 1970s, the smaller free churches also campaigned for greater control of broadcasting output. The Free Presbyterian Church of Scotland feared the 'subtle and undermining influence' of television on moral standards and blamed the 'licentious' attitude of broadcasters for corrupting youth and contributing to the rising incidence of teenage pregnancies, abortions and VD. As far as its Religion and Morals Committee was concerned, the proclivity of television to 'cater to the permissive society' was just another example of how active 'Satan [was] in the dissemination of sin and iniquity', and it strongly endorsed the work of Mary Whitehouse and the NVLA.[113]

Similarly, the Free Church of Scotland viewed broadcasters as 'purveyors of permissiveness', and as the architects of an insidious 'New Morality'. Its Committee on Public Questions blamed the depiction of nudity and promiscuity on television, and the preoccupation of broadcasters with the 'sordid, seamy and sensual way of life', for the increase in 'fornication, adultery and sexual perversity'. In its view, a group of amoral and avant-garde programme producers and planners were 'playing havoc with the morals of the young and gullible and draining words like immorality . . . and depravity of all meaning in the name of freedom'. The Free Church supported the establishment of a new Broadcasting Authority to protect standards of Christian morality, and, in collaboration with the NVLA, pressed for greater moral accountability to be built into the regulations governing the BBC and Independent Broadcasting Authority.[114]

For the most part, the Scottish departments of state merely acted as a post office for church representations on issues relating to broadcasting. Insofar as they became involved in policy making, their efforts were focused primarily on securing an adequate representation of Scottish interests and culture in programme scheduling and output. With respect to issues of sexual morality, their most important role, as in the 1960s, was to alert Home Office officials to the depth of concern in Scotland over what was viewed as the desertion of Christian family values in broadcasting, and to the importance of the Church assemblies as mediators of public opinion, in the absence of a devolved Parliament.

FILM

Throughout the 1970s, the Scottish Office was also pressed by the Church of Scotland to ensure more consistent and effective action against films and film posters that contained sexually explicit or pornographic content.[115] In its evidence to Lord Longford's inquiry, in the annual deliverances of its General Assembly and in its 1979 report entitled *Obscenity and Community Standards*, the Church advanced a range of proposals. While endorsing the non-statutory role of the

British Board of Film Censors (BBFC), it argued for the Board to 'strengthen its resolve' and to resist popular demand for a relaxation in the 'moral yardsticks' for granting X certification.[116] The Church of Scotland also campaigned for greater uniformity in licensing policy across Scotland, perhaps coordinated by the Council of Scottish Local Authorities. While it acknowledged that there might legitimately be some variation in practice allowing for cultural differences – as, for example, between Glasgow and the Highlands and Islands – it did not find it acceptable that anomalies should exist between adjacent local authorities in the central belt of Scotland. In addition, the Church sought new powers at local level to regulate private cinema clubs and to prevent the spread of Soho-style sex cinemas north of the Border. Finally, given that Scotland shared the same films and system of certification as the rest of the United Kingdom, the Church pressed for Scotland (and Scottish legal and moral perspectives) to be included in any future legislation dealing with obscenity and the cinema.

The response of the SHHD was cautious. In general, it sought to downplay the more sensational accusations levelled by purity activists against cinema entertainment while endorsing the need for vigilance. A circular issued by the Department in 1970 recommended the new categories introduced by the BBFC and revised the model licensing conditions, including those relating to the morality of film content.[117] In addition, the SHHD sought to address concerns surrounding advertising displays in cinemas. It reminded licensing bodies that, since 1955, they had possessed the power to 'prohibit the display of any advertisement which offend[ed] against good taste or decency or would be likely to be offensive to public feeling', and suggested that they review their procedures to ensure such conditions were imposed.[118] Finally, Scottish officials supported legislative initiatives to bring 'private' cinema clubs under the same licensing and censorship systems as commercial cinemas and prevent their more or less public exhibition of 'blue movies'.[119] However, for the most part, rather than espouse fresh legislation, the SHHD continued to devolve responsibility for moral issues relating to the cinema to local licensing and police authorities.

Edinburgh

As in the 1950s and 1960s, during the early 1970s a range of uncertificated films was submitted to the Edinburgh Magistrates' Committee in order to secure a licence for exhibition in the city. They fell broadly within four categories. First, there were sexually explicit films purporting to be instructional such as *Love Variations* and *Language of Love*. Such films tended to be granted an X certificate, but the magistrates required the distributors to show evidence of their educational value before they were previewed.[120] Second, there were serious films such as *Tropic of Cancer*, *Camille 2000* and *Last Tango in Paris* that explored either promiscuous or 'deviant' sexual relationships or practices.[121] A third category was made up of films with superficial plots that were, in reality, thinly disguised soft-core pornography, with a range of sexually explicit themes including lesbianism, female masturbation and sexual orgies. Examples of this genre included *Virgin Witch*, *Without a Stitch*, *Danish Blue*, *The Sex Adventures of the Three Musketeers* and *Sex Farm*.[122] Finally, there were films, such as *Oh! Calcutta!*, where the sexual content was interpreted as part of a broader political attack on civil society and the establishment.[123]

The Magistrates' Committee was also concerned to enforce the new categories formulated by the BBFC together with the model licensing conditions recommended by the SHHD. In particular, despite protests from the Cinematograph Exhibitors' Association, it reaffirmed that no person under 18 should be admitted to an X certificated film and no person under 14 to a film rated AA.[124] It also warned cinema operators that firm action would be taken against any cinema displays that were deemed indecent or offensive.[125]

An additional area of concern, shared by the Edinburgh Presbytery of the Church of Scotland and many civic leaders, was the showing of sexually explicit, uncertificated, avant-garde films during the Edinburgh International Film Festival.[126] In January 1971, contrary to a certificate of exemption from HM Customs and Excise allowing the Festival to exhibit uncertificated productions, the Magistrates' Committee refused to waive the censorship requirements for films in public premises, whether or not they were to be shown during the Festival.[127] Later the same year, it further resolved that it would only pass films for the Edinburgh International Film Festival that had been previewed by its Director and/or Viewing Panel.[128]

However, evidence suggests that the Edinburgh Magistrates were increasingly unhappy with their role as film censors, and increasingly polarised in their views when undertaking it. In 1971, they protested to the BBFC that, in liberalising its approach to the granting of X certificates, the BBFC was effectively devolving censorship back to local authorities:

In effect the Board appeared to be granting certificates on the basis that each licensing authority was entitled to prohibit the exhibit of any film in its own area. If their impression was correct, the Magistrates considered it to be a retrograde step as they anticipated that, as a Committee, they would, in future, have to devote much more time to the viewing of controversial films . . . a function, which, in their opinion, was fundamentally the responsibility of the Board.[129]

The view of the Lord Provost in 1972 was that magistrates should be relieved of such duties.[130] Thereafter, the Committee increasingly retreated from its role as film censor, refusing to preview any film certificated by the BBFC. As one councillor observed in 1973, he no longer considered himself 'the arbiter of the good or bad taste of the citizens of Edinburgh'.[131] In addition, unless justified as performing an educational function, uncertificated films were either disregarded or banned without a preview, purely on the basis of a written synopsis of their contents.[132] By 1975, this retreat had begun to attract public disquiet and a public petition was organised to lobby the City's magistrates to adopt a more proactive stance in proscribing indecent and offensive film exhibitions.[133] Nonetheless, while formally retaining the power to veto films that were regarded as 'obscene or offensive', for the remainder of the 1970s the Edinburgh magistrates continued to distance themselves from issues of film censorship.

Glasgow

In Glasgow, the operation of film censorship by the local authority was also a contentious issue. While the ban in March 1971 on *Tropic of Cancer* – described by one bailie as 'a filthy, disgusting, depraved film' – raised few objections,[134] there was little official or public agreement over the ban imposed later in the year by magistrates on Ken Russell's *The Devils*, awarded an X certificate by the BBFC. This was the first time that the Glasgow magistrates had banned a certificated film on the grounds that 'it offended good taste and decency and would be likely to be offensive to public feeling'.[135] The editor and film correspondent of the *Glasgow Herald* considered it inappropriate for the 'city bailies to challenge the censor in the name of Glasgow', pointing out that it had been licensed for exhibition in Edinburgh and that other semi-pornographic films, such as *Naughty*, had been approved for Glasgow cinemas.[136] The correspondence columns of the *Herald* reflected a wide range of views, some condemning the patronising interference of so-called 'city fathers' in dictating the viewing habits of the public, while others – notably representing the churches – strongly supported the ban as one blow in what they hoped would be a more general confrontation with declining moral standards in the performance arts.[137]

The issue resurfaced in 1974 when *The Sex Adventures of the Three Musketeers* and *Oh! Calcutta!* were submitted for consideration by the Glasgow Magistrates' Committee. On a narrow vote, the former was banned, partly because of its 'strong emphasis on immorality taking place behind the walls of convents and monasteries'. However, some magistrates considered that a ban would merely give the film a status it did not deserve and lead to busloads of Glaswegians satisfying their curiosity elsewhere in Scotland.[138] Views on *Oh! Calcutta!*, approved by eight votes to three, were also divided. Bailie Catherine Cantley considered it both a danger to children and an incitement to sexual violence against women, while the senior magistrate, Bailie McGrath, felt it was 'a safe release from sexual fantasy' and in keeping with changing moral values in society.[139]

These discussions prompted a proposal from Bailie Long that the magistrates should delegate all decisions relating to films to a special panel chosen by the public. This was objected to on the grounds that it would be problematic to establish an equitable selection process, given the range of special interests involved. The senior magistrate concluded that 'this tasteless burden' was one that the magistrates were bound to accept. However, in order to make the process seem less arbitrary, it was decided that, as far as possible, viewing of films would involve at least one third of the magistrates.[140] In the event, as in Edinburgh, little effort was made by Glasgow licensing authorities to censor films after the mid-1970s.

CONCLUSION

Moral censorship by the state in Scotland during the period 1950–80 shared many of the fears and assumptions that underpinned policy making towards other issues relating to sexual behaviour. Whether in the form of film, plays, broadcasts or literature, sexually provocative or explicit material was viewed as a threat not only to public morality but also to public order and public health. Such material was increasingly associated, in the media and in professional debate, with anti-social behaviour and with the deterioration in the sexual health of the nation. As with other areas of sexual regulation, the shaping and implementation of Scottish laws relating to censorship were informed by a set of norms that elevated heterosexual and familial values and continued to emphasise sexual restraint/sublimation rather than sexual expression. Some debates surrounding censorship also shared a preoccupation with the moral fibre and vulnerability of the young, albeit sometimes as an excuse for the imposition of controls on the general population. Finally, as with the regulation of sexual offences such as soliciting, the story of censorship policy in Scotland is very much a local story, with local statutes, law officers, and civic and church dignitaries, along with the local media, shaping the narrative.

In addressing the issue of censorship, policy makers within Scottish government sought to realise a variety of aims. First and foremost, they endeavoured to secure the moral integrity of the Scottish nation. Whether it was the regulation of films in the 1950s or of theatrical performances and broadcasting output in the 1960s and 1970s, a central concern was to protect the moral equilibrium of Scottish society against the invasion of metropolitan or foreign decadence. Underlying this policy was a fundamental belief in the distinctiveness of Scottish culture, and, in particular, the continuing hegemony of presbyterian values, so powerfully reaffirmed in the deliverances of the church synods and assemblies. As a result, there was an enduring commitment to powers that reflected the prevailing moral consensus north of the Border rather than a set of statutory norms imposed from Westminster.

A significant and related concern was to ensure that power to shape and interpret the law in relation to moral censorship remained at the level of the local community. Although the Burgh Police Act of 1892 and the corresponding provisions of local acts and Corporation Orders were to pose serious obstacles to those seeking to rationalise the laws on indecency and obscenity, they represented the lynchpin of Scottish civic governance. Whatever direction the national debate on censorship might take, Scottish officials retained local burgh interests as their point of reference. Likewise, Scottish law officers were intent on preserving the autonomy of local magistrates to judge what was obscene in the context of local community values rather than imposing any precise statutory definition or English processes that might enable more cosmopolitan (and thus suspect) views on literary merit to intrude.

More broadly, as in the debates surrounding the reform of the laws relating to abortion and homosexual and street offences, Scottish policy makers viewed Scots law on censorship more as a role model for English legislators than a suitable case for treatment. They considered that Scots law was far more flexible and responsive to public and professional opinion. In particular, they believed that Lord Cooper's judgement of 1953 had ensured that Scottish sheriffs and magistrates took appropriate account of the intention of the accused and the likely harm inflicted by offensive material. Nor, as in the case of pornographic literature or blue movies, was the Scottish Office prepared to sacrifice Scotland's legal processes for the sake of a knee-jerk response to moral panic in England, preferring instead to limit measures in accordance with the actual extent of the problem in Scotland.

As with sex education, censorship remained an area of acute social contest, reflecting competing moral ideologies and the enduring tension between public and private spheres. Scottish government was confronted on the one hand by the heavily censorious demands of the Kirk, of moral vigilantes and of many civic leaders, educationists and outraged correspondents, and, on the other, by the concerns of civil liberty groups, of the more liberal sections of the Scottish press and of a range of commercial and cultural groups associated with broadcasting, film, theatre and literature. For the most part, Scottish policy makers favoured a more restrictive rather than permissive regime. They opposed the more liberal aspects of the 1959 Obscene Publications Act, actively resisted the reform of theatre censorship and pressed for a more regulatory approach to broadcasting. Unsurprisingly, they were dismissive of the recommendations of the Williams Committee. When Scottish lawmakers were reluctant to espouse new legislation, as with the Indecent Displays Bill and Child Protection Act, or to extend existing powers or statutory orders to Scotland, as in the case of the more coercive clauses of the Obscene Publications Act and A film regulations, this did not reflect any libertarian agenda. Rather, it stemmed from their belief in the greater efficacy of existing Scots law and legal processes to confront issues of indecency and obscenity.

However, as with so many of the more contentious issues relating to sexual morality, civil servants and law officers frequently sought to evade direct confrontation with such a divisive issue by devolving responsibility in the main to local authorities and magistrates, or to semi-autonomous agencies such as the Broadcasting Council for Scotland. As a result, censorship in Scotland often remained fragmented and *ad hoc*. For the most part, the local state, whether in the form of licensing or library committees, the police or procurators fiscal, responded randomly to public complaint rather than implementing any systematic policy. The decision to prohibit or prosecute could therefore often be arbitrary, and at times unduly influenced by local puritanical, Presbyterian elites, but, arguably, it seldom formed part of any consistently repressive regime.

Notes

1 See, for example, Haste, *Rules of Desire*, ch. 10; Travis, *Bound and Gagged*, ch. 9; Weeks, *Sex, Politics and Society*, ch. 14; Holden, *Makers and Manners*, ch. 5.
2 According to Marcus Collins, by the early 1970s 'pornography [had] succeeded prostitution as the principal symbol of sexual malaise' [Collins, 'The pornography of permissiveness', 100].
3 General Assembly of the Free Church of Scotland (hereafter GAFCS), *Report of Committee on Public Questions, Religion and Morals for 1971*, 138; FPCS, *Proceedings of Synod for 1971*, 16; *1972*, 11.
4 *Glasgow Herald*, 6 January 1972.
5 GACS, *Report of Committee on Moral Welfare for 1972*, 480–1; *Glasgow Herald*, 3 and 17 February 1972; *Pornography: The Longford Report*, 390–1.
6 The following is based on NRS, HH43/287, Sex supermarkets: representations and enquiries, 1971; *Glasgow Herald*, 5, 11, 12 and 15 May 1971, 9, 10 and 17 June 1971, 15 July 1971, 6 January 1972.
7 In Edinburgh, Councillor Kidd, a leading purity activist, was leading a similar campaign to ban sex shops, with support from local church leaders [*Glasgow Herald*, 10 June 1971].
8 NRS, HH43/287, Minute by I. L. Sharp, 18 May 1971.
9 Ibid., R. J. Inglis to Mary Goldie, Draft letter, May 1971. The SHHD was equally sceptical of the efforts of David Steel to criminalise the circulation of unsolicited literature, including advertising material, which described or illustrated sexual techniques. There had been Scottish complaints, mainly relating to Julian Press (*A Manual of Sexual Technique*) and Running Man Press (*The Mouth and Oral Sex, How to Achieve Sexual Ecstasy*), but the Department viewed the problem to be 'comparatively minor' in Scotland. However, Steel's clause was successfully inserted into the 1971 Unsolicited Goods and Services Act [*Hansard* [*HC*], vol. 813, 19 March 1971, cols 1,875–97; NRS, AD63/953/1, Bill correspondence].
10 *Longford Report*, 387–405.
11 Ibid., 397–8.
12 Ibid., 398.

13 *Glasgow Herald*, 9 October 1972.
14 NRS, HH41/2503, Minute by I. L. Sharp, 11 October 1972.
15 *Glasgow Herald*, 21 and 26 September 1972; *The Scotsman*, 21 September 1972.
16 NRS, HH41/2503, Notes for meeting, 25 October 1972.
17 Ibid., Notes for meeting, 22 October 1972.
18 Ibid., Minute by I. L. Sharp, 11 October 1972.
19 Ibid., I. L. Sharp to W. K. Fraser, 25 October 1972.
20 See especially Ibid., I. L. Sharp to W. K. Fraser, 25 October 1972; Minutes of Working Party on Vagrancy and Street Offences, 24 November 1972.
21 Ibid., W. K. Fraser to Secretary, SHHD, 12 October 1972.
22 Ibid., Minutes of meeting with Chief Constables and Crown Agent, 7 November 1972.
23 Ibid., Minute R. J. Inglis to R. D. M. Calder, 16 November 1972.
24 *Glasgow Herald*, 21 September 1972.
25 *Hansard [HL]*, vol. 336, 29 November 1972, cols 1,330–3.
26 Ibid., cols 1,350–5; vol. 338, 30 January 1973, col. 579.
27 NRS, HH41/2503, Scottish Office to Russell Johnston MP, 29 December 1972.
28 NRS, AD63/1133, Indecent Displays Bill, briefing note, 24 July 1973.
29 Ibid., R. Brodie to G. I. Mitchell, 16 August 1973.
30 Ibid., Lord Advocate to Bruce Millan, 7 December 1973.
31 Ibid., Scottish Secretary of the National Federation of Retail Newsagents to Bruce Millan MP, 7 December 1973.
32 *Hansard [HC]*, vol. 864, 13 November 1973, cols 362–6.
33 NRS, HH41/2714, Draft consultative document on indecent and obscene displays in public places, May 1974.
34 Ibid., Working Party on Vagrancy and Street Offences 1974–5, correspondence and papers.
35 On the social politics of this moral panic, see especially Holden, *Makers and Manners*, ch. 5; Travis, *Bound and Gagged*, ch. 10; Weeks, *Sex, Politics and Society*, ch. 14.
36 GAFCS, *Report of Committee on Public Questions, Religion and Morals for 1976*, 149–50; *1977*, 144–5.
37 GACS, *Report of Social Responsibility Committee for 1977*, 304.
38 *Hansard [HL]*, vol. 646, 24 March 1976, cols 642–760; *[HC]*, vol. 908, 1 April 1976, col. 551.
39 NRS, HH41/2714, Consolidation of Criminal Law Amendment Acts (Sexual Offences), papers and correspondence, 1975.
40 Ibid., Minute by J. Borthwick, 20 March 1975.
41 The following account is based upon Church of Scotland Archives, File 740.13, 1976–9, Working Party of Executive (Social Responsibility) Committee (Obscenity) (hereafter SRCWPO).

42 Ibid., Bruce Millan to Rev. K. M. Steven, 25 July 1977.

43 For the history of the Bill, see especially Holden, *Makers and Manners*, 218–19.

44 GAFCS, *Report of Committee on Public Questions, Religion and Morals for 1978*, 169; GAUFCS, *Report of Public Questions Committee for 1978*, 20.

45 *Hansard* [HC], vol. 943, 10 February 1978, cols 1,863, 1,868, 1,915.

46 NRS, AD63/1434, J. H. F. Finnie to K. J. Mackenzie, 8 March 1978.

47 Ibid., J. H. F. Finnie to K. J. Mackenzie, 23 February 1978.

48 Under existing law in Scotland, on summary conviction, a penalty of up to three months' imprisonment or £1,000 fine could be imposed. Conviction on indictment could attract a sentence of up to two years' imprisonment and/or unlimited fine.

49 NRS, AD63/1434, K. J. Mackenzie to J. H. F. Finnie, 13 February and 14 April 1978.

50 *Hansard* [HC], vol. 953, 14 July 1978, col. 1964.

51 NRS, AD63/1495, Indecent Displays (Control) Bill 1978–9, papers and correspondence.

52 Social Responsibility Committee of the Church of Scotland, *Obscenity and Community Standards*, 4, 33.

53 Ibid., 36. The Committee firmly believed that there was a correlation between the incidence of pornography and sexual offences, including 'predatory behaviour', citing evidence from H. J. Eysenck and D. K. B. Nias, *Sex, Violence and the Media* [Ibid., 44, 86].

54 Ibid., 41–3.

55 Ibid., 25, 69–71, 73.

56 Ibid., 70.

57 Ibid., 49–50.

58 Ibid., 74–8.

59 Holden, *Makers and Manners*, 237–8.

60 *Report of Committee on Obscenity and Film Censorship*, 159–66.

61 See, for example, *Glasgow Herald*, 30 November 1979.

62 The Williams Committee did little to endear itself to the Scottish Office by arguing (p. 20) that, although it had not considered any Scottish evidence, the validity of its conclusions was not confined to England and Wales, and that any legislation based on its report would almost certainly embrace Scotland.

63 *Glasgow Herald*, 20 November 1979; *Hansard* [HL], vol. 404, 16 January 1980, cols 183–94.

64 SRCWPO papers, O. Whitley to J. Land, 31 January 1980.

65 Ibid., M. Rifkind to Rev. F. S. Gibson, 19 March 1980.

66 Ibid., Draft responses to SSS, March/April 1980; Rev F. S. Gibson to M. Rifkind, 6 July 1981.

67 Ibid., Indecent Display (Control) Bill, June 1981, correspondence and cuttings.

68 NRS, DD12/4188, Minute by J. D. Gallacher, 24 March 1981; AD63/1514/6, M. Rifkind to G. Shaw MP, 28 August 1981.
69 NRS, AD63/1514/18, Civic Government (Scotland) Bill, 1 July 1982, clauses 45, 51–2.
70 NRS, AD63/1514/6, I. Finlayson to Scottish Office, 8 September 1981.
71 *Hansard* [HC], vol. 999, 26 February 1981, col. 433; SRCWPO, Scottish Office to Rev F. S. Gibson, 8 April 1982.
72 *Longford Report*, 392.
73 Ibid., 392.
74 Ibid., 394.
75 Ibid., 392.
76 Social Responsibility Committee, *Obscenity and Community Standards*, 68.
77 NRS, HH41/2503, Minutes of meeting with Chief Constables and Crown Agent, 7 November 1972; SRCWPO papers, Evidence of Association of Chief Police Officers, 3 April 1978.
78 *8 & 9 Eliz. 2, c. III*, section 162.
79 *1971, c. LXXIII*, clause 6.
80 *Eliz. 2, 1967, c. V*, sections 451–4. On Lord Cooper's judgement, see Chapter 9 of this volume.
81 *Evening News*, 25 May 1973.
82 Ibid., 29 August 1973.
83 NRS, AD63/1514/7, Memorandum by Crown Office, 19 October 1981.
84 SRCWPO papers, SHHD to Church of Scotland, 22 July 1981.
85 NRS, AD63/1434, Scottish Office to T. Drummond, 16 May 1978.
86 *Evening News*, 17 January 1977.
87 Ibid., 13 September 1974. Aberdeen District Council narrowly voted in favour of a similar ban [*Glasgow Herald*, 11 April 1978].
88 *Evening News*, 22 February 1977.
89 *The Scotsman*, 7 January 1977.
90 Calder, *Pursuit*, 400.
91 NRS, ED61/101, Representations to Scottish Education Department, September 1970.
92 Ibid., Correspondence and papers relating to 'The Arts Council and the Public', February and March 1971.
93 *Hansard* [HL], vol. 336, 29 November 1972, cols 1,332–3.
94 FPCS, *Proceedings of Synod for 1977*, 9; *1978*, 38.
95 See, for example, GAFCS, *Reports from Presbyteries for 1979*, 105.
96 *Glasgow Herald*, 10, 17 and 18 September 1970.
97 Ibid., 21 November 1975.
98 Ibid., 14 March 1977.
99 Ibid., 15 March 1977.
100 *Longford Report*, 387.
101 Social Reponsibility Committee, *Obscenity and Community Standards*, 22–3.

102 Ibid., 76.

103 Ibid., 23.

104 *Longford Report*, 388.

105 See, for example, *Hansard [HL]*, vol. 336, 29 November 1972, cols 1,330–3, 1,350–5.

106 *Glasgow Herald*, 18 January 1973.

107 EUL, GB0237 E95.25, Minutes of BCS, 2 February 1973, 9 November 1973.

108 Social Responsibility Committee, *Obscenity and Community Standards*, 11.

109 Ibid., 12.

110 Ibid., 13.

111 Ibid., 11, 76.

112 GACS, *Report of Social Responsibility Committee for 1979*, 302.

113 FPCS, *Report of Religion and Morals Committee for 1970*, 58; *1974*, 73–4; *1979*, 36–7; *Proceedings of Synod for 1977*, 9; *1978*, 9.

114 GAFCS, *Report of Committee on Public Questions, Religion, and Morals for 1971*, 132–3; *1973*, 137; *1974*, 144–5; *1975*, 164; *1976*, 136; *1978*, 164.

115 The following is primarily based upon *Longford Report*, 378–9; GACS, *Report of Committee on Moral Welfare for 1975*, 341–2; Social Responsibility Committee, *Obscenity and Community Standards*, 17–21.

116 This was a view shared by many Scottish magistrates. See, for example, ECA, SL119/3/40, Minutes of EMC, 6 January 1971.

117 NRS, HH41/1709, SHHD circular no. 34/1970, 20 July 1970.

118 *Glasgow Herald*, 20 April 1971.

119 NRS, AD63/1133, papers relating to the Cinematograph and Indecent Displays Bill, 1973.

120 ECA, Minutes of EMC, SL119/3/40, 6 January 1971; SL119/3/41, 21 July 1971.

121 Ibid., SL119/3/41, 9 February 1972, 15 March 1972; SL119/3/42, 14 March 1973.

122 Ibid., SL119/3/41, 24 November 1971, 5 January 1972, 3 March 1972; SL119/3/45, 23 October 1974, 12 February 1975.

123 Ibid., SL119/3/45, 12 February 1975.

124 Ibid., SL119/3/40, 16 December 1970, 10 February 1971.

125 Ibid., 10 February 1971.

126 Ibid., 9 October 1970; *Edinburgh Evening News*, 3 February 1971.

127 ECA, SL119/3/40, Minutes of EMC, 6 January 1971.

128 Ibid., SL119/3/41, 4 August 1971.

129 Ibid., SL119/3/40, 6 January 1971.

130 *The Scotsman*, 6 January 1972.

131 *Glasgow Herald*, 15 March 1973.

132 See, for example, ECA, SL119/119/3/45, Minutes of EMC, 23 October 1974, 12 February and 23 April 1975.
133 Ibid., 8 January 1975.
134 *Glasgow Herald*, 3 March 1971.
135 Ibid., 25 October 1971.
136 Ibid., 16 and 25 October 1971.
137 Ibid., 19, 20, 21 and 23 October 1971; 16 November 1971.
138 Ibid., 15 October 1974.
139 Ibid., 6 November 1974.
140 Ibid., 20 November 1974.

12

CONCLUSION

What general insights can be drawn about the response of Scottish governance to issues of sexuality in the third quarter of the twentieth century? One outstanding feature was the degree of continuity between the ideology, assumptions and legal framework underpinning policy in pre-war Scotland and those prevailing in the 1950s and 1960s, and even, in some instances, the 1970s. Despite the socially disruptive effects of the Second World War, the wide-ranging review by the Wolfenden Committee of the relationship of the law to sexual behaviour, and the cultural impact of the so-called 'permissive sixties', policy continued to be shaped by a traditional medico-moral sexology that focused on the control of the sexual instinct, on the conflation of sexuality and pollution, and on a hierarchy of normality and deviance.

This continuity was most apparent in the Scottish evidence on homosexual offences and prostitution to the Wolfenden Committee. While much has been made of the innovative, albeit regulatory, medical and legal discourses of the Committee's proceedings, and its extensive classification of contemporary sexual pathologies,[1] Scottish submissions revealed a fundamental attachment to conventional values and perceptions. The medical evidence of agencies such as the Davidson Clinic and the Scottish Prison Service, and the legal testimonies of the Crown Agents and procurators fiscal sometimes embraced new taxonomies of deviance but remained within a quintessentially 'moral' framework of prescription with respect to policy. They still articulated the traditional rhetoric of degenerationism and social hygiene, and within Scottish governance, public order, public morality and public health remained inextricably linked both administratively and ideologically.

Similar patterns of continuity can be detected in other areas of policy making. The delegation of school sex education in the 1950s and early 1960s to a purity organisation (the Alliance-Scottish Council) and to a relic of the Social Hygiene Movement (the Scottish Council for Health Education) was symptomatic of an attachment to conventional norms in the content and delivery of sexual enlightenment. Thereafter, in the late 1960s and 1970s, one does detect a shift, albeit tentative and problematic, to a more progressive approach to sex education under the influence of the behavioural sciences and of social and medical activists within agencies such as the Scottish Health Education Unit and the Family Planning Association, concerned to reduce the so-called 'sex casualties' of a more permissive society and to empower the young with a broader sexual awareness. Nonetheless, even in the 1970s, within Scottish government, many advisers and officials were still articulating a discourse of sexual sublimation rather than sexual expression, with the sexual urge, especially amongst girls, still depicted as inherently dysfunctional unless controlled and deferred into the socially acceptable, heterosexual contexts of marriage and family formation. Their operational philosophy continued to be underpinned by a strong thread of what might be characterised as 'enlightened asceticism', in which increased access to sexual knowledge was predicated upon the need for self-control and discipline.

The response of the Scottish state to issues of sexual health and contraception during the period 1950–80 was also heavily informed by traditional values and moral imperatives. In spite of the introduction of new chemotherapies, the legal and medical discourses surrounding VD continued to be shaped by moral concerns, and issues of guilt and personal blame continued to influence policy making towards sexually transmitted diseases. Medical and moral viewpoints remained closely intertwined, with moral issues prescribing the boundaries within which debate took place and within which both social and medical strategies were formulated. Similarly, despite the expansion of family planning facilities within Scotland, policy making within the Scottish Office continued to be constrained by a culture of moral conservatism that resisted the provision of contraceptive advice to unmarried women and viewed 'abstinence' as an essential ingredient of any health education programme.

Continuities in policy also stemmed from the deference of government departments to the moral conservatism of Scottish society, articulated in the press, in council chambers across the land, in opinion polls and, above all, in the proceedings of the Scottish church assemblies, presbyteries and synods. Government archives reveal that the policy community in Scotland was convinced that there was a distinctive sexual culture in Scotland, heavily influenced by Calvinistic values. Notwithstanding the utilitarian distinction drawn by the Wolfenden

Committee between the spheres of 'public' and 'private' morality, in many instances policy makers continued to view private sexual behaviour as an appropriate territory for surveillance and regulation in the interests of society. Thus, the Scottish Office was reluctant to take the initiative in pushing for the decriminalisation of consensual homosexual behaviour after 1967 given the prevailing homophobia in Scotland. Any legislative advance in the relationship of the Scottish state to the 'homosexual citizen' would not be the outcome of any systematic appraisal of sexual law reform but of the protracted and convoluted efforts of the Scottish Minorities Group in liaison with 'private members' in Parliament. Similarly, the response of the Scottish Office to proposals to liberalise the law relating to abortion, family planning, censorship and sex education was heavily constrained by a concern not to alienate public opinion in Scotland that was resistant to a more permissive approach to sexual issues, an approach that, it was feared, might introduce metropolitan vice and licentiousness north of the Border.[2]

In resisting legislative change, in addition to citing the conservative tenor of Scottish public opinion, Scottish governance frequently argued that the greater efficacy, flexibility and equity of Scottish procedures rendered new powers unnecessary. Indeed, a *leitmotiv* of policy making across a range of issues such as prostitution, homosexual law reform, abortion and censorship was an appeal to the superiority of Scots law and legal practice. Just as the processes of evidence and investigation in Scotland were seen to neutralise the more draconic aspects of the criminal law in respect of private, consensual, male homosexual acts, and to mitigate the dangers of police corruption and blackmail, so the mix of care and coercion – of caution, rescue and prosecution – was seen to satisfy both the punitive and rehabilitative demands of professional and public opinion in respect of female prostitution. In both instances, such procedures were advanced, albeit at times somewhat disingenuously, as a rationale for resisting sexual law reform and for justifying the omission of Scotland from parliamentary legislation. Similarly, there were (unsuccessful) efforts to exclude Scotland from the 1967 Abortion Act, partly on the grounds that, under Scottish common law, there already existed considerable scope for medical discretion in the provision of terminations. Again, as we have seen, in addressing the issue of censorship, whether relating to theatre, cinema or obscene publications, Scottish policy makers viewed existing Scots law as consistent with the protection of public morality and cultural tastes north of the Border, and resisted new legislation – whether permissive or coercive – that failed to accord with either the perceived needs or values of Scottish society.

Another major feature displayed by the governance of sexual issues in Scotland in the period 1950–80 was the degree to which the policy-making process was devolved. Part of the reason for this devolvement of power was the reluctance of the Scottish Office to become involved in the more contentious areas of social politics relating to personal morality. These were issues where, as with abortion and sex education, in a conservative and sectarian society, direct engagement might incur political costs. As a result, what emerged was a pattern of government where the initiative came not primarily from the centre but from the periphery. The legal environment relating to sexual behaviour, whether with respect to street offences, homosexuality, reproduction, health education or the consumption of obscene materials, was configured primarily within the local state, by local health and education committees, by local magistrates and local byelaws, and by local civic and church leaders. The personality and proclivities of a Crown Agent or Lord Advocate could clearly be decisive at the end of the day, but the evidence would suggest that it was those who, in the broadest sense of the term, 'policed' the streets, the clinics, the cafés, the classrooms, the toilets and the magazine racks who proved the major impulses and constraints in the policy-making process.

In many ways this reliance on local powers, primarily under the Burgh Police (Scotland) Act of 1892 and the corresponding provisions of local acts and corporation orders, served to further reinforce the resistance of Scottish officials to legislative change. The incorporation of Scotland into a range of national statutes and regulations was inhibited by the presence of a complicated body of local law that was jealously guarded by local magistrates and law officers as reflecting community values rather than some distant imprimatur from London. Moreover, with the focus of much policy making residing in the local state, the ability of church and civic leaders to censure and regulate the sexual behaviour of the community was greatly enhanced. Access to reproductive strategies such as contraception and abortion, to sexually explicit literature, theatre performances and films, and to sex education and sexual health advice, was frequently determined by local police, health, education, library and licensing committees. In addition, their anxieties and prejudices could often prove decisive in influencing the rigour with which sexual offenders were pursued. Moreover, even where the Scottish Office chose to delegate responsibility for sexual policy to quasi-autonomous agencies such as the Alliance-Scottish Council or the Family Planning Association, in practice their role was largely defined by local government.

The degree of continuity and devolvement displayed by Scottish governance of sexual issues in the period 1950–80 reflected a more general lack of modernity in the policy-making process. First, although there were issues, such as the rejection of compulsory notification for venereal diseases, where a concern to protect civil liberties operated, the policy community, for the most part, continued to defend the right of the law to address matters of personal morality and sexual behaviour in the interests of social stability and justice. Despite the fact that, for practical and procedural reasons, few criminal proceedings were brought against private, consensual homosexual acts after 1950, there was an enduring resistance within the Scottish establishment to decriminalising homosexuality. Likewise, although there were instances of informal 'tolerance zones' for female prostitution being implemented by local police authorities, and they liaised with church and social work agencies to provide 'rescue' facilities, policy was primarily driven by a desire for more rigorous prosecution and penalties. Similar sentiments shaped the response of Scottish government to issues relating to censorship. It was resistant to concessions to artistic freedom in the Official Publications Acts and the Theatres Act of 1968. Where it distanced itself from more coercive measures, such as the Indecent Displays Bills of the 1970s, this was motivated more by a desire to tailor legislation to Scottish needs than any inclination to embrace a more permissive regime.

Second, if, as Jeffrey Weeks maintains, the Wolfenden Committee did proffer 'a new moral economy, responsive to underlying shifts' in post-war Britain,[3] it was not one readily embraced within Scottish governance in the 1950s. Although policy documents subsequently ranged over an increasing variety of sexual issues, they rarely addressed the moral relativism and sexual pluralism of the 1960s and 1970s. The concept of sexual citizenship enshrined within policy making at both the central and local levels remained exclusive and disempowering. Despite the growing influence of sexologists and medical sociologists, in accordance with the views of the Scottish churches, sexual activity continued to be validated narrowly within the context of heterosexual relationships, marriage and reproduction. A central theme in recent Scottish historiography has been the 'secularisation' of Scottish society after 1960 and the declining role of the churches in the shaping of policy.[4] However, although, as

Catriona Macdonald has observed, the responses of the Scottish churches to shifts in sexual mores and the 'parameters of popular morality' were not always 'uniform or predictable',[5] evidence suggests that the more traditional moral agendas of the presbyteries and Roman Catholic hierarchy continued to exert significant influence on the legislative process both in the Scottish Office and the offices of local government.

Accordingly, in its conditional clauses, the 1980 Criminal Law Amendment (Scotland) Act preserved the stigma associated with homosexual activity, as did the guidelines issued to police forces across Scotland. Premarital and extramarital sex continued to be treated, implicitly and, at times, explicitly, as transgressive in the framing and implementation of measures relating to abortion, family planning, sexually transmitted diseases and sexual health education. It also formed a prime target for censorship in the cinema, theatre and broadcasting. Meanwhile, within schools, sexual diversity and pleasure remained largely absent from the very limited amount of sex education on offer.

Third, although, as we have seen, by 1980, public discussion surrounding sexual issues had become more inclusive, embracing not only professional interest groups but also a wide spectrum of opinion within the general community, the policy-making process remained elitist and at best resembled a form of 'bounded pluralism'. As with sexual politics earlier in the twentieth century, there was no cohesive or unified state strategy, the state's view being fragmented and evolving as part of a symbiotic relationship with a range of pressure groups and ideologies. The process was primarily shaped by horizontal contests for power and prestige between competing professional groups in Scottish society, including educationists, medical practitioners, lawyers, social workers, local magistrates and church leaders. The interplay both within and between such groups at the local level was crucial, as was the negotiation between their imperatives and those of advisers and politicians in regional and central government. In contrast, sexual issues rarely impinged upon working-class politics and figured only fleetingly in representations made by the Scottish Trades Union Congress. Still less was there more than token, if any, consultation by the policy community with those most likely to be affected by its measures; with those indulging in homosexual relations or prostitution, seeking contraceptive advice or abortions, suffering from sexually transmitted diseases, searching for sexual enlightenment, patronising avant-garde films and plays, or perusing risqué literature.

Fourth, evidence suggests that the process of policy making in Scotland with respect to sexual issues remained heavily gendered throughout the period 1950–80. It was most apparent in the response of the state to soliciting and prostitution. Both in legal and medical discourses, prostitution continued to be constructed as a quintessentially female sexual aberration, requiring surveillance, proscription and/or treatment. Although several Scottish witnesses before the Wolfenden Committee called for heavier penalties for male pimps, procurers and kerb crawlers, in the main it was the female body of the 'common prostitute', with its perceived moral and physical corruption, that was reaffirmed as the vector of disease and debauchery. In the 1970s there *were* efforts to render the legal processes relating to street offences less discriminatory, and powers to penalise male clients were canvassed, but the basic asymmetry with which the issue was addressed endured. Similarly, although the social epidemiology of VD/STDs shifted markedly during the period, sexual health policy continued to focus on female sexuality and sexual behaviour. Sexually active adolescent girls and single women continued to be depicted in health education materials as 'reservoirs of infection' and to be perceived by policy makers as a threat to the moral stability and health of society. Sex education also remained, both in content and delivery, extremely gendered, with the onus of responsibility for sexual restraint predominantly placed on girls, and with a continuing double standard of expectations and censure.

Fifth, although many authorities have associated advances in medical knowledge and technologies with a liberalisation of social attitudes towards sexual issues in this period, in the Scottish context this association appears, in some areas of policy making, far more problematic. The taxonomies of sexual behaviour embraced within Scottish medical evidence to the Wolfenden Committee were in many ways as stigmatising as those previously articulated by the social purity and hygiene movements. While many witnesses did recognise the need for the medical treatment and rehabilitation of homosexual offenders, their mindset remained rooted in established notions of sexual pathology rather than in more progressive ideas of sexual expression and inclusion. Cure or sublimation, with their implications of self-rejection or self-denial, remained at the basis of therapy.[6] Similarly, while sex education policy had, by the late 1960s, partially been freed from the legacy of social purity and social hygiene, medical experts advising Scottish health and education departments sustained an ideology in which sexual enlightenment remained more an issue of self-restraint than self-awareness. As with the provision of medical termination of pregnancy, officials were acutely conscious that the medical establishment in Scotland remained divided over the content and delivery of sex education, the appropriate balance between medical and moral considerations, and the degree to which the medical profession should assume responsibility for contentious issues relating to sexual development and behaviour.

In many respects sexual health policy did adapt to a more permissive age. The campaign for the compulsory notification and/or treatment of VD, that had featured so prominently in Scottish sexual politics during the first half of the twentieth century, had run its course by 1960 in favour of a voluntarist strategy of treatment, health education and contact tracing. In addition, a new, less judgemental generation of clinicians had emerged to help shape public health provisions. Nonetheless, underpinning medical policy was a moral epidemiology that implicitly, if not overtly, censured certain lifestyles. Moreover, on the eve of the onset of AIDS, the stigma associated within the policy community with sexually transmitted infections was still clearly reflected in the marginalisation of sexual health issues.

Finally, it might appropriately be asked how far, if at all, the lack of constitutional autonomy inhibited a more progressive approach to sexual issues by policy makers in Scotland after 1950. As the Labour MP Robin Cook rightly observed in 1977, there was no convincing evidence that more permissive legislation relating to sexual behaviour in Scotland had been impeded by the minority position of Scottish MPs or by parliamentary procedures at Westminster.[7] On the contrary, on a range of topics, pre-eminently homosexual law reform and the relaxation of censorship, the apathy or outright opposition of Scottish MPs had been a major factor in delaying measures. This was, as Cook noted, partly because the Presbyterian Church in Scotland was so dominant and possessed its own formalised democratic structure. In his view, many seeking change in the field of sexual morality failed to lobby at Westminster and 'regarded as their goal the approval of a Deliverance by the General Assembly, rather than the passage of a statute by the secular chamber'.[8] However, as we have seen, the General Assembly frequently saw its role as primarily the preservation of traditional morality and resisted sexual law reform and the loosening of community controls. As Cook concluded, given this moral conservatism entrenched within Scottish civil society, devolution might well have provided the forum for *more* rather than *less* illiberal attitudes to sexual issues.[9] It awaits a social historian of Scottish governance in the age of HIV/AIDS to have the final say on whether this was to be a justified fear.

Notes

1 See especially Mort, 'Mapping sexual London', 94–5.
2 For a discussion of this juxtaposing of provincial virtue with the decadence of London's society, see Mort, *Capital Affairs*, 333.
3 Weeks, *Sex, Politics and Society*, 242.
4 See, for example, Brown, *Religion and Society*, chs 6–7; Cameron, *Impaled upon a Thistle*, 226–8.
5 Macdonald, *Whaur Extremes Meet*, 285.
6 This was also reflected in much of the psychiatric evidence submitted to the Scottish High Court in cases involving homosexual offences during the period 1950–80 [Davidson, 'Law, medicine and the treatment of homosexual offenders', 125–42].
7 NRS, GD467/2/2/7, Robin Cook, 'Personal Law Reform for Scotland', 30 June 1977.
8 Ibid.
9 Ibid. It is significant that, in 1978, anti-abortionists were angered by an amendment to the Scotland Act that removed from any future Scottish Assembly responsibility for abortion policy. Their assumption was that a devolved Scottish Parliament would be far less permissive in its approach to the issue [*Scottish Catholic Observer*, 21 July 1978].

SOURCES AND SELECT BIBLIOGRAPHY

ARCHIVE SOURCES

Central government archives

National Records of Scotland

Cabinet Papers, Home Affairs Committee Minutes.
Edinburgh Women Citizens' Association, Minutes.
Lord Advocate's Department:
     Crown Agent's Files.
     Legal and General Case Files.
     Parliamentary Bills' Files.
     Parliamentary Bills' Files Series B.
Scottish Education Department:
     Arts Files.
     Child Care Files.
     Educational Research Files.
     Primary and Secondary Education Files.
Scottish Home Department/Department of Health for Scotland/Scottish Home
   and Health Department:
     Criminal Justice and Procedure Files.
     Departmental Circulars.
     Infectious Disease and Public Health Files.
     Legal and General Files.
     Licensing Files.
     Local Authority Health Services (Health and Welfare) Files.
     Medical Services Files.
     National Health Service, Administrative Files.
     National Health Service, Services Files.
     National Health Service, Specific Diseases Files.
     Prison and Borstal Services General Files.
Scottish Minorities Group and Scottish Homosexual Rights Group, Papers.
Scottish Office Development Department, Planning Files.

The National Archives, Public Record Office, Kew

Cabinet Papers.
Home Office Criminal Files.
Home Office, Papers of Wolfenden Committee on Homosexual Offences and
   Prostitution.

Local government archives

Edinburgh City Archives

Burgh Court Records.
Edinburgh City Police, Annual Reports.
Edinburgh Education Committee, Minutes.
Edinburgh Library and Museums Committee, Minutes.
Edinburgh Magistrates' Committee, Minutes.

Glasgow City Archives

Chief Constable of the City of Glasgow, Annual Reports.
Chief Constable of Strathclyde Police, Annual Reports.
Glasgow Corporation Education Committee, Minutes.
Glasgow Corporation Police Committee, Minutes.

Medical archives and papers

British Medical Association archive (Edinburgh and London)

Committee on Homosexuality and Prostitution, Minutes and Agenda.
Scottish Committee for Hospital Medical Services.
Venereologists' Committee, Minutes and Agenda.

Lothian Health Services Archive

NHS Greater Glasgow and Clyde Archives

Northern Health Services Archives

Wellcome Library for the History and Understanding of Medicine

Records of Abortion Law Reform Association.
Records of the Family Planning Association.

In private possession

R. C. L. Batchelor Papers.
Medical Society for the Study of Venereal Diseases, Scottish Branch,
　Minutes and Papers.

Other archives

Church of Scotland Archives (Charis House, Edinburgh)

Working Party on Obscenity, Papers and Correspondence.

Edinburgh Central Library

Press cuttings.

Edinburgh University Library, Centre for Research Collections

Broadcasting Council for Scotland, Minutes.

National Library of Scotland
Ian C. Dunn Papers.
Scottish Council for Health Education, Pamphlets.

University of Aberdeen, Special Libraries and Archives
Interview with Sir Dugald Baird.

PRINTED SOURCES

Official publications

Public General Acts and Regulations
Criminal Law Amendment Act 1885 (48 & 49 Vict. c. 69).
Burgh Police (Scotland) Act 1892 (55 & 56 Vict. c. 55).
Immoral Traffic (Scotland) Act 1902 (2 Edw. VII c. 11).
Licensing (Scotland) Act 1903 (3 Edw. VII c. 25).
Criminal Law Amendment Act 1912 (2 & 3 Geo. V c. 20).
Infant Life (Preservation) Act 1929 (19 & 20 Geo. V c. 34).
Children and Young Persons (Scotland) Act 1937 (1 Edw. 8 & 1 Geo. VI c. 37).
Defence Regulation 33B, 1943 (S. R. and 0. no. 2277).
National Health Service (Scotland) Act 1947 (10 & 11 Geo. VI c. 27).
Criminal Justice (Scotland) Act 1949 (12, 13 & 14 Geo. VI c. 94).
Cinematograph Act 1952 (15 & 16 Geo. VI & 1 Eliz. II c. 68).
Children and Young Persons (Harmful Publications) Act 1955 (3 & 4 Eliz. 2 c. 28).
Cinematograph (Children) (Scotland) (no. 2) Regulations, 1955 (S. R. and O. no. 1125).
Street Offences Act 1959 (7 & 8 Eliz. 2 c. 57).
Obscene Publications Act 1959 (7 & 8 Eliz. 2 c. 66).
Criminal Justice (Scotland) Act 1963 (c. 39).
Obscene Publications Act 1964 (c. 74).
Sexual Offences Act 1967 (c. 60).
Abortion Act 1967 (c. 87).
Social Work (Scotland) Act 1968 (c. 49).
Control of Venereal Diseases Bill, 1968 (Bill 40).
Health Services and Public Health Act 1968 (c. 46).
Theatres Act 1968 (c. 54).
Unsolicited Goods and Services Act 1971 (c. 30).
Cinematograph and Indecent Displays Bill, 1973 (Bill 6).
Sexual Offences (Scotland) Act 1976 (c. 67).
Protection of Children Act 1978 (c. 37).
Criminal Justice (Scotland) Act 1980 (c. 62).
Indecent Display (Control) Act 1981 (c. 42).
Civic Government (Scotland) Act 1982 (c. 45).

Local and Private Acts

Edinburgh Corporation Order Confirmation Act 1933 (23 & 24 Geo. V c. v).

Glasgow Corporation (General Powers) Order Confirmation Act 1960 (8 & 9 Eliz. 2 c. iii).

Edinburgh Corporation Order Confirmation Act 1961 (10 Eliz. 2 c. ii).

Edinburgh Corporation Order Confirmation Act 1967 (Eliz. 2 c. v).

Glasgow Corporation Order Confirmation Act 1971 (c. lxxiii).

Circulars and pamphlets

Board of Education Pamphlet no. 119. Sex Education in Schools and Youth Organisations (London: HMSO, 1943).

Ministry of Education Pamphlet no. 31. Health Education: Handbook of Suggestions for the Consideration of Teachers and Others Concerned in the Health and Education of Children and Young People (London: HMSO, 1957).

Department of Health for Scotland Circular (64) 1960, Venereal Disease in Scotland: Increase in Incidence of Gonorrhoea, 2 September 1960.

Ministry of Health Circular, Control of Venereal Diseases, HM (68) 84, November 1968.

Reports and minutes of evidence (annual)

Department of Health for Scotland, *Annual Reports.*

Department of Health for Scotland/Scottish Home and Health Department, *Scottish Health Statistics.*

Ministry of Health/Department of Health and Social Security, *Report on the State of Public Health for England and Wales.*

Scottish Education Department, *Report of the Secretary of State for Scotland on Education in Scotland.*

Scottish Health Education Unit, *Annual Reports.*

Scottish Home/Home and Health Department, *Criminal Statistics Scotland.*

Scottish Home and Health Department, *Health and Welfare Services in Scotland.*

Reports and minutes of evidence (occasional)

Report of Departmental Committee on Sexual Offences Against Children and Young People in Scotland, PP 1926 (Cmd 2592) XV.

Report of the Street Offences Committee, PP 1928–9 (Cmd 3231) IX.

Report of the Committee on Scottish Health Services, PP 1936 (Cmd 5204) XI.

Training for Citizenship: A Report of the Advisory Council on Education in Scotland, PP 1943–4 (Cmd 6495) III.

Report of Medical Advisory Committee (Scotland) on Venereal Diseases, PP 1943–4 (Cmd 6518) IV.

The Needs of Youth in These Times: A Report of the Scottish Youth Advisory Committee (Edinburgh: HMSO, 1945).

Scottish Advisory Council on the Treatment and Rehabilitation of Offenders: Psycho-Therapeutic Treatment of Certain Offenders with Special Reference to the Case of Persons Convicted of Sexual and Unnatural Offences (Edinburgh: HMSO, 1948).

Report of Departmental Committee on Children and the Cinema, PP 1950 (Cmd 7945) VII.

Report of Royal Commission on Marriage and Divorce, PP 1955–6 (Cmd 9678) XXIII.

Report of the Committee on Homosexual Offences and Prostitution, PP 1956–7 (Cmnd 247) XIV.

Report and Minutes of Evidence of the Committee on Broadcasting, PP 1961–2 (Cmnd 1819) X.

Health Education – Report of a Joint Committee of the Central and Scottish Health Services Councils (London: HMSO, 1964).

Report of Joint Committee on Censorship of the Theatre, PP 1966–7 (HC 503), 31.

Moral and Religious Education in Scottish Schools (Edinburgh: HMSO, 1972).

Report of Joint Sub-Committee on Sexually Transmitted Diseases (Edinburgh: HMSO, 1973).

Scottish Education Department Curriculum Paper 14: Health Education in Schools (Edinburgh: HMSO, 1974).

Report of the Committee on the Working of the Abortion Act, PP 1974 (Cmnd 5579) 16.

Scottish Education Department, *Health Education in Primary, Secondary and Special Schools in Scotland. A Report by HM Inspectors of Schools* (Edinburgh: HMSO, 1979).

Report of the Committee on Obscenity and Film Censorship, PP 1979–80 (Cmnd 7772) 49.

House of Commons Social Services Committee, *Problems Associated with AIDS, Minutes of Evidence* (London: HMSO, 1987).

Other central government publications

Parliamentary Debates (Hansard) House of Commons Official Reports (London: HMSO).

Parliamentary Debates (Hansard) House of Lords Official Reports (London: HMSO).

Local government reports

Edinburgh Health and Social Services Department, *Annual Reports*.

Edinburgh Public Health Department, *Annual Reports*.

Medical Officer of Health for Aberdeen, *Annual Reports*.

Medical Officer of Health for Dundee, *Annual Reports*.

Medical Officer of Health for Glasgow, *Annual Reports*.

Church reports

Church of Scotland, *Reports and Proceedings of General Assembly*.
Social Responsibility Committee of the Church of Scotland, *Obscenity and Community Standards* (Edinburgh: Saint Andrew Press, 1979).
Congregational Union of Scotland, *Annual Reports of Temperance and Social Questions Committee*.
Congregational Union of Scotland, *Year Book*.
Free Church of Scotland, *Acts and Proceedings of General Assembly*.
Free Presbyterian Church of Scotland, *Proceedings of Synod*.
United Free Church of Scotland, *Reports and Proceedings of General Assembly*.

Other printed reports and proceedings

Pornography: The Longford Report (London: Coronet Books, 1972).

Medical journals*

British Journal of Psychiatry.
British Journal of Venereal Diseases.
British Medical Journal.
Edinburgh Medical Journal.
Health Bulletin.
Health Education.
Journal of Biosocial Science.
Lancet.
Medico-Legal and Criminological Review.
Midwives' Chronicle.
New England Journal of Medicine.
Royal Society of Health Journal.

*References to articles and reports appearing in these journals are given in the notes. With a few exceptions, these are not included in the bibliography.

Scottish newspapers

Aberdeen Press and Journal.
Bulletin and Scots Pictorial.
Dumfries and Galloway Standard and Advertiser.
Dundee Courier and Advertiser.
Edinburgh Evening News (1950–63).
Edinburgh Evening News and Dispatch (1963–7).
Evening Dispatch (Edinburgh, 1950–63).
Evening Express (Aberdeen).
Evening News (Edinburgh, 1967–80).

Gay News.
Gay Scotland.
Glasgow Herald.
Glasgow Observer and Scottish Catholic Herald (1950–66).
Glasgow Observer (1966–8).
Greenock Telegraph.
Inverness Courier.
Kilmarnock Standard.
Leven Mail.
Scottish Catholic Observer (1968–80).
Scottish Daily Express.
Scottish Daily Record.
Scottish Educational Journal.
Scottish Sunday Express.
SMG News.
The Scotsman.

Books and articles

Abrams, L. and C. G. Brown (eds), *A History of Everyday Life in Twentieth-Century Scotland* (Edinburgh: Edinburgh University Press, 2010).

Aitken-Swan, J., *Fertility Control and the Medical Profession* (London: Croom Helm, 1977).

Aldgate, A., *Censorship and the Permissive Society: British Cinema and Theatre 1955–1965* (Oxford: Oxford University Press, 1995).

Aldgate, A. and J. C. Robertson, *Censorship in Theatre and Cinema* (Edinburgh: Edinburgh University Press, 2005).

Anderson, S., 'The most important place in the history of British birth control – community pharmacy and sexual health in 20th–century Britain', *The Pharmaceutical Journal*, 266 (2001), 23–9.

Baird, D., 'Preventive medicine in obstetrics', *New England Journal of Medicine*, 246 (1952), 561–8.

Baird, D., 'Sterilization and therapeutic abortion in Aberdeen', *British Journal of Psychiatry*, 113 (1967), 701–9.

Baird, D., 'The Abortion Act 1967: the advantages and disadvantages', *Royal Society of Health Journal*, 90 (1970), 291–5.

Baird, D.,'The changing pattern of human reproduction in Scotland, 1928–72', *Journal of Biosocial Science*, 7 (1975), 77–97.

Barrie, D. G., *Police in the Age of Improvement: Police Development and the Civic Tradition in Scotland, 1775–1865* (Collompton: Willan Publishing, 2008).

Batchelor, R. C. L. and M. Murrell, *Venereal Diseases Described for Nurses* (Edinburgh: Livingstone, 1951).

Bell, D. and J. Binnie, *The Sexual Citizen: Queer Politics and Beyond* (Oxford: Polity, 2000).

Billington, D. R. and J. Bell (eds), *Research in Health Education* (Edinburgh: SHEU, 1978).

Bland, L. and F. Mort, 'Look out for the "Good Time" girl: dangerous sexualities as a threat to national health', in Open University (ed.), *Formations of Nation and People* (London: Routledge and Kegan Paul, 1984), 131–51.

Bone, M., *Family Planning in Scotland in 1982: A Survey Carried out on Behalf of the Scottish Home and Health Department* (London: HMSO, 1985).

Brookes, B., *Abortion in England 1900–1967* (London: Croom Helm, 1988).

Brookes, B. and P. Roth, 'Rex v. Bourne and the medicalization of abortion', in M. Clark and C. Crawford (eds), *Legal Medicine in History* (Cambridge: Cambridge University Press, 1994), 314–43.

Brown, C. G., *Religion and Society in Twentieth-Century Britain* (Harlow: Pearson Longman, 2006).

Calder, J., *Pursuit: The Uncensored Memoirs of John Calder* (London: Calder Publications, 2001).

Cameron, E., *Impaled upon a Thistle: Scotland since 1880* (Edinburgh: Edinburgh University Press, 2010).

Cant, B. (ed.), *Footsteps and Witnesses: Lesbian and Gay Lifestories from Scotland* (Edinburgh: Polygon, 1993).

Carver, T. and V. Mottier (eds), *Politics of Sexuality: Identity, Gender, Citizenship* (London: Routledge, 1998).

Cocks, H. G. and M. Houlbrook (eds), *The Modern History of Sexuality* (Basingstoke: Palgrave Macmillan, 2006).

Cohan, A., 'Abortion as a marginal issue: the use of peripheral mechanisms in Britain and the United States', in J. Lovenduski and J. Outshoorn (eds), *The New Politics of Abortion* (London: Sage, 1986).

Collins, M., 'The pornography of permissiveness: men's sexuality and women's emancipation in mid twentieth-century Britain', *History Workshop Journal*, 47 (1999), 99–120.

Collins, M., *Modern Love: An Intimate History of Men and Women in Twentieth-Century Britain* (London: Atlantic Books, 2003).

Collins, M. (ed.), *The Permissive Society and Its Enemies: Sixties British Culture* (London: Rivers Oram Press, 2007).

Cook, H., *The Long Sexual Revolution: English Women, Sex and Contraception 1800–1975* (Oxford: Oxford University Press, 2004).

Coveney, M., *The Citz: 21 Years of the Glasgow Citizens Theatre* (London: Hern, 1990).

Cree, V., *From Public Street to Private Life: The Changing Task of Social Work* (Aldershot: Avebury, 1995).

Currie, J. R. and A. G. Mearns, *Manual of Public Health Hygiene* (Edinburgh: Livingstone, 1948).

Davenport-Hines, R., *Sex, Death and Punishment: Attitudes to Sex and Sexuality in Britain since the Renaissance* (London: Fontana Press, 1991).

Davidson, R., 'Searching for "Mary, Glasgow": contact tracing for sexually transmitted diseases in twentieth-century Scotland', *Social History of Medicine*, 9 (1996), 195–214.

Davidson, R., *Dangerous Liaisons: A Social History of Venereal Disease in Twentieth-Century Scotland* (Amsterdam & Atlanta, GA: Rodopi, 2000).

Davidson, R., 'Law, medicine and the treatment of homosexual offenders in Scotland', in I. Goold and C. Kelly (eds), *Lawyers' Medicine: The Legislature, the Courts and Medical Practice, 1760–2000* (Oxford: Hart Publishing, 2009), 125–42.

Davidson, R. and L. A. Hall (eds), *Sex, Sin and Suffering: Venereal Disease and European Society since 1870* (London & New York: Routledge, 2001).

De Jongh, N., *Politics, Prudery and Perversions: The Censoring of the English Stage 1901–1968* (London: Methuen, 2000).

De Moerloose, J. and H. Rahm, 'A survey of VD legislation in Europe', *Acta Dermato-Venereologica*, 44 (1964), 146–63.

Dempsey, B., *Thon Wey: Aspects of Scottish Lesbian and Gay Activism, 1968 to 1992* (Edinburgh: Outright Scotland, 1995).

Douglas, C. and P. McKinlay, *Report on Maternal Morbidity and Mortality in Scotland* (Edinburgh: HMSO, 1935).

Durham, M., *Sex and Politics: The Family and Morality in the Thatcher Years* (Basingstoke: Macmillan, 1991).

Evans. D., 'Sexually transmitted disease policy in the English National Health Service, 1948–2000: Continuity and social change', in R. Davidson and L. A. Hall (eds), *Sex, Sin and Suffering: Venereal Disease and European Society since 1870* (London & New York: Routledge, 2001).

Evans, D. T., *Sexual Citizenship: The Material Construction of Sexualities* (London: Routledge, 1993).

Farrell, C. and L. Kellaher, *My Mother Said . . . The Way People Learned About Sex and Birth Control* (London: Routledge and Kegan Paul, 1978).

Ferris, P., *Sex and the British: A Twentieth-Century History* (London: Michael Joseph, 1993).

Fisher, K., *Birth Control, Sex and Marriage in Britain 1918–60* (Oxford: Oxford University Press, 2006).

Foucault, M., *The History of Sexuality, Volume 1: An Introduction* (London: Penguin Books, 1990 reprint).

Freshwater, H., *Theatre Censorship in Britain: Silencing, Censure and Suppression* (London: Palgrave Macmillan, 2009).

Gane, C. H. W., *Sexual Offences* (Edinburgh: Butterworths, 1992).

Garton, S., *Histories of Sexuality: Antiquity to Sexual Revolution* (London: Equinox, 2004).

Giarchi, G. C., *Between McAlpine and Polaris* (London: Routledge and Kegan Paul, 1984).

Glaister, J., *Medical Jurisprudence and Toxicology*, twelfth edition (Edinburgh & London: E. and S. Livingstone, 1966).

Glover, E., *The Psycho-Pathology of Prostitution*, second edition (London: Institute for the Study and Treatment of Delinquency, 1947).

Gordon, G. H., *The Criminal Law of Scotland*, first and second editions (Edinburgh: W. Green and Son, 1967; 1978).

Gorsky, M., '"Threshold of a new era": the development of an integrated hospital system in northeast Scotland, 1900–39', *Social History of Medicine*, 17 (2004), 247–67.

Hall, L., *Sex, Gender and Social Change in Britain since 1880* (Basingstoke: Macmillan Press, 2000).

Hall, L., 'Birds, bees and general embarrassment: sex education in Britain from social purity to section 28', in R. Aldrich (ed.), *Public or Private Education? Lessons from History* (London: Woburn, 2004), 98–115.

Hampshire, J., 'The politics of sex education policy in England and Wales from the late 1940s to the 1960s', *Social History of Medicine*, 18 (2005), 87–105.

Hampshire, J. and J. Lewis, '"The ravages of permissiveness": sex education and the permissive society', *Twentieth Century British History*, 15 (2004), 290–312.

Harvie, C., *No Gods and Precious Few Heroes: Scotland 1914–1980* (London: Arnold, 1981).

Haste, C., *Rules of Desire: Sex in Britain: World War 1 to the Present* (London: Chatto and Windus, 1992).

Higgins, P., *Heterosexual Dictatorship: Male Homosexuality in Postwar Britain* (London: Fourth Estate Ltd, 1996).

Hindell, K. and S. Simms, *Abortion Law Reformed* (London: Owen, 1971).

Hoggart, L., *Feminist Campaigns for Birth Control and Abortion Rights in Britain* (Lewiston and Lampeter: Edwin Mellen Press, 2003).

Holden, A., *Makers and Manners: Politics and Morality in Post-War Britain* (London: Politico's Publishing, 2004).

Homans, H. (ed.), *The Sexual Politics of Reproduction* (Aldershot: Gower, 1985).

Houlbrook, M., *Queer London: Perils and Pleasures in the Sexual Metropolis* (Chicago, IL & London: Chicago University Press, 2005).

Hughes, A., *Gender and Political Identities in Scotland, 1919–1939* (Edinburgh: Edinburgh University Press, 2010).

Hunter, J., S. Bain and D. H. H. Robertson, 'Sexually transmitted diseases in Edinburgh: a changing pattern 1961–76', *Health Bulletin*, 36 (1978), 251–9.

Hunter, J. and M. Neilson, 'Sexually transmitted diseases in Edinburgh: patients under 18 years of age', *Health Bulletin*, 38 (1980), 23–8.

Irvine, J. M., *Talk About Sex: The Battles over Sex Education in the United States* (Berkeley, CA & Los Angeles, CA: University of California Press, 2002).

James., T. E., *Prostitution and the Law* (London: William Heinemann, 1951).

Jarvis, M., *Conservative Governments, Morality and Social Change in Affluent Britain* (Manchester: Manchester University Press, 2005).

Jeffery-Poulter, S., *Peers, Queers & Commons: The Struggle for Gay Law Reform from 1950 to the Present* (London: Routledge, 1991).

Jivani, A., *It's Not Unusual: A History of Lesbian and Gay Britain in the Twentieth Century* (London: Michael O'Mara Books, 1997).

Johnston, J., *The Lord Chamberlain's Blue Pencil* (London: Hodder and Stoughton, 1990).

Kandiah, M. and G. Staerck (eds), *The Abortion Act 1967* (London: ICBH, 2002).

Kellas, J. G., *The Scottish Political System*, fourth edition (Cambridge: Cambridge University Press, 1989).

Keown, J., *Abortion, Doctors and the Law: Some Aspects of the Legal Regulation of Abortion in England from 1803 to 1982* (Cambridge: Cambridge University Press, 1988).

Kuhn, A., *Cinema, Censorship and Sexuality 1909–1925* (London: Routledge, 1988).

Latham, M., *Regulating Reproduction: A Century of Conflict in Britain and France* (Manchester & New York: Manchester University Press, 2002).

Leathard, A., *The Fight for Family Planning: The Development of Family Planning Services in Britain 1921–74* (London: Macmillan, 1980).

Lees, R., 'VD – some random reflections of a venereologist', *British Journal of Venereal Diseases*, 26 (1950), 157–63.

Lovenduski, J. and J. Outshoorn (eds), *The New Politics of Abortion* (London: Sage, 1986).

Mahood, L., *The Magdalenes: Prostitution in the Nineteenth Century* (London: Routledge, 1990).

Marks, L., *Sexual Chemistry: A History of the Contraceptive Pill* (New Haven, CT & London: Yale University Press, 2001).

Mayer, T. (ed.), *Gender Ironies of Nationalism: Sexing the Nation* (London: Routledge, 2000).

McClintock, A., *Imperial Leather: Race, Gender and Sexuality in the Colonial Contest* (New York & London: Routledge, 1995).

Macdonald, C. M. M., *Whaur Extremes Meet: Scotland's Twentieth Century* (Edinburgh: John Donald, 2009).

McLaren, A., *Twentieth-Century Sexuality: A History* (Oxford: Blackwell Publishers, 1999).

Mcmillan, A. and D. H. H. Robertson, 'Sexually-transmitted diseases in homosexual males in Edinburgh', *Health Bulletin*, 35 (1977), 266–71.

McMillan, J., *The Traverse Theatre Story: 1963–1988* (London: Methuen Drama, 1988).

Mearns, A. G., *Teaching Health: A Working Guide* (Edinburgh: Scottish Council for Health Education, 1961).

Mearns, A. G., *The Whole Child* (London: National Children's Home, 1962).

Meredith, P., *Sex Education: Political Issues in Britain and Europe* (London & New York, Routledge, 1989).

Merrilees, W., *The Short Arm of the Law: The Memoirs of William Merrilees OBE: Chief Constable The Lothians and Peebles Constabulary* (London: John Long, 1966).

Mooij, A., *Out of Otherness: Characters and Narrators in the Dutch Venereal Disease Debates* (Amsterdam & Atlanta, GA: Rodopi, 1998).

Moran, L. J., *The Homosexual(ity) of Law* (London: Routledge, 1996).

Mort, F., *Dangerous Sexualities: Medico-Moral Politics in England since 1830* (London: Routledge & Kegan Paul, 1987).

Mort, F., 'Mapping sexual London: the Wolfenden Committee on homosexual offences and prostitution 1954–57', *New Formations*, 37 (1999), 92–110.

Mort, F., *Capital Affairs: London and the Making of the Permissive Society* (New Haven, CT & London: Yale University Press, 2010).

Newburn, T., *Permission and Regulation: Law and Morals in Post-War Britain* (London & New York: Routledge, 1992).

Pilcher, J., 'School sex education: policy and practice in England 1870 to 2000', *Sex Education*, 5 (2005), 153–70.

Robertson, D. H. H., 'Medical and legal problems in the treatment of delinquent girls in Scotland: I. Girls in custodial institutions', *British Journal of Venereal Diseases*, 45 (1969), 129–39.

Robertson, D. H. H. and G. George, 'Medical and legal problems in the treatment of delinquent girls in Scotland: II. Sexually transmitted disease in girls in custodial institutions', *British Journal of Venereal Diseases*, 46 (1970), 46–53.

Robertson, J. C., *The Hidden Cinema: British Film Censorship 1913–1975* (London & New York: Routledge, 1989).

Rowbotham, S., *A New World for Women: Stella Brown – Socialist Feminist* (London: Pluto Press, 1977).

Sauerteig, L. D. H. and R. Davidson (eds), *Shaping Sexual Knowledge: A Cultural History of Sex Education in Twentieth Century Europe* (London & New York: Routledge, 2009).

Schofield, C. B. S. and N. McNeil, 'Venereal disease in Scotland', *Health Bulletin*, 28 (1970), 19–25.

Schofield, C. B. S., *Sexually Transmitted Disease*, second and third editions (Edinburgh: Churchill Livingstone, 1975; 1979).

Schofield, M., *The Sexual Behaviour of Young People* (London: Longman, 1965).

Self, H. J., *Prostitution, Women and the Misuse of the Law: The Fallen Daughters of Eve* (London: Frank Cass, 2003).

Sheldon, S., *Beyond Control: Medical Power and Abortion Law* (London: Pluto Press, 1997).

Smart, C., 'Law and the control of women's sexuality: the case of the 1950s', in B. Hutter and G. Williams (eds), *Controlling Women: The Normal and the Deviant* (London: Croom Helm, 1992), 40–60.

Smith, S. J., *Children, Cinema and Censorship: From Dracula to the Dead End Kids* (London & New York: I. B. Tauris, 2005).

Springhall, J., *Youth, Popular Culture and Moral Panics: Penny Gaffs to Gangsta-Rap, 1830–1996* (London: Macmillan Press, 1998).

Steel, D., *Against Goliath: David Steel's Story* (London: Weidenfeld and Nicolson, 1989).

Sutherland, J., *Offensive Literature, Decensorship in Britain, 1960–1982* (London: Junction Books Ltd, 1982).

Swanson, G., *Drunk with the Glitter: Space, Consumption and Sexual Instability in Modern Urban Culture* (London & New York: Routledge, 2007).

Szreter, S. and K. Fisher, *Sex before the Sexual Revolution: Intimate Life in England 1918–1963* (Cambridge: Cambridge University Press, 2010).

Thomas, D., D. Carlton and A. Etienne, *Theatre Censorship from Walpole to Wilson* (Oxford: Oxford University Press, 2007).

Towers, B., 'Politics and policy: historical perspectives on screening', in V. Berridge and P. Strong (eds), *AIDS and Contemporary History* (Cambridge: Cambridge University Press, 1993), 55–73.

Travis, A., *Bound and Gagged: A Secret History of Obscenity in Britain* (London: Profile Books, 2000).

Trevelyan, J., *What the Censor Saw*, second edition (London: Joseph, 1977).

Webster, C., *The Health Services Since the War, Volume Two, Government and Health Care: The National Health Service, 1958–1979* (London: HMSO, 1996).

Webster, C., *The National Health Service: A Political History* (Oxford: Oxford University Press, 2002).

Weeks, J., *Sexuality and its Discontents: Meanings, Myths and Modern Sexualities* (London: Routledge and Kegan Paul, 1985).

Weeks, J., *Sex, Politics and Society: The Regulation of Sexuality since 1800*, second edition (London: Longman Group, 1989).

Weeks, J., *Coming Out: Homosexual Politics in Britain from the Nineteenth Century to the Present*, second edition (London: Quartet Books, 1990).

Weeks, J., *Making Sexual History* (Oxford: Polity Press, 2000).

Wilcox, M., *Rents* (London: Methuen Drama, 1983).

Wilson, L., *Sex on the Rates: Memoirs of a Family Planning Doctor* (Glendaruel: Argyll Publishing, 2004).

Wivel, A., 'Abortion policy and politics on the Lane Committee of enquiry, 1971–1974', *Social History of Medicine*, 11 (1998), 109–35.

Wolfenden, J., *Turning Points: The Memoirs of Lord Wolfenden* (London: The Bodley Head, 1976).

UNPUBLISHED THESES AND ARTICLES

Bartie, A., 'Festival city: the arts, culture and moral conflict in Edinburgh, 1947–67', PhD dissertation, University of Dundee, 2007.

Bhatia, G., 'Social obstetrics, maternal health care policies and reproductive rights: the role of Dugald Baird in Great Britain, 1937–65', MPhil dissertation, University of Oxford, 1996.

Debenham, C., 'Grassroots feminism: a study of the campaigning of the

Society for the Provision of Birth Control Clinics, 1924–1938', PhD dissertation, University of Manchester, 2010.

Elliott, K., 'Birth control clinics in Scotland, 1926–1939', MSc dissertation, University of Edinburgh, 2011.

Orr, R. W., 'Capitalism, patriarchy and gay oppression: a study of the Scottish Minorities Group', MA dissertation, University of Edinburgh, 1980.

Wallis, G. P., 'Some ideological issues in sex education in post-war Britain', MA dissertation, University of London, Institute of Education, 1984.

RADIO PROGRAMMES

Scotland the Gay, BBC Radio Scotland, 15 and 22 June 2004.

INDEX

121n12, 128–31, 135–9, 142, 147,
159–60, 164, 166, 169, 172,
176–9, 187–8, 204, 207, 207n4,
211n100, 215–17, 221–8, 232n26,
243, 253, 258n46, 258n47, 271–2,
274–5, 287, 290n62, 296–7
eugenics, 7, 59, 128, 136, 167, 187, 202
European Court of Human Rights, 83

Faculty of Advocates, 16, 51
Fairbairn, Nicholas, 73, 119, 245
Falkirk, 15, 32, 129, 254
family planning, 4–5, 7–8, 97–8, 100,
127–55, 139, 162–4, 174–5, 196,
201–4, 206, 231, 268, 295–9
domiciliary service, 135, 144
Health and Welfare Services Circular
No.10/1966, 137
Health Care Circular 74(3) (1974),
143–5
Memorandum 153 M. C. W. (1930),
128–9
Scottish clinics, 127–36, 148,
151n50, 151n57
sterilisation, 128, 136, 142, 145,
150n44
see also oral contraceptive pill
Family Planning Association, 131–9,
143–5, 148, 174, 202, 204–6, 295,
297–8
fertility control *see* abortion, family
planning
Festival of Light, 85, 262, 264, 269
Fife, 120–1, 200
Finlayson, Alan, 3
Foucault, Michel, 7, 215

Galpern, Myer, 165, 186
Gay Liberation Front, 68, 88
Gellatly v. *Laird* (1953), 219, 221–2,
244, 276
Gilloran Committee on Sexually
Transmitted Diseases (1971–3),
164, 170–1, 179, 203–4
Glaister, John, 48–50, 100
Glasgow, 17–18, 20, 22, 24, 26,
29–32, 39n85, 44–5, 48, 50, 57,
65n56, 67–8, 71–2, 85, 100–1,

106, 108–14, 116–18, 120,
121n12, 127–31, 133–5, 139–40,
145–6, 151n50, 165, 174, 178–9,
194, 200–1, 204–5, 216, 218–19,
223, 230, 234n, 241, 245–6, 249,
254–6, 257n14, 262–3, 270–1,
274, 276, 278–9, 282, 284–5
Glasgow Consolidation (General
Powers) Order Confirmation Act
(1960), 276
Glasgow Order Confirmation Act
(1971), 276
Glasgow United Evangelical
Association, 30
Gordon, Lionel, 51
Grangemouth, 15
Grant, William, 236
Greenock, 16, 74, 100, 113

Hall, Lesley, 3, 186
Hamilton, Willie, 120–1
Hart, Judith, 136–7
health boards, 100–1, 111, 114,
116–18, 143–5, 171, 174, 204, 206
health education, 5, 135, 141–2, 146,
168, 171–6, 180–1, 189–91,
194–6, 198–203, 205–6, 294–5,
297, 299–301
Health Services and Public Health Act
(1968), 138, 141
Heath, Edward, 249
Heatly, James, 237–8
Helensburgh, 254
heterosexuality, 7–9, 47, 51, 53, 69,
73, 75, 83–4, 175, 286, 295, 298
Higgins, Patrick, 46–7, 58
Highlands and Islands, 117, 135–6,
138, 145, 230, 233n47, 263, 282
historiography, 1–3, 13, 67, 97, 145,
207n4, 211n97, 211n100, 215, 262
HM Advocate v. *Anderson* (1928),
121n7
Holbrook, David, 269
Home Affairs Committee, 138, 224
Home Office, 25, 27, 34, 83, 102, 215,
218, 223–5, 240–2, 250, 264–5,
271, 275, 281
homosexuality, 4, 7, 38n65, 41–94,